Recent Advancements in Multimedia Data Processing and Security:

Issues, Challenges, and Techniques

Ahmed A. Abd El-Latif
Menoufia University, Egypt & Prince Sultan University, Saudi Arabia

Mudasir Ahmad Wani
Prince Sultan University, Saudi Arabia

Yassine Maleh
Sultan Moulay Slimane University, Morocco

Mohammed A. El-Affendi
Prince Sultan University, Saudi Arabia

A volume in the Advances in Data
Mining and Database Management
(ADMDM) Book Series

IGI Global
PUBLISHER of TIMELY KNOWLEDGE

Published in the United States of America by
    IGI Global
    Information Science Reference (an imprint of IGI Global)
    701 E. Chocolate Avenue
    Hershey PA, USA 17033
    Tel: 717-533-8845
    Fax: 717-533-8661
    E-mail: cust@igi-global.com
    Web site: http://www.igi-global.com

Library of Congress Cataloging-in-Publication Data

Names: Abd El-Latif, Ahmed A., 1984- editor. | Wani, Mudasir Ahman, 1987-
   editor. | Maleh, Yassine, 1987- editor. | El-Affendi, Mohammed, 1971- editor.
Title: Recent advancements in multimedia data processing and security :
   issues, challenges, and techniques / edited by: Ahmed A. Abd El-Latif,
   Mudasir Ahmad Wani, Yassine Maleh, Mohammed A. El-Affendi.
Description: Hershey, PA : Information Science Reference, [2023] | Includes
   bibliographical references and index. | Summary: "The purpose of this
   book is to demonstrate the new development and application of Artificial
   intelligent algorithms for multimedia data processing, to solve the
   problem from multimedia analysis and multimedia processing to multimedia
   cybersecurity. This book bridges the gap between AI techniques,
   Multimedia Signal Processing and cybersecurity. This book connects
   various interdisciplinary domains related to Multimedia signal
   processing, cybersecurity for media data particularly the social data
   and will be highly beneficial for the students, researchers and
   academicians working in this area as this book will cover state-of-the
   art technologies around multimedia processing and cybersecurity
   techniques and their role in Media Data Analysis and performance.
   Furthermore, this book will be highly beneficial to IT experts working
   in security management and enhancement from cyber-security point of view
   as this book will present recent advancements and methods developed and
   deployed to ensure the high level cyber-security"-- Provided by publisher.
Identifiers: LCCN 2023029626 (print) | LCCN 2023029627 (ebook) | ISBN
   9781668472163 (hardcover) | ISBN 9781668472170 (paperback) | ISBN
   9781668472187 (ebook)
Subjects: LCSH: Multimedia systems--Data processing. | Multimedia
   systems--Security measures. | Artificial intelligence.
Classification: LCC QA76.575 .R435 2023 (print) | LCC QA76.575 (ebook) |
   DDC 006.7--dc23/eng/20230711
LC record available at https://lccn.loc.gov/2023029626
LC ebook record available at https://lccn.loc.gov/2023029627

This book is published in the IGI Global book series Advances in Data Mining and Database Management (ADMDM) (ISSN: 2327-1981; eISSN: 2327-199X)

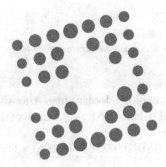

Advances in Data Mining and Database Management (ADMDM) Book Series

ISSN:2327-1981
EISSN:2327-199X

Editor-in-Chief: David Taniar, Monash University, Australia

MISSION

With the large amounts of information available to organizations in today's digital world, there is a need for continual research surrounding emerging methods and tools for collecting, analyzing, and storing data.

The **Advances in Data Mining & Database Management (ADMDM)** series aims to bring together research in information retrieval, data analysis, data warehousing, and related areas in order to become an ideal resource for those working and studying in these fields. IT professionals, software engineers, academicians and upper-level students will find titles within the ADMDM book series particularly useful for staying up-to-date on emerging research, theories, and applications in the fields of data mining and database management.

COVERAGE

- Text Mining
- Web-based information systems
- Heterogeneous and Distributed Databases
- Neural Networks
- Sequence analysis
- Cluster Analysis
- Information Extraction
- Data Mining
- Enterprise Systems
- Data Analysis

IGI Global is currently accepting manuscripts for publication within this series. To submit a proposal for a volume in this series, please contact our Acquisition Editors at Acquisitions@igi-global.com or visit: http://www.igi-global.com/publish/.

Titles in this Series

For a list of additional titles in this series, please visit:
http://www.igi-global.com/book-series/advances-data-mining-database-management/37146

Recent Developments in Data Science Tools and Applications
Shadi A. Aljawarneh (Jordan University of Science and Technology, Jordan) Juan Alfonso Lara Torralbo (UDIMA, Spain) and Vangipuram Radhakrishna (VNR Vignana Jyothi Institute of Engineering and Technology, Hyderaba, India)
Engineering Science Reference • © 2023 • 300pp • H/C (ISBN: 9781668462096) • US $265.00

Handbook of Research on the Applications of Neutrosophic Sets Theory and Their Extensions in Education
Said Broumi (Laboratory of Information Processing, Faculty of Science Ben M'Sik, University of Hassan II, Casablanca, Morocco & Regional Center for the Professions of Education and Training (CRMEF), Morocco)
Engineering Science Reference • © 2023 • 365pp • H/C (ISBN: 9781668478363) • US $325.00

Handbook of Research on Driving Socioeconomic Development With Big Data
Zhaohao Sun (Papua New Guinea University of Technology, Papua New Guinea)
Information Science Reference • © 2023 • 421pp • H/C (ISBN: 9781668459591) • US $295.00

Handbook of Research on Data-Driven Mathematical Modeling in Smart Cities
Sabyasachi Pramanik (Haldia Institute of Technology, India) and K. Martin Sagayam (Karunya Institute of Technology and Sciences, India)
Engineering Science Reference • © 2023 • 468pp • H/C (ISBN: 9781668464083) • US $325.00

Advancements in Quantum Blockchain With Real-Time Applications
Mahendra Kumar Shrivas (Department of Personnel and Administrative Reforms (E-Governance), Government of Karnataka, Bangalore, India) Kamal Kant Hiran (Aalborg University, Denmark) Ashok Bhansali (Department of Computer Engineering and Applications, GLA University, Mathura, India) and Ruchi Doshi (Azteca University, Mexico)
Engineering Science Reference • © 2022 • 312pp • H/C (ISBN: 9781668450727) • US $300.00

701 East Chocolate Avenue, Hershey, PA 17033, USA
Tel: 717-533-8845 x100 • Fax: 717-533-8661
E-Mail: cust@igi-global.com • www.igi-global.com

Table of Contents

Muhammad Asim, Prince Sultan University, Saudi Arabia
Younas Aziz, Central South University, China
Muhammad Ejaz, Central South University, China
Adeel Ahmed Abbasi, Central South University, China
Anbar Hussain, Central South University, China
Aasim Danish, Central South University, China

Mohammed Amin Almaiah, Department of Computer Science, Aqaba
  University of Technology, Aqaba, Jordan
Tayseer Alkdour, Department of Computer Networks, College of
  Computer Sciences and Information Technology, King Faisal
  University, Al Hofuf, Saudi Arabia

Section 3
Advanced Applications and Analysis in Multimedia Data Processing

Ishrat Nabi, Cluster University of Srinagar, India
Akib Mohi Ud Din Khanday, United Arab Emirates University, UAE
Ishrat Rashid, Cluster University of Srinagar, India
Fayaz Ahmed Khan, Cluster University of Srinagar, India
Rumaan Bashir, Islamic University of Science and Technology, India

G. Ananthi, Mepco Schlenk Engineering College, India
T. Balaji, Mepco Schlenk Engineering College, India
M. Pugalenthi, Mepco Schlenk Engineering College, India
M. Rajkumar, Mepco Schlenk Engineering College, India

Detailed Table of Contents

Section 1
Multimedia Security and Data Processing

The use of 1D chaotic maps in multimedia security applications is becoming increasingly attractive due to their advantages, including the high sensitivity to both initial and control parameters, rich dynamical behavior and ease of implementation for both software and hardware. This chapter presents a survey and analysis of recent multimedia encryption, watermarking, zero-watermarking and data hiding schemes involving the use of 1D chaotic maps. The present work also attempts to identify some drawbacks of existing 1D chaotic maps and multimedia security schemes involved the use of such maps, with suggestions for overcoming the identified limitations.

In this study, a comprehensive framework emerges, interweaving the capabilities of deep learning and NLP. This framework stands as a cornerstone in the pursuit of elevating the safety and security of individuals and organizations navigating the multifaceted realm of social cyberspace. The framework's architecture sets the stage for efficient threat detection and the preemptive identification of vulnerabilities, heralding a new era of cybersecurity strategies. As this conceptual framework unfolds, future endeavors will bridge theory and practice, ushering in the application of this paradigm to real-world data scenarios. The projected outcome of these efforts is the provision of pragmatic security services tailored to individuals and groups. This chapter encapsulates a visionary approach to social cybersecurity, where the synergy of NLP, deep learning, and AI converges to fortify digital landscapes against emergent threats, thereby safeguarding the interconnected fabric of the modern online world.

Chapter 3

In the face of escalating cyber threats posed by malware, advanced detection techniques are crucial. This study introduces a cutting-edge approach that merges convolutional neural networks (CNNs) and long short-term memory recurrent neural networks (LSTMs) for enhanced malware classification. The effectiveness of this method is rigorously examined using Microsoft's BIG Cup 2015 dataset. By combining CNN's ability to capture local features and LSTM's proficiency in processing sequence data, our approach achieves remarkable accuracy (98.73%) in identifying malicious behaviors. This research contributes an extensive exploration of deep learning models, an innovative CNN-LSTM hybrid architecture, and a comprehensive case study showcasing its superior performance. The presented approach signifies a significant stride in bolstering cybersecurity against the ever-evolving threat of malware.

Section 2
Advanced Techniques in Multimedia Data Processing

This book chapter is a vital guide for understanding today's complex landscape of booming multimedia data and growing cybersecurity risks. It focuses on the transformative roles of natural language processing (NLP) and deep learning in both areas. The chapter starts by discussing deep learning's capabilities in multimedia data analysis before moving to its applications in cybersecurity. It then shifts to examine how NLP is revolutionizing multimedia data management through semantic understanding and context awareness. The chapter also explores the emerging area of social cybersecurity, spotlighting NLP's role in identifying and mitigating social engineering attacks and disinformation. It wraps up with key insights into future trends. Overall, this chapter serves as a comprehensive resource for applying NLP and Deep Learning techniques to multimedia data and cybersecurity challenges.

Chapter 5

Muhammad Asim, Prince Sultan University, Saudi Arabia
Younas Aziz, Central South University, China
Muhammad Ejaz, Central South University, China
Adeel Ahmed Abbasi, Central South University, China
Anbar Hussain, Central South University, China
Aasim Danish, Central South University, China

Change detection (CD) and security plays a crucial role in remote sensing applications. The proposed change detection approach focuses on detecting the changes in synthetic aperture radar (SAR) images. The SAR images suffer from speckle noise which affects the classification accuracy. The proposed approach focuses on improving the model's accuracy by removing speckle noise with k-means clustering and an improved threshold approach based on curvelet transform and designing a stacked U-Net model. The stacked U-Net is designed with the help of a 2-dimensional convolutional neural network (2D-CNN). The proposed change detection strategy is evaluated via performing extensive experiments on three SAR datasets. The obtained results reveal that the proposed approach achieves better results than the several state-of-art works in terms of percentage of correct classification (PCC), overall error (OE), and kappa coefficient (KC).

Chapter 6

Mohammed Amin Almaiah, Department of Computer Science, Aqaba
University of Technology, Aqaba, Jordan
Tayseer Alkdour, Department of Computer Networks, College of
Computer Sciences and Information Technology, King Faisal
University, Al Hofuf, Saudi Arabia

The authors have developed an innovative topology by amalgamating consortium blockchain, often referred to as supervisory blockchain, with fog computing. The proposed system is organized into three distinct layers: the application layer, the fog layer, and the blockchain security layer. To accommodate this model effectively, the authors introduce the novel proof of enhanced concept (PoEC) consensus mechanism. This approach employs homomorphic encryption to secure transactions, which are then outsourced to the fog layer or fog devices. This strategy mitigates various security threats, including collusion attacks, phishing attacks, and replay attacks, bolstering the resilience of each layer against such incursions. To bolster security measures further, our model adopts a hybrid-deep learning protocol for safeguarding electronic medical records against potential breaches while concurrently reducing latency through a decentralized fog computing system.

Section 3
Advanced Applications and Analysis in Multimedia Data Processing

Chapter 7

Ishrat Nabi, Cluster University of Srinagar, India
Akib Mohi Ud Din Khanday, United Arab Emirates University, UAE
Ishrat Rashid, Cluster University of Srinagar, India
Fayaz Ahmed Khan, Cluster University of Srinagar, India
Rumaan Bashir, Islamic University of Science and Technology, India

Signature recognition is the process of automatically identifying or verifying an individual's signature to determine its authenticity. The basic motivation of developing signature recognition systems is to check whether a signature has been done by an authorized user /genuine user or an unauthorized user/a forger. The objective of this chapter is to study different algorithms that are used to authenticate and authorize the signatures of the individual. For personal identification and verification, Signatures are the most acceptable and economical way that is used for this purpose. Signature verification is used for documents like bank transactions and in offices as well. It is a huge time-consuming task for verifying a large number of documents. Hence the verification systems led to huge dramatic changes based on the physical characteristics and the behavioural characteristics of the individual. The verification methods used in the past suffer from flaws. This chapter provides a comparative analysis of various techniques used for recognizing signatures.

Chapter 8

G. Ananthi, Mepco Schlenk Engineering College, India
T. Balaji, Mepco Schlenk Engineering College, India
M. Pugalenthi, Mepco Schlenk Engineering College, India
M. Rajkumar, Mepco Schlenk Engineering College, India

Detection of faces from low light image is challenging. Such images often suffer from poor contrast, poor intensity, and high noise make it challenging to gather information and identify people or objects. The proposed method uses a deep learning-based approach to enhance the images by capturing multiple exposures and combining them to generate a high-quality image. Max-margin object detection (MMOD) human face detector, a face detection algorithm is used to identify and enhance the faces in the images. MMOD algorithm is a deep learning-based object detection approach which accurately detects human faces in images. By identifying and enhancing the faces in the images, they are made more visible and recognizable, even in low light conditions. The experimental results of this proposed approach demonstrate its effectiveness in enhancing face visibility and raising the quality of low-light images. This method has practical applications in areas such as security surveillance, where capturing high-quality images under low light conditions is critical.

Chapter 9

Valeria P. Pisarkova, Independent Researcher, Russia
Denis N. Garaev, Independent Researcher, Russia
Ekaterina A. Lopukhova, Independent Researcher, Russia
Azat R. Bilyalov, Independent Researcher, Russia
Ruslan V. Kutluyarov, Independent Researcher, Russia
Alexey S. Kovtunenko, Independent Researcher, Russia

The chapter presents a method for diagnosing oncourological diseases based on machine learning algorithms. MobileNet50, ResNet50 convolutional neural networks are used to solve the problem of classifying patient biopsy image segments according to the Gleason scale. Augmentation technologies were applied to the existing data set for better performance of the neural network. The accuracy of the algorithm was estimated by the total error and the Cohen's Kappa coefficient. The results of the algorithm in software show a good level of accuracy: in 65% of cases, the algorithm accurately determined the Gleason index, and the rest of the data had a slight deviation of the confusion matrix.

Chapter 10

Tariq Ahmad, Guilin University of Electronic Technology, China
Sadique Ahmad, Prince Sultan University, Saudi Arabia
Asif Rahim, Guilin University of Electronic Technology, China
Neelofar Shah, NUST University, Pakistan

The importance of early brain stroke detection cannot be overstated in terms of patient outcomes and mortality rates. Although computed tomography (CT) scan images are frequently used to identify brain strokes, radiologists may not always be accurate in their assessments. Since the advent of deep convolutional neural network (DCNN) models, automated brain stroke detection from CT scan images has advanced significantly. It's probable that current deep convolutional neural network

(DCNN) models aren't the best for detecting strokes early on. The authors present a novel deep convolutional neural network model for computed tomography (CT) images-based brain stroke early detection. The ability to extract features, fuse those features, and then recognize strokes is key to the proposed deep convolutional neural network model. To extract high-level information from CT scan images, a feature extractor with numerous convolutional and pooling layers is used.

Chapter 11

V. Stella Mary, Anna University, Chennai, India
P. Jayashree, MIT, Anna University, Chennai, India
G. Rajesh, MIT, Anna University, Chennai, India
V. Viswanath Shenoi, CSE, Koneru Lakshmaiah Education Foundation, Vaddeswaram, India

Object detection or shape reconstruction of an object from images plays a vital role in computer vision, computer graphics, optics, optimization theory, statistics, and various fields. The goal of object detection is to empower the machines to locate and identify the items or things in the given image or video. An object forms the image in human eyes or on a camera sensor is defined by its shape, reflectance, and illumination. This overview covers the estimation of the object shape, reflectance, illumination, recent object detection algorithms and data sets used in recent research works. The classic photometric stereo is aimed to reconstruct the surface orientation from the known parameters of reflectance and illumination in multiple images. Object detection approaches are used to find various pertinent objects in a given single image and location of the objects. There are various datasets for objection detection, some of them are addressed here.

Preface

This book comprehensively explores the dynamic and evolving multimedia data processing and security field. At its core, it delves into the intricate interplay between the processing and safeguarding multimedia data, a domain characterized by continual innovation, growing complexity, and the ever-pressing need for data protection.

Multimedia data, encompassing various forms such as images, videos, audio, and text, occupies a central position in today's digital landscape. The digital age has witnessed an unprecedented surge in the creation, consumption, and sharing of multimedia content across many platforms, including social media, e-commerce, healthcare, and entertainment. This surge has ushered in an era where multimedia data has become both an invaluable asset and a potential vulnerability.

The significance of multimedia data processing and security becomes evident when we consider the profound impact of this data on our daily lives. From personalized content recommendations and online communication to medical imaging and critical infrastructure, multimedia data permeates every facet of contemporary society. Its proper handling, analysis, and protection are not merely desirable but essential, given the vast array of applications and the potential risks associated with misuse or compromise.

In today's interconnected world, the processing and security of multimedia data have assumed paramount importance. As multimedia data's volume, variety, and velocity continue to escalate, so do the challenges and opportunities presented by this data. It is in this context that our exploration finds its relevance.

The primary aim of this book is to showcase the latest advancements in the development and utilization of Artificial Intelligence (AI) algorithms for multimedia data processing, specifically focusing on addressing challenges in multimedia analysis, processing, and cybersecurity. This book is a vital link connecting AI techniques, Multimedia Signal Processing, and the field of cybersecurity, creating a cohesive framework for addressing critical issues in the digital landscape.

Multimedia data plays a pivotal role in various industries, serving as a means to convey information across diverse domains. In an era characterized by increased internet usage and advanced communication technologies, safeguarding transmitted information, particularly high-quality image streaming, has become imperative. Effective processing and analysis of image and signal data are essential components of modern technology, facilitating tasks such as information embedding, retrieval, monitoring, video surveillance, data concealment, confidentiality enhancement, tracking, object detection, and data integrity verification.

Despite extensive image and signal processing work for these applications, existing theories and algorithms often fail to deliver satisfactory results. Transplanting conventional methods directly into cybersecurity also proves challenging, demanding the development of novel theories and algorithms to enhance the efficiency and effectiveness of image and signal processing for cybersecurity purposes. Consequently, this book addresses these pressing issues by inviting authors to submit original and unpublished research manuscripts highlighting the latest breakthroughs in image and signal processing for cybersecurity applications, thus presenting a comprehensive overview of the field's current research landscape.

Emerging technologies such as artificial intelligence (AI), machine learning, big data analytics, and the Internet of Things (IoT) have heightened the demand for advanced techniques in multimedia data processing. These techniques empower us to extract valuable insights from multimedia content, enabling applications ranging from content recommendation systems and sentiment analysis to autonomous vehicles and medical diagnostics.

Concurrently, the escalating cybersecurity threats targeting multimedia data necessitate innovative approaches to secure this data. The world has witnessed a proliferation of cyberattacks, data breaches, and privacy infringements, highlighting the criticality of robust security measures. The intersection of multimedia data and security requires pioneering research and practical solutions to mitigate risks and fortify the digital infrastructure.

In essence, multimedia data processing and security is not confined to a niche; it is a pervasive concern that resonates across industries, academia, government agencies, and society. Understanding and addressing these concerns is pivotal for individuals, organizations, and governments seeking to harness the potential of multimedia data while safeguarding against threats.

This book is designed to cater to a diverse audience with a shared interest in the multifaceted world of multimedia data. Researchers will discover in-depth insights into emerging trends and methodologies, while practitioners will find practical solutions to enhance their real-world applications. Students will gain a holistic understanding of the field, equipping themselves to meet the challenges ahead.

Each chapter of this book advances our understanding of multimedia data processing and security. They offer unique perspectives, innovative techniques, and practical applications.

Chapter 1: Multimedia Security Through 1D Chaotic Systems – Review and Analysis

This chapter conducts a comprehensive survey and analysis of multimedia encryption, watermarking, zero-watermarking, and data-hiding schemes employing 1D chaotic maps. It identifies existing limitations and suggests strategies to enhance multimedia data security.

Chapter 2: AI and NLP Empowered Framework for Strengthening Social Cyber Security

This visionary chapter introduces a framework that integrates the capabilities of Deep Learning and Natural Language Processing (NLP) to fortify social cybersecurity. It paves the way for proactive threat detection and vulnerability identification, safeguarding the digital world.

Chapter 3: Deep Learning Fusion for Multimedia Malware Classification

In response to the escalating cyber threats posed by malware, this chapter presents a cutting-edge approach that merges Convolutional Neural Networks (CNNs) and Long Short-Term Memory Recurrent Neural Networks (LSTMs). It achieves remarkable accuracy in malware classification, advancing cybersecurity defenses.

Chapter 4: Role of NLP and Deep Learning for Multimedia Data Processing and Security

This pivotal chapter explores the transformative roles of Natural Language Processing (NLP) and Deep Learning in multimedia data analysis and cybersecurity. It offers insights into their applications and future trends.

Chapter 5: Enhancing Remote Sensing Image Change Detection and Security With Stacked U-Net

Addressing the critical domains of change detection and security in remote sensing, this chapter introduces a novel approach to detecting changes in Synthetic Aperture Radar (SAR) images. It improves the accuracy of environmental monitoring and security.

Chapter 6: Securing Fog Computing Through Consortium Blockchain Integration – The Proof of Enhanced Concept (PoEC) Approach

This chapter presents an innovative topology that amalgamates consortium blockchain with fog computing, introducing the novel Proof of Enhanced Concept (PoEC) consensus mechanism. It mitigates security threats and enhances fog computing.

Chapter 7: A Comparative Analysis of Signature Recognition Methods

Signature recognition for authentication and authorization is the focus of this chapter. It compares various techniques for recognizing signatures, offering insights into improving document verification processes.

Chapter 8: Low Light Face Detection System

Detecting faces in low-light conditions poses challenges, addressed by this chapter's deep learning-based approach. It enhances image visibility, with applications in security surveillance.

Chapter 9: Determination of Oncourological Pathologies Based on the Analysis of Medical Images Using Machine Learning Methods

In healthcare, this chapter demonstrates the potential of machine learning in diagnosing oncourological diseases based on medical image analysis, contributing to early detection and improved patient care.

Chapter 10: Development of a Novel Deep Convolutional Neural Network Model for Early Detection of Brain Stroke Using CT Scan Images

Early detection of brain strokes is paramount, and this chapter presents a novel deep convolutional neural network model for this purpose, promising advancements in medical imaging and patient care.

Chapter 11: Deep Learning Techniques for Computer Vision - An Overview

This chapter provides an expansive overview of object detection, algorithms, and datasets, serving as a valuable resource for computer vision enthusiasts and researchers.

Recent Advancements in Multimedia Data Processing and Security: Issues, Challenges, and Techniques stands as a pioneering endeavor that resonates deeply with the dynamic landscape of multimedia data processing and security. This book is a comprehensive guide that navigates through the intricacies of safeguarding and harnessing multimedia data—a domain where precision and protection are paramount. It is a testament to this field's ever-expanding boundaries of knowledge and innovation.

In today's digitally interconnected world, the relevance of this book is undeniable. Multimedia data has permeated every facet of our daily lives, from personalized content recommendations and telemedicine to autonomous vehicles and entertainment. Multimedia data's sheer volume and diversity present both immense opportunities and formidable challenges. Our book positions itself at the forefront of this evolving landscape.

As a resource that bridges the gap between theory and practice, research and application, this book impacts the field in multifaceted ways. It advances knowledge through the dissemination of cutting-edge research and methodologies. It offers practical solutions to address real-world challenges, empowering professionals and practitioners. It serves as a foundational educational tool, shaping the future generation of experts. It also informs policy and governance, fosters interdisciplinary collaboration, and inspires future directions and innovation. The influence of this book extends beyond its pages, shaping the discourse and practice of multimedia data processing and security for years to come.

We would like to sincerely thank the authors of the contributing chapters and reviewers for their valuable suggestions and feedback. The editors would like to thank Mrs. Elizabeth Barrantes (Development Editor - IGI Global) and Mrs. Jocelynn Hessler (Managing Editor of book Development - IGI Global), for the editorial assistance and support in producing this important scientific work. Without this collective effort, this book would not have been possible to be completed.

We hope you will enjoy this book and this amazing research field multimedia data processing and security.

Ahmed A. Abd El-Latif
Menoufia University, Egypt & Prince Sultan University, Saudi Arabia

Mudasir Ahmad Wani
Prince Sultan University, Saudi Arabia

Yassine Maleh
Sultan Moulay Slimane University, Morocco

Mohammed A. El-Affendi
Prince Sultan University, Saudi Arabia

Section 1
Multimedia Security and Data Processing

Chapter 1
Multimedia Security Through 1D Chaotic Systems:
Review and Analysis

Achraf Daoui
National School of Applied Sciences, Sidi Mohamed Ben Abdellah-Fez University, Morocco

Ahmed A. Abd El-Latif
EIAS Data Science Lab, College of Computer and Information Sciences, Prince Sultan University, Saudi Arabia

ABSTRACT

The use of 1D chaotic maps in multimedia security applications is becoming increasingly attractive due to their advantages, including the high sensitivity to both initial and control parameters, rich dynamical behavior and ease of implementation for both software and hardware. This chapter presents a survey and analysis of recent multimedia encryption, watermarking, zero-watermarking and data hiding schemes involving the use of 1D chaotic maps. The present work also attempts to identify some drawbacks of existing 1D chaotic maps and multimedia security schemes involved the use of such maps, with suggestions for overcoming the identified limitations.

1. INTRODUCTION

Multimedia data such as text, images, audio and video, or their combination, are widely used in real-life situations. Indeed, Multimedia is used in a variety of real-life situations, including: education (Abdulrahaman et al., 2020), business (Koko

DOI: 10.4018/978-1-6684-7216-3.ch001

& Ogechi, 2019), communication (Sodhro et al., 2019), healthcare (Mahajan & Junnarkar, 2023), internet of things (IoT) (Nauman et al., 2020), manufacturing (Ko et al., 2021), etc. However, sharing multimedia content over unsecured communication channels is generally associated with several major problems, including: (i) Copyright issues: multimedia content is often protected by copyright law, and any unauthorized use of this content may constitute copyright infringement (Agilandeeswari et al., 2023). Examples of such issues include the unauthorized downloading, sharing or the use of copyrighted multimedia content without permission (Qureshi & Megías Jiménez, 2021). (ii) Data security concerns, as multimedia data can be voluminous and challenging to protect against manipulation by unauthorized parties (Taloba et al., 2023). This problem can cause serious damage to companies and organizations that use multimedia data (Sood, 2020). (iii) Privacy problems (Ma et al., 2019) as the multimedia data can be used to track people's movements, activities and so on. This can be challenging for the privacy-conscious of individuals (Liu et al., 2019). It is therefore extremely important to protect multimedia data from unauthorized access, modification or distribution (Dhar et al., 2022). To this end, multimedia security applications can be successfully incorporated. These applications include watermarking (Yamni, Daoui, Karmouni et al, 2020), zero-watermarking (Yamni, Karmouni, Daoui et al, 2020), encryption (Daoui, 2022)–(Abd EL-Latif et al., 2019), data hiding (Abd-El-Atty et al., 2020), (El-Latif et al., 2018) and multi-purpose (hybrid) applications (Daoui, Karmouni, El ogri et al, 2022)–(Wang, Song, & El-Latif, 2022). Figure 1 illustrates the main applications involved for multimedia security purposes.

Figure 1. Overview on multimedia security applications

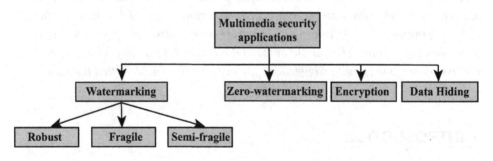

Watermarking is generally a technology that incorporates invisible data, called the watermark, into a multimedia file (image, video, audio, etc.) for the purposes of copyright protection and authentication (Amrit & Singh, 2022). In the literature, various types of watermarking schemes can be found, such as robust (Amrit & Singh,

2022), fragile (Molina-Garcia et al., 2020) and semi-fragile watermarking (Lefèvre et al., 2022). Robust watermarking schemes are generally designed to resist various attacks (geometric, noise, filtering, compression, etc.) (Li & Zhang, 2020). This type of watermark is often used for copyright protection. Fragile watermarking schemes are generally designed to be sensitive to minor modifications to the media file (Benrhouma et al., 2016). This watermarking kind is often used for authentication (Gul & Ozturk, 2021). Semi-fragile watermarking can be seen as a compromise between robust and fragile watermarking. This watermarking type is designed to resist some distortions caused by noise, compression, etc. However, is also sensitive to intentional attack (Agilandeeswari et al., 2023). Semi-fragile watermarking is often used for tracking and fingerprinting applications. In this application, it is essential that the watermark should be protected against unauthorized access or modification, in order to guarantee the security features of the designed watermarking scheme.

Unlike traditional watermarking, where the watermark is embedded into the cover multimedia file, which can degrade the quality of this file, the zero-watermarking application does not embed the watermark directly into a digital media signal (Daoui, Karmouni, Sayyouri, & Qjidaa, 2022). In this application, the watermark is embedded in features (vector/matrix) extracted from the input file. This guarantees the imperceptibility of the input file, i.e. no degradation is caused to this file. The main purpose of zero-watermarking is to protect the copyright of input media (Daoui, Karmouni, Sayyouri, & Qjidaa, 2022). To achieve this, the zero-watermarking schemes are expected to provide good robustness against various types of signal processing attacks. In this application, the embedded and extracted watermark is achieved by using a secure method (Yamni, Daoui, Karmouni, Sayyouri et al, 2023).

The encryption application can be used to protect the confidentiality, integrity and authenticity of multimedia data (Wang, Song, & El-Latif, 2022). For this, the input multimedia data is encrypted/decrypted using a secret key, so that unauthorized reading or modification of the encrypted data is impossible without the correct security key (Serag Eldin, 2023).

Data hiding is a valuable application for protecting the security and confidentiality of secret data being communicated over communication channels (Abd-El-Atty et al., 2020). As the use of multimedia continues to grow, so will the need for multimedia-based data hiding/steganography schemes (Hassanien et al., 2017). These schemes involve the integration of secret data into a cover medium (Abd El-Latif, Abd-El-Atty, Elseuofi et al, 2020), considering the need to achieve a high level of security for the integrated data, and to preserve the high quality of the cover medium to avoid attracting the attention of attackers (Peng, El-Atty, Khalifa, & El-Latif, 2019).

It appears that in the above multimedia applications, the security aspect is a fundamental requirement that needs to be satisfied before employing a designed application for practical use in real-life situations. To meet the security requirement in multimedia security applications, chaotic systems that are non-linear dynamic systems, can be used successfully, as they are highly sensitive to their initial conditions and control parameters. These can be used as security keys for communication between authorized users of multimedia files. Chaotic systems can be classified into one-dimensional (1D) and n-dimensional (nD) systems with n>1. nD chaotic systems include 2D (Daoui, Yamni, Karmouni, Sayyouri, Qjidaa, Motahhir et al, 2022), (Daoui, Yamni, Karmouni, Sayyouri, Qjidaa, Ahmad et al, 2022), 3D (Peng, El-Atty, Khalifa, & El-Latif, 2019), (Veeman et al., 2022), and more high-dimensional ones (Benkouider et al., 2022), (Abd-El-Atty et al., 2022). In general, high-dimensional chaotic maps can guarantee a high security level, as they contain a large number of control parameters and initial values (Talhaoui & Wang, 2021). However, the mathematical complexity of nD chaotic maps makes them challenging to implement both in software and hardware (Daoui, Yamni, Chelloug et al, 2023). To overcome this limitation, 1D chaotic maps are frequently incorporated, as they are easy to implement either in software or hardware (Daoui, Mao, Yamni et al, 2023).

This work focuses on the use 1D chaotic systems in multimedia security applications. Indeed, this work presents a summary of the latest watermarking, zero-watermarking, data hiding and multimedia encryption schemes. These summarizations present the main features of the considered schemes, as well as the role of 1D chaotic maps in these schemes, while showing some drawbacks of the reviewed schemes. Critical discussions of the reviewed schemes are also provided. In addition, some suggested guidelines are given for future work of multimedia security applications involving 1D chaotic maps. The remainder of this chapter is organized as follows: the second section presents the mathematical background of classical 1D chaotic maps. The third section is devoted to a review of recently designed 1D chaotic maps. The fourth section reviews recent multimedia encryption schemes based on 1D chaotic systems. The fifth section is devoted to reviewing some recent watermarking schemes that involve 1D chaotic systems. The sixth section is preserved to review recent zero-watermarking schemes using 1D chaotic systems. The seventh section presents a survey of recent data hiding schemes involving 1D chaotic maps. The final section concludes the present chapter and offers suggestions for future work concerning the incorporation of 1D chaotic systems in multimedia security applications.

2. CLASSICAL 1D CHAOTIC MAPS

One-dimensional chaotic maps are frequently used in multimedia security applications. The popularity of 1D maps in the field on multimedia security can be linked to their simple mathematical models and rich dynamics, making them an effective tool for a wide range of multimedia security applications. Extensive one-dimensional chaotic maps have been explored in the field of multimedia security. Here, some mathematical models of popular 1-D chaotic systems are presented.

2.1 Logistic Map

Mathematically, the logistic map's (LM) model is defined as follows (Pareek et al., 2006):

$$L_i = \lambda L_{i-1}(1 - L_{i-1}), \ L_i \in (0,1) \tag{1}$$

where $L_0 \in (0,1)$ is LM's initial condition and $\lambda \in [0-4]$ represents its control parameter. LM exhibits a highly chaotic behavior when $\lambda \in [3.54,4]$. Figure 2 illustrates the bifurcation diagram of LM.

Figure 2. Bifurcation diagram of LM

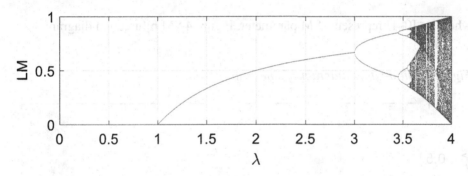

2.2 Tent Map

Tent map TM is one of the most popular 1D chaotic systems, which is defined by the next formula (Kanso, 2011):

$$T_i = \begin{cases} \lambda T_{i-1} & \text{for } T_{i-1} < 0.5 \\ \lambda(1 - T_{i-1}) & \text{for } T_{i-1} \geq 0.5 \end{cases} \quad \text{with } 0 \leq T_0 \leq 1 \tag{2}$$

where $\lambda \in [0-2]$ represents TM control parameter. Figure 3 shows TM bifurcation diagram.

Figure 3. Bifurcation diagram of the tent map

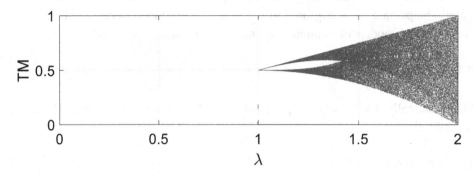

2.3 Sine Map

The 1D Sine chaotic map (SM) is defined by the next model (Hua & Zhou, 2016):

$$S_i = \lambda sin\left(\pi S_{i-1}\right) \text{ with } S_0 \in \left[0-1\right] \tag{3}$$

where $\lambda \in [0–1]$ represents SM parameter. Figure 4 SM bifurcation diagram.

Figure 4. Bifurcation diagram of sine map

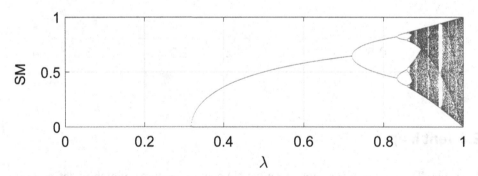

2.4 Chebyshev Map

The 1D Chebychev map (CM) is defined by the next mathematical formula (Geisel & Fairen, 1984):

$$C_i = cos\left(\lambda \times acos\left(C_{i-1}\right)\right) \text{ with } C_0 \in [0-1] \quad (4)$$

where $\lambda > 0$ represents CM parameter. Figure 5 illustrates CM bifurcation diagram.

Figure 5. Bifurcation diagram of Chebychev map

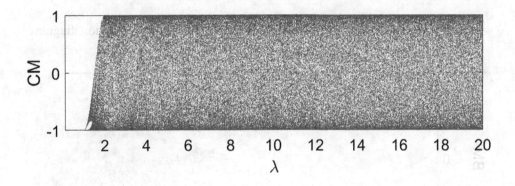

2.5 Quadratic Map

The 1D chaotic quadratic map (QM) model is given as follows (Panahi et al., 2018):

$$Q_i = \lambda - Q_{i-1}^2 \text{ with } Q_0 \in [0-1] \quad (5)$$

where $\lambda \in [0-2]$ represents CM parameter. Figure 6 illustrates CM bifurcation diagram.

Figure 6. Bifurcation diagram of QM

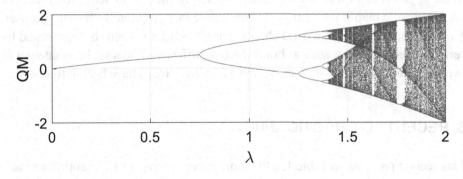

2.6 Bernoulli Map

The 1D Bernoulli map (BM) is defined as follows (Hernández-García et al., 2002):

$$B_i = \begin{cases} \lambda B_{i-1} + 0.5 & \text{for } B_{i-1} < 0 \\ \lambda B_{i-1} - 0.5 & \text{for } B_{i-1} \geq 0 \end{cases} \quad \text{with } 0 \leq B_0 \leq 1 \tag{6}$$

where $\lambda > 0$ represents CM parameter. Figure 7 illustrates CM bifurcation diagram.

Figure 7. Bifurcation diagram of BM

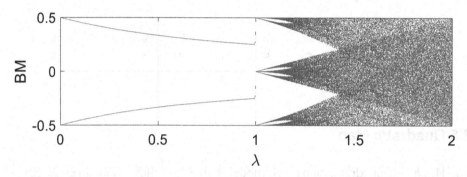

Although the classical 1D chaotic systems are easy to implement, both in hardware and software, they are still limited by the limited number of their control parameters, which makes the majority of 1D chaotic-based applications vulnerable to brute-force cracking attacks. In addition, most 1D chaotic systems have a limited range of their parameters, leading to the generation of chaotic sequences. This problem can lead to the appearance of a periodicity phenomenon in the output sequence values of the 1D chaotic map if its control parameters are inappropriately chosen by a user. This problem can lead to the 1D chaotic-based security systems being cracked by certain types of attacks, such as brute-force or differential attacks. In an attempt to overcome these limitations, some recent 1D chaotic maps have been introduced.

3. RECENT 1D CHAOTIC MAPS

This section presents, in Table 1, a literature survey on recent 1D chaotic maps and their key features.

Table 1. Literature review of recent 1D chaotic maps with their characteristics

Reference	Used Chaotic Map	Control Parameters Number	Interval of the Control Parameters
(Talhaoui & Wang, 2021)	Fractional 1D chaotic map	2	Limited
(Talhaoui et al., 2021)	1D cosine fractional chaotic map.	2	Infinite
(Muñoz-Guillermo, 2021)	q-deformed logistic map	2	Limited
(Kumar, 2022)	Novel 1D chaotic map	1	Limited
(Wang, Liu, Xu et al, 2022)	1D LS chaotic model	2	Limited
(Belazi et al., 2022)	Improved 1D chaotic map	1	Limited
(Daoui, Karmouni, El ogri et al, 2022)	Modified logistic map	2	Limited
(Zhu et al., 2022)	1D memristive chaotic map	1	Infinite
(Rong et al., 2022)	Newly designed 1D chaotic map	1	Infinite
(Zhu et al., 2023)	1D PWQPCM map	3	Limited
(Liu & Wang, 2023)	1D Quadratic map	3	Limited
(Daoui, Yamni, Chelloug et al, 2023)	1D Multi-parametric Tent map	6	Infinite

From Table 1, it can be deduced that some recently introduced 1D chaotic maps (Talhaoui & Wang, 2021), (Muñoz-Guillermo, 2021), (Kumar, 2022), (Wang, Liu, Xu et al, 2022), (Daoui, Karmouni, El ogri et al, 2022), (Belazi et al., 2022), (Zhu et al., 2023), (Liu & Wang, 2023) are still limited by the previously mentioned problems in Section 2. By contrast, other recent maps introduced in (Talhaoui et al., 2021), (Zhu et al., 2022), (Rong et al., 2022), effectively overcome the limitations of the 1D chaotic map's limited-range control parameters. In fact, these maps contain control parameters that are defined over infinite range (R-domain). However, these cards are still limited by the small number of control parameters (less than 3), making them vulnerable to cyber-attacks. To overcome both the limited number of control parameters and the restricted range of such parameters, Daoui et al. recently introduced the 1D Multiparametric Tent Map (MTM) (Daoui, Yamni, Chelloug et al, 2023) as an extended version of the existing 1D tent map. The MTM contains six control parameters defined over an infinite interval, making the MTM superior to existing 1D chaotic maps in both number of control parameters. Consequently, the use of MTM in security systems can provide superior security performance compared to existing 1D chaotic maps.

Apparently, the trend in the design of new 1D chaotic maps is to create new models of chaotic maps incorporating a large number of control parameters defined over an unlimited range. However, when designing these maps, it is important to ensure that any small variation in the control parameters results in a large variation in the resultant chaotic sequence, thus guaranteeing the use of these parameters as security keys in security systems. It's also worth considering the histogram shape of the output chaotic sequence. This shape should be uniform for effective use of the chaotic sequences in certain security applications, particularly multimedia encryption.

4. MULTIMEDIA ENCRYPTION BY 1D CHAOTIC MAPS

Multimedia encryption is considered a powerful tool that can be used to protect digital multimedia content against a variety of cyber-attacks. It is a key security solution for organizations that handle sensitive data or need to guarantee the authenticity of their communications. Multimedia encryption schemes can be divided into two categories: symmetrical and asymmetrical. In the case of symmetrical encryption, the same security key is used for both encryption and decryption of the input data. It is therefore relatively easy to implement, but is also vulnerable to cyber-attack if the used security key is not sufficiently resistant to brute-force attacks. For asymmetric encryption systems, two security keys are required: a public key and a private one. The public key is used to encrypt the input multimedia data, and the private key is employed to decrypt the data. This type of encryption is generally more secure than symmetrical encryption, but it is also more complex to implement. Typically, the majority of multimedia encrypted schemes are symmetric. These schemes include the next main phases: (i) the generation of a pseudo-rando sequence, which is often produced by using a chaotic system. (ii) The confusion phase, during which the values of the multimedia files (pixels, samples, etc.) are confused/scrambled in order to break their natural correlation and also to hide their visual information. (iii) Diffusion phase: during this phase, the values of the multimedia files (pixels, samples, etc.) are modified to cancel their statistical information for the purpose of preventing any statistical attack. The confusion and diffusion phases can be repeatedly repeated n-rounds by using a pseudo-random sequence to ensure a maximum level of security. Figure 8 summarizes the basic steps involved in symmetrical multimedia encryption and decryption phases. Although multimedia cryptosystems are good tools for the secure transmission of multimedia content over unsecured communication channels, they can be vulnerability to cyber-attacks such as brute-force attacks and differential cryptanalysis. These attacks can be used to crack encryption schemes if these schemes do not provide a strong enough security standard. It is therefore important to consider this drawback when designing any encryption scheme. In multimedia encryption applications, the use of 1D chaotic maps is popular due to their advantages, including the simple mathematical nature of their models, which make them easy to implement in both software and hardware. This property is also desirable for real-time applications, where the fast data processing is highly valued.

Figure 8. General phases of symmetric multimedia encryption

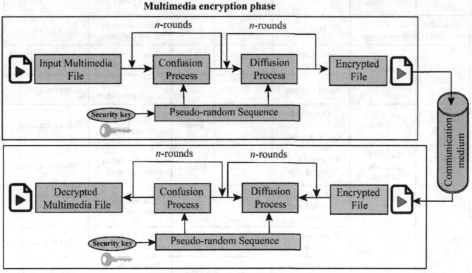

Table 2 lists recent 1D chaotic-based encryption schemes with their specifications including the type of the encrypted multimedia, the used chaotic map, its number of parameters and the range of these parameters (Limited/Infinite).

From Table 2, it's apparent that the use of 1D chaotic systems is becoming increasingly successful in multimedia encryption application. The popularity of 1D chaotic systems is essentially due to their ease of implementation, both in software and hardware. In addition, the discrete nature of these schemes and their rich chaotic behavior make them preferable for use in multimedia cryptosystems. However, the use of 1D chaotic systems in multimedia cryptosystems also presents certain challenges. In fact, the main limitation of using 1D chaotic maps in multimedia encryption systems is their vulnerability to brute-force attacks, as the majority of these maps contain only a small number of parameters and their chaotic behavior is limited to certain restricted ranges of their control parameters. This problem means that the key space of the chaos-based 1D cryptosystem is small. To overcome this limitation, cryptosystem designers can follow several paths: (i) the generation of

11

Table 2. Review of recent 1D chaotic-based encryption schemes

Scheme	Encrypted Multimedia	Chaotic Map Feautures				
		Used 1D Chaotic Map	Number of Control Parameters	Chaotic Range	Limitation	Histogram Shape
(Midoun et al., 2021)	Grayscale and color images	1-DFCS	1	Infinite	Low number of control parameters	Not mentioned
(Liu & Wang, 2023)	Grayscale and binary images	1D quadratic map	1	Finite	Low number of control parameters	Not mentioned
(Khairullah et al., 2021)	Grayscale and color images	1D-IQM	1	Finite	Low number of control parameters	Uniform
(Dou & Li, 2021)	Grayscale images	novel Logistic map	1	Finite	Low number of control parameters	Not mentioned
		novel sine map	1	Finite	Low number of control parameters	Not mentioned
(Dou & Li, 2020)	Color images	Combined logistic, sine and Chebyshev maps	3	Finite	Complex mathematical form	Not mentioned
(Belazi et al., 2022)	Grayscale medical images	Improved Sine-Tangent map	1	Infinite	Low number of control parameters	Not mentioned
(Trujillo-Toledo et al., 2021)	Color images	Improved Bernoulli shift map	1	Finite	Low number of control parameters	Not mentioned
		Improved Tent map	1	Finite	Low number of control parameters	Not mentioned
		Improved Zigzag map	1	Finite	Low number of control parameters	Not mentioned
		Improved Logistic map	1	Finite	Low number of control parameters	Not mentioned
(Daoui, Yamni, Chelloug et al, 2023)	Grayscale and color images	Multiparametric Tent map	6	Infinite	Non-uniform histogram	Uniform after histogram equalization
(Daoui, Mao, Yamni et al, 2023)	Grayscale and color medical images	Multiparametric Piecewise Linear Chaotic Map	8	Infinite	-	Not mentioned

several chaotic sequences via the use of 1D chaotic system, and for each generated sequence a different value of the control parameter is used. The generated chaotic sequences are then used for different roles (e.g. confusion and diffusion) in the designed encryption algorithm. This method can increase the key space of the encryption algorithm, but also increases the encryption algorithm's complexity and fails to solve the problem of the limited range of the control parameter that lead to a chaotic behavior. Another way of designing 1D chaotic systems is to use combined/ coupled 1D chaotic maps. This method can be used to increase the number of the chaotic map's control parameters, thereby increasing the key space of encryption systems. However, designing 1D chaotic maps with coupled 1D systems can increase the complexity of the designed maps, thus losing the easy-to-implement property of the designed 1D map. Recently, Daoui et al. proposed a way of designing 1D chaotic maps with a large number of parameters defined over infinite range. The authors' method extends existing classical chaotic maps by increasing the number of their control parameters and ensuring that these parameters are defined over an infinite range. This method has proven its ability to significantly improve the key space of multimedia encryption algorithms. In addition, the ease of implementation of the improved multiparametric chaotic maps is also preserved. The authors' method can be extensively used to boost the security level of encryption schemes, designed on the basis of 1D chaotic maps. Another problem associated with most 1D chaotic maps is the non-uniform histogram of the generated chaotic sequences. This failure can reduce the security level of the designed cryptosystems in terms of statistical strength. To solve this problem, a general method proposed in XX can be applied to make the histogram of a chaotic sequence uniform and, consequently, this sequence becomes suitable for multimedia encryption. It seems that the use of 1D chaotic maps with a large number of parameters and rich dynamic behavior will continue to develop in the field of multimedia encryption.

5. MULTIMEDIA WATERMARKING BY 1D CHAOTIC MAPS

Basically, multimedia watermarking application consists of two main phases: watermark embedding and the watermark extraction. The watermark embedding phase consists in incorporating a secret data (e.g. binary image), known as the watermark, into the original/host multimedia file (signal, image, video), producing the watermarked multimedia file. To guarantee the security of the embedded information in this stage, a secret key can be used for the watermark embedding. This key can be produced using chaotic maps, as these maps produce pseudo-random sequences, making them highly unpredictable and hard for reproduction by attackers. The watermarked file can then be communicated over unsecured communication channels. The second phase of the watermarking application is designed to extract the watermark data from the watermarked image. In this phase, the same key used in the previous phase must be used to successfully extract the watermark data. The extracted watermark is then compared to the original one in order to confirm or deny the originality of the communicated multimedia file. Figure 9 gives an overview of the multimedia watermaking phases.

Figure 9. Overview of image watermarking phases

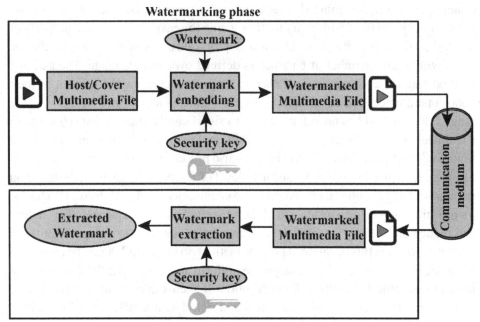

Table 3 summarizes some recent multimedia watermarking systems involving the use of 1D chaotic maps. This table also presents some specifications of the surveyed schemes, focusing on the used chaotic system.

Table 3 shows that the use of 1D chaotic systems is becoming increasingly popular in the field of multimedia watermarking to guarantee a good security level of the proposed scheme. The main use of 1D chaotic systems in multimedia watermarking can be summarized as follows: the encryption of watermark bits, the generation of chaotic sequences for secure integration and extraction of the watermark data, and the generation of chaotic watermarks for use in multimedia authentication purposes. Thus, 1D chaotic systems can considerably improve the security level of watermarking schemes, and their control parameters can be used as security keys. However, the majority of 1D chaotic-based watermarking systems remain vulnerable to cyberattacks, as these systems involve the use of 1D chaotic systems of small number of parameters and a limited chaotic range. Therefore, when considering the use of a 1D chaotic map in a watermarking scheme, it's important to consider the need to use a 1D chaotic systems with a large number of parameters and extensive chaotic behavior, which ensures a maximum-security level to resist cyber-attacks.

Table 3. Review of digital multimedia watermarking schemes including 1D chaotic maps.

Watermarking Scheme			Used 1D Chaotic Map			
Scheme	Watermarking Type	Role	Used Maps	Role	Number of Control Parameters	Chaotic Behavior
(Haghighi et al., 2019)	Fragile	Detection and recovery of tampered images	Chebyshev-Chebyshev System	Watermark generation, insertion and extraction	2	Limited
(Nazari & Maneshi, 2021)	Fragile	Tampering detection of medical images	Chaotic Logistic-Sine map	Watermark bits generation, integration and data extraction	1	Limited
(Huang et al., 2022)	Fragile	Tamper detection and image recovery	Logistic-Logistic map	Generate chaotic sequences for watermark insertion/extraction	1	Limited
(Nouioua et al., 2018)	Robust	Copyright protection for videos	Logistic map	Watermark encryption	1	Limited
(Ravichandran et al., 2021)	Robust	Ensuring medical image and data integrity and authentication	Coupled Logistic-Sine map	Watermark and data encryption, embedding and extraction	1	Limited
(Hosny et al., 2021)	Robust	Copyright protection for color images	Sine chaotic map	Watermark image scrambling	1	Limited
(Yuan et al., 2021)	Robust	Grayscale image copyrights protection	Logistic map	Watermark encryption, data embedding and extraction	1	Limited
(Yamni, Karmouni, Sayyouri, & Qjidaa, 2022)	Robust	Audio/speech copyrights protection	MLNCML map	Watermark encryption	3	Limited
(Yamni, Karmouni, Sayyouri, & Qjidaa, 2022)	Robust	Audio copyrights protection	MLNCML map	Watermark encryption	3	Limited
(Fan et al., 2022)	Robust	Video copyright protection	Logistic map	Watermark encryption	1	Limited
(Borah & Borah, 2019)	Semi-fragile	3D models authentication	logistic map	watermark encryption	1	Limited

6. MULTIMEDIA ZERO-WATERMARKING BY 1D CHAOTIC MAPS

The zero-watermarking multimedia application can be considered as a type of digital watermarking, but with the advantage of keeping the original multimedia file unchanged. Thus, the zero-watermarking application guarantees a perfect imperceptibility of the protected multimedia file. This application comprises two main phases, illustrated in Figure 10. The first phase involves extracting features from the original multimedia file. This phase can be implemented in the spatial domain, or in the transform domain. Typically, the extracted features in the transformation domain are more resistant to various attacks than those extracted in the spatial domain. Then, the watermark file is embedded in the extracted features (coefficients). This process requires the use of a security key to guarantee that the designed scheme is secure against attacks. At this stage, 1D chaotic systems can be employed for encrypting the watermark file and/or for securely integrating this file into the extracted multimedia features. Finally, a master share, called "zero watermark is generated for future use during the copyright verification phase. The zero-watermark and the original multimedia can be communicated between the sender and the recipient via different communication channels. In the copyright verification phase, which is carried out by the receiver, the received multimedia file and the zero-watermark are used to confirm or deny the originality of the received file. In this phase, the same process carried out by the sender is followed by the received image to create the zero-watermark. It should be noted that the zero-watermarking application is symmetric, so the same security keys must be used in both phases of this application. To confirm or deny the originality of the received file, a comparison is necessary between the zero-watermark extracted from the original file and that extracted from the received multimedia file.

Figure 10. Overview of image zero-watermarking phases

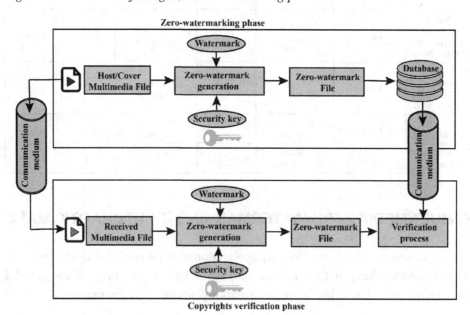

Table 4 provides a summary of recent zero-watermarking schemes, which incorporate 1D chaotic maps. This table lists certain characteristics related to the surveyed scheme as well as to the used 1D chaotic map.

Table 4. Review of digital multimedia watermarking schemes including 1D chaotic maps

Zero-Watermarking Scheme			Used 1D Chaotic Map			
Scheme	Role	Implementation Domain	Used Maps	Role	Number of Control Parameters	Chaotic Behavior
(Wang et al., 2019)	Copyright protection of grayscale stereo images	Transform	Logistic map	Encrypting the watermark and the feature vectors	1	Limited
(Xia et al., 2019)	Medical images copyright protection	Transform	Logistic map	Feature vector selection, watermark encryption and insertion	1	Limited
(Wang et al., 2020)	Copyright protection of grayscale images	Transform	Logistic map and Tent map	Feature vector selection, watermark and feature vector encryption	2	Limited
(Xia et al., 2021)	Color medical images copyrights protection	Transform	1D ICMIC map	Feature vector and watermark encryption	1	Infinite
(Khafaga et al., 2022)	Copyright protection of Color medical images	Transform	1D Chebyshev map	Watermark scrambling	1	Infinite
(Liu et al., 2021)	Volumetric medical imaging copyrights protection	Spatial	Logistic-logistic system	Feature vector encryption	2	Limited
(Liu et al., 2022)	Copyright protection of DIBR 3D videos	Spatial	Logistic-logistic system	Feature vectors encryption	2	Limited
(Dai et al., 2022)	Copyright protection of grayscale medical images	Spatial	Logistic-logistic system	Scrambling the feature vector	2	Limited
(Huang et al., 2023)	Grayscale medical images copyrights protection	Spatial	Improved logistic map	Watermark encryption	2	Limited
(Xia et al., 2023)	Grayscale image copyrights protection	Transform	Coupled 1D Logistic map and Sine map	Watermark encryption	1	Limited

Table 4 clearly shows that the development of new, robust zero-watermarking schemes is becoming a hot topic in copyright protection technology area. The particular attention paid to zero-watermarking technology is due in particular to its ability to achieve perfect imperceptibility and its excellent resistance to various types of attack. Table 4 also shows that the majority of zero-watermarking schemes have been developed for medical images copyrights protection. The reason for this is that the protected medical multimedia must be preserved unchanged to prevent any misinterpretation by healthcare professionals. Given the advantages of zero-watermarking applications, it seems that researchers will continue to suggest new schemes that are highly robust against various types of attack (geometric, signal processing attacks, filtering, noise, etc.). Another point to emerge from Table 4 analysis is that the use of 1D chaotic systems in zero-watermarking schemes is popular and fundamental. Indeed, 1D chaotic systems are generally deployed in zero-watermarking scheme to provide certain security level to avoid third-party attacks. The use of a 1D chaotic systems in the zero-watermarking application can be summarized as follows: (i) the encryption of watermark data, which is essential for copyright verification. (ii) The encryption of feature vectors extracted from multimedia files. (iii) The pseudo-random selection of feature vector coefficients computed from copyrighted files. Furthermore, the initial values and control parameters of the used chaotic systems are provided security keys that are needed for both zero-watermarking and copyright verification phases. However, the majority of 1D chaotic maps employed in zero-watermarking schemes can be vulnerable to cyber-attacks, as these maps contain only a small number of parameters and these parameters have a restricted range, which results in chaotic behavior. In future zero-watermarking work using 1D chaotic maps, it is essential to consider the key-space strength of the system security key. Indeed, the key-space should be able to withstand different attacks, in particular brute-force ones.

7. DATA HIDING IN MULTIMEDIA BY 1D CHAOTIC MAPS

Secret message data hiding is considered as important application in the field of cybersecurity. The data hiding involves concealing a secret information/message in a digital medium/cover, usually a multimedia file such as an image, audio or video file. The secret information, called stego-text, is typically of lower size than the cover file. The integrated stego-text is designed to preserve a high-quality of the multimedia files. There are two main types of steganography: spatial steganography and frequency steganography. In spatial steganography, the stego-text is cancelled out in the spatial domain of the carrier multimedia file. Frequency steganography involves hiding the secret data in the carrier's frequency domain computed from the cover multimedia file. This means that the original multimedia file is first transformed into the frequency domain through transformations, generally orthogonal transforms, such as Discrete Wavelet Transform (DWT), Discrete Cosine Transform

(DCT), Discrete Orthogonal Moments, etc. Next, the stego-text is hidden in the frequency coefficients by using a secret method. Finally, a reconstruction process is carried out to produce the stego-multimedia file containing the secret data. The latter is then safely forwarded from the sender to the receiver via an unsecured communication channel. On the receiver side, an extraction process is performed to retrieve the secret message. Figure 11 summarizes the entire process of data hiding in multimedia files. 1D chaotic maps can be useful in the context of data hiding to ensure a secret data incorporation process. Indeed, more secure data integration techniques increase the difficulty for attackers to identify, remove or extract secret data from the cover multimedia medium.

Figure 11. Overview of multimedia data hiding phases

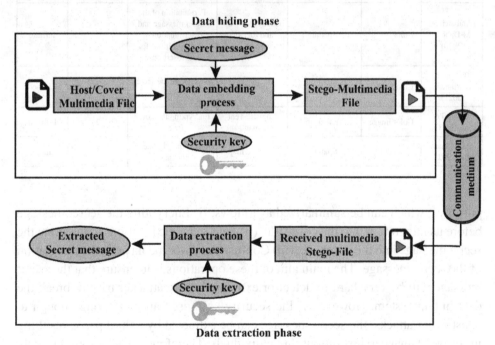

Table 5 summarizes recent work of data hiding schemes that involve the use of 1D chaotic maps. The table highlights some important features related to both the summarized scheme as well as the employed 1D chaotic map.

Table 5 confirms that 1D chaotic systems are fundamental and popular tools in data hiding applications. The initial values and local parameters of these maps are given as secret keys to be shared between the sender and receiver of the secret message. Chaotic maps can be used in multimedia data hiding for a variety of

Table 5. Review of digital multimedia watermarking schemes including 1D chaotic maps

Data Hiding Scheme			Used 1D Chaotic Map			
Scheme	Cover File	Implementation Domain	Used Maps	Role	Number of Control Parameters	Chaotic Behavior
(Kaur & Singh, 2021)	Grayscale image	Transform	Logistic map, Sine map and Coupled chaotic map	Random embedding of the secret data in the cover image	3	Limited
(Abdel-Aziz et al., 2021)	Color image	Transform	Logistic map	Cover image rows and columns confusion	1	Limited
(Pak et al., 2020)	Color image	Transform	Improved 1D chaotic map	Selection of secret message integration positions	2	Limited
(Alabaichi & Al-Dabbas, 2020)	Color image	Spatial	Chebyshev map and logistic map	Permutation of the secret message and determination of secret positions for its insertion.	2	Infinite
(Gambhir & Mandal, 2021)	Color image	Spatial	Tent map	Encrypting the secret message	1	Limited
(Sharafi et al., 2021)	Color image	Transform	Logistic-Tent map	Encrypting the cover image	2	Limited
(Manjunath et al., 2022)	Audio	Spatial	Logistic map	Encrypting the secret message	1	Limited

purposes, which can be summarized as follows: (i) Encrypting the secret message before its integration into the cover file. (ii) Select chaotic positions to integrate the secret message into the cover file. (iii) Confuse the cover media prior the integration of the secret message. The main aim of these operations is to ensure that the secret message will be very hard to detect or extract when an attacker tries to break the data hiding system. However, if the security keys used are not strong enough to resist cyber-attacks, the secret message can be extracted by a third party, resulting in serious damage to institutions and individuals. Therefore, when designing a data hiding scheme, it is essential to ensure a high security standard while maximizing the key space of used security keys. However, Table 5 content shows also that the majority of 1D chaotic system-based data hiding schemes use a small number of security keys, that are the control parameters of the chaotic maps. This problem can make such schemes highly vulnerable to cyber-attacks, especially when using brute-force attacks with modern computers. It is therefore strongly recommended that future data hiding schemes relying on 1D chaotic systems should envisage the use of high-parameter chaotic systems, which are highly sensitive to small variations, thus guaranteeing the robustness of the developed schemes to various attacks.

8. CONCLUSION

This chapter presents a survey and analysis of recent multimedia encryption, watermarking, zero-watermarking and data hiding schemes involving the use of 1D chaotic maps. The survey and analysis carried out showed that the use of 1D chaotic maps in multimedia security applications is becoming increasingly attractive due to their benefits, which include the high sensitivity to the initial and control parameters, the rich dynamical behavior and the ease of implementation for both software and hardware. The present work has also identified some drawbacks of the reviewed 1D chaotic maps, security multimedia security schemes, as well as the way in which chaotic maps are integrated into multimedia security systems. To overcome these drawbacks, a number of suggestions are made for consideration in future work. which have the disadvantages of high dimensions and weight (not possible), high energy consumption and undesirable use of the Internet of Things environment. Consequently, future trends in multimedia security systems based on 1D chaotic can be oriented towards the design of low-cost hardware implementations based on low-cost embedded system boards.

REFERENCES

Abd-El-Atty, B., Abd El-Latif, A. A., & Amin, M. (2017). New Quantum Image Steganography Scheme with Hadamard Transformation. *Proceedings of the International Conference on Advanced Intelligent Systems and Informatics 2016*, 533, 342-352. 10.1007/978-3-319-48308-5_33

Abd-El-Atty, B., Belazi, A., & Abd El-Latif, A. A. (2022). A Novel Approach for Robust S-Box Construction Using a 5-D Chaotic Map and Its Application to Image Cryptosystem. In Cybersecurity: A New Approach Using Chaotic Systems. Springer International Publishing. doi:10.1007/978-3-030-92166-8_1

Abd-El-Atty, B., Iliyasu, A. M., Alaskar, H., & Abd El-Latif, A. A. (2020, January). A Robust Quasi-Quantum Walks-based Steganography Protocol for Secure Transmission of Images on Cloud-based E-healthcare Platforms. *Sensors (Basel)*, *20*(11), 11. Advance online publication. doi:10.339020113108 PMID:32486383

Abd El-Latif, A. A., Abd-El-Atty, B., Amin, M., & Iliyasu, A. M. (2020, February). Quantum-inspired cascaded discrete-time quantum walks with induced chaotic dynamics and cryptographic applications. *Scientific Reports*, *10*(1), 1. doi:10.103841598-020-58636-w PMID:32029798

Abd El-Latif, A. A., Abd-El-Atty, B., Elseuofi, S., Khalifa, H. S., Alghamdi, A. S., Polat, K., & Amin, M. (2020, March). Secret images transfer in cloud system based on investigating quantum walks in steganography approaches. *Physica A*, *541*, 123687. doi:10.1016/j.physa.2019.123687

Abd EL-Latif, A. A., Abd-El-Atty, B., & Venegas-Andraca, S. E. (2019, August). A novel image steganography technique based on quantum substitution boxes. *Optics & Laser Technology*, *116*, 92–102. doi:10.1016/j.optlastec.2019.03.005

Abdel-Aziz, M. M., Hosny, K. M., & Lashin, N. A. (2021, March). Improved data hiding method for securing color images. *Multimedia Tools and Applications*, *80*(8), 12641–12670. doi:10.100711042-020-10217-9

Abdulrahaman, M. D., Faruk, N., Oloyede, A. A., Surajudeen-Bakinde, N. T., Olawoyin, L. A., Mejabi, O. V., Imam-Fulani, Y. O., Fahm, A. O., & Azeez, A. L. (2020, November). Multimedia tools in the teaching and learning processes: A systematic review. *Heliyon*, *6*(11), e05312. doi:10.1016/j.heliyon.2020.e05312 PMID:33195834

Agilandeeswari, L., Prabukumar, M., & Alenizi, F. A. (2023). A robust semi-fragile watermarking system using Pseudo-Zernike moments and dual tree complex wavelet transform for social media content authentication. *Multimedia Tools and Applications*. doi:10.100711042-023-15177-4 PMID:37362657

Alabaichi, M. A. A. K. & Al-Dabbas, A. S. (2020). Image steganography using least significant bit and secret map techniques. *Int. J. Electr. Comput. Eng.*, *10*(1).

Amrit, P., & Singh, A. K. (2022, April). Survey on watermarking methods in the artificial intelligence domain and beyond. *Computer Communications*, *188*, 52–65. doi:10.1016/j.comcom.2022.02.023

Belazi, A., Kharbech, S., Aslam, M. N., Talha, M., Xiang, W., Iliyasu, A. M., & El-Latif, A. A. A. (2022, May). Improved Sine-Tangent chaotic map with application in medical images encryption. *J. Inf. Secur. Appl.*, *66*, 103131. doi:10.1016/j.jisa.2022.103131

Benkouider, K., Vaidyanathan, S., Sambas, A., Tlelo-Cuautle, E., El-Latif, A. A. A., Abd-El-Atty, B., Bermudez-Marquez, C. F., Sulaiman, I. M., Awwal, A. M., & Kumam, P. (2022). A New 5-D Multistable Hyperchaotic System With Three Positive Lyapunov Exponents: Bifurcation Analysis, Circuit Design, FPGA Realization and Image Encryption. *IEEE Access : Practical Innovations, Open Solutions, 10*, 90111–90132. doi:10.1109/ACCESS.2022.3197790

Benrhouma, O., Hermassi, H., Abd El-Latif, A. A., & Belghith, S. (2016, July). Chaotic watermark for blind forgery detection in images. *Multimedia Tools and Applications, 75*(14), 8695–8718. doi:10.100711042-015-2786-z

Borah, S., & Borah, B. (2019). A blind, semi-fragile 3d mesh watermarking algorithm using minimum distortion angle quantization index modulation (3d-mdaqim). *Arabian Journal for Science and Engineering, 44*(4), 3867–3882. doi:10.100713369-018-03714-5

Dai, Z., Lian, C., He, Z., Jiang, H., & Wang, Y. (2022). A Novel Hybrid Reversible-Zero Watermarking Scheme to Protect Medical Image. *IEEE Access : Practical Innovations, Open Solutions, 10*, 58005–58016. doi:10.1109/ACCESS.2022.3170030

Daoui, A. (2022). Color stereo image encryption and local zero-watermarking schemes using octonion Hahn moments and modified Henon map. *J. King Saud Univ.- Comput. Inf. Sci., 34*(10), 8927–8954.

Daoui, A., Karmouni, H., El ogri, O., Sayyouri, M., & Qjidaa, H. (2022, March). Robust image encryption and zero-watermarking scheme using SCA and modified logistic map ». *Expert Systems with Applications, 190*, 116193. doi:10.1016/j.eswa.2021.116193

Daoui, A., Karmouni, H., Sayyouri, M., & Qjidaa, H. (2022a). New method for bio-signals zero-watermarking using quaternion shmaliy moments and short-time fourier transform. *Multimedia Tools and Applications, 81*(12), 17369–17399. doi:10.100711042-022-12660-2

Daoui, A., Karmouni, H., Sayyouri, M., & Qjidaa, H. (2022b). Robust 2D and 3D images zero-watermarking using dual Hahn moment invariants and Sine Cosine Algorithm. *Multimedia Tools and Applications, 81*(18), 25581–25611. doi:10.100711042-022-12298-0 PMID:35345547

Daoui, A., Mao, H., Yamni, M., Li, Q., Alfarraj, O., & Abd El-Latif, A. A. (2023, January). Novel Integer Shmaliy Transform and New Multiparametric Piecewise Linear Chaotic Map for Joint Lossless Compression and Encryption of Medical Images in IoMTs. *Mathematics, 11*(16), 16. doi:10.3390/math11163619

Daoui, A., Yamni, M., Chelloug, S. A., Wani, M. A., & El-Latif, A. A. A. (2023). Efficient image encryption scheme using novel 1D multiparametric dynamical tent map and parallel computing. *Mathematics, 11*(7), 1589. doi:10.3390/math11071589

Daoui, A., Yamni, M., Karmouni, H., Sayyouri, M., Qjidaa, H., Ahmad, M., & Abd El-Latif, A. A. (2022). Biomedical Multimedia Encryption by Fractional-Order Meixner Polynomials Map and Quaternion Fractional-Order Meixner Moments. *IEEE Access : Practical Innovations, Open Solutions, 10*, 102599–102617. doi:10.1109/ACCESS.2022.3203067

Daoui, A., Yamni, M., Karmouni, H., Sayyouri, M., Qjidaa, H., Motahhir, S., Jamil, O., El-Shafai, W., Algarni, A. D., Soliman, N. F., & Aly, M. H. (2022). Efficient Biomedical Signal Security Algorithm for Smart Internet of Medical Things (IoMTs) Applications. *Electronics (Basel), 11*(23), 3867. doi:10.3390/electronics11233867

Dhar, S., Khare, A., & Singh, R. (2022). Advanced security model for multimedia data sharing in Internet of Things. *Trans. Emerg. Telecommun. Technology,* e4621, . doi:10.1002/ett.4621

Dou, Y., & Li, M. (2020, January). Cryptanalysis of a New Color Image Encryption Using Combination of the 1D Chaotic Map. *Applied Sciences (Basel, Switzerland), 10*(6), 6. doi:10.3390/app10062187

Dou, Y., & Li, M. (2021, July). An image encryption algorithm based on a novel 1D chaotic map and compressive sensing. *Multimedia Tools and Applications, 80*(16), 24437–24454. doi:10.100711042-021-10850-y

El-Latif, A. A. A., Abd-El-Atty, B., Hossain, M. S., Elmougy, S., & Ghoneim, A. (2018). Secure Quantum Steganography Protocol for Fog Cloud Internet of Things. *IEEE Access : Practical Innovations, Open Solutions, 6*, 10332–10340. doi:10.1109/ACCESS.2018.2799879

Fan, D., Zhang, X., Kang, W., Zhao, H., & Lv, Y. (2022, January). Video Watermarking Algorithm Based on NSCT, Pseudo 3D-DCT and NMF. *Sensors (Basel), 22*(13), 13. doi:10.339022134752 PMID:35808245

Gambhir, G., & Mandal, J. K. (2021, December). Shared memory implementation and performance analysis of LSB steganography based on chaotic tent map. *Innovations in Systems and Software Engineering, 17*(4), 333–342. doi:10.100711334-021-00385-8

Geisel, T., & Fairen, V. (1984, October). Statistical properties of chaos in Chebyshev maps. *Physics Letters. [Part A], 105*(6), 263–266. doi:10.1016/0375-9601(84)90993-9

Gul, E., & Ozturk, S. (2021, June). A novel pixel-wise authentication-based self-embedding fragile watermarking method. *Multimedia Systems*, *27*(3), 531–545. doi:10.100700530-021-00751-3

Haghighi, B. B., Taherinia, A. H., & Mohajerzadeh, A. H. (2019). TRLG: Fragile blind quad watermarking for image tamper detection and recovery by providing compact digests with optimized quality using LWT and GA. *Information Sciences*, *486*, 204–230. doi:10.1016/j.ins.2019.02.055

Hernández-García, E., Masoller, C., & Mirasso, C. R. (2002, March). Anticipating the dynamics of chaotic maps. *Physics Letters. [Part A]*, *295*(1), 39–43. doi:10.1016/S0375-9601(02)00147-0

Hosny, K. M., Darwish, M. M., & Fouda, M. M. (2021). Robust color images watermarking using new fractional-order exponent moments. *IEEE Access : Practical Innovations, Open Solutions*, *9*, 47425–47435. doi:10.1109/ACCESS.2021.3068211

Hua, Z., & Zhou, Y. (2016, April). Image encryption using 2D Logistic-adjusted-Sine map. *Information Sciences*, *339*, 237–253. doi:10.1016/j.ins.2016.01.017

Huang, L., Kuang, D., Li, C., Zhuang, Y., Duan, S., & Zhou, X. (2022, February). A self-embedding secure fragile watermarking scheme with high quality recovery. *Journal of Visual Communication and Image Representation*, *83*, 103437. doi:10.1016/j.jvcir.2022.103437

Huang, T., Xu, J., Tu, S., & Han, B. (2023, March). Robust zero-watermarking scheme based on a depthwise overparameterized VGG network in healthcare information security. *Biomedical Signal Processing and Control*, *81*, 104478. doi:10.1016/j.bspc.2022.104478

Kanso, A. (2011). Self-shrinking chaotic stream ciphers. *Communications in Nonlinear Science and Numerical Simulation*, *16*(2), 822–836. doi:10.1016/j.cnsns.2010.04.039

Kaur, R., & Singh, B. (2021). A novel approach for data hiding based on combined application of discrete cosine transform and coupled chaotic map. *Multimedia Tools and Applications*, *80*(10), 14665–14691. doi:10.100711042-021-10528-5

Khafaga, D. S., Karim, F. K., Darwish, M. M., & Hosny, K. M. (2022, January). Robust Zero-Watermarking of Color Medical Images Using Multi-Channel Gaussian-Hermite Moments and 1D Chebyshev Chaotic Map. *Sensors (Basel)*, *22*(15), 15. Advance online publication. doi:10.339022155612 PMID:35957177

Khairullah, M. K., Alkahtani, A. A., Bin Baharuddin, M. Z., & Al-Jubari, A. M. (2021, January). Designing 1D Chaotic Maps for Fast Chaotic Image Encryption. *Electronics (Basel)*, *10*(17), 17. Advance online publication. doi:10.3390/electronics10172116

Ko, D., Lee, S., & Park, J. (2021, November). A study on manufacturing facility safety system using multimedia tools for cyber physical systems. *Multimedia Tools and Applications*, *80*(26), 34553–34570. doi:10.100711042-020-09925-z

Koko, M. N., & Ogechi, N. (2019). Perceived Influence of Mobile Learning and Multimedia on Business Education Students' Academic Performance in Rivers State Universities. *Int. J. Innov. Inf. Syst. Technol. Res.*, *7*(4), 40–46.

Kumar, A. (2022). Dynamical properties of a novel one dimensional chaotic map. Math. Biosci. Eng., 19(3). doi:10.3934/mbe.2022115

Lefèvre, P., Carré, P., Fontaine, C., Gaborit, P., & Huang, J. (2022, January). Efficient image tampering localization using semi-fragile watermarking and error control codes. *Signal Processing*, *190*, 108342. doi:10.1016/j.sigpro.2021.108342

Li, J.-Y., & Zhang, C.-Z. (2020, October). Blind watermarking scheme based on Schur decomposition and non-subsampled contourlet transform. *Multimedia Tools and Applications*, *79*(39), 30007–30021. doi:10.100711042-020-09389-1

Liu, B., Xiong, J., Wu, Y., Ding, M., & Wu, C. M. (2019). Protecting Multimedia Privacy from Both Humans and AI. In *IEEE International Symposium on Broadband Multimedia Systems and Broadcasting (BMSB)*, (pp. 1-6). IEEE. 10.1109/BMSB47279.2019.8971914

Liu, L., & Wang, J. (2023, February). A cluster of 1D quadratic chaotic map and its applications in image encryption. *Mathematics and Computers in Simulation*, *204*, 89–114. doi:10.1016/j.matcom.2022.07.030

Liu, X., Sun, Y., Wang, J., Yang, C., Zhang, Y., Wang, L., Chen, Y., & Fang, H. (2021). A novel zero-watermarking scheme with enhanced distinguishability and robustness for volumetric medical imaging. *Signal Processing Image Communication*, *92*, 116124. doi:10.1016/j.image.2020.116124

Liu, X., Zhang, Y., Wang, J., Sun, Y., Zhang, W., Zhou, D., Schaefer, G., & Fang, H. (2022). Multiple-feature-based zero-watermarking for robust and discriminative copyright protection of DIBR 3D videos. *Information Sciences*, *604*, 97–114. doi:10.1016/j.ins.2022.05.010

Ma, S., Zhang, T., Wu, A., & Zhao, X. (2019). Lightweight and Privacy-Preserving Data Aggregation for Mobile Multimedia Security. *IEEE Access : Practical Innovations, Open Solutions*, *7*, 114131–114140. doi:10.1109/ACCESS.2019.2935513

Mahajan, H. B., & Junnarkar, A. A. (2023). Smart healthcare system using integrated and lightweight ECC with private blockchain for multimedia medical data processing. *Multimedia Tools and Applications*, (avr). doi:10.100711042-023-15204-4 PMID:37362704

Manjunath, K., Kodanda Ramaiah, G. N., & GiriPrasad, M. N. (2022, April). Backward movement oriented shark smell optimization-based audio steganography using encryption and compression strategies. *Digital Signal Processing*, *122*, 103335. doi:10.1016/j.dsp.2021.103335

Midoun, M. A., Wang, X., & Talhaoui, M. Z. (2021, April). A sensitive dynamic mutual encryption system based on a new 1D chaotic map. *Optics and Lasers in Engineering*, *139*, 106485. doi:10.1016/j.optlaseng.2020.106485

Molina-Garcia, J., Garcia-Salgado, B. P., Ponomaryov, V., Reyes-Reyes, R., Sadovnychiy, S., & Cruz-Ramos, C. (2020, February). An effective fragile watermarking scheme for color image tampering detection and self-recovery. *Signal Processing Image Communication*, *81*, 115725. doi:10.1016/j.image.2019.115725

Muñoz-Guillermo, M. (2021). Image encryption using q-deformed logistic map. *Information Sciences*, *552*, 352–364. doi:10.1016/j.ins.2020.11.045

Nauman, A., Qadri, Y. A., Amjad, M., Zikria, Y. B., Afzal, M. K., & Kim, S. W. (2020). Multimedia Internet of Things: A Comprehensive Survey. *IEEE Access : Practical Innovations, Open Solutions*, *8*, 8202–8250. doi:10.1109/ACCESS.2020.2964280

Nazari, M., & Maneshi, A. (2021). Chaotic reversible watermarking method based on iwt with tamper detection for transferring electronic health record. *Security and Communication Networks*, *2021*, 1–15. doi:10.1155/2021/5514944

Nouioua, I., Amardjia, N., & Belilita, S. (2018, November). A Novel Blind and Robust Video Watermarking Technique in Fast Motion Frames Based on SVD and MR-SVD. *Security and Communication Networks*, *2018*, e6712065. doi:10.1155/2018/6712065

Pak, C., Kim, J., An, K., Kim, C., Kim, K., & Pak, C. (2020, January). A novel color image LSB steganography using improved 1D chaotic map. *Multimedia Tools and Applications*, *79*(1-2), 1409–1425. doi:10.100711042-019-08103-0

Panahi, S., Sprott, J. C., & Jafari, S. (2018, November). Two Simplest Quadratic Chaotic Maps Without Equilibrium. *International Journal of Bifurcation and Chaos in Applied Sciences and Engineering, 28*(12), 1850144. doi:10.1142/S0218127418501444

Pareek, N. K., Patidar, V., & Sud, K. K. (2006). Image encryption using chaotic logistic map. *Image and Vision Computing, 24*(9), 926–934. doi:10.1016/j.imavis.2006.02.021

Peng, J., El-Atty, B. A., Khalifa, H. S., & El-Latif, A. A. A. (2019). Image steganography algorithm based on key matrix generated by quantum walks. *Eleventh International Conference on Digital Image Processing (ICDIP 2019)* (pp. 24-28). Spie Digital Library. 10.1117/12.2539630

Peng, J., El-Atty, B. A., Khalifa, H. S., & El-Latif, A. A. A. (2019). Image watermarking algorithm based on quaternion and chaotic Lorenz system. *Eleventh International Conference on Digital Image Processing (ICDIP 2019)* (pp. 234-239). Spie Digital Library. 10.1117/12.2539753

Qureshi, A., & Megías Jiménez, D. (2021, January). Blockchain-Based Multimedia Content Protection: Review and Open Challenges. *Applied Sciences (Basel, Switzerland), 11*(1), 1. doi:10.3390/app11010001

Ravichandran, D., Praveenkumar, P., Rajagopalan, S., Rayappan, J. B. B., & Amirtharajan, R. (2021). ROI-based medical image watermarking for accurate tamper detection, localisation and recovery. *Medical & Biological Engineering & Computing, 59*(6), 1355–1372. doi:10.100711517-021-02374-2 PMID:33990889

Rong, X., Jiang, D., Zheng, M., Yu, X., & Wang, X. (2022, November). Meaningful data encryption scheme based on newly designed chaotic map and P-tensor product compressive sensing in WBANs. *Nonlinear Dynamics, 110*(3), 2831–2847. doi:10.100711071-022-07736-5

Serag Eldin, S. M. (2023). Design and Analysis of New Version of Cryptographic Hash Function Based on Improved Chaotic Maps with Induced DNA Sequences. IEEE Access. doi:10.1109/ACCESS.2023.3298545

Sharafi, J., Khedmati, Y., & Shabani, M. M. (2021, January). Image steganography based on a new hybrid chaos map and discrete transforms. *Optik (Stuttgart), 226*, 165492. doi:10.1016/j.ijleo.2020.165492

Sodhro, A. H., Luo, Z., Sodhro, G. H., Muzamal, M., Rodrigues, J. J. P. C., & de Albuquerque, V. H. C. (2019, June). Artificial Intelligence based QoS optimization for multimedia communication in IoV systems. *Future Generation Computer Systems, 95*, 667–680. doi:10.1016/j.future.2018.12.008

Sood, S. K. (2020, April). Mobile fog based secure cloud-IoT framework for enterprise multimedia security. *Multimedia Tools and Applications, 79*(15), 10717–10732. doi:10.100711042-019-08573-2

Talhaoui, M. Z., & Wang, X. (2021, March). A new fractional one dimensional chaotic map and its application in high-speed image encryption. *Information Sciences, 550,* 13–26. doi:10.1016/j.ins.2020.10.048

Talhaoui, M. Z., Wang, X., & Talhaoui, A. (2021, July). A new one-dimensional chaotic map and its application in a novel permutation-less image encryption scheme. *The Visual Computer, 37*(7), 1757–1768. doi:10.100700371-020-01936-z

Taloba, A. I., Elhadad, A., Rayan, A., Abd El-Aziz, R. M., Salem, M., Alzahrani, A. A., Alharithi, F. S., & Park, C. (2023, February). A blockchain-based hybrid platform for multimedia data processing in IoT-Healthcare. *Alexandria Engineering Journal, 65,* 263–274. doi:10.1016/j.aej.2022.09.031

Trujillo-Toledo, D. A., López-Bonilla, O. R., García-Guerrero, E. E., Tlelo-Cuautle, E., López-Mancilla, D., Guillén-Fernández, O., & Inzunza-González, E. (2021, December). Real-time RGB image encryption for IoT applications using enhanced sequences from chaotic maps. *Chaos, Solitons, and Fractals, 153,* 111506. doi:10.1016/j.chaos.2021.111506

Veeman, D., Alanezi, A., Natiq, H., Jafari, S., & Abd El-Latif, A. A. (2022, February). A Chaotic Quadratic Oscillator with Only Squared Terms: Multistability, Impulsive Control, and Circuit Design. *Symmetry, 14*(2), 2. doi:10.3390ym14020259

Wang, C., Wang, X., Xia, Z., & Zhang, C. (2019). Ternary radial harmonic Fourier moments based robust stereo image zero-watermarking algorithm. *Information Sciences, 470,* 109–120. doi:10.1016/j.ins.2018.08.028

Wang, J., Liu, L., Xu, M., & Li, X. (2022). A novel content-selected image encryption algorithm based on the LS chaotic model », *J. King Saud Univ. - Comput. Inf. Sci., 34*(nov), 8245–8259. doi:10.1016/j.jksuci.2022.08.007

Wang, J., Song, X., & El-Latif, A. A. A. (2022, July). Efficient Entropic Security with Joint Compression and Encryption Approach Based on Compressed Sensing with Multiple Chaotic Systems. *Entropy (Basel, Switzerland), 24*(7), 7. Advance online publication. doi:10.3390/e24070885 PMID:35885109

Wang, J., Song, X., & El-Latif, A. A. A. (2022, January). Single-Objective Particle Swarm Optimization-Based Chaotic Image Encryption Scheme. *Electronics (Basel), 11*(16), 16. Advance online publication. doi:10.3390/electronics11162628

Wang, R., Shaocheng, H., Zhang, P., Yue, M., Cheng, Z., & Zhang, Y. (2020). A novel zero-watermarking scheme based on variable parameter chaotic mapping in NSPD-DCT domain. *IEEE Access : Practical Innovations, Open Solutions, 8*, 182391–182411. doi:10.1109/ACCESS.2020.3004841

Xia, Z., Wang, C., Ma, B., Li, Q., Zhang, H., Wang, M., & Wang, X. (2023, August). Geometric attacks resistant double zero-watermarking using discrete Fourier transform and fractional-order Exponent-Fourier moments. *Digital Signal Processing, 140*, 104097. doi:10.1016/j.dsp.2023.104097

Xia, Z., Wang, X., Li, X., Wang, C., Unar, S., Wang, M., & Zhao, T. (2019, November). Efficient copyright protection for three CT images based on quaternion polar harmonic Fourier moments. *Signal Processing, 164*, 368–379. doi:10.1016/j.sigpro.2019.06.025

Xia, Z., Wang, X., Wang, C., Ma, B., Wang, M., & Shi, Y.-Q. (2021, March). Local quaternion polar harmonic Fourier moments-based multiple zero-watermarking scheme for color medical images. *Knowledge-Based Systems, 216*, 106568. doi:10.1016/j.knosys.2020.106568

Yamni, M., Daoui, A., Karmouni, H., Elmalih, S., Ben-fares, A., Sayyouri, M., Qjidaa, H., Maaroufi, M., Alami, B., & Jamil, M. O. (2023). Copyright protection of multiple CT images using Octonion Krawtchouk moments and grey Wolf optimizer. *Journal of the Franklin Institute, 360*(7), 4719–4752. doi:10.1016/j.jfranklin.2023.03.008

Yamni, M., Daoui, A., Karmouni, H., Sayyouri, M., Qjidaa, H., & Flusser, J. (2020). Fractional Charlier moments for image reconstruction and image watermarking. *Signal Processing, 171*, 107509. doi:10.1016/j.sigpro.2020.107509

Yamni, M., Daoui, A., Karmouni, H., Sayyouri, M., Qjidaa, H., Wang, C., & Jamil, M. O. (2023). A Powerful Zero-Watermarking Algorithm for Copyright Protection of Color Images Based on Quaternion Radial Fractional Hahn Moments and Artificial Bee Colony Algorithm. *Circuits, Systems, and Signal Processing, 42*(9), 1–32. doi:10.100700034-023-02379-2

Yamni, M., Karmouni, H., Daoui, A., Sayyouri, M., & Qjidaa, H. (2020). Blind image zero-watermarking algorithm based on radial krawtchouk moments and chaotic system. In *2020 International Conference on Intelligent Systems and Computer Vision (ISCV)*. IEEE. 10.1109/ISCV49265.2020.9204071

Yamni, M., Karmouni, H., Sayyouri, M., & Qjidaa, H. (2022, January). Efficient watermarking algorithm for digital audio/speech signal. *Digital Signal Processing, 120*, 103251. doi:10.1016/j.dsp.2021.103251

Yamni, M., Karmouni, H., Sayyouri, M., & Qjidaa, H. (2022, October). Robust audio watermarking scheme based on fractional Charlier moment transform and dual tree complex wavelet transform. *Expert Systems with Applications*, *203*, 117325. doi:10.1016/j.eswa.2022.117325

Yuan, S., Magayane, D. A., Liu, X., Zhou, X., Lu, G., Wang, Z., Zhang, H., & Li, Z. (2021). A blind watermarking scheme based on computational ghost imaging in wavelet domain. *Optics Communications*, *482*, 126568. doi:10.1016/j.optcom.2020.126568

Zhu, L., Jiang, D., Ni, J., Wang, X., Rong, X., & Ahmad, M. (2022, August). A visually secure image encryption scheme using adaptive-thresholding sparsification compression sensing model and newly-designed memristive chaotic map. *Information Sciences*, *607*, 1001–1022. doi:10.1016/j.ins.2022.06.011

Zhu, S., Deng, X., Zhang, W., & Zhu, C. (2023, May). Secure image encryption scheme based on a new robust chaotic map and strong S-box. *Mathematics and Computers in Simulation*, *207*, 322–346. doi:10.1016/j.matcom.2022.12.025

Chapter 2
AI and NLP–Empowered Framework for Strengthening Social Cyber Security

Mudasir Ahmad Wani

(iD) https://orcid.org/0000-0002-6947-3717
Prince Sultan University, Saudi Arabia

ABSTRACT

In this study, a comprehensive framework emerges, interweaving the capabilities of deep learning and NLP. This framework stands as a cornerstone in the pursuit of elevating the safety and security of individuals and organizations navigating the multifaceted realm of social cyberspace. The framework's architecture sets the stage for efficient threat detection and the preemptive identification of vulnerabilities, heralding a new era of cybersecurity strategies. As this conceptual framework unfolds, future endeavors will bridge theory and practice, ushering in the application of this paradigm to real-world data scenarios. The projected outcome of these efforts is the provision of pragmatic security services tailored to individuals and groups. This chapter encapsulates a visionary approach to social cybersecurity, where the synergy of NLP, deep learning, and AI converges to fortify digital landscapes against emergent threats, thereby safeguarding the interconnected fabric of the modern online world.

DOI: 10.4018/978-1-6684-7216-3.ch002

1. INTRODUCTION

In an era characterized by the pervasive influence of digital connectivity, social media platforms have emerged as dynamic landscapes that shape personal interactions, global conversations, and even economic landscapes. However, this digital evolution is not without its pitfalls. The expansive reach and interactive nature of social media platforms offer a breeding ground for cyber threats that range from phishing attacks and identity theft to the dissemination of misinformation and the manipulation of user behavior. This underscores the crucial importance of Social Cyber Security with Artificial Intelligence (AI) (Charniak, 1985) and Natural Language Processing (NLP) (Nadkarni et al., 2011) in mitigating the intricate challenges posed by the confluence of social media dynamics and cyber threats. The transformative impact of social media on the fabric of modern society is undeniable. Individuals, organizations, and even governments leverage these platforms to communicate, share ideas, and influence opinions on a global scale. Yet, beneath this digital tapestry lies an intricate web of vulnerabilities that threat actors are adept at exploiting. In response, the integration of cutting-edge technologies becomes an essential strategy for safeguarding personal privacy, securing sensitive data, and fortifying digital infrastructure against emerging cyber threats.

At the heart of this synergy is Artificial Intelligence, a driving force in the evolution of cybersecurity strategies. By leveraging AI's capacity to analyze data patterns and predict potential threats, cybersecurity professionals can anticipate cyber-attacks, identify vulnerabilities, and respond with unparalleled agility. Deep learning algorithms, a subset of AI, enable the automatic extraction of features from complex datasets, allowing for the discernment of subtle nuances within the massive volumes of data generated by social media interactions. When coupled with Natural Language Processing, AI is poised to revolutionize threat detection.

Natural Language Processing (NLP), a branch of AI, empowers machines to understand, interpret, and generate human language. In the context of cybersecurity, NLP offers a transformative lens through which to analyze the textual content pervading social media platforms. By employing sentiment analysis, entity recognition, and language models, NLP facilitates the discernment of intent, sentiment, and contextual meaning behind user interactions. Consequently, this technology can pinpoint potential threats, identify anomalies, and distinguish genuine user engagements from malicious activities. The ability to detect linguistic shifts, emergent threats, and patterns of misinformation positions NLP as an indispensable asset in the arsenal of social cyber security.

The convergence of AI and NLP not only enhances threat detection but also empowers proactive defense strategies. By analyzing user behavior, linguistic cues, and sentiment dynamics, cybersecurity professionals can preemptively identify emerging threats, preventing the amplification of malicious campaigns. Moreover, these technologies enable the rapid assessment of potential risks and vulnerabilities, allowing for informed decision-making and adaptive responses.

2. IMPORTANCE OF SOCIAL CYBERSECURITY

Social cybersecurity, also known as social media security, is a crucial aspect of maintaining digital safety and privacy in the modern era. It involves protecting personal and organizational information while using social media platforms. The Figure 1 provides a brief overview of the importance of social cybersecurity:

i)   *Protection of Personal Information*: Social media platforms often require users to share personal information, such as names, birthdates, and locations. Ensuring the security of this information is essential to prevent identity theft, fraud, and other cybercrimes.

ii) *Mitigation of Social Engineering Attacks*: Cybercriminals use social engineering techniques to manipulate individuals into divulging sensitive information or performing actions that compromise security. Social cybersecurity educates users to recognize and resist these tactics.

iii) *Prevention of Account Compromise*: Unauthorized access to social media accounts can lead to unauthorized posts, identity theft, and spam distribution. Strong security practices, including unique passwords and two-factor authentication, help prevent account compromise.

iv) *Privacy Management*: Social media platforms often have complex privacy settings. Users must understand how to manage their privacy preferences to control who can view their posts, personal information, and interactions.

v)   *Reputation Management*: What individuals or organizations post on social media can have lasting effects on their reputation. Social cybersecurity encourages responsible posting to avoid sharing content that could harm the personal or professional image.

vi) *Defending Against Online Harassment*: Cyberbullying and online harassment are significant concerns on social media. Social cybersecurity emphasizes strategies to protect oneself from such negative interactions and report abusive behavior.

vii) *Avoiding Phishing Scams*: Cybercriminals create fake profiles or messages to trick users into sharing sensitive information or clicking on malicious links. Social cybersecurity helps users recognize and avoid these phishing attempts.

viii) *Educating Youth and Vulnerable Populations*: Children and elderly individuals are often more vulnerable to online threats due to their lack of experience or familiarity with technology. Social cybersecurity includes educating these populations about safe online practices.

ix) *Business and Organizational Security*: Many organizations use social media for branding, marketing, and customer engagement. Social cybersecurity ensures that employees understand the company's social media policies to prevent data breaches or reputational damage.

x) *Data Privacy Compliance*: In some regions, social media platforms are subject to data protection regulations. Businesses and individuals must understand and adhere to these regulations to avoid legal consequences.

xi) *Protection from Location-based Threats*: Sharing real-time location information can expose users to physical risks, such as stalking or burglary. Social cybersecurity emphasizes the importance of limiting location sharing.

xii) *Balancing Connectivity and Security*: While social media facilitates connection, oversharing personal information can lead to security risks. Social cybersecurity encourages users to strike a balance between sharing and protecting their information.

Figure 1. Dimensions of social cyber security

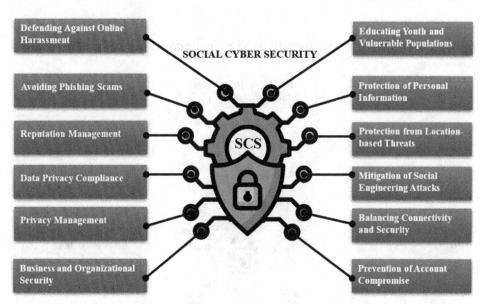

In summary, social cybersecurity is vital for maintaining digital safety and privacy in an age of widespread social media use. By educating individuals about potential risks, providing guidance on secure practices, and fostering responsible online behavior, social cybersecurity helps users navigate the digital landscape with confidence and minimize the chances of falling victim to cyber threats.

3. NATURAL LANGUAGE PROCESSING (NLP) FOR SOCIAL CYBERSECURITY

Natural Language Processing (NLP) stands as a pivotal tool within the realm of Social Cybersecurity, enabling computers to understand, interpret, and analyze human language in textual form. As social media platforms become hubs of communication, NLP empowers cybersecurity professionals to dissect vast volumes of textual content – including posts, comments, and messages to discern patterns, sentiments, and intentions. This proficiency allows for the detection of linguistic cues that may signify phishing attempts, misinformation campaigns, or even the manipulation of user behavior. NLP's ability to comprehend context, sentiment, and intent is harnessed to enhance threat detection, enabling rapid response and proactive defense against emerging cyber threats within the intricate landscape of social media interactions.

Figure 2. Natural language processing (NLP) in the domain of social cybersecurity

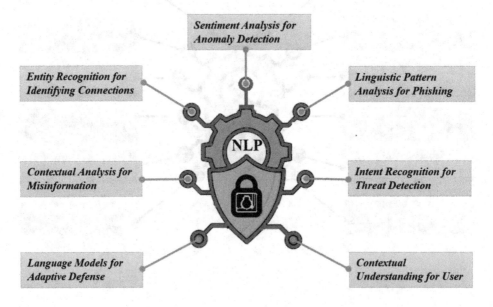

There are various ways in which Natural Language Processing (NLP) is utilized in the domain of Social Cybersecurity. Some commonly known are shown in the figure 2 and are briefly discussed as under:

Sentiment Analysis for Anomaly Detection:

Sentiment analysis, a foundational NLP technique, is used to gauge the emotional tone expressed within social media content. In "Social Cybersecurity," this technique is harnessed to detect anomalies or sudden shifts in sentiment that might indicate malicious activities. Sudden spikes in negative sentiment or unusual emotional responses can signify potential cyber threats, enabling security analysts to investigate further and take proactive measures.

Entity Recognition for Identifying Connections:

NLP's entity recognition capabilities are employed to identify and categorize entities within social media content, such as people, organizations, and locations. By identifying these entities and their relationships, security professionals can uncover potential patterns of communication, connections, or affiliations that might be indicative of malicious intent or coordinated attacks.

Linguistic Pattern Analysis for Phishing Detection:

NLP algorithms analyze linguistic patterns, syntax, and vocabulary to identify common characteristics of phishing messages or social engineering tactics. Certain linguistic cues, such as urgent requests for sensitive information or suspicious URLs, can be recognized through NLP techniques. By flagging such patterns, NLP aids in the identification and prevention of phishing attempts, safeguarding users from falling victim to cybercriminals.

Contextual Analysis for Misinformation Detection:

NLP's ability to understand contextual nuances enables the detection of misinformation and fake news within social media content. By analyzing the content, sources, and context of posts, NLP algorithms can identify inconsistencies, contradictions, or misleading information. This helps in curbing the spread of false information that could lead to panic or compromise users' trust.

Intent Recognition for Threat Detection:

NLP's capacity to discern the intent behind language is crucial for identifying potentially harmful messages. By analyzing the phrasing and context of social media interactions, NLP can identify messages that suggest threats, violence, or illegal activities. This proactive approach aids in preventing situations where users may be exposed to harmful content or actions.

Language Models for Adaptive Defense:

NLP-based language models, developed through machine learning, can be trained on vast datasets of legitimate and malicious social media content. These models learn to distinguish between typical user interactions and content that exhibits characteristics of cyber threats. By applying these models in real time, organizations can quickly classify and respond to potentially harmful content, improving their overall cybersecurity posture.

Contextual Understanding for User Profiling:

NLP techniques can analyze users' language usage and preferences, allowing for the creation of linguistic profiles. These profiles aid in identifying deviations from users' typical behavior, helping to detect compromised accounts or unauthorized access. By leveraging these profiles, organizations can enhance their ability to detect and prevent unauthorized activities.

Table 1 presents a list of commonly known categories of NLP techniques used in the direction of social cybersecurity. This table also presents specific techniques used by different researcher working in this direction.

Table 1. Commonly known categories

Broad Category/Technique	The Specific Technique (s)	Reference	Year
Sentiment Analysis	Gated Recurrent Unit (GRU) networks, Tomek Link method	(Studiawan et al., 2020)	2020
Named Entity Recognition (NER)	Bidirectional Long Short-Term Memory with Conditional Random Fields (Bi-LSTM with CRF)	(Ma et al., 2020)	2020
Phishing Detection	Chi-Square statistics, Mutual Information, Component Analysis (PCA) and Latent Semantic Analysis (LSA)	(Gualberto et al., 2020)	2020
Contextual Analysis	Support Vector Machine, Random Forest, BERT	(Wani et al., 2023)	2023
Threat Detection	Random Forest, Linear Support Vector Classifier, Multinomial-NB, Logistic Regression	(Marinho & Holanda, 2023)	2023
User Behavior Analysis	Principle Component Analysis (PCA)	(Najafabadi et al., 2017)	2017
User Profiling	Emotion Analysis, Plutchik's emotion wheel	(Ahmad Wani et al., 2023)	2021
User Profiling	CNN, LSTM Depression Detection	(Shakil et al., 2021)	2023

4. PROPOSED DEEP LEARNING AND NLP-BASED FRAMEWORK FOR SOCIAL CYBERSECURITY

Building a deep learning framework for social cybersecurity using Natural Language Processing (NLP) involves several key components to effectively detect, analyze, and mitigate potential security threats arising from social media and other text-based platforms. Here we proposed the main components one should consider while dealing with mitigating social cybersecurity threats. The conceptual framework in shown in the Figure 3.

Data Collection and Preprocessing

Collecting data involves scraping or using APIs to gather text content from social media platforms and other sources. This data needs preprocessing to ensure consistency and remove noise.

a.   *Data Collection:* Utilize web scraping tools or APIs to gather data from social media platforms, forums, blogs, and other relevant sources. Collect a diverse range of text content to ensure comprehensive coverage.

b.   *Data Filtering:* Apply filters to exclude irrelevant or duplicate content. You might also consider sentiment analysis or preliminary anomaly detection to prioritize potentially malicious or unusual content.

Text Preprocessing involves cleaning and standardizing the collected text. Convert all text to lowercase to ensure case-insensitive processing. Remove special characters, emojis, URLs, and punctuation marks. Tokenize the text into words or subword units.

Feature Extraction

Feature extraction transforms raw text into numerical representations suitable for machine learning. A few commonly known feature extraction techniques include the following:

a.   *Term Frequency - Inverse Document Frequency (TF-IDF)* (Ahmad Wani et al., 2023): Calculate the Term Frequency-Inverse Document Frequency values for each word in the corpus. This assigns weights to words based on their frequency and rarity in the dataset.

b.   *Word Embeddings:* Train word embeddings using models like Word2Vec (Shakil et al., 2021), GloVe, or use pre-trained embeddings. These embeddings capture semantic relationships between words and are represented as dense vectors.

c.   *Contextual Embeddings:* Implement pre-trained transformer models like BERT (Tenney et al., 2019) or GPT to generate contextual embeddings. These embeddings capture word meanings in the context of the entire sentence.

Model Architecture

Model architecture is the blueprint that defines the structure and organization of a neural network within a deep learning framework. Just as the architecture of a building dictates its layout and functionality, the model architecture determines how data flows through the network and how it processes information. Following sections briefly discuss the popular model architectures.

a. *Recurrent Neural Networks (RNNs):* One can use Recurrent Neural Networks (RNNs) to process sequential data, such as text. Long Short-Term Memory (LSTM) and Gated Recurrent Unit (GRU) are variants of RNNs that help capture longer-term dependencies in text.

b. *Convolutional Neural Networks (CNNs):* We can apply Convolutional Neural Networks (CNNs) to capture local patterns in text. These are often used for text classification tasks.

c. *Transformers*: Transformers are a revolutionary type of neural network architecture focuses on handling sequential data by leveraging a novel attention mechanism that captures contextual relationships between words regardless of their position in the sequence. We can use transformer-based architectures, such as BERT and GPT, to capture contextual information and relationships across long spans of text. Transformers use self-attention mechanisms to achieve this.

After selecting the appropriate model architecture, we can apply it to several social cybersecurity tasks. In the following sub-sections, we have discussed a few of tasks such tasks.

Social Cybersecurity Domains

Sentiment Analysis (SA)

Sentiment analysis, also known as opinion mining, is a Natural Language Processing (NLP) technique that involves determining the emotional tone or sentiment expressed in a piece of text. The goal of sentiment analysis is to classify the sentiment of text as positive, negative, neutral, or sometimes even more nuanced emotions like joy, anger, sadness, etc. This technique plays a crucial role in understanding public opinion, customer feedback, and user sentiments expressed in social media, reviews, comments, and other forms of text data. The following two steps are involved in SA process.

Dataset Labeling: Create a labeled dataset where each text snippet is annotated with its corresponding sentiment label (positive, negative, neutral).

Model Training: Train a classification model (such as LSTM or a transformer-based classifier) on the sentiment-labeled dataset. The model learns to predict sentiment labels for new text inputs.

Named Entity Recognition (NER)

Named Entity Recognition (NER) is a critical Natural Language Processing (NLP) task that involves identifying and categorizing named entities within text. Named entities are specific words or phrases that refer to entities such as names of people, organizations, locations, dates, quantities, and more. NER plays a pivotal role in understanding the structure and context of text, making it valuable for various applications, including information retrieval, text summarization, and, in the context of social cybersecurity, threat detection and analysis. The following two steps are involved in the NER process.

Data Annotation: Annotate the collected text data with labeled named entities like names, locations, dates, and organizations.

Model Training: Train a sequence tagging model (e.g., LSTM-CRF or transformer with a CRF layer) to identify and categorize named entities within the text.

Figure 3. Conceptual deep learning-based framework for social cybersecurity

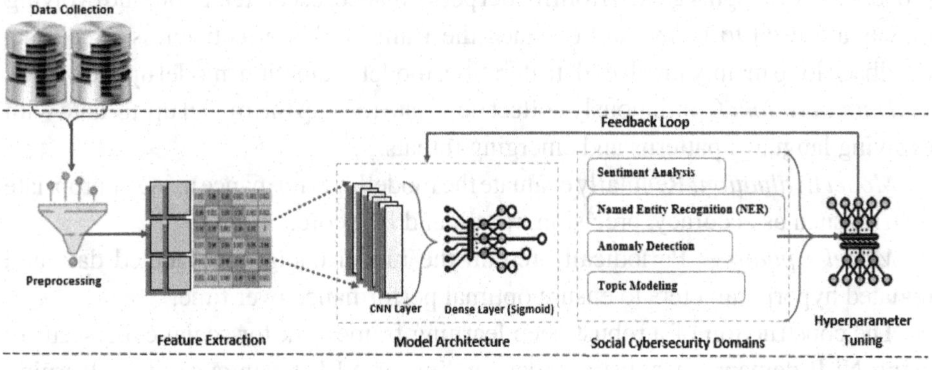

Anomaly Detection

Anomaly detection is a vital technique used in various fields, including cybersecurity, to identify patterns or instances that deviate significantly from the norm or expected behavior. In the context of social cybersecurity, anomaly detection plays a crucial role in identifying unusual or potentially malicious activities, behaviors, or content within social media platforms and other text-based communication channels. Anomaly detection involves the following two steps.

Data Labeling: Manually label a subset of the data as normal or anomalous based on predefined criteria. This labeled data serves as the basis for training anomaly detection models.

Model Training: Train an anomaly detection model (autoencoders, Isolation Forest, etc.) on the labeled data to learn the normal patterns in the text. The model can then identify deviations as anomalies.

Hyperparameter Tuning

Hyperparameter tuning involves optimizing the parameters of a machine learning model that are not learned during training but set before training. These parameters, known as hyperparameters, influence how the model learns and generalizes from data. Experiment with different hyperparameters such as learning rate, batch size, and model architecture to find the best combination for your specific task.

Feedback Loop

The feedback loop is a continuous cycle of learning, adaptation, and improvement within a deep learning framework for social cybersecurity. It involves a dynamic process where insights gained from model performance, user interaction, and evolving threats are used to refine and enhance the framework's effectiveness over time. Feedback loop mainly involves data iteration, model evaluation, model updating, etc.

Data Iteration: Continuously collect new data to keep the model up-to-date with evolving language patterns and emerging threats.

Model Evaluation: Regularly evaluate the model's performance using appropriate metrics such as accuracy, precision, recall, and F1-score.

Model Updating: Periodically retrain the model using new labeled data and updated hyperparameters to ensure optimal performance over time.

The construction of a robust deep learning framework for social cybersecurity using NLP demands a holistic understanding of NLP techniques, deep learning concepts, and cybersecurity challenges. Adaptation and refinement are essential to keeping the framework effective and aligned with changing trends and threats in the digital landscape.

5. CONCLUSION

This study underscores the pivotal role of the symbiotic relationship between Natural Language Processing (NLP) and Deep Learning in tackling social cyber threats. Through their integration, cybersecurity experts can anticipate potential threats promptly, bolstering preemptive defense mechanisms. In this study we have proposed an NLP and AI-based comprehensive framework with the potential to revolutionize threat detection. This framework is systematically designed, comprising six integral modules—Data collection and preprocessing, feature extraction, Model Architecture, the Social Cybersecurity track, Hyperparameter tuning, and a Feedback loop. This holistic framework embodies a proactive cybersecurity strategy, adeptly tailored to enhance the security posture of individuals and organizations within the digital setting. The Social Cybersecurity track module within this framework encapsulates a repository of strategic tasks aimed at preemptively mitigating evolving risks. Serving as a roadmap for proactive risk mitigation, this module provides a structured approach to enhancing cybersecurity measures in an ever-dynamic digital sphere.

As this study culminates, its trajectory extends toward practical application. The logical progression involves the operationalization of this conceptual framework with real-world data sets. In essence, the objective is to translate theoretical prowess into actionable outcomes, safeguarding digital experiences in a tangible and measurable manner.

In summation, this study encapsulates the transformative potential of the convergence between NLP and Deep Learning in the range of cybersecurity. The comprehensive framework and its practical implementation unite to clear a pathway to cybersecurity excellence, characterized by its proactive nature, adaptability, and robustness. Through this integrated approach, the study underscores the commitment to defending the digital realm against emergent threats, ushering in an era of enhanced digital safety and security for all stakeholders.

Key Abbreviations

Several key abbreviations utilized in this study are enumerated as follows:

BERT: Bidirectional Encoder Representations from Transformers
GloVe: Global Vectors for Word Representation
TF-IDF: Term Frequency - Inverse Document Frequency
NLP: Natural Language Processing
AI: Artificial Intelligence
DT: Decision Tree
KNN: K-Nearest Neighbor

LR: Logistic Regression
LSVM: Linear Support Vector
MNB: Machines Multinomial Naïve Bayes
BNB: Bernoulli Naïve Bayes
NN: Neural Network
ERF: Ensemble Random Forest

ACKNOWLEDGMENT

This research work is supported by the EIAS, Data Science and Blockchain Laboratory, Prince Sultan University, Riyadh, Saudi Arabia.

REFERENCES

Abd El-Latif, A. A., Ahmad Wani, M., & El-Affendi, M. A. (2023). *Advanced Applications of NLP and Deep Learning in Social Media Data.* IGI Global. [https://www.igi-global.com/book/advanced-applications-nlp-deep-learning/304800 doi:10.4018/978-1-6684-6909-5

Ahmad Wani, M., ELAffendi, M. A., Shakil, K. A., Shariq Imran, A., & Abd El-Latif, A. A. (2023, August). Depression Screening in Humans With AI and Deep Learning Techniques. *IEEE Transactions on Computational Social Systems*, *10*(4), 2074–2089. doi:10.1109/TCSS.2022.3200213

Charniak, E. (1985). *Introduction to artificial intelligence.* Pearson Education India.

Floridi, L., & Chiriatti, M. (2020). GPT-3: Its nature, scope, limits, and consequences. *Minds and Machines*, *30*(4), 681–694. doi:10.100711023-020-09548-1

Gualberto, E. S., De Sousa, R. T., Vieira, T. P. D. B., Da Costa, J. P. C. L., & Duque, C. G. (2020). The answer is in the text: Multi-stage methods for phishing detection based on feature engineering. *IEEE Access : Practical Innovations, Open Solutions*, *8*, 223529–223547. doi:10.1109/ACCESS.2020.3043396

Ma, P., Jiang, B., Lu, Z., Li, N., & Jiang, Z. (2020). Cybersecurity named entity recognition using bidirectional long short-term memory with conditional random fields. *Tsinghua Science and Technology*, *26*(3), 259–265. doi:10.26599/TST.2019.9010033

Marinho, R., & Holanda, R. (2023). Automated Emerging Cyber Threat Identification and Profiling Based on Natural Language Processing. *IEEE Access : Practical Innovations, Open Solutions*, *11*, 58915–58936. doi:10.1109/ACCESS.2023.3260020

Nadkarni, P. M., Ohno-Machado, L., & Chapman, W. W. (2011). Natural language processing: An introduction. *Journal of the American Medical Informatics Association : JAMIA*, *18*(5), 544–551. doi:10.1136/amiajnl-2011-000464 PMID:21846786

Najafabadi, M. M., Khoshgoftaar, T. M., Calvert, C., & Kemp, C. (2017, August). User behavior anomaly detection for application layer ddos attacks. In *2017 IEEE International Conference on Information Reuse and Integration (IRI)* (pp. 154-161). IEEE. 10.1109/IRI.2017.44

Shakil, K. A., Tabassum, K., Alqahtani, F. S., & Wani, M. A. (2021). Analyzing user digital emotions from a holy versus non-pilgrimage city in Saudi Arabia on twitter platform. *Applied Sciences (Basel, Switzerland)*, *11*(15), 6846. doi:10.3390/app11156846

Studiawan, H., Sohel, F., & Payne, C. (2020). Anomaly detection in operating system logs with deep learning-based sentiment analysis. *IEEE Transactions on Dependable and Secure Computing*, *18*(5), 2136–2148. doi:10.1109/TDSC.2020.3037903

Tenney, I., Das, D., & Pavlick, E. (2019). *BERT rediscovers the classical NLP pipeline*. arXiv preprint arXiv:1905.05950. doi:10.18653/v1/P19-1452

Wani, M. A., ELAffendi, M., Shakil, K. A., Abuhaimed, I. M., Nayyar, A., Hussain, A., & El-Latif, A. A. A. (2023). Toxic Fake News Detection and Classification for Combating COVID-19 Misinformation. *IEEE Transactions on Computational Social Systems*, 1. doi:10.1109/TCSS.2023.3276764

Chapter 3
Deep Learning Fusion for Multimedia Malware Classification

Yassine Maleh

ⒾD https://orcid.org/0000-0003-4704-5364
Sultan Moulay Slimane University, Morocco

ABSTRACT

In the face of escalating cyber threats posed by malware, advanced detection techniques are crucial. This study introduces a cutting-edge approach that merges convolutional neural networks (CNNs) and long short-term memory recurrent neural networks (LSTMs) for enhanced malware classification. The effectiveness of this method is rigorously examined using Microsoft's BIG Cup 2015 dataset. By combining CNN's ability to capture local features and LSTM's proficiency in processing sequence data, our approach achieves remarkable accuracy (98.73%) in identifying malicious behaviors. This research contributes an extensive exploration of deep learning models, an innovative CNN-LSTM hybrid architecture, and a comprehensive case study showcasing its superior performance. The presented approach signifies a significant stride in bolstering cybersecurity against the ever-evolving threat of malware.

1. INTRODUCTION

In the rapidly evolving digital landscape, the proliferation of malicious software, commonly called malware, has emerged as a pervasive cybersecurity challenge. (Sadqi & Maleh, 2022) With the potential to inflict a broad spectrum of threats,

DOI: 10.4018/978-1-6684-7216-3.ch003

from data breaches to covert surveillance, the need for accurate and robust malware classification methods has grown more critical than ever. Traditional approaches often fall short in the face of the escalating sophistication of malware variants, driving researchers to explore cutting-edge technologies to fortify cybersecurity defenses (Maleh, 2019).

In this context, the convergence of deep learning techniques presents a promising avenue for enhancing the accuracy and resilience of malware classification systems. By harnessing the power of neural networks, specifically Convolutional Neural Networks (CNNs) and Long Short-Term Memory Recurrent Neural Networks (LSTMs), a novel paradigm of "Deep Learning Fusion" emerges. This amalgamation capitalizes on the strengths of both CNNs in capturing local features and LSTMs in modeling temporal dependencies, thus enabling the creation of a potent classifier capable of discerning intricate patterns within malicious code. Furthermore, the democratization of malware development has diminished the skill barrier, owing to the widespread availability of attack tools on the Internet (Maleh et al., 2021). The proliferation of anti-detection techniques and the accessibility of black-market malware has made it feasible for virtually anyone to become an attacker, regardless of technical expertise. The landscape is witnessing increased attacks initiated by script kiddies or automated agents (Aliyev, 2010).

In light of these developments, safeguarding computer systems against malware has become a paramount cybersecurity imperative for individuals and businesses. A single breach can compromise critical data and trigger substantial losses. The prevalence of attacks and their profound repercussions underscore the urgency of precise and prompt detection strategies. Established static and dynamic approaches often fall short, especially in the realm of zero-day attacks, prompting an exploration of machine-learning techniques (Chumachenko & Technology, 2017).

When classifying families of malicious code, the process hinges on identifying unique attributes while aptly selecting classification algorithms for accurate outcomes. Remarkably, the arena of deep neural networks (DNNs) has emerged as a focal point for classification and recognition methodologies. The extension to deep neural network models, achieved by augmenting the hidden layer depths of neural networks, has yielded exceptional performance gains in areas like image and speech recognition. This trend has found its way into malicious code analysis, although incorporating DNN-based models in this field remains relatively limited, particularly concerning malware and intrusion detection (M. & Sethuraman, 2023).

This chapter explores the intricate domain of malware classification, presenting a pioneering approach that unites Convolutional Neural Networks (CNNs) with Long Short-Term Memory Recurrent Neural Networks (LSTMs). The effectiveness of this novel approach is rigorously evaluated using data sourced from Microsoft's BIG Cup 2015 dataset. The main contributions of this chapter encompass the following:

- An in-depth exploration of diverse deep learning models tailored to address the complex challenge of malware classification.
- The introduction of an innovative deep neural network model fusing CNN and LSTM layers to discern and classify malicious behaviors.
- A detailed case study involving the Microsoft Malware Dataset, showcases the exceptional detection accuracy (98.73%) achieved by our proposed model compared to some related works.

In the forthcoming section, the chapter initiates by setting the research backdrop. Subsequently, Section 3 delves into an examination of pertinent literature encompassing techniques for classifying malware. Section 4 offers an intricate exposition of the envisaged methodology, presenting a detailed account of the proposed approach. Section 5 meticulously delineates the experimental procedures utilizing the proposed model. Lastly, Section 6 encapsulates conclusive insights from the research findings and outlines prospective directions for further scholarly inquiry.

2. BACKGROUND

In artificial intelligence and machine learning, Convolutional Neural Networks (CNNs) have emerged as a pivotal breakthrough, revolutionizing various fields such as computer vision, image recognition, and malware analysis. CNNs are a specialized neural network uniquely suited to handle grid-like data, such as images, due to their inherent ability to capture local patterns and hierarchies of features within such data.

Originating from the seminal work of LeCun et al. (2015) in the 1990s, CNNs were initially designed to mimic the human visual system's ability to discern visual patterns. Their hierarchical architecture involves layers of interconnected nodes that learn to recognize increasingly abstract features, ultimately culminating in high-level representations. This characteristic makes CNNs adept at capturing spatial and hierarchical relationships within images, effectively allowing them to learn complex features autonomously from raw pixel data.

Key components of a CNN include convolutional layers, pooling layers, and fully connected layers. Convolutional layers employ a set of filters or kernels to scan the input data, extracting relevant features through a process known as convolution. Pooling layers downsample the extracted features, reducing the computational load while retaining the essential information. Fully connected layers, resembling traditional neural networks, amalgamate the extracted features to make final predictions.

The rise of CNNs has been underpinned by their capacity to automatically learn feature representations, negating the need for manual feature engineering. This attribute has empowered CNNs to excel in diverse image-related tasks, including object recognition, segmentation, and localization. Consequently, CNNs have found applications beyond computer vision, influencing domains such as natural language processing and medical image analysis.

In the context of malware analysis, CNNs offer a potent avenue for discerning patterns and attributes that distinguish malicious code from benign software. The innate ability of CNNs to capture intricate spatial relationships in data makes them an excellent choice for analyzing binary representations of malware samples, encoded as images. Researchers have used this ability to use CNN-based models that effectively classify and detect malware, contributing to enhancing cybersecurity measures.

In the subsequent sections, we delve deeper into the intersection of CNNs with malware analysis, elucidating how these networks are harnessed to bolster our understanding of malware behavior and facilitate accurate classification. Through our proposed approach, we amalgamate the power of CNNs with Long Short-Term Memory Recurrent Neural Networks (LSTMs) to develop a comprehensive model for malware classification.

2.1 Convolutional Neural Networks (CNN)

A Convolutional Neural Network (CNN) falls within the category of neural networks designed for downstream processing. Its neural connectivity takes inspiration from the structural arrangement of neurons within the visual cortex of animals, responding to overlapping segments of the visual field to create a holistic representation.

CNNs comprise three fundamental types of layers: (i) fully connected, (ii) convolutional, and (iii) pooling layers. Various CNN implementations can be conceptualized through a common sequence of steps:

- Employ multiple compact filters across the input image.
- Downsample the resultant filter activation space.
- Iteratively apply these steps until a sufficient number of high-level features are retained.
- Utilize a conventional neural network feedforward process on the derived features.

Illustrated in Figure 1 is the architectural configuration employed by Krizhevsky et al. (2012) for the ImageNet classification competition. This architecture incorporates 8 layers of learning, with the initial five being convolutional layers and the subsequent fully connected ones.

Figure 1. AlexNet architecture

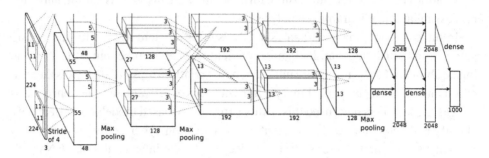

2.2 Convolutional Layer

Illustrated in Figure 2 is the operational process of convolution. In the context of the depicted 5x5 pixel image, where values range from 0 (denoting complete black) to 255 (representing absolute white), a 3x3 pixel kernel is centered within the image. The kernel is composed of eight 0s and a single 1. The outcome emerges from the computation of this kernel at every conceivable position within the image. The stride parameter guides the kernel's convolution across the image, which dictates the spacing between applications. Notably, a stride of 1 yield the customary convolution, while a stride of 2 circumvents half of the convolutions by mandating a 2-pixel gap between kernel centers.

The output's dimensions following the convolution of an N-sized image with a Z-sized kernel and a stride of S are meticulously defined as:

$$output = \frac{N - Z}{S} + 1$$

At the core of a CNN lies the convolutional layer, a pivotal component that embodies its essence. Comprising an ensemble of learning kernels, a convolutional layer executes convolution across the breadth and height of the input features during the forward pass. This process yields a two-dimensional activation map associated with the specific kernel.

In summary, a core consists of a connection weight layer, the input having the size of a small 2D patch and the output being a single unit.

Figure 2. Convolutional layer

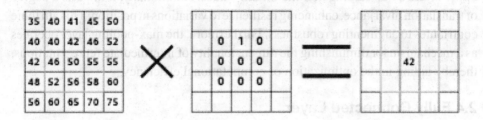

2.3 Pooling Layer

This particular layer is assigned the role of subsampling, entailing a reduction in the spatial resolution of input layers. The rationale behind this operation is to expedite processing and ensure computational resources are effectively utilized to handle the scale of the data. Notably, pooling contributes to reducing teachable parameters within subsequent network layers. The method of choice, max pooling, involves partitioning the image into non-overlapping rectangles. Within each sub-region, the maximum value is extracted, resulting in the retention of only the highest value and the omission of others. This widely employed pooling technique is illustrated in Figure 3, underscoring its function.

Figure 3. Max_pooling with 2x2 filter and stride =2

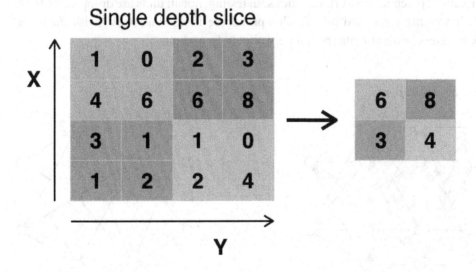

The utilization of a max-pooling layer serves to streamline computations in upper layers by discarding non-maximum values. Additionally, it imparts a degree of translation invariance, enhancing resilience to variations in position. This attribute contributes to augmenting robustness. Furthermore, the max-pooling layer operates as a mechanism for diminishing the dimensionality of intermediate representations, thereby aiding in the optimization of computational efficiency.

2.4 Fully Connected Layer

Convolutional neural networks inherently incorporate several layers interlinked through convolutional layers, followed by fully connected layers. Within these fully connected layers, neurons establish comprehensive connections with all neurons from the preceding layer. The structural composition of a fully connected layer mirrors that of a conventional neural network layer. This layer executes classification based on the outcomes stemming from the convolutional and pooling layers. Each neuron within this layer establishes links with every neuron within the previous layer.

In practice, a Dropout layer typically succeeds a fully connected layer. This addition is pivotal in bolstering the model's generalizability by mitigating the risk of overfitting, a prevalent concern in deep learning. Dropout, as elucidated by Hinton (2014), functions as a mechanism to curb overfitting and effectively amalgamates diverse neural network architectures. During model formation, a unit has a probability 'p' of being temporarily excluded from the network, as depicted in Figure 4. This exclusion encompasses the forward and backward propagation calculations during the training process for a specific sample. This approach prevents units from becoming excessively tailored to the training data. With 'n' units in a layer, the mechanism creates 2^n potential network variations. In testing, not all units are dropped; instead, their weights are scaled by 'p'. This procedure fuses 2^n networks with the same parameters into a singular neural network configuration.

Figure 4. Dropout

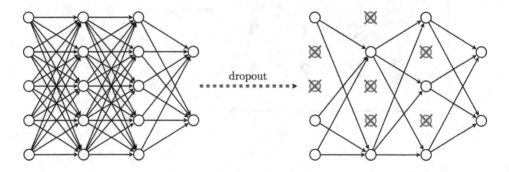

Recurrent Neural Network (RNN)

A recurrent neural network (RNN), or simply recurrent network, is a deep neural network architecture in which there is at least one recurrent connection (loop or cycle) in its structure. In a recurrent network, signals can go backward (via a loop or cycle) and feed neurons from a previous or the same layer.

Recurrent neural networks can process data of any size. They are particularly suited to the analysis of sequences of data over time (time series). RNNs are used in automatic speech recognition, automatic natural language processing on character strings and texts, and automatic translation, which are good examples of sequential data processing.

In general, RNN consider $x = (x_1, x_2, \ldots, x_{T-1}, x_T)$ as input and maps them to hidden and output vector sequences as:

$$hl = (hl_1, hl_2, \ldots, hl_{T-1}, hl_T) \text{ and } op = (op_1, op_2, \ldots, op_{T-1}, op_T)$$

from $t=1$ to T through the following equations in the forward direction.

$$HL(x, hl) = A(w_{xhl}x + w_{hlhl}hl + b)$$

$$HL : \mathbb{R}^m \times \mathbb{R}^n \to \mathbb{R}^n \quad w_{hx} \in \mathbb{R}^{n \times m} \quad w_{hh} \in \mathbb{R}^{n \times n} \quad b \in \mathbb{R}^k$$

where A, b, w denotes activation function, bias vector and weight matrices respectively.

To learn the temporal dependencies, RNN feds the initial step $hl0$ layer value to the next time step hidden layer $hl_1 = HL(x_1, hl_0)$, which is defined recursively as $hl_T = HL(x_T, hl_{T-1})$. Next, we can feed hl_T to stacked recurrent hidden or output layers through *soft*max or *sigmoid* as non-linear activation functions. At each time-step t, the output node op value is estimated using the hidden node value hl at time-step t as:

$$op_t = sf(w_{ophl}hl + b_{op})$$

RNN are converted to FFN using Unfolding or Unrolling. This helps to understand the inherent dynamics of each time-step t. Unfolded RNN contains hl hidden layers for the input sequences of length l.

As shown in figure 5, the unfolded RNN looks similar to deep neural network except that the weights w_{xh}, w_{hh}, w_{ho} are shared across time steps.

RNN is a parameterized function and to find the right parameters loss function is used. Loss function gives the units of difference between the predicted and target values. This is defined for subnet in unfolded RNN at each time-step t as:

Figure 5. Unfolded over time steps t=0, t=1 and RNN

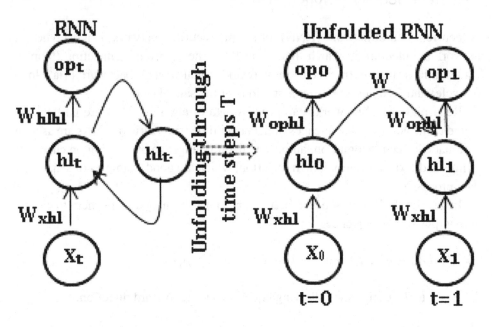

$$L = d(tv, pv) = \sum_{i=1}^{T} d(tv, pv)$$

The complete sequence is treated as a single training vector, for example $(x_1, \dots, x_{41}, cl)$. Consequently, the total loss is computed by summing individual losses at each time-step. To minimize this loss, the gradient of the loss is calculated with respect to the weight parameters. These weight parameters are then adjusted using stochastic gradient descent (SGD). Similarly, during the backpropagation process for the total loss, each training vector requires the summation of gradient vectors at every time step. The gradient is derived using backpropagation, employing the chain rule to compute it through an unfolded computational graph iteratively. However, unfolded RNNs share weight parameters across time-steps, resulting in a process termed as backpropagation through time (BPTT), as explained by Sutskever (2013).

While propagating errors across multiple time-steps, the gradient signal is multiplied by the weight matrix. This can lead to vanishing gradients when the gradient becomes extremely small, or exploding gradients when it becomes excessively large, a phenomenon discussed by Cho (2014). Consequently, RNNs struggle with effectively capturing long-range contextual information in sequence data modeling. To address these issues, researchers recommend regularization to automatically determine suitable values at each time step (Pascanu et al., 2013).

They also propose techniques such as gradient clipping and soft constraints to tackle vanishing and exploding gradients.

An alternative approach called Real-time Recurrent Learning (RTRL) is introduced by Williams and Zipser (1989), which estimates error derivatives at each time step for a single forward-direction update. However, due to increased computational costs compared to BPTT, RTRL remained less popular. Truncated Backpropagation Through Time (TBPTT), an extension of BPTT proposed by Williams and Peng (1990), addresses the issue of exploding gradients in continuously running networks by limiting the number of time steps over which the error is propagated.

Despite these advancements, traditional RNNs still struggle with long-term dependencies. Neural Recurrent Networks (NRNs) cannot effectively retain information from distant pasts, leading to a disconnection between relevant information and its point of use, a problem highlighted by Bengio et al. (1994). Long Short-Term Memory networks (LSTMs), introduced by Hochreiter and Schmidhuber (1997) are designed to mitigate this problem. LSTMs possess a chain structure akin to NRNs. Still, they include memory cells with adaptive multiplicative gating units such as input, forget, and output gates, allowing them to control memory retention. These gates determine which information should flow to other LSTM cells, enabling LSTMs to extract pertinent past information for effective decision-making selectively. In summary, LSTMs address the challenges of long-term dependencies by utilizing memory blocks and adaptive gating units to control memory cells. Their forward pass is generally formulated as follows:

$$x_t, hl_{t-1}, mc_{t-1} \rightarrow hl_t, mc_t$$

$$in\_g_t = \sigma(w_{xin\_g}x_t + w_{hlin\_g}hl_{t-1} + w_{mcin\_g}ml_{t-1} + b_{in\_g})$$

$$fr\_g_t = \sigma(w_{xfr\_g}x_t + w_{hlfr\_g}hl_{t-1} + w_{mcfr\_g}ml_{t-1} + b_{fr\_g})$$

$$mc_t = fr\_g_t \odot mc_{t-1} + in\_g_t \odot \tanh(w_{xmc}x_t + w_{hlmc}hl_{t-1} + b_{mc})$$

$$op_t = \sigma(w_{xop}x_t + w_{hlop}hl_{t-1} + w_{mcop}mc_t + b_{op})$$

$$hl_t = op_t \odot \tanh(mc_t)$$

where in_g, fr_g, op are input, forget and output gating functions respectively, mc denotes memory cell, hl output of hidden layer.

Figure 6. RNN unit and LSTM memory block scheme

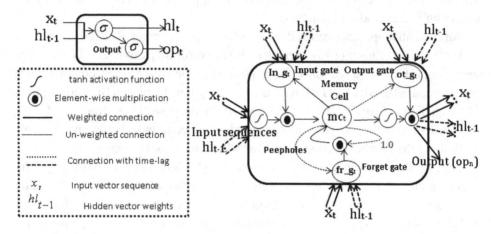

As depicted in Figure 6, a memory cell encapsulates a intricate array of operations, featuring a solitary memory cell, three adaptive multiplicative units, and a self-connection with a steadfast weight of 1.0. Various iterations of the LSTM have been introduced to streamline the number of units involved, among which the CWRNN and GRU stand out.

The Gated Recurrent Unit (GRU) emerges as a distinct adaptation within the realm of LSTM networks (Cho et al., 2014). Encompassing the forward pass of a GRU is a formulation that unfolds as follows:

$$x_t, hl_{t-1} \rightarrow hl_t$$

$$i\_f_t = \sigma(w_{xi\_f} x_t + w_{hli\_f} hl_{t-1} + b_{i\_f}) \quad \text{(Update gate)}$$

$$f_t = \sigma(w_{xf} x_t + w_{hlf} hl_{t-1} + b_f) \quad \text{(Forget or reset gate)}$$

$$ml_t = \tanh(w_{xml} x_t + w_{hlml}(fr \odot hl_{t-1}) + b_{ml}) \quad \text{(Current memory)}$$

$$hl_t = f \odot hl_{t-1} + (1 - f) \odot ml \quad \text{(Updated memory)}$$

The GRU comprises gates (update and forget) dissimilar to LSTM memory cell gate list (input, output and forget) that collaboratively balance the inflow as far as data within the unit.

Figure 7. Architecture of gated recurrent unit

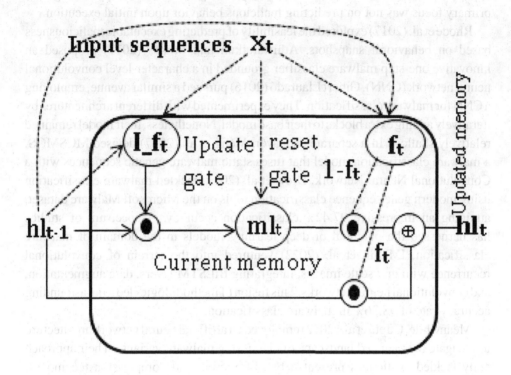

3. RELATED WORKS

Many approaches have been proposed to integrate deep learning into the malware detection and classification domain. Notably, Saxe et al. (2013) introduced a malware detection technique employing a Deep Neural Network (DNN) on histograms of byte sequences and metadata derived from headers. Huang and Stokes (2016) adopted a bag-of-words feature encompassing API call n-grams as input for a multi-task DNN, which simultaneously predicts malware presence and assigns it to a family. Numerous methodologies focusing on Android apps have also been put forth (Yuan et al., 2014; 2016; Li et al., 2018; Alzaylaee et al., 2020; Kim et al., 2022).

Kolsnaji et al. (2016) ingeniously combined convolutional neural networks with long-term memory cells (LSTMs), achieving a remarkable 89.4% recall rate. They tackled the intricate task of classifying malware into families using deep neural networks, including recurrent networks, to decipher API call sequences. Pascanu et al. (2015) ventured into determining whether files were malicious or benign, utilizing RNNs and Echo State Networks. Tobiyama et al. (2016) devised a malware detection technique centered on process behavior within potentially infected terminals. Their approach leveraged Echo State Networks, yielding a 95% accuracy, although the primary focus was not on predicting malicious behavior upon initial execution.

Rhode et al. (2017) explored the feasibility of predicting executable maliciousness based on behavioral snapshots. Athiwaratkun and Stokes (2017) proposed an innovative one-step malware classifier grounded in a character-level convolutional neural network (CNN). Gibert Llauradó (2016) pursued a similar avenue, employing a CNN for malware classification. They experimented with different architectures by iteratively adding extra blocks to their base model. Nonetheless, their model remained relatively shallow. In a separate endeavor, Meng et al. (2017) devised MCSMGS, a malware classification model that fuses static malware genetic sequences with a Convolutional Neural Network. Drew et al. (2017) tackled malware classification using modern gene sequence classification tools on the Microsoft Malware dataset, attaining an impressive 97.42% classification accuracy. A spectrum of studies has harnessed the potential of deep learning models in the domain of malware classification. IMallik et al. (2022) ventured into the terrain of convolutional recurrence with grayscale images, integrating BiLSTM layers, data augmentation, and convolutional neural networks. This fusion of methodologies led to an astounding accuracy rate of 98.36% in malware classification.

Meanwhile, Gupta et al. (2022) employed an artificial neural network architecture to navigate the nuanced landscape of classifying malware variants. Their approach aptly tackled challenges presented by obfuscation and compression techniques. Empirical findings underscored the prowess of their method, showcasing an accuracy of 90.80%. In recent works, Yaseen et al. (2023) delved into this realm, adopting convolutional neural networks (CNNs) as their weapon of choice. Through the ingenious transformation of malware binaries into grayscale images and the application of CNNs, their method achieved a commendable accuracy of 97.4%.

This chapter introduces a novel hybrid approach, intertwining Convolutional Neural Networks (CNNs) and Long Short-Term Memory (LSTM) networks, to effectively classify malware activities.

4. METHODOLOGY

4.1 Malware Dataset

In this scholarly work, we have utilized the prominent malware dataset BIG 2015 (Ronen et al., 2015), sourced from the Microsoft Malware Classification Challenge hosted on Kaggle. This dataset encompasses two fundamental components: a training dataset and a testing dataset. The training dataset includes 10,868 distinct malware programs, meticulously categorized into nine discernible classes. Each malware sample is represented by two distinct files: a .bytes file and a .asm file. The former encapsulates the raw hexadecimal code representation, whereas the latter presents the disassembled assembly code of the malware specimen. For our experimental, we opted to work exclusively with the .bytes files, which enabled us to facilitate the creation of images, as visually depicted in Figure 9. This image-generation procedure adeptly encapsulated the inherent nature of the malware samples, consequently reducing the extraction of pertinent and meaningful features for our comprehensive analysis.

To provide a visual insight into the diversity and characteristics inherent in our dataset, Figure 8 portrays a subset of image samples drawn from our dataset. This visual representation allows for a better comprehension of the visual attributes harnessed throughout our analysis, thereby establishing a foundational framework for our investigative pursuits.

In the subsequent depiction, Table 1 shows the different families in the dataset, each distinctly emblematic of diverse classes within our dataset. These images are emblematic of the following malware families: (a) Adialer.C, (b) Autorun.K, (c) Obfuscator.ACY, (d) Ramnit, (e) Dinwold, and (f) Regrun. Through these visual representations, we capture and delineate each malware family's unique attributes and characteristics. These images not only serve as means of identification but also empower our researchers to scrutinize their behaviors and potential implications deeply.

Table 1. Malware families in the dataset

Family Name	# Train Samples	Type
Ramnit	1541	Worm
Lollipop	2478	Adware
Kelihos_ver3	2942	Backdoor
Vundo	475	Trojan
Simda	42	Backdoor
Tracur	751	TrojanDownloader
Kelihos_ver1	398	Backdoor
Obfuscator.ACY	1228	Any kind of obfuscated malware
Gatak	1013	Backdoor

The dataset architecture adhered to a dual-file representation for each malware sample. Precisely, a .bytes file encapsulated the unprocessed hexadecimal manifestation of the binary content, with the executable headers excluded. Complementing this, a

.asm file was employed to house the disassembled code, extracted via the employment of the IDA disassembler tool. Our experimental endeavors primarily focused on the utilization of the .bytes files, which were instrumental in the creation of grayscale images of malware specimens. An exemplar illustration of such a .bytes file snapshot is furnished below, exemplifying the nature of our data processing methodology.

Figure 8. (a) Snapshot of one-byte file; (b) Snapshot of one assembly code file

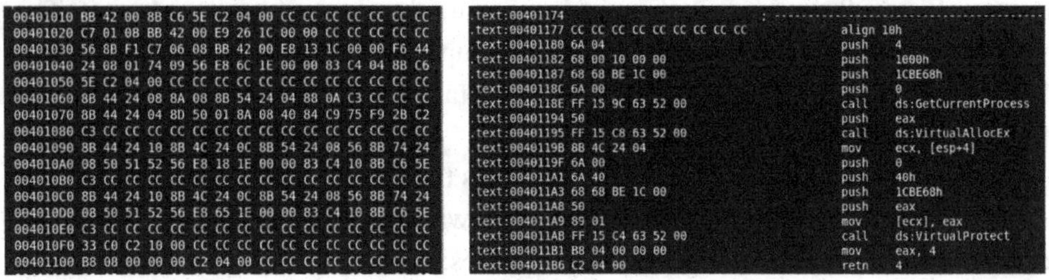

4.2 Data Pre-Processing

This study employed the GIST (Oliva & Torralba, 2001) framework. The outcome of this endeavor materialized in the form of characteristic vectors, which subsequently formed the basis for a nearest-neighbor classifier employing Euclidean distance metrics. The methodology adopted encompassed the conversion of a given malicious binary file into an array of unsigned 8-bit integers. This array was then organized into a 2D matrix structure, effectively shaping the data into a grayscale image within the range of [0, 255], as elucidated by Nataraj et al. (2011) This innovative approach facilitated the transformation of malware data into a visual context, thus enabling the application of image analysis techniques for adequate characterization and classification.

Figure 9. Visualizing Malware as a Gray-Scale Image

**Malware
Binary**
011100110101
100101011010
10100001....
➡ Segmentation to 8 bit vector ➡ 8 bits represents one grayscale pixel ➡

Malware developers often modify previously available code slightly to generate new malware instances (Nataraj et al., 2015). Representing malware as images offers a means to trace these minor alterations readily. Drawing from this notion and previous research (Nataraj et al., 2011), our approach involves visualizing malware binary files as grayscale images.

To execute this process, an initial malware binary file is interpreted as a vector of 8-bit unsigned integers. Subsequently, the binary values of each element within this vector are converted into their corresponding decimal equivalents (e.g., binary [00000000] corresponds to decimal [0], and [11111111] corresponds to [255]). These decimal values are then collated into a new vector, effectively representing the malware sample in decimal form. Lastly, this decimal vector is reconfigured into a 2D matrix, rendering it into a grayscale image. The dimensions (width and height) of this matrix, delineating the spatial resolution of the image, primarily hinge upon the size of the malware binary file. Following Nataraj et al. (2011), we adhere to their specified spatial resolution while reshaping the decimal vectors. This approach capitalizes on the intrinsic similarity in texture (visual characteristics) exhibited by malware variants sharing a common family lineage.

Figure 10. (a) Lollipop samples; (b) Rammit samples

Employing malware visualization as images brings forth a pivotal advantage: discerning distinct sections within a binary becomes facile. This approach is especially adept at identifying slight modifications introduced by malware authors to spawn new iterations. By utilizing images, we effectively detect these minor variations while preserving the overall structure. This practice culminates in a scenario where malware variants sharing a common lineage exhibit striking visual similarity as images, yet remain discernibly distinct from images representing divergent families.

A preliminary pre-processing of the grayscale image is conducted to align with the input data requirements of Convolutional Neural Networks (CNNs). When CNNs are tasked with objectives such as image classification, the input image data is expected to be uniform in size. Specifically, it's advantageous for the image data to possess equal dimensions in terms of length and width, establishing a 1:1 ratio. This standardization facilitates subsequent convolutional operations. However, executable files vary significantly in size, consequently leading to substantial discrepancies in the dimensions of grayscale images. The dimensions of a grayscale image can span from a large 1.04 MB (2048 × 1036 pixels) to a modest 120 KB (512 × 472 pixels). Consequently, the standardization of all grayscale images becomes imperative.

We adopt a bilinear interpolation algorithm for image scaling in our standardization process. This method leverages the four nearest pixel values from the original image to compute a virtual pixel for the target image. This technique produces superior results compared to direct scaling to the target dimensions. To culminate these considerations, we establish the standard dimensions for grayscale images as 64×64 pixels, a judicious selection that harmonizes varying image sizes into a standardized framework.

4.3 The Proposed Model

Inspired by Tsironi et al.'s (2017) work in gesture recognition utilizing a recurrent short-term convolutional memory neural network (CNN-LSTM), we present a deep neural network model designed for malware classification and analysis. This model exhibits a structured architecture, with malware images serving as input and generating scores corresponding to distinct malware classes as output.

Our design integrates two convolutional layers, each executing convolution, and subsequent max-pooling operations. The flattened output from the final convolutional layer is the input for a hidden recurrent LSTM neural network. This LSTM network, in turn, connects to a dense layer featuring a softmax output layer. Training is realized through the BackPropagation algorithm, underpinned by subsequence analysis. Activation of each output layer unit corresponds to a specific malware class. A squashing function is employed to fuse the convolutional and max-pooling layers. Another convolutional-max-pooling layer succeeds this first tier.

To synchronize with the LSTM layer, the CNN layers are temporally distributed. This necessitated the adaptation of Convolution2D, MaxPooling2D, and Flatten into versions compatible with distributed time configurations. Our experimentation encompassed diverse network architectures involving varying layers, filters, and pooling parameters. Ultimately, the CNN-LSTM configuration depicted in Figure 11 emerged as the optimal performer.

In our post-preprocessing phase, our dataset comprised 10,868 labeled samples. Given this relatively modest number, we opted for a robust assessment approach: five-fold cross-validation. This technique entailed the division of the dataset into five equivalent segments, ensuring approximate class distribution parity with the main dataset. During training, drop layers were incorporated after convolutional and dense layers, mitigating overfitting and fostering independence between different convolutional filters.

Our convolutional and max-pooling layers are harmonized through a squashing function, merging max-pooling outputs with an additive bias. This integration mechanism ensures coherence within the network's operations.

$$x_j^l = \tanh\left(pooling_{max}\left(\sum_i^{X_j^{l-1}} * k_{ij} \right) + b_j^l \right)$$

where x_j^l are the feature maps produced by the convolutional layer l, x_j^{l-1} are the feature maps of the previous convolutional layer $l-1$, k_{ij} are the i trained convolution kernels and b_j^l the additive bias. Finally, $pooling_{max}$ is the max-pooling function and tanh is the hyperbolic activation function.

The optimization process was executed employing Adaptive Moment Estimation (ADAM). This technique effectively curbs overfitting during the concluding training stages by calibrating adaptive learning rates for each parameter (Kingma & Ba, 2014). ADAM extends its utility by administering updates to the learning rate parameter-wise. The implementation of both the CNN architecture and the training regimen utilized the widely available Theano (Bergstra et al., 2010) and Lasagne (Dieleman et al., 2015) libraries within the Python programming environment. This choice facilitates the seamless replication of outcomes by fellow researchers, ensuring heightened consistency and comparability across studies.

Figure 11. The proposed CNN LSTM model

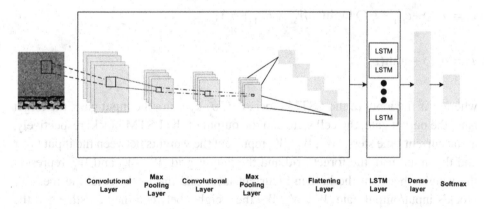

63

LSTM is applied in our context due to its aptitude for handling network traffic events that exhibit time series patterns. Given that network connection records are sequential, the present classification of a network connection can significantly benefit from insights gleaned from past traffic connection records. We utilize LSTM with newly generated features stemming from the max-pooling operation within the CNN framework to capture the temporal relationships embedded in time series data effectively.

These newly formed feature vectors undergo transmission to an LSTM layer. The architecture of Long Short-Term Memory (CNN-LSTM) represents an enhanced evolution of traditional Recurrent Neural Networks (RNNs), devised to address challenges such as the vanishing and exploding gradient dilemma (Schmidhuber, 1997). Notably, CNN-LSTM incorporates memory blocks, encompassing memory cells and an array of gates, offering an effective solution for handling long-range dependencies within sequences. This mechanism stands in contrast to conventional simple RNN units.

$$i_t = \sigma\left(x^t W_{xi} + h_{t-1} W_{hi} + c_{t-1} W_{ci} + b_i\right),$$

$$f_t = \sigma\left(x^t W_{xf} + h_{t-1} W_{hf} + c_{t-1} W_{cf} + b_i\right),$$

$$o_t = \sigma\left(x^t W_{xo} + h_{t-1} W_{ho} + c_{t-1} W_{co} + b_o\right),$$

$$c_t = f_t \odot + c_{t-1} + i_t \odot \tanh(x^t W_{xc} + h_{t-1} + b_c),$$

$$h_t = o_t \odot + \tanh(c_t),$$

where x^t is the input to the LSTM block, i_t, f_t, o_t, c_t, h_t are the input gate, the forget gate, the output gate, the cell state and the output of the LSTM block, respectively, at the current time step t. W_{xi}, W_{xf}, W_{xo} represent the weights between the input layer and the input grid, the forget grid and the output grid. W_{hi}, W_{hf} and W_{ho} represent the weights between the hidden recurrent layer and the forget gate, the memory block's input/output gate, W_{ci}, W_{cf}, W_{co} the weights between the cell state and the input gate, the forget gate and the output gate, and finally, b_i, b_i, b_o are the additive biases of the input gate, the forget gate, and the output gate. The activation functions comprise a sigmoid function. $\sigma(\bullet)$, the hyperbolic activation function tan h(.), and the element-wise multiplication $\odot$.

To counteract the issue of overfitting, we integrate L2 regularization as a means to restrict the weights within the convolutional layers. Additionally, we apply dropout across both the dense and LSTM layers. Without such regularization techniques, the representations learned by a neural network might not exhibit robust generalization capabilities. In our pursuit of regularization, we explore a combination of dropout and L2 regularization applied to the weights and bias terms within the network.

Dropout, as introduced by Hinton (2014), strategically omits a predetermined fraction of nodes during each training iteration, serving as an effective countermeasure against overfitting. By doing so, the network's propensity to adapt too specifically to individual instances is mitigated. L2 regularization, on the other hand, promotes the maintenance of manageable weight magnitudes. This regularization technique prevents a small subset of weights from attaining excessively large values, thereby curbing the potential for overfitting while facilitating a more balanced learning process.

5. EXPERIMENTS AND RESULTS

This section discusses the malware datasets, experiments, and evaluation schemes.

5.1 Experimental Setup

Our experimentation utilizes the Microsoft Malware Dataset, sourced from a Kaggle competition centered on malware classification (Ronen et al., 2015). This challenge, orchestrated by Microsoft in 2015, unveiled a substantial dataset containing 21,741 instances of malware samples. The dataset is further partitioned into distinct subsets, encompassing 10,868 samples earmarked for training purposes and 10,873 for subsequent testing. The dataset allocated for training, as supplied by Kaggle, was itself bifurcated into two segments:

- The training set of size $(N - N/10) = 9781$
- The validation set of size $M = N/10 = 1086$

Where N is the total size of the dataset, $N = 10868$ and $M = 1086$. The validation set was used to search the parameters of the networks and to know when to stop training. In particular, we stopped training the network if the validation loss increased in 10 iterations.

Our experiments were conducted within the Deep Learning Virtual Machine on the Windows Azure platform. The environment featured a 64-bit Ubuntu 22.04 operating system, supported by an Intel(R) Core i9-9900 CPU @ 4.00GHz ⇥ 8, 64GB RAM, and an NVIDIA Titan X GPU equipped with 12GB of memory. To facilitate GPU-based experimentation, the installation of the CUDA driver and CUDA Toolkit, components of Nvidia's GPU programming toolkit, was necessary.

The Keras library (Chollet, 2015) was employed for constructing the CNN-LSTM model. During the 5-fold cross-validation, each model underwent 100 training epochs on an Nvidia 1080 Ti GPU. The model's weights were adjusted using the Adam optimization method (Kingma & Ba, 2014) to minimize the average log-loss criteria.

5.2 Results

Our proposed CNN-LSTM network was trained throughout 100 epochs, utilizing a batch size 16 when applied to the Microsoft malware dataset. Notably, CNN-LSTM demonstrated exceptional performance, attaining a classification accuracy of 98.73% when evaluated on the validation data from the Microsoft malware dataset. This achievement stands out significantly against various baseline methods, as indicated by the substantial gap in performance, as detailed in Table 2. Figure 12 and Figure 13 illustrate the trajectory of accuracy and loss during training and validation for the final CNN-LSTM model, which persisted for 100 epochs. The culmination of this model resulted in an average log loss of 0.0698 on the validation data, thus demonstrating its robustness and effectiveness.

Figure 12. Training and validation accuracy of CNN-LSTM model

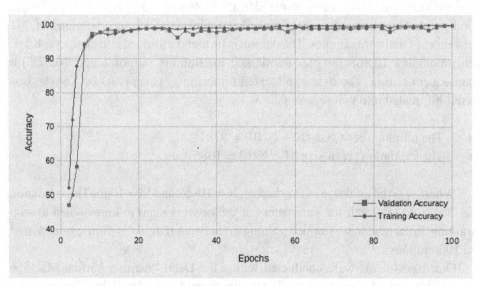

Figure 13. Loss of training and validation of CNN-LSTM model

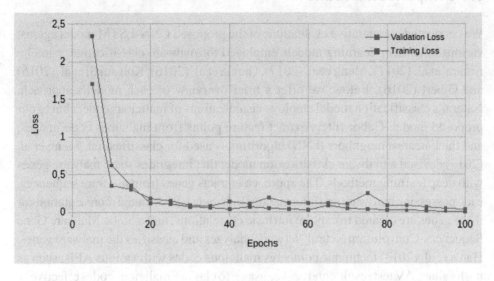

5.3 Testing

A test set devoid of labels is commonly provided in typical Kaggle competitions, including the Microsoft Malware Classification Challenge. A file containing predicted probabilities for each class must be submitted to Kaggle to assess our model's performance on this test set. The evaluation process on Kaggle involves the computation of two distinct scores: the public and private scores. The former is derived from approximately 30% of the test data, while the latter is computed using the remaining 70%. The evaluation process employs the multi-class logarithmic loss as the metric. Specifically, the logarithmic loss is defined as follows:

$$logloss = -\frac{1}{N} \sum_{i=1}^{N} \sum_{j=1}^{M} y_{i,j} \log\left(p_{i,j}\right)$$

where N is the number of malware samples, M is the number of malware classes, $y_{i,j}$ is 1 if the prediction is correct and 0 otherwise, and $p_{i,j}$ is the predicted probability (Ronen et al., 2015). Upon submitting the predictions of this model for the test malware files to Kaggle, we receive two average log-loss scores: a public score of 0.0691 calculated from 30% of the test dataset and a privates score of 0.0743 calculated from 70% of the test dataset. These results align with the log-loss we obtained on the validation data, which means our final model generalizes well on new data.

5.4 Comparison Results

We conducted comparative evaluations of the proposed CNN-LSTM model against various other deep learning models employed for malware classification, namely: Nataraj et al. (2011), Meng et al. (2017), Garcia et al. (2016), Kolosnjaji et al. (2016) and Gibert (2016). Below, we offer a brief overview of each model's approach. Nataraj's classification model employs visualizations of malicious code, akin to our proposed model. Gabor filters extract feature points from malicious code images, and the k-nearest neighbors (kNN) algorithm is used for classification. Meng et al. (2017) devised a malware classification model that integrates static malware genes with deep learning methods. The approach extracts genes from malware sequences, each possessing hardware and informational attributes. Distributed representations of these genes are created to capture intrinsic correlations, and a Static Malware Gene Sequences-Convolution Neural Network analyzes and classifies the malware genes. Han's et al. (2013) technique compares malicious codes with various APIs, such as hash values, AV test results, and packer usage, to classify malicious codes effectively. Drew et al. (2017) employed modern gene sequence classification tools for malware classification on the Microsoft Malware dataset. Garcia et al. (2016) introduced a novel approach that converts malware binaries into images and employs Random Forest for classifying various malware families. Kolosnjaji et al. (2016) designed a neural network featuring convolutional and recurrent layers for classifying system call sequences, focusing on the best characteristics for classification. Performance evaluation across these models relies on commonly used accuracy metrics in each study. S Yaseen et al. (2023) employed deep learning models, particularly convolutional neural networks (CNNs), to effectively categorize various malware families. By converting malware binaries into grayscale images and using CNNs, the researchers achieved a commendable accuracy rate of 97.4%. Meanwhile, Mallik et al. (2022) pursued an intricate avenue by combining convolutional recurrence with grayscale images, utilizing Bidirectional Long Short-Term Memory (BiLSTM) layers, data augmentation techniques, and convolutional neural networks. This comprehensive methodology yielded an impressive accuracy rate of 98.36% in the field of malware classification

Table 2 presents a comparative analysis of our proposed classification technique alongside previous research outcomes.

Compared to existing methods and experimental results, our combined CNN and LSTM architecture demonstrates superior performance over individual CNN and RNN models in malware classification. By harnessing the strengths of both the CNN and LSTM models, we achieve heightened classification accuracy compared to existing approaches. The CNN adeptly captures local features from the input data, while the LSTM effectively handles sequential inputs by learning long-term

Table 2. Performance of different methods on validation test

Model	Accuracy
Meng et al.	98%
Nataraj	97.18%
Yaseen	97.4%
Han	75%
Drew	97.42%
Garcia	95.62%
Kolosnjaji	85,6%
Mallik	98.36%
CNN-LSTM (ours)	**98,73%**

dependencies and deriving feature representations for malware. This symbiotic integration of CNN and LSTM thus affords us the advantage of enhanced accuracy in malware classification.

6. CONCLUSION AND FUTURE WORK

It is crucial to examine the actions of malicious software and classify instances to facilitate the creation of robust programs for deterring malware attacks. With this goal in mind, we have introduced a novel architecture based on convolutional neural networks (CNN) and long short-term memory (LSTM) networks to undertake malware analysis and classification. Our initial step involves transforming malware samples into grayscale images for training the CNN in classification tasks. Empirical findings from assessments of Microsoft's malware classification datasets underscore that our novel model outperforms existing benchmarks. The effectiveness of our proposed CNN-LSTM approach has been extensively validated through various experiments, yielding an impressive accuracy of 98.73% during cross-validation procedures. Notably, our model exhibits swift performance in categorizing the malware class of binary files, enhancing its practicality.

We are committed to refining and evaluating our deep learning model by exploring more intricate architectures to enhance its efficacy. Additionally, we intend to evaluate the performance of our approach on larger datasets encompassing a more comprehensive array of malware classes, aiming for further heightened accuracy levels.

REFERENCES

Aliyev, V. (2010). *Using honeypots to study skill level of attackers based on the exploited vulnerabilities in the network*. Chalmers University of Technology.

Alzaylaee, M. K., Yerima, S. Y., & Sezer, S. (2020). DL-Droid: Deep learning based android malware detection using real devices. *Computers & Security*, *89*, 101663. doi:10.1016/j.cose.2019.101663

Athiwaratkun, B., & Stokes, J. W. (2017). Malware classification with LSTM and GRU language models and a character-level CNN. *2017 IEEE International Conference on Acoustics, Speech and Signal Processing (ICASSP)*, (pp. 2482–2486). IEEE. 10.1109/ICASSP.2017.7952603

Bengio, Y., Simard, P., & Frasconi, P. (1994). Learning long-term dependencies with gradient descent is difficult. *IEEE Transactions on Neural Networks*, *5*(2), 157–166. doi:10.1109/72.279181 PMID:18267787

Bergstra, J., Breuleux, O., Bastien, F. F., Lamblin, P., Pascanu, R., Desjardins, G., Turian, J., Warde-Farley, D., & Bengio, Y. (2010). *Theano: a CPU and GPU math compiler in Python*. Proceedings of the Python for Scientific Computing Conference (SciPy), Montreal. http://www-etud.iro.umontreal.ca/~wardefar/publications/theano_scipy2010.pdf

Cho, K., Van Merriënboer, B., Gulcehre, C., Bahdanau, D., Bougares, F., Schwenk, H., & Bengio, Y. (2014). Learning phrase representations using RNN encoder-decoder for statistical machine translation. *ArXiv Preprint ArXiv:1406.1078*. doi:10.3115/v1/D14-1179

Chollet, F. (2015). *Deep learning library for theano and tensorflow*. Keras.

Chumachenko, K., & Technology, I. (2017). *Machine Learning for Malware Detection and Classification*. [Bachelor's Thesis Information Technology, Southeast Finland University of Applied Sciences].

Dieleman, S., Schlüter, J., Raffel, C., Olson, E., Sønderby, S. K., Nouri, D., & De Fauw, J. (2015). *Lasagne: first release*.

Drew, J., Hahsler, M., & Moore, T. (2017). Polymorphic malware detection using sequence classification methods and ensembles. *EURASIP Journal on Multimedia and Information Security*, *2017*(1), 2. doi:10.118613635-017-0055-6

Garcia, F. C. C., Muga, I. I., & Felix, P. (2016). Random Forest for Malware Classification. *ArXiv Preprint ArXiv:1609.07770*.

Gibert, D. (2016). *Convolutional Neural Networks for Malware Classification.* [Thesis, University of Barcelona].

Gupta, K., Jiwani, N., Sharif, M. H. U., Datta, R., & Afreen, N. (2022). A Neural Network Approach For Malware Classification. *2022 International Conference on Computing, Communication, and Intelligent Systems (ICCCIS)*, (pp. 681–684). IEEE. 10.1109/ICCCIS56430.2022.10037653

Hinton, G. (2014). Dropout : A Simple Way to Prevent Neural Networks from Overfitting. *Journal of Machine Learning Research, 15*, 1929–1958.

Hochreiter, S., & Schmidhuber, J. (1997). Long short-term memory. *Neural Computation, 9*(8), 1735–1780. doi:10.1162/neco.1997.9.8.1735 PMID:9377276

Huang, W., & Stokes, J. W. (2016). MtNet : A Multi-Task Neural Network for Dynamic Malware Classification. *International Conference on Detection of Intrusions and Malware, and Vulnerability Assessment*, (pp. 399–418). Springer. 10.1007/978-3-319-40667-1_20

Kim, J., Ban, Y., Ko, E., Cho, H., & Yi, J. H. (2022). MAPAS: A practical deep learning-based android malware detection system. *International Journal of Information Security, 21*(4), 725–738. doi:10.100710207-022-00579-6

Kingma, D. P., & Ba, J. (2014). Adam: A method for stochastic optimization. *ArXiv Preprint ArXiv:1412.6980.*

Kolosnjaji, B., Zarras, A., Webster, G., & Eckert, C. (2016). Deep Learning for Classification of Malware System Call Sequences. In B. H. Kang, & Q. Bai (Eds.), *Australasian Joint Conference on Artificial Intelligence* (pp. 137–149). Springer International Publishing. 10.1007/978-3-319-50127-7_11

Krizhevsky, A., Sutskever, I., & Hinton, G. E. (2012). ImageNet Classification with Deep Convolutional Neural Networks. In F. Pereira, C. J. C. Burges, L. Bottou, & K. Q. Weinberger (Eds.), Vol. 25, pp. 1097–1105). Advances in Neural Information Processing Systems. Curran Associates, Inc., http://papers.nips.cc/paper/4824-imagenet-classification-with-deep-convolutional-neural-networks.pdf

LeCun, Y., Bengio, Y., & Hinton, G. (2015). Deep learning. *Nature, 521*(7553), 436–444. doi:10.1038/nature14539 PMID:26017442

Li, C., Wu, Y., Yuan, X., Sun, Z., Wang, W., Li, X., & Gong, L. (2018). Detection and defense of DDoS attack–based on deep learning in OpenFlow-based SDN. *International Journal of Communication Systems, 31*(5), e3497. doi:10.1002/dac.3497

M., G., & Sethuraman, S. C. (2023). A comprehensive survey on deep learning based malware detection techniques. *Computer Science Review, 47*, 100529. https://doi.org/https://doi.org/10.1016/j.cosrev.2022.100529

Maleh, Y. (2019). Malware classification and analysis using convolutional and recurrent neural network. In *Handbook of Research on Deep Learning Innovations and Trends* (pp. 233–255). IGI Global. doi:10.4018/978-1-5225-7862-8.ch014

Maleh, Y., Shojafar, M., Alazab, M., & Baddi, Y. (2021). *Machine Intelligence and Big Data Analytics for Cybersecurity Applications*. Springer International Publishing AG. doi:10.1007/978-3-030-57024-8

Mallik, A., Khetarpal, A., & Kumar, S. (2022). ConRec: Malware classification using convolutional recurrence. *Journal of Computer Virology and Hacking Techniques, 18*(4), 297–313. doi:10.100711416-022-00416-3

Meng, X., Shan, Z., Liu, F., Zhao, B., Han, J., Wang, H., & Wang, J. (2017). MCSMGS: Malware Classification Model Based on Deep Learning. *2017 International Conference on Cyber-Enabled Distributed Computing and Knowledge Discovery (CyberC)*, (pp. 272–275). IEEE. 10.1109/CyberC.2017.21

Nataraj, L., Karthikeyan, S., Jacob, G., & Manjunath, B. S. (2011). Malware Images: Visualization and Automatic Classification. *Proceedings of the 8th International Symposium on Visualization for Cyber Security*. ACM. 10.1145/2016904.2016908

Nataraj, L., Karthikeyan, S., & Manjunath, B. S. (2015). SATTVA: SpArsiTy inspired classificaTion of malware VAriants. *In Proceedings of the 3rd ACM Workshop on Information Hiding and Multimedia Security* (pp. 135-140). ACM. 10.1145/2756601.2756616

Oliva, A., & Torralba, A. (2001). Modeling the Shape of the Scene: A Holistic Representation of the Spatial Envelope. *International Journal of Computer Vision, 42*(3), 145–175. doi:10.1023/A:1011139631724

Pascanu, R., Mikolov, T., & Bengio, Y. (2013). On the difficulty of training recurrent neural networks. *In International Conference on Machine Learning*, (pp. 1310–1318). Springer.

Pascanu, R., Stokes, J. W., Sanossian, H., Marinescu, M., & Thomas, A. (2015). Malware classification with recurrent networks. *2015 IEEE International Conference on Acoustics, Speech and Signal Processing (ICASSP)*, (pp. 1916–1920). IEEE. 10.1109/ICASSP.2015.7178304

Rhode, M., Burnap, P., & Jones, K. (2017). Early-Stage Malware Prediction Using Recurrent Neural Networks. *ArXiv Preprint ArXiv:1708.03513*, 1–28.

Ronen, R., Radu, M., Feuerstein, C., & Yom-tov, E. (2015). Microsoft Malware Classification Challenge. *Microsoft Kaggle*, 1–7. doi:10.1145/2857705.2857713

Sadqi, Y., & Maleh, Y. (2022). A systematic review and taxonomy of web applications threats. *Information Security Journal: A Global Perspective, 31*(1), 1–27. doi:10.1080/19393555.2020.1853855

Saxe, A. M., McClelland, J. L., & Ganguli, S. (2013). *Malware Analysis of Imaged Binary Samples by Convolutional Neural Network with Attention Mechanism.* 127–134.

Sutskever, I. (2013). *Training recurrent neural networks.* University of Toronto.

Tobiyama, S., Yamaguchi, Y., Shimada, H., Ikuse, T., & Yagi, T. (2016). Malware Detection with Deep Neural Network Using Process Behavior. *2016 IEEE 40th Annual Computer Software and Applications Conference (COMPSAC).* IEEE. 10.1109/COMPSAC.2016.151

Tsironi, E., Barros, P., Weber, C., & Wermter, S. (2017). An analysis of Convolutional Long Short-Term Memory Recurrent Neural Networks for gesture recognition. *Neurocomputing, 268*, 76–86. doi:10.1016/j.neucom.2016.12.088

Williams, R. J., & Zipser, D. (1989). A learning algorithm for continually running fully recurrent neural networks. *Neural Computation, 1*(2), 270–280. doi:10.1162/neco.1989.1.2.270

Yaseen, S., Aslam, M. M., Farhan, M., Naeem, M. R., & Raza, A. (2023). A Deep Learning-based Approach for Malware Classification using Machine Code to Image Conversion. *Technical Journal, 28*(01), 36–46.

Yuan, Z., Lu, Y., & Xue, Y. (2016). DroidDetector. *Android Malware Characterization and Detection Using Deep Learning., 21*(1), 114–123.

Yuan, Z., Lyu, Y., Wang, Z., & Xue, Y. (2014). *Droid-Sec: deep learning in android malware detection.* SIGCOMM. doi:10.1145/2619239.2631434

Section 2
Advanced Techniques in Multimedia Data Processing

Chapter 4
Role of NLP and Deep Learning for Multimedia Data Processing and Security

Mudasir Ahmad Wani

ⓘ https://orcid.org/0000-0002-6947-3717
Prince Sultan University, Saudi Arabia

Sarah Kaleem
Prince Sultan University, Saudi Arabia

Ahmed A. Abd El-Latif
Menoufia University, Egypt

ABSTRACT

This book chapter is a vital guide for understanding today's complex landscape of booming multimedia data and growing cybersecurity risks. It focuses on the transformative roles of natural language processing (NLP) and deep learning in both areas. The chapter starts by discussing deep learning's capabilities in multimedia data analysis before moving to its applications in cybersecurity. It then shifts to examine how NLP is revolutionizing multimedia data management through semantic understanding and context awareness. The chapter also explores the emerging area of social cybersecurity, spotlighting NLP's role in identifying and mitigating social engineering attacks and disinformation. It wraps up with key insights into future trends. Overall, this chapter serves as a comprehensive resource for applying NLP and Deep Learning techniques to multimedia data and cybersecurity challenges.

DOI: 10.4018/978-1-6684-7216-3.ch004

1. INTRODUCTION

Multimedia data represents different media formats and content types (Usman et al., 2019; Zhang et al., 2019). This data type encompasses various forms of unimodal and multimodal content, including text, images, video, audio, and more. Unlike traditional data, which may be strictly numerical or textual, multimedia data is often complex, high-dimensional, and contains rich information that can be unstructured and semi-structured. Multimedia data is widely used in various applications such as entertainment, education, advertising, and communication, leveraging multiple sensory channels to convey complex information more effectively (Li & Liu, 2023). Understanding the complexities of multimedia data is crucial for fields such as computer science, communications, entertainment, and digital media technologies. Multimedia data processing involves capturing, storing, transmitting, and manipulating various media types like text, audio, images, and video (Abd El-Latif et al., 2023). Multimedia data processing involves the analysis and interpretation of different forms of media, such as images, videos, audio, and text. Traditional techniques have been limited, especially when dealing with large, complex, unstructured multimedia datasets. Multimedia data processing uses computational algorithms and hardware to analyze and transform this diverse data into an easily accessed, edited, or shared format. This field is essential for streaming services, video conferencing, and augmented reality applications.

Deep learning employs neural networks with multiple layers to analyze various forms of data. It excels at pattern recognition, enabling applications like image and speech recognition, NLP, and autonomous vehicles. Deep learning algorithms automatically learn to identify features and make decisions, reducing the need for manual feature extraction (Ahmad Wani et al., 2023; Balaji, 2021; Islam, Liu, Wang et al, 2020). With the advent of deep learning, the processing and understanding of multimedia data have seen significant breakthroughs. Deep learning has recently emerged as a powerful tool for tackling the challenges, improving the efficiency and accuracy of multimedia data processing tasks (Hiriyannaiah, 2020). Deep learning for multimedia data processing utilizes neural networks to analyze and interpret complex data types like images, audio, and video. Automated feature extraction and pattern recognition significantly enhance tasks such as image classification, speech recognition, and video analysis. This approach has revolutionized applications ranging from content recommendation to autonomous vehicles, offering improved accuracy and efficiency over traditional methods.

Cybersecurity protects digital systems, networks, and data from unauthorized access, damage, or theft (El Latif, 2023). It encompasses a range of practices and technologies designed to safeguard personal, corporate, and governmental information (Islam, Uddin, Islam et al, 2020). Given the increasing prevalence of cyber threats, cybersecurity has become critical for ensuring information integrity, confidentiality, and availability in the digital age. Deep learning for cybersecurity employs neural networks to detect and mitigate cyber threats in real time (Cavallaro et al., 2020). It excels at pattern recognition, enabling it to identify anomalies and potential vulnerabilities in large datasets quickly and accurately. This advanced approach enhances traditional security measures, providing a more dynamic defense against increasingly sophisticated cyberattacks.

NLP is a field of artificial intelligence focusing on the interaction between computers and human language. It permits machines to recognize, infer, and produce text, paving the way for applications like chatbots, translation services, behavioral analysis, and sentiment analysis (Gosal et al., 2019; Mackey et al., 2020), (Wani, 2022). NLP uses machine learning algorithms to turn unstructured text into actionable data, enhancing user experience and business intelligence. NLP for multimedia data processing applies language algorithms to analyze and interpret text alongside other forms of media like images and videos. This integrated approach enables automatic captioning, semantic tagging, and sentiment analysis within multimedia content. It enhances searchability and accessibility, providing a richer, more interactive user experience across various platforms and applications.

Social cybersecurity protects social media platforms and online communities from cyber threats like misinformation, phishing, and harassment (Chen et al., 2020) (Wani et al., 2023). It employs various technologies and practices to monitor, detect, and mitigate malicious activities that exploit human interaction in digital social spaces. The field is increasingly important due to the pervasive use of social media and its potential impact on individual and societal well-being. NLP for social cybersecurity utilizes NLP algorithms to analyze text-based communications on social media platforms and other online forums. It aims to identify cyber threats like phishing scams, fake news, and hate speech, thereby enhancing the security and integrity of social networks. By examining linguistic patterns and contextual cues, NLP provides an additional defense against increasingly sophisticated cyberattacks in the social domain.

1.1 Contributions

- Examine the evolving impact of Deep Learning and Natural Language Processing (NLP) in handling large volumes of multimedia data, including state-of-the-art developments and their potential integrations.
- Identify multiple avenues through which Deep Learning and NLP can benefit various multimedia services, transforming the data processing landscape and the security of expansive multimedia datasets generated from diverse sources.

- Evaluate the ability of Deep Learning and techniques to manage cybersecurity and social cybersecurity concerns. and secure. This includes a detailed analysis of their unique features, advantages, and shortcomings.
- Synthesize key takeaways from our review, pointing out substantial research challenges that manifest as research questions aimed at furthering our understanding of Deep Learning and NLP applications for multimedia data processing and cybersecurity.

1.2 Chapter Organization

This book chapter is organized as follows: Section 2 delves into the applications and methodologies of Deep Learning for Multimedia Data Processing, offering a comprehensive overview of its evolving role in managing large datasets. Section 3 focuses on the critical intersection of Deep Learning and cybersecurity, examining how these advanced techniques enhance cybersecurity features. In Section 4, the discussion pivots to NLP and its applications in Multimedia Data Processing, providing a detailed exploration of how NLP is revolutionizing how we interact with and analyze multimedia content. Section 5 further expands on the applications of NLP but specifically focuses types on analysis with NLP for multimedia data. Section 6 outlines key points for future perspectives in NLP for multimedia data processing. Finally, Section 7 provides a conclusion that synthesizes the key takeaways from the chapter and offers final thoughts on the future trajectory.

2. DEEP LEARNING FOR MULTIMEDIA DATA PROCESSING

This section comprehensively overviews various deep-learning approaches applied to multimedia data processing. This is a curated repository of seminal and recent research efforts detailing their specific contributions and limitations. The aim is to offer a succinct yet informative reference point for scholars, practitioners, and enthusiasts interested in the intersection of deep learning technologies and multimedia applications. Details of each study, including the methodologies used and the results achieved, provide a more in-depth understanding. The emerging field of Deep Learning for Multimedia Data Processing combines sophisticated neural network models to analyze and generate various multimedia forms, including images, videos, audio, and text (Rathee et al., 2020). Utilizing specialized techniques like CNNs for visual content, RNNs for sequential forms like audio, and Transformer models for text and multi-modal data. This field offers unprecedented capabilities in areas such as image recognition, natural language processing, audio synthesis, and even the creation of new multimedia content (Ghantasala et al., 2022). However, the field also grapples with challenges such as high computational costs, the requirement for extensive, labeled datasets, and ethical and interpretability issues. Despite these hurdles, the potential for significant advances in various domains, from healthcare and surveillance to entertainment and social media analytics, is promising.

An inclusive proposal on multimedia data processing presents deep learning methods mostly suited for multimedia data (Li & Liu, 2023). Despite its depth, it needs a discussion on computational requirements and the specifics of the datasets used, and it fails to provide a comparative analysis with other methodologies. A novel hybrid architecture for suggesting hashtags for orphaned tweets is proposed (Djenouri et al., 2022). This system blends CNNs, frequent pattern mining, and genetic algorithms for fine-tuning parameters. Although the work backs its claims with solid experiments, it should tackle issues like the scope and diversity of the Twitter datasets used, computational needs, and ethical considerations. Another paper focuses on the healthcare sector, particularly against the COVID-19 pandemic and rising chronic illnesses (Tobon et al., 2022). While pushing for deep learning applications in healthcare, the paper falls short by not delving into technical specifics or discussing the quality and variety of healthcare data used. It also sidesteps the ethical and privacy concerns of applying deep learning in healthcare.

An Adaptive-weighted Multiview Deep Basis Matrix Factorization (AMDBMF) is proposed to handle the weights dynamically (Li et al., 2021). This model blends matrix factorization, deep learning, and view fusion to learn feature representations in multiview multimedia data. While the approach is creative, it would be beneficial for the model to delve into computational demands and scalability. Additionally, it could provide more insights into how the model handles typical multimedia issues like data noise. Similarly, an approach that employs edge computing coupled with Deep Reinforcement Learning (DRL) to enhance task offloading is presented (Yang et al., 2022). It tackles hurdles in the Internet of Vehicles (IoV) sector, including concerns about time lags and energy use. The model could be strengthened by discussing its scalability and the possible security risks. It would also benefit from comparing this approach to other cutting-edge algorithms. Separate concerns about scalability are raised in the context of image and video processing tools, and a cloud-based platform for computer vision applications is suggested (Mahmoudi et al., 2020). While promising, the research neglects information on the platform's security protocols and resilience against system failures or disruptions. The paper also doesn't state the scalability limits or compare its platform against existing ones. A unique method for enhancing video quality is proposed that focuses on the growing Multimedia IoT (M-IoT) domain (Bouaafia et al., 2022). The proposal has potential but would improve by comparing its techniques to other methods, detailing how much computing power it requires, and discussing how well it performs in various network conditions. Another study provides a secure storage framework that melds multi-biometrics, deep learning, and cryptographic mapping for increased security (Sedik et al., 2023). The LW-DeepFakeNe, a lean network that combines CNN and LSTM technologies detect DeepFake videos in real-time is introduced (Masud et al., 2023). Additionally, deep learning algorithms predict Alzheimer's disease (Jabeen et al., 2023). The key issues and challenges in pedestrian detection for autonomous vehicles using deep learning are discussed (Iftikhar et al., 2022). A sophisticated drowsiness detection system for drivers is presented, leveraging multiple CNN models and facial subsampling to enhance traffic safety (Ahmed et al., 2021).

3. DEEP LEARNING FOR CYBERSECURITY

Deep learning has also significantly impacted the field of cybersecurity. This technology's capacity for analyzing large data sets has changed how organizations protect against cyber risks that identify complex patterns and make precise predictions. By using artificial neural networks that mimic the human brain's architecture, deep learning enables computers to tackle tasks once deemed too difficult. One of its key advantages in cybersecurity is real-time detection and prevention of cyber-attacks. Unlike traditional methods, which often lag behind in identifying new threats, deep learning models can spot minor changes that could indicate a security issue. These models can spot irregularities in network activity, flag abnormal user actions, and even forecast likely future attacks based on past data. Deep learning is particularly effective in handling unstructured data types, such as text and images, which are prevalent in cybersecurity. Deep learning techniques can analyze and categorize textual data from various sources, including emails, social media, and websites, to uncover potential threats or phishing attempts.

Furthermore, deep learning models can analyze and categorize images that may contain harmful code or signs of a cyber-attack, thereby improving malware identification and stopping its distribution. Deep learning's proficiency in automating decision-making is also invaluable in dealing with incidents and reducing threats. Security experts often have to sift through massive amounts of data and make rapid, precise judgments. Deep learning aids in ranking alerts, recommending effective countermeasures, and even independently halting suspect activities, freeing human professionals to concentrate on higher-level tasks. Nevertheless, it's worth mentioning that deep learning comes with its own set of challenges. These models need extensive training on big datasets, and their intricacy can expose them to vulnerabilities and targeted attacks. The considerable computational power required for training and running these models may also hinder smaller firms with restricted resources.

3.1. Applying Deep Learning to Cybersecurity

Applying deep learning for cybersecurity involves a systematic process incorporating various stages, from data collection to model deployment. To implement deep learning for cybersecurity, there are some critical steps, which are shown in Figure 1 and briefly discussed in the following subsections.

Figure 1. Basic steps to apply deep learning to cybersecurity

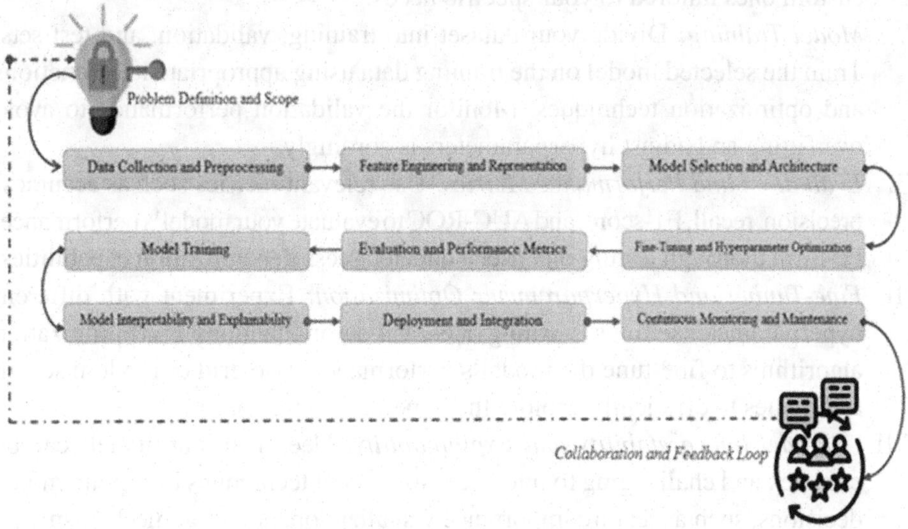

I. *Problem Definition and Scope*: Clearly define the cybersecurity problem you aim to address using deep learning. This could include tasks like malware detection, intrusion detection, phishing detection, or vulnerability assessment. Determine the scope, objectives, and success criteria for your project.

II. *Data Collection and Preprocessing:* Gather relevant and representative datasets for training, validation, and testing. These datasets could include network traffic logs, text data, images, or any other relevant sources. Clean, preprocess, and transform the data to ensure it's suitable for deep learning models. Data preprocessing might involve data augmentation, normalization, and feature extraction.

III. *Feature Engineering and Representation:* For structured data, design appropriate features that capture the characteristics of the problem. Use techniques like word embeddings or convolutional filters to create meaningful representations for unstructured data like text or images. Proper feature engineering can significantly impact the performance of deep learning models.

IV. *Model Selection and Architecture:* Choose the appropriate deep-learning architecture for your problem. Convolutional Neural Networks (CNNs) are effective for image analysis, Recurrent Neural Networks (RNNs) for sequential data, and Transformers for NLP tasks. Research existing architectures or design custom ones tailored to your specific needs.

V. *Model Training:* Divide your dataset into training, validation, and test sets. Train the selected model on the training data using appropriate loss functions and optimization techniques. Monitor the validation performance to avoid overfitting and adjust hyperparameters accordingly.

VI. *Evaluation and Performance Metrics:* Use relevant metrics such as accuracy, precision, recall, F1-score, and AUC-ROC to evaluate your model's performance. Perform thorough testing on unseen data to assess generalization capabilities.

VII. *Fine-Tuning and Hyperparameter Optimization:* Experiment with different hyperparameter settings, learning rates, activation functions, and optimization algorithms to fine-tune the model's performance. Use grid or random search techniques to efficiently explore the hyperparameter space.

VIII. *Model Interpretability and Explainability:* Deep learning models can be complex and challenging to interpret. Implement techniques to explain model decisions, such as feature importance visualization, attention mechanisms, or SHAP (SHapley Additive exPlanations) values.

IX. *Deployment and Integration:* Once the model performs satisfactorily, deploy it in a real-world environment. This might involve integrating it with cybersecurity systems, such as SIEM (Security Information and Event Management) tools. Ensure the model's scalability, reliability, and security during deployment.

X. *Continuous Monitoring and Maintenance:* Cyber threats and attack patterns evolve. Regularly monitor the model's performance in the production environment and retrain it if necessary. Stay updated with the latest research and techniques to adapt the model to new challenges.

XI. *Collaboration and Feedback Loop:* Encourage collaboration between data scientists, cybersecurity experts, and IT teams. Create a feedback loop based on real-world incidents and emerging threats to improve the model's accuracy and effectiveness.

By following these steps, organizations can effectively apply deep learning techniques to enhance their cybersecurity strategies and proactively defend against evolving cyber threats.

4. NLP FOR MULTIMEDIA DATA PROCESSING

Natural Language Processing (NLP) has traditionally been associated with the analysis and understanding of textual data. However, the scope of NLP has expanded beyond text to encompass the realm of multimedia data processing, ushering in a new era of interdisciplinary research and applications. NLP for multimedia data processing involves the integration of language understanding and analysis techniques with various forms of multimedia content, such as images, videos, and audio files. This convergence enables machines to not only comprehend textual context but also interpret and extract meaning from the rich information present in multimedia sources. One of the key challenges in multimedia data processing is the heterogeneity of information types. Integrating NLP techniques with multimedia content demands the ability to understand and extract insights from multiple data modalities simultaneously. For instance, the combination of images and accompanying captions, or videos and spoken descriptions, necessitates the development of models that can jointly process textual and visual information. This interdisciplinary approach holds immense potential for applications such as multimedia search, content recommendation, video summarization, and sentiment analysis of audiovisual content. Multimodal sentiment analysis (Shakil et al., 2021) is a compelling application that showcases the capabilities of NLP in multimedia data processing. By fusing textual content with visual cues, such as facial expressions and gestures, sentiment analysis can yield more accurate insights into the emotions and attitudes conveyed in multimedia content. This enables businesses to gauge customer sentiment in online videos or analyze user reactions to multimedia advertisements more comprehensively.

The integration of NLP and multimedia data also plays a pivotal role in accessibility and content understanding. Automated speech recognition (ASR) and audio-to-text transcription technologies, which are often a part of NLP systems, can be applied to convert spoken content in videos and podcasts into textual transcripts. These transcripts make multimedia content more accessible to individuals with hearing impairments and enable content creators to index, search, and analyze spoken information more effectively. Moreover, multimedia content often comes with metadata, captions, and contextual information that can be leveraged by NLP techniques. Named Entity Recognition (NER) applied to images, for instance, can identify objects, locations, and people, enriching the textual description of visual data. This integration opens doors to applications like automated image captioning, where NLP models generate coherent and contextually relevant textual descriptions for images.

As with any emerging field, challenges persist in NLP for multimedia data processing. Models must handle the inherent complexity and variability of multimedia content, accounting for noise, ambiguity, and context. Additionally, multimodal datasets are typically larger and more diverse, demanding robust preprocessing and novel techniques for representation learning. In conclusion, NLP's expansion into multimedia data processing marks a significant paradigm shift, facilitating the seamless integration of textual and visual information for a comprehensive understanding of multimedia content. As researchers and practitioners delve deeper into this interdisciplinary domain, the potential for transformative applications that harness the synergy between NLP and multimedia data becomes increasingly evident, enriching our interactions with a vast array of audiovisual information.

5. TYPES OF ANALYSIS WITH NLP FOR MULTIMEDIA DATA

NLP for multimedia data processing offers a diverse range of analyses that can be performed to extract insights from the combination of textual and visual information. These analyses enable a deeper understanding of multimedia content, enhancing applications such as content recommendation, sentiment analysis, and content summarization. There are several types of analyses that can be performed with NLP for multimedia data processing, some are shown in figure 2, and discussed in following subsections.

Figure 2. Types of analysis with NLP for multimedia data

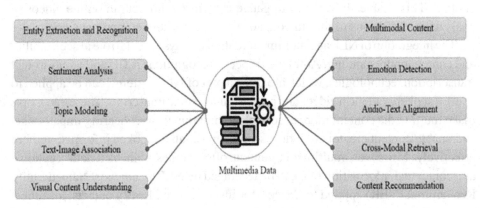

I.   *Sentiment Analysis:* Determine the sentiment expressed in multimedia content, including images, videos, and audio. By analyzing both textual and visual cues, you can ascertain whether the content conveys positive, negative, or neutral sentiments, offering a comprehensive perspective.

II.   *Emotion Detection:* Identify emotions depicted in multimedia data, such as facial expressions in images and videos or voice tones in audio. This analysis can reveal emotional nuances and help gauge the emotional impact of the content on viewers.

III.   *Entity Extraction and Recognition:* Extract entities, such as names of people, locations, organizations, and more, from multimedia data. This analysis enhances understanding by identifying key elements and entities present in the content.

IV.   *Topic Modeling:* Uncover the underlying topics or themes present in multimedia content. By combining textual and visual information, you can identify the main subject matters discussed or depicted in the content.

V.   *Text-Image Association:* Analyze how textual descriptions or captions relate to the associated images. This helps verify the accuracy of image descriptions and identify cases of mismatch or inconsistency.

VI.   *Visual Content Understanding:* Interpret and describe the content of images and videos using natural language. This involves generating captions or textual descriptions that accurately convey the visual information.

VII.   *Multimodal Content Summarization:* Generate concise summaries that capture the essence of multimedia content. By analyzing both textual and visual cues, you can create more informative and contextually rich summaries.

VIII. *Audio-Text Alignment:* Align transcribed audio content with corresponding textual information. This enables the extraction of insights from spoken content and facilitates search and retrieval based on audio context.

IX.   *Cross-Modal Retrieval:* Retrieve relevant content from one modality (e.g., images) based on queries from another modality (e.g., text). This analysis enables applications like finding images based on textual descriptions.

X.   *Content Recommendation:* Leverage insights from both textual and visual elements to make accurate recommendations. For instance, recommend videos or articles that match user preferences and interests.

6. FEATURE PERSPECTIVES IN NLP FOR MULTIMEDIA DATA PROCESSING.

Utilizing Natural Language Processing (NLP) for multimedia data processing holds the potential to uncover intricate insights within the realm of multimedia content. This integration of NLP with various forms of media such as images, videos, and audio opens avenues to delve deeper into the underlying context, sentiment, and semantics present in the data. By combining textual understanding with visual and auditory cues, NLP enables the extraction of nuanced details that might otherwise remain hidden. In the following subsections, we have briefly discussed future perspectives in NLP for multimedia data processing. These viewpoints are also presented in Figure 3.

6.1. Multimodal Fusion Advances

Advances in multimodal fusion techniques will lead to the development of models that effectively combine textual, visual, and audio information. Techniques like attention mechanisms and graph neural networks will be refined to capture intricate relationships between different modalities, enabling more comprehensive content analysis.

6.2. Interdisciplinary Collaborations

Collaborations among experts from linguistics, computer vision, audio processing, and various domains will lead to more holistic and accurate analyses. Combining insights from different disciplines will contribute to better understanding the complexities of multimedia data.

6.3. Deep Learning Evolution

Deep learning architectures will evolve to better accommodate the complexities of multimodal data. Architectures like Transformers will be extended to handle multiple modalities, enabling seamless integration of text, images, and audio.

6.4. Emotion and Intention Understanding

Understanding emotions and intentions from multimodal data will become more nuanced. Advanced algorithms will consider fine-grained cues, such as microexpressions in videos and subtle tonal shifts in audio, to infer emotions and intentions accurately. Models capable of understanding the contextual nuances of multimodal data will emerge. These models will capture how textual, visual, and audio elements interact within a specific context, leading to more accurate and contextually relevant analyses.

Figure 3. NLP domains for multimedia data

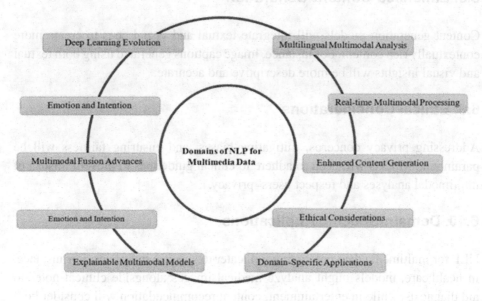

6.5. Explainable Multimodal Models

Explainability will be integrated into multimodal models to enhance transparency. Techniques like attention visualization and feature attribution will enable users to understand why certain decisions or analyses were made.

6.6. Multilingual Multimodal Analysis

Multilingual approaches will be developed to analyze content in multiple languages across different modalities. Models will need to account for language-specific semantics while interpreting textual and visual information.

6.7. Real-time Multimodal Processing

Real-time processing capabilities will enable instant analysis of multimedia data. Applications like live video captioning and sentiment analysis of social media streams will leverage the integration of text, images, and audio.

6.8. Enhanced Content Generation

Content generation models will integrate textual and visual cues to create more contextually rich content. For instance, image captions generated using both textual and visual insights will be more descriptive and accurate.

6.9. Ethical Considerations

Addressing privacy concerns, mitigating biases, and ensuring fairness will be paramount. Models will need to adhere to ethical guidelines to prevent misuse of multimodal analyses and respect users' privacy.

6.10. Domain-Specific Applications

NLP for multimedia data processing will cater to specific industries. For instance, in healthcare, models might analyze medical images alongside clinical notes to aid diagnosis, while in entertainment, content recommendation will consider both textual preferences and visual preferences.

7. CONCLUSION

This paper has shed light on the pivotal role of Natural Language Processing (NLP) and Deep Learning in the domain of multimedia data processing and cybersecurity. With the contemporary landscape characterized by an unprecedented surge in multimedia data and an ever-growing spectrum of cybersecurity threats, the insights presented in this paper hold significant implications. By unraveling the innovative facets of NLP and Deep Learning, this paper has highlighted their transformative impact on multimedia data management and cybersecurity. The exploration journey embarked upon in this paper encompassed deep learning techniques tailored for multimedia data analytics, traversing through the intricate realm of cybersecurity. As elucidated, the integration of NLP injects a layer of semantic understanding and contextual awareness into multimedia data processing, enabling a more nuanced comprehension of content. The comprehensive insights provided in this chapter underscore the potential of NLP to not only decipher textual and visual cues but also to contribute to a safer online ecosystem. Looking forward, the future perspectives presented in this paper signify the evolution of NLP for multimedia data processing. These emerging directions promise to further enhance the depth and accuracy of analyses, fostering interdisciplinary collaborations that harness the synergies of linguistics, computer vision, and audio processing. In summary, this paper has navigated through the complex interplay of NLP, Deep Learning, multimedia data, and cybersecurity. By offering a comprehensive overview of their transformative potential, the paper contributes to the discourse on how these technologies shape the digital landscape, ultimately paving the way for more sophisticated analyses, enhanced content understanding, and a more secure cyberspace.

REFERENCES

El-Latif, A. (2023). *Artificial Intelligence for Biometrics and Cybersecurity*. IET. https://shop.theiet.org/artificial-intelligence-for-biometrics-and-cybersecurity

Abd El-Latif, A. A., Ahmad Wani, M., & El-Affendi, M. A. (2023). *Advanced Applications of NLP and Deep Learning in Social Media Data*. IGI Global. [https://www.igi-global.com/book/advanced-applications-nlp-deep-learning/304800 doi:10.4018/978-1-6684-6909-5

Ahmad Wani, M., ELAffendi, M. A., Shakil, K. A., Shariq Imran, A., & Abd El-Latif, A. A. (2023, August). Depression Screening in Humans With AI and Deep Learning Techniques. *IEEE Transactions on Computational Social Systems*, *10*(4), 2074–2089. doi:10.1109/TCSS.2022.3200213

Ahmed, M., Masood, S., Ahmad, M., & Abd El-Latif, A. A. (2021). Intelligent driver drowsiness detection for traffic safety based on multi CNN deep model and facial subsampling. *IEEE Transactions on Intelligent Transportation Systems*, *23*(10), 19743–19752. doi:10.1109/TITS.2021.3134222

Balaji, T. K. (2021). Chandra Sekhara Rao Annavarapu, and Annushree Bablani. "Machine learning algorithms for social media analysis: A survey.". *Computer Science Review*, *40*, 100395. doi:10.1016/j.cosrev.2021.100395

Bouaafia, S., Khemiri, R., Messaoud, S., Ben Ahmed, O., & Sayadi, F. E. (2022). Deep learning-based video quality enhancement for the new versatile video coding. *Neural Computing & Applications*, *34*(17), 14135–14149. doi:10.100700521-021-06491-9 PMID:34511732

Cavallaro, A., Malekzadeh, M., & Shamsabadi, A. S. (2020). Deep learning for privacy in multimedia. In *Proceedings of the 28th ACM International Conference on Multimedia*, (pp. 4777-4778). ACM. 10.1145/3394171.3418551

Chen, L.-C., Lee, C.-M., & Chen, M.-Y. (2020). Exploration of social media for sentiment analysis using deep learning. *Soft Computing*, *24*(11), 8187–8197. doi:10.100700500-019-04402-8

Djenouri, Y., Belhadi, A., Srivastava, G., & Lin, J. C.-W. (2022). Deep learning-based hashtag recommendation system for multimedia data. *Information Sciences, 609*, 1506–1517. doi:10.1016/j.ins.2022.07.132

Ghantasala, G. P., Sudha, L. R., Priya, T. V., Deepan, P., & Vignesh, R. R. (2022). An Efficient Deep Learning Framework for Multimedia Big Data Analytics. In *Multimedia Computing Systems and Virtual Reality* (pp. 99–127). CRC Press. doi:10.1201/9781003196686-5

Gosal, A. S., Geijzendorffer, I. R., Václavík, T., Poulin, B., & Ziv, G. (2019). Using social media, machine learning and natural language processing to map multiple recreational beneficiaries. *Ecosystem Services, 38*, 100958. doi:10.1016/j.ecoser.2019.100958

Hiriyannaiah, S. (2020). Deep learning for multimedia data in IoT. Multimedia Big Data Computing for IoT Applications: Concepts. Paradigms and Solutions.

Iftikhar, S., Zhang, Z., Asim, M., Muthanna, A., Koucheryavy, A., & Abd El-Latif, A. A. (2022). Deep Learning-Based Pedestrian Detection in Autonomous Vehicles: Substantial Issues and Challenges. *Electronics (Basel), 11*(21), 3551. doi:10.3390/electronics11213551

Islam, M. M., Uddin, M. A., Islam, L., Akter, A., Sharmin, S., & Acharjee, U. K. (2020). Cyberbullying detection on social networks using machine learning approaches. In *2020 IEEE Asia-Pacific Conference on Computer Science and Data Engineering (CSDE),* (pp. 1-6). IEEE. 10.1109/CSDE50874.2020.9411601

Islam, M. R., Liu, S., Wang, X., & Xu, G. (2020). Deep learning for misinformation detection on online social networks: A survey and new perspectives. *Social Network Analysis and Mining, 10*(1), 1–20. doi:10.100713278-020-00696-x PMID:33014173

Jabeen, F., Ur Rehman, Z., Shah, S., Alharthy, R. D., Jalil, S., Ali Khan, I., Iqbal, J., & Abd El-Latif, A. A. (2023). Deep learning-based prediction of inhibitors interaction with Butyrylcholinesterase for the treatment of Alzheimer's disease. *Computers & Electrical Engineering, 105*, 108475. doi:10.1016/j.compeleceng.2022.108475

Li, G., & Liu, W. (2023). Multimedia data processing technology and application based on deep learning. *Advances in Multimedia, 2023*, 2023. doi:10.1155/2023/4184425

Li, S., Liu, Q., Dai, J., Wang, W., Gui, X., & Yi, Y. (2021). Adaptive-weighted multiview deep basis matrix factorization for multimedia data analysis. *Wireless Communications and Mobile Computing, 2021*, 1–12. doi:10.1155/2021/7264264

Mackey, T. K., Li, J., Purushothaman, V., Nali, M., Shah, N., Bardier, C., Cai, M., & Liang, B. (2020). Big data, natural language processing, and deep learning to detect and characterize illicit COVID-19 product sales: Infoveillance study on Twitter and Instagram. *JMIR Public Health and Surveillance*, 6(3), e20794. doi:10.2196/20794 PMID:32750006

Mahmoudi, S. A., Belarbi, M. A., Mahmoudi, S., Belalem, G., & Manneback, P. (2020). Multimedia processing using deep learning technologies, high-performance computing cloud resources, and Big Data volumes. *Concurrency and Computation*, 32(17), e5699. doi:10.1002/cpe.5699

Masud, U., Sadiq, M., Masood, S., Ahmad, M., El-Latif, A., & Ahmed, A. (2023). LW-DeepFakeNet: A lightweight time distributed CNN-LSTM network for real-time DeepFake video detection. *Signal, Image and Video Processing*, 17(8), 1–9. doi:10.100711760-023-02633-9

Rathee, G., Sharma, A., Saini, H., Kumar, R., & Iqbal, R. (2020). A hybrid framework for multimedia data processing in IoT-healthcare using blockchain technology. *Multimedia Tools and Applications*, 79(15-16), 9711–9733. doi:10.100711042-019-07835-3

Sedik, A., Abd El-Latif, A. A., Ahmad Wani, M., Abd El-Samie, F. E., Abdel-Salam Bauomy, N., & Hashad, F. G. (2023). Efficient Multi-Biometric Secure-Storage Scheme Based on Deep Learning and Crypto-Mapping Techniques. *Mathematics*, 11(3), 703. doi:10.3390/math11030703

Shakil, K. A., Tabassum, K., Alqahtani, F. S., & Wani, M. A. (2021). Analyzing user digital emotions from a holy versus non-pilgrimage city in Saudi Arabia on twitter platform. *Applied Sciences (Basel, Switzerland)*, 11(15), 6846. doi:10.3390/app11156846

Tobon, D. P., Hossain, M. S., Muhammad, G., Bilbao, J., & El Saddik, A. (2022). Deep learning in multimedia healthcare applications: A review. *Multimedia Systems*, 28(4), 1465–1479. doi:10.100700530-022-00948-0 PMID:35645465

Usman, M., Jan, M. A., He, X., & Chen, J. (2019). A survey on big multimedia data processing and management in smart cities. *ACM Computing Surveys*, 52(3), 1–29. doi:10.1145/3323334

Wani, M. A., ELAffendi, M. A., Shakil, K. A., Imran, A. S., & Abd El-Latif, A. A. (2022). Depression screening in humans with AI and deep learning techniques. *IEEE Transactions on Computational Social Systems*.

Wani, M. A., ELAffendi, M., Shakil, K. A., Abuhaimed, I. M., Nayyar, A., Hussain, A., & El-Latif, A. A. A. (2023). Toxic Fake News Detection and Classification for Combating COVID-19 Misinformation. *IEEE Transactions on Computational Social Systems*, 1. Advance online publication. doi:10.1109/TCSS.2023.3276764

Yang, C., Xu, X., Zhou, X., & Qi, L. (2022). Deep Q Network–Driven Task Offloading for Efficient Multimedia Data Analysis in Edge Computing–Assisted IoV. *ACM Transactions on Multimedia Computing Communications and Applications*, *18*(2s, no. 2s), 1–24. doi:10.1145/3548687

Zhang, W., Yao, T., Zhu, S., & El Saddik, A. (2019). Deep learning–based multimedia analytics: A review. *ACM Transactions on Multimedia Computing Communications and Applications*, *15*(no. 1s), 1–26.

Chapter 5
Enhancing Remote Sensing Image Change Detection and Security With Stacked U–Net

Muhammad Asim
Prince Sultan University, Saudi Arabia

Younas Aziz
Central South University, China

Muhammad Ejaz
Central South University, China

Adeel Ahmed Abbasi
iD https://orcid.org/0000-0001-7826-9278
Central South University, China

Anbar Hussain
Central South University, China

Aasim Danish
Central South University, China

ABSTRACT

Change detection (CD) and security plays a crucial role in remote sensing applications. The proposed change detection approach focuses on detecting the changes in synthetic aperture radar (SAR) images. The SAR images suffer from speckle noise which affects the classification accuracy. The proposed approach focuses on improving the model's accuracy by removing speckle noise with k-means clustering and an improved threshold approach based on curvelet transform and designing a stacked U-Net model. The stacked U-Net is designed with the help of a 2-dimensional convolutional neural network (2D-CNN). The proposed change detection strategy is evaluated via performing extensive experiments on three SAR datasets. The obtained results reveal that the proposed approach achieves better results than the several state-of-art works in terms of percentage of correct classification (PCC), overall error (OE), and kappa coefficient (KC).

DOI: 10.4018/978-1-6684-7216-3.ch005

1. INTRODUCTION

Change detection is a technique for identifying the dissimilarities in the images taken at different times. CD method is applied in various fields like remote sensing, disaster evaluation, medical diagnosis, etc. The change detection scheme's outcomes help provide information in policymaking, area planning, etc. (Kalaiselvi & Gomathi, 2020). The change detection on the earth's surface involves monitoring and comparing two images obtained at different times in the same area. In remote sensing, SAR images acquired for change detection are divided into microwave remote sensing and optical image sensing (Mu et al., 2019). SAR images in remote sensing have advantages over optical images since they can penetrate through clouds and work without light. The optical image resolution is affected by natural factors such as clouds, rain, fog, etc. However, the problem with SAR images is speckle noise (Mu et al., 2019), (Jiang et al., 2007). In conventional approaches, several methods are employed to remove speckle noise. Conventional methods to remove speckle noise with a filter process are spatial adaptive filtering, Lee filter, Pre-test filter, wiener filter, etc. (Ahmed et al., 2010; Chen et al., 2011; Fracastoro et al., 2020; Lee, 1980). These approaches have encountered a loss of resolution and speckle reduction (Fracastoro et al., 2020). The wavelet-based approaches improve the speckle rejection, but problems such as visible filtering artifacts like ringing occur (Fracastoro et al., 2020), (Bianchi et al., 2008). Signal artifacts are observed in methods that model image de-speckling as an optimization problem (Aubert & Aujol, 2008; Bioucas-Dias & Figueiredo, 2010; Shi & Osher, 2008).

Moreover, the conventional approaches to removing the speckle noise cannot be applicable in fields where the number of data is significant. Change detection with the neural network has been a primary area of research in recent years. The deep neural network (DNN) has been widely used in SAR image CD (Minematsu et al., 2017). A deep belief network (DBN) has been utilized to detect the changes in SAR images (Li et al., 2018). In (Keshk & Yin, 2019), an automatic CD method for flood mapping with SAR data with an Expectation maximization-based Gaussian mixture model (GMM) was proposed. Change detection of SAR images with deep learning focused on identifying the changes with the CNN approach (Touati et al., 2019). The neural network approaches have improved the basic models and detected the image changes for enhanced accuracy.

In this research, we proposed a Stacked U-Net where a 2D-CNN is used for SAR change detection. In this approach, SAR images are de-speckled with k means clustering and Curvelet Transform-based threshold method. The de-speckling and change detection are handled separately, so the deep learning method has to focus only on detecting the changes, significantly reducing the complexity. The two-dimensional CNN has been used to learn the features in depth. The contributions of the approach are as follows.

- First, the images are pre-processed with k- means clustering and an improved thresholding approach to remove the speckle noise.
- Second, the 2D CNN has been used in the encoder part of the Stacked U-Net to obtain better features.
- Finally, the experiments on the proposed approach are conducted with various datasets to reveal the proposed strategies' effectiveness on SAR change detection.

The paper is organized as follows. In Section 2, the related works are discussed. The proposed methodology is discussed in Section 3. In Section 4, the results and discussion of the experiments are provided. Finally, the Section ends with a conclusion.

2. RELATED WORK

Some of the recent works carried out in the CD estimation scheme are discussed in this section. Annabelle *et al.* (Keshk & Yin, 2019) presented a Very High-Resolution image change detection method for seismic changes after an earthquake. The approach compared the performance with two classification models: Bayesian Maximum A Posteriori (MAP) and Support Vector Machine (SVM). The approach compared the results of change detection with the ground survey reports. The simulation results obtained a better accuracy with SVM classifier than with the Bayesian classifier. The approach infers the problems while handling the manual survey. Touati *et al.* (Touati et al., 2019) proposed a CD technique with an Unsupervised Pixel Pairwise based Markov Random Field (MRF) model. The change detection problem with heterogeneous data is less addressed. The proposed Markovian-based multimodal change detection method decreases the computation load with a sub-sample of pixels. The maximum posterior solution is computed with the stochastic optimization process. Li *et al.* (Li et al., 2019) presented a deep learning (DL) based CD method in SAR images. The difference image (DI) influence on classification results is eliminated in the proposed approach without handling pre-processing operations. The false labels are produced with the help of an unsupervised spatial fuzzy clustering approach. The detection results are obtained with the help of a convolutional network. Usha *et al.* (Gandhimathi Alias Usha & Vasuki, 2017) presented a CD technique with multispectral satellite images using a graph cut-based clustering method and multiclass SVM. The inconsistency in the clustering algorithm is solved with the spatial-spectral method in segmenting the images. The CD approach is based on the graph-cut-based clustering approach. The change detection problem is solved with the proposed new multiclass SVM approach. Mou *et al.* (Mou et al., 2019) presented a change detection with recurrent CNN. The approach utilized the CNN and recurrent neural network (RNN) to generate rich spectral-spatial feature representation and analyze the temporal dependence in bi-temporal images. Lv *et al.* (Lv et al., 2016) proposed a CD strategy with a hybrid conditional random field model.

The research work performed CD for high spatial resolution remote sensing images. The research focused on obtaining the change detection in HSR images with limited spectral information. The changed and unchanged pixels are separated with a soft clustering method. Geng *et al.* (Geng et al., 2019) presented a saliency-guided deep neural network for SAR image CD. The SAR images containing speckle noise may lead to false changed points, affecting the CD performance. The speckle Noise problem is solved using the salient region extracted from the different images. The proposed DNN model extracts the discriminative feature from two SAR images and a difference image (DI). Lv *et al.* (Lv et al., 2018) proposed a deep learning and super pixel feature extraction for CD in SAR images with a Contractive Autoencoder. The proposed research has focussed on reducing the performance degradation due to speckle noise. The proposed strategy extracts the feature with a stacked contractive autoencoder. Saha *et al.* (Saha et al., 2020) presented a VHR SAR image-based CD with cycle consistent generative adversarial network (CycleGAN). The absence of labeled SAR data is a challenge in CD. The proposed approach focusses on solving this challenge using Cycle GAN. The changes in the building are found with deep change vector analysis and fuzzy rules. Zhan *et al.* (Zhan et al., 2020) proposed a CD strategy for VHR images. A CNN is used to extract the information from the images. A change map is generated with the aid of deep spatial features and image spectral features. With SVM, the samples are trained to detect the changes. Luppino *et al.* (Luppino et al., 2020) proposed a code-aligned autoencoder for the unsupervised CD method. The approach focussed on extracting the relational pixel information instead of supervised information of the changing area. However, the approach performs poorly with limited features. The code layers of two autoencoders are combined such that the output of one of the encoders can be fed to both decoders in order to reconstruct the data and transform them into another domain. Chen *et al.* (Chen et al., 2020) proposed a CD method with a hybrid DL-based method. The proposed method employed deep Siamese Convolutional multiple layers recurrent neural network (SiamCRNN), which can extract the features from homogeneous and heterogeneous VHR images. The change information is obtained with the LSTM unit. The fully connected layer predicts the change probability. Liu *et al.* (Liu et al., 2019) proposed a stacked fisher autoencoder (SFAE) for SAR image CD. The SFAE consists of two stages. Where the first helps to suit multiplicative noise, and then in the second, the features extracted are discriminant due to the Fisher discriminant criterion.

3. METHODOLOGY

A system model of the proposed CD model is provided in this section. The proposed CD approach consists of a series of steps before generating a final change map. Fig 1 shows the framework of proposed change detection model.

3.1 Data Set

The SAR dataset publicly available is obtained from the city of Bern and Switzerland in the year April and May 1999 respectively (Gong et al., 2014). The Ottawa dataset (Gong et al., 2014) is captured over the city of Ottawa. The images were captured in the period of May and August 1997. The Mexico dataset (Gao et al., 2017) captured in April 2000 and May 2002 consists of images with 512x512 pixels. The SZADA consists of images captured by FOMI in the year 2000 and 2005. The image is taken in an area of 9.5km per square at a pixel of 1.5m/pixel resolution. The size of the images is 952*640 pixels (Zhang et al., 2018). The test set TISZADOB consists of five pairs of images taken from the years 2000 and 2007 with the same size and resolution as that of SZADA over an area of 6.8-kilometer square (Zhang et al., 2018). The dataset archive (Zhang et al., 2018) consists of two images taken in the year 1984 by FOMI and in 2007 by Google Earth photo. Though there are a lot of changes due to the long year gap the image taken in 1984 has poor resolution. The changes considered are building regions, planting of trees or forests, and fresh cultivable lands before the presence of buildings. The yellow river dataset (Gong et al., 2014) obtained in June 2008 and 2009 consists of SAR images with the size of 7666*7692. The dataset is divided into smaller areas and is used as 2 datasets.

Initially, the pre-processing is carried out where the image is first converted to matrix value. The process involves merging two image samples into one by extracting pixel values. It is carried out with the help of reference information, which we obtain from the ground truth image. The speckle noise in the SAR image affects the accuracy of the change detection process. Therefore, removing the speckle noise in the images is necessary. The speckle noise is removed with k means clustering and an improved threshold method. The advantage of using the K means clustering process is that the data dimensionality can be reduced, and features can be easily found. The huge range of variables demands an increase in memory and computation power. Finally, the denoised images are normalized before feeding the data into the deep neural network.

Figure 1. Proposed change detection model

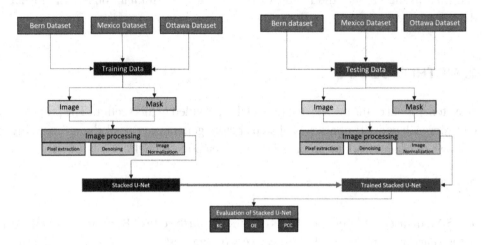

3.2 Stacked U-Net Based change detection of SAR images

The proposed change detection method utilizes U-Net which was developed by Olaf Ranneberger *et al* (Ronneberger et al., 2015). The U shape of the architecture gives the name U-Net. The basic U-Net consists of an encoder, bridge, and decoder. The encoder part handles the down sampling with the CNN. The encoder consists of CNN and max pooling with stride=2. The proposed U-Net model is designed with 2 dimensional convolutional and max pool layers. The encoder in the CNN network is constructed with 2 two-dimensional 3*3 convolution layers which are followed by ReLU and two dimensional 2*2 max pooling with stride 2. The down-sampling part focuses to learn the features of the images. The up-sampling portion consists of 2*2 convolutions which reduces the feature map into half and two 3*3 convolutions followed by ReLU. The final layer employs 1*1 convolutions to map the feature vector to the number of classes. The details of 2D CNN are discussed in this section. The 2D CNN which has filters is used in the decoder part for feature extraction. The 2D convolution and 2D max pooling operation of 2D CNN helps to extract the features which are more meaningful.

The neurons in convolution and pooling layers are constructed as a matrix that can perform convolution and pooling operations. The convolution operations performed by these matrices or filters can extract a feature from each part of the feature map. The spatial structure relationship can be preserved through this process. The input of the convolution layers which have 64 filters is first fed to the max pooling layer and then to the second convolutional layer where we have used about 96 filters to obtain the higher-level representation. Convolution filters are applied to a window to feature units and pixels to obtain the dependencies between the k_1 pixels and feature units. The feature obtained by the vector window is given as $M^{n,k}$. The N convolution filters learn the features and each of them generates a feature map given as

$$M^k = [M^{1,k}, M^{2,k}, ... M^{N,k}]$$

The dimension of the feature map is reduced by the 2D max pooling operation. Max (.) 2D max pooling function is applied to the convoluted features obtained from 2D convolution layers. The pooling operation when applied on a window to obtain a maximum value is given as

$$P^{n,k} = \max(M^{n,k})$$

The feature map obtained from 2d max pooling is passed through the SoftMax layer to predict the relation between the labels and the classes. After clustering and removal of speckle noise with the help of filters the training data is created by converting the processed data into vectors. The data can again be turned into images with the same mapping procedure. The structural integrity of the image can be preserved with the help of this process.

d) Evaluation Metrics

The performance is evaluated in terms of the percentage of correct classification (PCC), Overall Error (OE), and kappa Coefficient (KC).

3.3 Overall Error (OE)

The OE is defined as the sum of the false positive with the false negative which is given as

$$OE = FP + FN$$

FP and FN are the false positive and false negative.

3.4 Percentage of Correct Classification (PCC)

The PCC is computed as follows.

$$PCC = \frac{NT - OE}{NT} \times 100\%$$

Where *NT* is the pixel representation in the ground truth.

3.5 Kappa Coefficient (KC)

The KP is computed as follows.

$$KC = \frac{PCC - PRE}{1 - PRE}$$

The KC gives the percentage of the expected chance.

4. EXPERIMENTAL RESULTS

4.1 Implementation Details

The stacked U-Net implementation is carried out in MATLAB 2019a on a 64-bit Intel (R) I5 2.30 GHz GPU with 16GB RAM. The dataset was divided was divided into training (80%) and testing (20%). The training was carried out for 500 epochs with a learning rate of 0.0002. SoftMax loss function is utilized during training of stacked U-Net.

4.2 Quantitative and Qualitative Performance

The Detection performance by the four different techniques is quantitatively evaluated in terms of PCC and KC values, averaged over all test images. The KP, FN, OE, PCC, and KC values for datasets Bern, Mexico, and Ottawa are shown in Table 1. In subsequent paragraphs provide an analysis of detection results for all the datasets.

The U-Net network was trained and tested with three different datasets. To determine the efficacy of the proposed process, we use false positives (FPs), false negatives (FNs), overall error (OE), and Kappa coefficient (KC) as indicators. The KP, FN, OE, PCC, and KC values for datasets Bern, Mexico, and Ottawa are presented in Table 1. The KP, FN, OE, PCC, and KC values in Table 1 indicate that the extraction patches have enhanced the detection results mainly because it has increased the amount of training data hence, enriching the networks with more data.

The KC, FN, OE, and PCC are analyzed and it is found that PCC attained better value when $r=8$ and 14. The final change from different changes is observed based on the changed region mapping and finding the missed pixels with reference to the ground truth. The PCA method generalizes the vector pixel and forms a statistical analysis for finding the changed parameters. In K-means the clustering techniques are used for sorting the group of mapping regions and based on the changes in pixels it observes the important pixels. The CNN method is the basic neural method that forms a neural network and depending on the weight and bias calculation the change detection is considered but this does not provide much accurate result so the U-Net model is classified with the U shape of the pooling and the ReLU this results in the segmentation of the proposed method. The custom U-Net proposed model redraws the balance between the FP and the FN at the best result at the PCC and KC values. With the introduction of residual learning from the neural network, the model is improved by 20% over the CNN and 40% from the K means, respectively. As the results are drawn the conclusion with the proposed changed detection in the dataset is analyzed.

Table 1. Analysis of the results with various datasets

Method	The Result of the Bern Dataset			
	KC	FN	OE	PCC
Stacked U-Net	0.98	.87	1.004	98.9
Method	**The result of the Mexico City**			
	KC	**FN**	**OE**	**PCC**
Stacked U-Net	0.85	.79	1.004	99.3
Method	**The result of the Ottawa**			
	KC	**FN**	**OE**	**PCC**
Stacked U-Net	0.66	.61	1.66	99.7

Figure 2. Visualized results of berlin dataset for changed detection method

Figure 3. Visualized results of Mexico dataset for the changed detection method

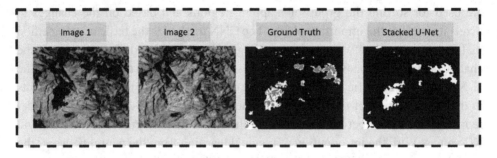

Figure 4. Visualized results of Ottawa dataset for the change detection method.

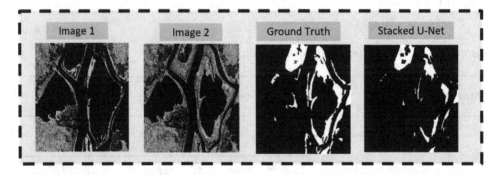

Table 2. Comparison of proposed network with literature work

Work	Dataset	Network	Evaluation		
			KC	OE	PCC
(Geng et al., 2019)	SAR Dataset	SGDNNs	32.1	6.0	98.73
(Touati et al., 2019)	SAR images	MRF Model	-	-	64.2
(Li et al., 2019)	SAR images	CD with DL	49.0	1.33	98.67
(Gandhimathi Alias Usha & Vasuki, 2017)	SAR dataset	CD with SVM	-	-	92.79
(Mou et al., 2019)	SAR dataset	RNN and LSTM	-	-	92.56
Our Work	**Bern Dataset**	**Stacked U-Net**	98.0	1.004	98.9
Our Work	**Mexico Dataset**	**Stacked U-Net**	85.0	1.004	99.3
Our Work	**Ottawa dataset**	**Stacked U-Net**	66.6	1.664	99.7

Table 3 displays the quantitative test results for all three data sets, showing that the proposed method's PCC and KC values are clearly superior to the other methods. The proposed method can use effective feature representations from multitemporal SAR images, and its KC value is higher than the state of art work. Furthermore, in terms of PCC and KC, the proposed approach outperforms machine learning approaches, demonstrating that the proposed Stacked U-Net is a strong tool for SAR image change detection. As a result, we can conclude that on all three data sets, the proposed approach outperforms the other methods. The proposed method's effectiveness is shown by visual and quantitative comparisons of both data sets.

5. CONCLUSION

The proposed change detection strategy of SAR images with an improved Stacked U-Net focused on removing the speckle noise and improving the change detection accuracy. The speckle noise has been reduced with the k means clustering and thresholding approach in the preprocessing stage. The preprocessing handled in this research has avoided the burden on neural networks in removing the speckle noise. The Stacked U-Net is improved by adding two dimensional CNN that learns the image's in-depth features, resulting in enhanced accuracy in detecting changes.

The experimental results have proved that the proposed approach has reduced the effect of speckle noise, and the accuracy of the model has been improved than the conventional approaches.

Conﬂicts of Interest: The authors declare no conﬂict of interest.

REFERENCES

Ahmed, S. M., Eldin, F. A. E., & Tarek, A. M. (2010). *Speckle noise reduction in SAR images using adaptive morphological filter*. 2010 10th International Conference on Intelligent Systems Design and Applications, Cairo. 10.1109/ISDA.2010.5687254

Aubert, G., & Aujol, J.-F. (2008). A Variational Approach to Removing Multiplicative Noise. *SIAM Journal on Applied Mathematics*, 68(4), 925–946. doi:10.1137/060671814

Bianchi, T., Argenti, F., & Alparone, L. (2008). Segmentation-Based MAP Despeckling of SAR Images in the Undecimated Wavelet Domain. *IEEE Transactions on Geoscience and Remote Sensing*, 46(9), 2728–2742. doi:10.1109/TGRS.2008.920018

Bioucas-Dias, J. M., & Figueiredo, M. A. T. (2010). Multiplicative Noise Removal Using Variable Splitting and Constrained Optimization. *IEEE Transactions on Image Processing, 19*(7), 1720–1730. doi:10.1109/TIP.2010.2045029 PMID:20215071

Chen, H., Wu, C., Du, B., Zhang, L., & Wang, L. (2020, April). Change Detection in Multisource VHR Images via Deep Siamese Convolutional Multiple-Layers Recurrent Neural Network. *IEEE Transactions on Geoscience and Remote Sensing, 58*(4), 2848–2864. doi:10.1109/TGRS.2019.2956756

Chen, J., Chen, Y., An, W., Cui, Y., & Yang, J. (2011). Nonlocal Filtering for Polarimetric SAR Data: A Pretest Approach. *IEEE Transactions on Geoscience and Remote Sensing, 49*(5), 1744–1754. doi:10.1109/TGRS.2010.2087763

Fracastoro, G., Magli, E., Poggi, G., Scarpa, G., Valsesia, D., & Verdoliva, L. (2020). Deep learning methods for SAR image despeckling: trends and perspectives. arXiv preprint arXiv:2012.05508.

Gandhimathi Alias Usha, S., & Vasuki, S. (2017). Improved segmentation and change detection of multi-spectral satellite imagery using graph cut based clustering and multiclass SVM. *Multimedia Tools and Applications, 77*(12), 15353–15383. doi:10.100711042-017-5120-0

Gao, F., Liu, X., Dong, J., Zhong, G., & Jian, M. (2017). Change Detection in SAR Images Based on Deep Semi-NMF and SVD Networks. *Remote Sensing (Basel), 9*(5), 435. doi:10.3390/rs9050435

Geng, J., Ma, X., Zhou, X., & Wang, H. (2019, October). Saliency-Guided Deep Neural Networks for SAR Image Change Detection. *IEEE Transactions on Geoscience and Remote Sensing, 57*(10), 7365–7377. doi:10.1109/TGRS.2019.2913095

Gong, M., Su, L., Jia, M., & Chen, W. (2014). Fuzzy Clustering With a Modified MRF Energy Function for Change Detection in Synthetic Aperture Radar Images. *IEEE Transactions on Fuzzy Systems, 22*(1), 98–109. doi:10.1109/TFUZZ.2013.2249072

Jiang, L., Liao, M., Zhang, L., & Lin, H. (2007). Unsupervised change detection in multitemporal SAR images using MRF models. *Geo-Spatial Information Science, 10*(2), 111–116. doi:10.100711806-007-0051-y

Kalaiselvi, S., & Gomathi, V. (2020). α-cut induced Fuzzy Deep Neural Network for change detection of SAR images. *Applied Soft Computing, 95*, 106510. doi:10.1016/j.asoc.2020.106510

Keshk, H. M., & Yin, X.-C. (2019). Change Detection in SAR Images Based on Deep Learning. *International Journal of Aeronautical and Space Sciences*, *21*(2), 549–559. doi:10.100742405-019-00222-0

Lee, J. S. (1980). Digital image enhancement and noise filtering by use of local statistics. *IEEE Transactions on Pattern Analysis and Machine Intelligence*, *PAMI-2*(2), 165–168. doi:10.1109/TPAMI.1980.4766994 PMID:21868887

Li, Y., Martinis, S., Plank, S., & Ludwig, R. (2018). An automatic change detection approach for rapid flood mapping in Sentinel-1 SAR data. *International Journal of Applied Earth Observation and Geoinformation*, *73*, 123–135. doi:10.1016/j. jag.2018.05.023

Li, Y., Peng, C., Chen, Y., Jiao, L., Zhou, L., & Shang, R. (2019). A Deep Learning Method for Change Detection in Synthetic Aperture Radar Images. *IEEE Transactions on Geoscience and Remote Sensing*, *57*(8), 5751–5763. doi:10.1109/ TGRS.2019.2901945

Liu, G., Li, L., Jiao, L., Dong, Y., & Li, X. (2019). Stacked Fisher autoencoder for SAR change detection. *Pattern Recognition*, *96*, 106971. doi:10.1016/j. patcog.2019.106971

Luppino, L. T., Hansen, M. A., Kampffmeyer, M., Bianchi, F. M., Moser, G., Jenssen, R., & Anfinsen, S. N. (2020). Code-Aligned Autoencoders for Unsupervised Change Detection in Multimodal Remote Sensing Images. arXiv preprint arXiv:2004.07011.

Lv, N., Chen, C., Qiu, T., & Sangaiah, A. K. (2018, December). Deep Learning and Superpixel Feature Extraction Based on Contractive Autoencoder for Change Detection in SAR Images. *IEEE Transactions on Industrial Informatics*, *14*(12), 5530–5538. doi:10.1109/TII.2018.2873492

Lv, P., Zhong, Y., Zhao, J., & Zhang, L. (2016). Unsupervised change detection model based on hybrid conditional random field for high spatial resolution remote sensing imagery. *2016 IEEE International Geoscience and Remote Sensing Symposium (IGARSS)*. IEEE. 10.1109/IGARSS.2016.7729478

Minematsu, T., Shimada, A., & Taniguchi, R. I. (2017, August). Analytics of deep neural network in change detection. In *2017 14th IEEE International Conference on Advanced Video and Signal Based Surveillance (AVSS)* (pp. 1-6). IEEE. 10.1109/ AVSS.2017.8078550

Mou, L., Bruzzone, L., & Zhu, X. X. (2019). Learning Spectral-Spatial-Temporal Features via a Recurrent Convolutional Neural Network for Change Detection in Multispectral Imagery. *IEEE Transactions on Geoscience and Remote Sensing*, *57*(2), 924–935. doi:10.1109/TGRS.2018.2863224

Mu, C.-H., Li, C.-Z., Liu, Y., Qu, R., & Jiao, L.-C. (2019). Accelerated genetic algorithm based on search-space decomposition for change detection in remote sensing images. *Applied Soft Computing, 84*, 105727. doi:10.1016/j.asoc.2019.105727

Ronneberger, O., Fischer, P., & Brox, T. (2015, October). U-net: Convolutional networks for biomedical image segmentation. In *International Conference on Medical image computing and computer-assisted intervention* (pp. 234-241). Springer. 10.1007/978-3-319-24574-4_28

Saha, S., Bovolo, F., & Bruzzone, L. (2020). Building Change Detection in VHR SAR Images via Unsupervised Deep Transcoding. *IEEE Transactions on Geoscience and Remote Sensing*, 1–13. doi:10.1109/TGRS.2020.3000296

Shi, J., & Osher, S. (2008). A Nonlinear Inverse Scale Space Method for a Convex Multiplicative Noise Model. *SIAM Journal on Imaging Sciences*, *1*(3), 294–321. doi:10.1137/070689954

Swamy, P. S., & Vani, K. (2016). A novel thresholding technique in the curvelet domain for improved speckle removal in SAR images. *Optik (Stuttgart)*, *127*(2), 634–637. doi:10.1016/j.ijleo.2015.10.057

Touati, R., Mignotte, M., & Dahmane, M. (2019). Multimodal Change Detection in Remote Sensing Images Using an Unsupervised Pixel Pairwise Based Markov Random Field Model. *IEEE Transactions on Image Processing*, 1–1. doi:10.1109/TIP.2019.2933747 PMID:31425034

Zhan, T., Gong, M., Jiang, X., & Zhang, M. (2020). Unsupervised Scale-Driven Change Detection With Deep Spatial–Spectral Features for VHR Images. *IEEE Transactions on Geoscience and Remote Sensing*, *58*(8), 5653–5665. doi:10.1109/TGRS.2020.2968098

Zhang, M., Xu, G., Chen, K., Yan, M., & Sun, X. (2018). Triplet-based semantic relation learning for aerial remote sensing image change detection. *IEEE Geoscience and Remote Sensing Letters*, *16*(2), 266–270. doi:10.1109/LGRS.2018.2869608

Chapter 6
Securing Fog Computing Through Consortium Blockchain Integration:
The Proof of Enhanced Concept (PoEC) Approach

Mohammed Amin Almaiah
Department of Computer Science, Aqaba University of Technology, Aqaba, Jordan

Tayseer Alkdour
Department of Computer Networks, College of Computer Sciences and Information Technology, King Faisal University, Al Hofuf, Saudi Arabia

ABSTRACT

The authors have developed an innovative topology by amalgamating consortium blockchain, often referred to as supervisory blockchain, with fog computing. The proposed system is organized into three distinct layers: the application layer, the fog layer, and the blockchain security layer. To accommodate this model effectively, the authors introduce the novel proof of enhanced concept (PoEC) consensus mechanism. This approach employs homomorphic encryption to secure transactions, which are then outsourced to the fog layer or fog devices. This strategy mitigates various security threats, including collusion attacks, phishing attacks, and replay attacks, bolstering the resilience of each layer against such incursions. To bolster security measures further, our model adopts a hybrid-deep learning protocol for safeguarding electronic medical records against potential breaches while concurrently reducing latency through a decentralized fog computing system.

DOI: 10.4018/978-1-6684-7216-3.ch006

INTRODUCTION

In the realm of IoT (internet of things) and IoMT (internet of medical things), where data traffic is increasingly centralized within cloud-based systems, significant concerns have emerged (Al Hwaitat et al., 2023). These concerns encompass patient safety and confidentiality, as issues like data ownership, data collection, and location privacy are put at risk. One alarming vulnerability is the potential for hackers to target 5G-enabled IoMT networks by copying data and altering the identification of healthcare equipment. Currently, IoMT-Cloud systems face challenges related to single points of failure, malicious attacks, and privacy breaches (Mushtaq et al., 2016). To ensure the security of networks and the safe transmission of Personal Health Data (PHD), it is imperative that data exchanges between IoMT and the Cloud incorporate robust mechanisms for trust, device identification, and user authentication (UA) (Azaria et al., 2016). The safeguarding of individuals' private data has long been a focal point within the field of computer science. However, the rise of deep learning (DL) algorithms has, in some instances, led to their application without adequate consideration for data privacy. While these algorithms have delivered improved learning accuracy, privacy concerns have often been deferred. It was only with the deployment of remote DL models over the internet that a heightened interest in data privacy emerged. In response, various cloud platforms were developed, utilizing DL models for both training and inference phases. Subsequently, this service became known as Deep Learning as a Service (DLaaS) (Hasnain et al., 2020). Hence, the transmission and storage of private data over the internet pose significant risks, as servers holding this data are susceptible to vulnerabilities that could result in leakage. Such leaks may occur intentionally or unintentionally (Ali, Rahim, Pasha et al, 2021). Intentional breaches can happen through hacking, piracy, or social engineering tactics, whereas unintentional leaks may be attributed to users themselves or the employees of service providers. Remarkably, a substantial portion of data leakage incidents, totaling 43%, is attributed to employee actions, as reported by Intel Security (Ali & Mehboob, ; Ali et al., 2017; Hameed et al., 2016). Figure 1 illustrates the application of Fog and Cloud Computing, which aids planners in the establishment and delivery of services, thereby enhancing resource allocation and reducing service latency.

2. RESEARCH MOTIVATION

Nowadays, the existing research on data security and privacy preservation for IoT and healthcare system relies on central device which are more vulnerable to security threats and breaches. Moreover, the most popular security threats associated with

Figure 1. Application of fog and cloud environment

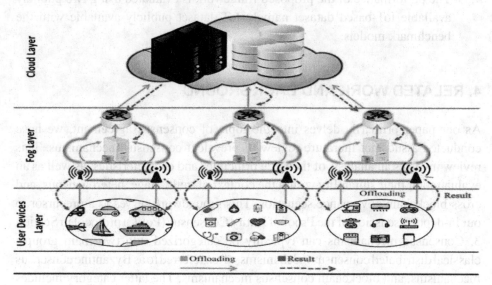

such model consist of DDoS, replay attack, Phishing attack and collusion attack (Liu et al., 2018). Similarly ensuring a secure transaction from one node to another node is of great importance (Kim et al., 2019). In order to tackle such issue and research problem we have designed a novel hybrid-deep learning based IoMT fog computing system which pre-train the model in the cloud and then transfer the global model to the local edge as well as fog computing devices. The proposed research design provides security, privacy, low latency and reduce computational as well as storage overhead.

3. RESEARCH CONTRIBUTION

This paper addresses the aforementioned challenges by introducing a novel blockchain-based deep-learning framework aimed at enhancing security and privacy within the context of supervisory blockchain-based fog computing. The primary contributions of this study encompass:

1. The development of a novel privacy preservation and intrusion detection framework, constructed upon a consortium blockchain framework.
2. The design of novel (PoEC) provides resistant to phishing and collusion attack.
3. In second level, an intrusion detection model was introduced to validate the proposed model against security attacks.

4.   The performance of the proposed framework is evaluated using two publicly available IoT-based dataset namely IoT-dataset publicly available with the benchmark models.

4. RELATED WORK AND BACKGROUND

As our paper primarily delves into the topic of consensus agreement, we have conducted a succinct literature review of prevalent consensus mechanisms. This review involves an analysis of their key principles and characteristics, as well as an evaluation of their suitability within the context of multi-stage, heterogeneous, and cross-blockchain governance scenarios. This groundwork serves as a precursor to our in-depth discussion of the Proof of Entity Consensus (PoEC) protocol in Section 3. Consensus mechanisms can typically be categorized into two main groups: classical distributed consensus mechanisms, often referred to as Byzantine consensus mechanisms, and blockchain consensus mechanisms. The latter category includes Proof of X (PoX) consensus mechanisms, permissioned consensus mechanisms, and hybrid consensus mechanisms.

4.1 Classic Distributed Consensus Mechanisms

The classical distributed consensus mechanism is employed in conventional distributed networks, facilitating distributed consensus through state machine replication among network nodes. This concept traces back to the Byzantine General problem, introduced by (Kim et al., 2019), which addressed the challenge of achieving consensus on specific data when potential node failures or malicious attacks were a concern. This laid the foundation for consensus mechanism research. (Jiang et al., 2019) Subsequently presented the Paxos algorithm, offering a solution to the Byzantine generals' problem. The Paxos algorithm is capable of tolerating the failure of a certain number of network nodes, allowing agreement on a specific value within a distributed system. Building upon this, (Chen et al., 2018) proposed Practical Byzantine Fault Tolerance (PBFT), which achieved final consensus among honest nodes when the number of adversarial nodes did not exceed one-third of the total node count.

Moreover, (Chakraborty et al., 2019) introduced the Mixed Byzantine Fault Tolerance (MBFT) algorithm. Functionally, MBFT partitions participating nodes in the consensus process, enhancing scalability and efficiency without compromising security. MBFT also incorporates a random node selection mechanism and a credit system to bolster security and fault tolerance. Expanding upon this, (Yazdinejad et al., 2020) proposed a dynamic reputation-based Practical Byzantine Fault Tolerance algorithm. This dynamic reputation-based approach employs a consensus election method rooted in credit. Monitoring nodes classify remaining nodes into two categories based on reputation scores: consensus nodes and auxiliary nodes. These nodes participate in distinct stages of the block generation process, with consensus nodes receiving dynamic updates based on their reputation scores.

4.2. PoX Consensus Mechanism

The Proof of X (PoX) consensus mechanism is primarily oriented towards public blockchain networks. Its fundamental concept involves assessing the probability and expectation of nodes acquiring the right to validate transactions based on their ownership of specific key resources. This approach aims to enhance the security of public blockchain networks. This concept originates from the design of the Bitcoin system, as realized by (Jiang et al., 2018), which is founded on the traditional Proof of Work (PoW) consensus mechanism, with blockchain technology introduced as its underlying framework. (Jiang et al., 2020) introduced Proof of Stake (PoS) and introduced the notion of 'currency age.' In PoS, nodes with a greater quantity of coins and a longer duration of coin ownership are more likely to be selected as validators. Additionally, (Dorri et al., 2017) proposed Permacoin, founded on Proof of Capacity (PoC). In PoC, participants are required to possess the capability to store a segment of a large file. (Lazaroiu & Roscia, 2017) Presented an innovative lightweight consensus algorithm known as Proof of Block Trade (PoBT), tailored for blockchain networks within the Internet of Things (IoT) framework. PoBT offers the ability to verify transactions and blocks with reduced computational time. Furthermore, (Lacity, 2018) introduced a novel consensus mechanism named Proof of Negotiation (PoN). PoN introduced a trust-based mechanism to facilitate the random selection of honest miners and conducted a round of block creation through a negotiation-based approach.

4.3. Authorization Consensus Mechanism

An authorization consensus mechanism is a type of consensus mechanism used in blockchain and distributed ledger technologies (Sengupta et al., 2020). Unlike some other consensus mechanisms, which primarily focus on validating and agreeing upon the order of transactions or blocks, authorization consensus mechanisms emphasize authentication and access control (Honar Pajooh et al., 2021). These mechanisms are designed to ensure that only authorized participants can perform specific actions within a blockchain network. There are three key aspects and characteristics of authorization consensus mechanisms including: (1) Authentication and Authorization: Authorization consensus mechanisms are primarily concerned with verifying the identity and permissions of participants within a blockchain network. Participants must authenticate themselves to prove their identity, and their actions within the network are authorized based on predefined rules and permissions. (2) Access Control: Access control plays a central role in authorization consensus mechanisms. It involves defining who can read data, submit transactions, validate blocks, and perform other actions within the blockchain network. Access control lists (ACLs) or smart contracts are often used to enforce these rules. (3) Role-Based Permissions: Many authorization consensus mechanisms employ role-based access control. In this approach, participants are assigned specific roles, and each role has a set of associated permissions. For example, there may be roles for network administrators, validators, and regular users, each with different levels of access.

The fundamental concept behind authorization consensus mechanisms is to execute block generation and maintenance via distributed consistency algorithms after authenticating participating nodes. For instance, (Sengupta et al., 2020) introduced the foundational framework for Hyperledger Fabric, which is part of the Hyperledger project initiated by the Linux Foundation. Hyperledger aims to deliver an enterprise-grade open-source distributed ledger framework and associated source code. Within this ecosystem, Hyperledger Fabric serves as a community-driven project that offers essential infrastructure for blockchain applications. Another notable example is the DFINITY consensus mechanism proposed by (Honar Pajooh et al., 2021). The DFINITY protocol operates in distinct periods, organizing participating nodes into various groups. In each period, a random committee assumes responsibility for processing transactions and overseeing the consensus process. At the conclusion of each period, a random number function is employed to select the committee for the subsequent period. Additionally, (Peng et al., 2020) introduced the PaLa consensus mechanism, which facilitates rapid consensus within authorized networks. PaLa utilizes parallel pipelines to enhance the efficiency of block processing. It also incorporates a sub-committee sliding window reconfiguration method to ensure sustained transaction processing during reconfiguration.

4.4. Hybrid Consensus Mechanism

A hybrid consensus mechanism is a type of consensus mechanism used in blockchain technology. It combines elements from different traditional consensus mechanisms to achieve a balance between security, scalability, and efficiency (Esposito et al., 2018). Hybrid consensus mechanisms are designed to address some of the limitations and challenges associated with single-consensus algorithms (Patel, 2019). Hybrid consensus mechanisms typically combine two or more traditional consensus algorithms. These could include Proof of Work (PoW), Proof of Stake (PoS), Practical Byzantine Fault Tolerance (PBFT), Delegated Proof of Stake (DPoS), and more.

The core concept of hybrid consensus mechanisms involves the selection of specific nodes as the consensus committee via a PoX consensus mechanism, followed by the execution of a Byzantine consensus mechanism within this committee to facilitate block generation. One of the early instances of combining the classical distributed consistency algorithm, PBFT, with blockchain technology was introduced by (Esposito et al., 2018) through the PeerCensus consensus algorithm. This algorithm leverages Bitcoin as the underlying chain to authenticate a designated set of nodes. Subsequently, these authenticated nodes employ the Chain Agreement (CA) algorithm to finalize block generation. (Patel, 2019) Introduced the Hybrid Consensus mechanism, which achieves state machine replication in an unauthorized environment through workload proof. This approach marks the first instance of applying a formal security model and modular design to model hybrid consensus mechanisms while demonstrating their capability to meet safety requirements such as consistency and liveness. Another notable hybrid consensus mechanism is ELASTICO, proposed by (Kim et al., 2021). ELASTICO employs a fragmentation consensus approach, dividing participating nodes into multiple groups. Each group generates a block, and these individual blocks are combined to form the overall block. The Rapid Chain consensus mechanism, presented by (Hang & Kim, 2019), focuses on sharding for computation, communication, and storage. Its core modules encompass startup, consensus, and reconfiguration. (Figorilli et al., 2018) Introduced Proof of QoS (PoQ), which relies on Quality of Service (QoS). In this validation protocol, the network is divided into small regions, with each region designating a node based on its QoS. Subsequently, deterministic Byzantine fault-tolerant consensus is executed among the specified nodes. While the aforementioned consensus mechanisms demonstrate excellent performance in terms of security and efficiency, they are primarily tailored for single-chain or homogeneous blockchain environments. They face challenges when applied to multi-tiered, heterogeneous, and cross-blockchain application scenarios in governing blockchain-by-blockchain frameworks. Consequently, there remains a need for a secure, efficient, and scalable cross-blockchain mechanism designed for governing blockchain-by-blockchain frameworks. In response, we propose the Proof-of-Endorse-Contract (PoEC) consensus mechanism, specifically designed for cross-blockchain consensus scenarios.

4.5. Design Requirements for PoEC

In the context of governing blockchain-by-blockchain models, two primary functional requirements emerge: (1) Supporting Supervision Chain: This entails the ability to acquire data from the supervised blockchain. (2) Implementing Reward and Penalty Measures: The supervised blockchain must execute the reward and penalty measures defined by the governing blockchain. Reward and penalty measures encompass both incentives and sanctions. Incentives primarily target public chain nodes participating in the consensus mechanism. The configuration of incentive measures is determined by the incentive mechanism, typically a straightforward process. Once consensus is reached on these incentive measures within the supervised blockchain, a transfer transaction can be initiated by a minimum of m out of N supervision nodes, relying on a multi-signature algorithm. Penalties can take various forms, including fines, trade restrictions, and frozen balances (with rollbacks being a less practical option). In terms of the consensus mechanism, the core objective when imposing penalties is to compel the supervised blockchain to accept specific transactions. Conversely, measures related to prohibited transactions and frozen balances aim to prevent the supervised blockchain from processing certain transactions. Additionally, the consensus mechanism is subject to non-functional requirements, ensuring its own security, scalability, and efficiency.

4.6. Architecture of PoEC Consensus Process

The architecture of the Proof-of-Enhanced-Contract (PoEC) model involves the integration of supervisory nodes into the supervised blockchain. This composition includes supervisory nodes alongside other node types, enabling the oversight and auditing of the supervised blockchain. It also facilitates the implementation of pertinent reward and penalty measures, as illustrated in Figure 2. In this diagram, the leftmost block represents the supervisory blockchain network. Typically, this network operates as an open public chain where any node has the capacity to initiate smart contracts or transactions. Conversely, the rightmost block corresponds to a supervisory zone chain network, often structured as a licensed consortium chain or a private network. It comprises representative nodes, various regulatory bodies, notaries, or other stakeholders from the supervised blockchain. The supervisory node is deployed within both the supervisory blockchain network and the supervised blockchain network. It acts as the gateway node, enabling cross-blockchain communication between the supervised and supervisory blockchains. This architecture readily fulfills the first functional requirement - supporting the supervisory chain in acquiring data from the supervised blockchain. This is achieved by introducing N supervisory nodes into the supervised blockchain. Each supervisory node locally maintains the data of the entire public chain. For real-time monitoring, when a new block receives confirmation within the supervisory blockchain, supervisory nodes broadcast this information across the supervisory blockchain network. In terms of active review, nodes within the supervisory blockchain can issue data requests to supervisory nodes. Notably, the quantity of supervisory nodes can be dynamically adjusted to strike a balance between scalability and efficiency (Jiang et al., 2018). A privacy preservation model was presented by the author in (Jiang et al., 2020), the author used novel secure algorithm for privacy preservation for IoT data but the issue related to this existing model is computational cost and more latency during transaction. A secure surveillance system was proposed by Dorri et.al (Honar Pajooh et al., 2021). The author explored the concept of deep convolutions neural network (Peng et al., 2020). According to performance trials, the author's explored method reduces Aggarwal S. et al (Peng et al., 2020) X. Cheng et al. (Esposito et al., 2018) proposed a node security identity authentication; provide a secure and reliable updating method for authentication keys and session keys. Ejaz, Muneeb et al. (Patel, 2019) work on Smart remote healthcare systems that require long working periods, low cost, network resilience, security, and confidence in highly dynamic network environments. J. Fu et al. (Kim et al., 2021) highlight the rising issues in IIoT information processing, storage, querying, and dynamic data collecting. Y. Sun et al. (Hang & Kim, 2019) proposed the case database and the current patient's privacy are protected whether the abstracts match or not. A blockchain based healthcare system survey was provided by the authors in references (Dorri et al., 2017) (Lazaroiu & Roscia, 2017) (Lacity, 2018) (Sengupta et al., 2020). The main objectives and themes of these surveys are to highlight the issues related to the current centralized system and the application of decentralized approach such as blockchain technology. Moreover, the authors in these surveys provided more detail and intensive comparative analysis of the existing state of the art models. Similarly, the security breaches associated with IoT and IoMT healthcare systems and its impact are been highlighted. Keeping all these in view, we have proposed hybrid deep learning model using fog computing for IoMT systems to provide privacy preservation and low latency. Xu et al. (Honar Pajooh et al., 2021; Peng et al., 2020) proposed privacy-protection model for fine-grained access control of healthcare data based on blockchain. Rahman et al. (Esposito et al., 2018) presented a secure and provenance enhanced framework for healthcare systems based on federated learning and differential privacy (DP). In this approach blockchain and smart contracts performs the trust management, edge training, and authenticates the federated participating entities. Various studies have been conducted to demonstrate data privacy along with the application of intrusion detection in IoT and its applications (Patel, 2019) (Kim et al., 2021).

4.7 Homomorphic Encryption

Homomorphic encryption is a cryptographic technique that enables computation on encrypted data without the need for decryption (Hang & Kim, 2019). In simpler terms, it allows you to perform operations on data while it remains encrypted, and only the results are revealed when the data is decrypted. This is a powerful tool for maintaining data privacy and security in scenarios where sensitive information needs to be processed, such as in cloud computing, medical research, or secure data analysis. Homomorphic encryption is based on advanced mathematical principles and algorithms (Hang & Kim, 2019). It enables mathematical operations to be carried out on encrypted data, and the results are also encrypted. These encrypted results can then be decrypted to obtain the final result. Properties of Homomorphic Encryption including: (1) Homomorphism: The core property of homomorphic encryption is its homomorphic nature, meaning it preserves the mathematical structure of data even when encrypted (Hang & Kim, 2019). (2) Security: Homomorphic encryption ensures that even though mathematical operations are performed on encrypted data, it remains secure. Only authorized parties with the decryption keys can access the final results (Hang & Kim, 2019). (3) Secure Outsourcing of Computation: Homomorphic encryption is often used when you want to perform computations on data that you don't want to reveal in its decrypted form. For example, a medical researcher can perform analyses on encrypted patient data stored in the cloud without accessing the actual patient records (Hang & Kim, 2019). (4) Privacy-Preserving Data Analysis: In scenarios where multiple parties need to collaborate and analyze data while preserving individual data privacy, homomorphic encryption can be used. It allows computations to be performed on encrypted data, and only the final results are shared (Hang & Kim, 2019). (5) Secure Voting Systems: Homomorphic encryption can be employed in electronic voting systems to ensure that votes remain confidential while enabling the aggregation of results (Hang & Kim, 2019).

5. PROPOSED METHODOLOGY

The methodology presented in this section within two subsections: '5G-enabled IoMT Communication' and 'Blockchain and Fog-Based Architecture for IoMT Communication.' A significant application within 5G networks is the domain of smart healthcare. The general architecture and essential components of the 5G intelligent healthcare network are illustrated in Figure 2, which showcases the necessity of smart antennas for 5G-enabled IoMT communication. Smart antennas have seen notable advancements in recent times, significantly enhancing 5G network coverage and capacity (Figorilli et al., 2018). An innovative development in this context is beam shaping, a technology that focuses RF (Radio Frequency) energy into a concentrated beam, and precisely targeting areas where it's needed instead of dispersing it over a broader area. This is especially crucial for mm-Wave RF, as improper beamforming can lead to signal loss and diminished connectivity over extended distances, due to potential obstructions like vehicles or buildings. A well-coordinated RF beam ensures optimal signal quality and transmission capabilities. However, maintaining the focus over longer distances still poses challenges.

Figure 2. Essential entities of the 5G intelligent health network

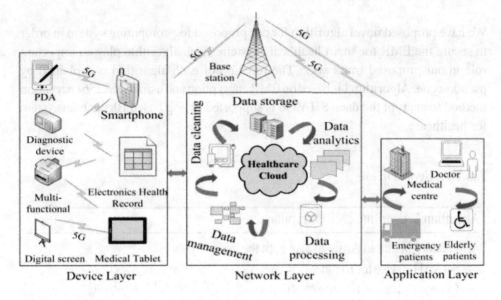

Machine-to-machine (M2M) connections and the Internet of Medical Things (IoMT) are expected to form the foundation of intelligent healthcare within 5G networks (Zhu & Badr, 2018). Figure 3 depicts the Fog-IoMT Architecture, which leverages blockchain technology to enhance the security of healthcare records for IoT devices.

Figure 3. Generic fog-based IoT architecture

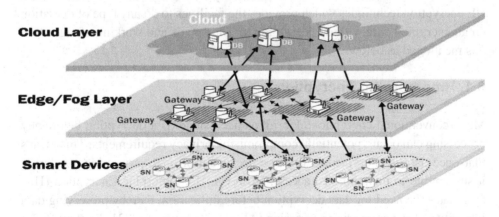

6. PROPOSED ALGORITHMS

We have proposed novel algorithm for our proposed fog computing system in order to secure the EMR for smart healthcare system. Each algorithm play an important role in our proposed framework. The function of each algorithm is explained by pseudo-code. Algorithm 1 is based on EMR encryption and using SHA256 encryption method to encrypt the data. SHA256 is supported by fog based Blockchain system for healthcare.

Table 1. Algorithm one

Algorithm 1 Algorithm EMR encryption

1: Enhance Manifold Analy Eval of both the IoMT end
2: Set IoMT device for comm
3: Get acquisition, ω, $electronicmedicalrecords(EMR)ExtractEMRfromBC$
EMR, valid SHA256 checkHash if EMR, $valid \leq T, thenGettheLusingConnectlength(CL)$
Generate(CL)
IF Blockchain $trans \leq addAnalysis(i, \omega)delLocalEMRendif(EMR)$
end
end

Algorithm 2 is based on Homomorphic encryption (HE). We have implemented HE encryption techniques which provides the facilities to do any type of operation on an encrypted data without decryption it. The details and working of algorithm 2 is mentioned as below:

6.1. Hmomorphic Encryption

Many conventional encryption algorithms necessitate data decryption before any processing can occur, potentially compromising privacy requirements. This means that once data is encrypted, it must be decrypted prior to processing, rendering it susceptible to unauthorized access. However, Homomorphic Encryption (HE) eliminates the need for data decryption before utilization, thereby preserving data integrity and privacy during processing (Ali, Rahim, Ali et al, 2021; Jia et al., 2020; Lin, An, Niu et al, 2022; Lin et al., 2021; Lin, Niu, An et al, 2022; Niu et al., 2022; Tan et al., 2021). HE is a cryptographic technique that empowers Deep Learning (DL)

Table 2. Algorithm two

Algorithm 2 Algorithm Homomorphic Encryption

1: Init an arr T_{Set} of size B
2: Each val is an arr of S rec of type rec
3: Init an arr free of size B whose value are int
4: Init all set to $1, ..., S$
5: Choose a rand k K_T of (PRF) F
6: Let W be the set of keyw in D_B
7: For every w belongs to W do
8: Set $s_{tag} \longleftarrow F(K_T, w)$ and $t \longleftarrow T|w|$
9: For each $i = 1$
10: Set s_i as the i-th string in t
11: Set $(b, L, K) \longleftarrow H(F(s_{tag}, i))$
12: If empty array b is an empty set
13: restart $T_{Set_{Setup}}(T)$ with fresh key K_T
14: Choose j belongs to r free array b and remove j from set free array b
15: Set bit β as 1 if i less than $|t|$ and 0 if i equal $|t|$
16: Set $T_{Set}[b, j]$ label appr L
17: $T_{Set}[b, j]$ label $\longleftarrow (\beta | s_i)$
18: Output (T_{Set}, K_T)
19: Output $s_{tag} \longleftarrow F(K_T, w)$
20: $1-$ Init t as an empty list, bit β as 1, and counter i as 1
21: $2-$ Rept the following loop while $\beta = 1$
22: Set $((b, L, K) \longleftarrow H(F(s_{tag}, i))$
23: Retrieve an array $B \longleftarrow T_{Set}[b]$
24: Search for index j belongs to $1, ..., S$ s.t. $B[j]$ lable $= L$
25: Let $v \longleftarrow B[j]$ value K
26: Let β be the first bit of v and s the remaining $n \omega$ bits of v
27: Add str s to the list t and increment i
28: Output t
29: End procd

---

methodologies to operate on encrypted data without losing the underlying context. It effectively removes the trade-off between data usability and privacy, ensuring data security even in untrusted environments. In the context of DL, HE permits the training and testing of algorithms using encrypted data. If the DL algorithm achieves satisfactory prediction accuracy, it can be deployed in real-world scenarios to make decisions based on the encrypted data (Peng et al., 2021; Peng, Xu, Hu et al, 2022; Peng, Zhang, Xu et al, 2022; Ruan et al., 2020; Ruan et al., 2019; Wang et al., ; Yu et al., 2021). The end user can then decrypt the data using a unique secret key, maintaining both data privacy and security. HE techniques can be categorized into three primary subtypes: Partially Homomorphic Encryption (PHE), Somewhat Homomorphic Encryption (SWHE), and Fully Homomorphic Encryption (FHE) (Adil, Almaiah, Omar Alsayed et al, 2020; Adil, Khan, Ali et al, 2020; Adil, Khan, Almaiah, Al-Zahrani et al, 2020; Adil, Khan, Almaiah, Binsawad et al, 2020; Alrawad, Lutfi, Almaiah, Alsyouf, Al-Khasawneh et al, 2023; Alrawad, Lutfi, Alyatama et al, 2023; Khan, Rahman, Almaiah et al, 2020; Lutfi, Alqudah, Alrawad et al, 2023; Lutfi, Alrawad, Alsyouf et al, 2023; Lutfi, Alshira'h, Alshirah et al, 2023). Figure

Figure 4. Classification of homomorphic encryption

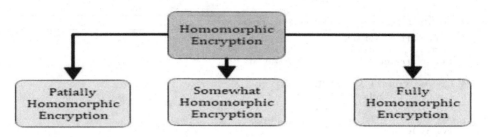

4 illustrates the classification structure of homomorphic encryption. PHE facilitates only one type of mathematical operation on the encrypted data.

PHE schemes are generally more computationally efficient than SHE and FHE due to their homomorphism with respect to only one type of operation, either addition or multiplication (Khan, Asif, Ahmad et al, 2020; Sharma, 2020). SHE offers greater generality than PHE as it supports a wider range of operations; however, its applicability is constrained to a limited set. The primary drawback of FHE lies in its slow computational speed. The entirety of our proposed methodology is divided into two subsections: 5G-enabled IoMT communication and the Blockchain and Fog-based architecture for IoMT communication. SHE permits all addition and multiplication operations but with a limited range on the encrypted data (Al Hwaitat et al., 2020; Ali et al., 2022; Almaiah et al., 2020; Dwivedi et al., 2020; Nkenyereye, 2020). In contrast, FHE allows for a broader range of evaluation operations on encrypted data without limits. Figure 5 illustrates the proposed fog computing architectures and their functionality, including the devices at each layer, as detailed in Figure 5.

Figure 5. Proposed fog and cloud system architecture and its function and IoT devices

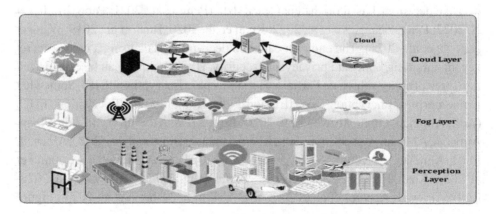

6.2. Privacy-Preserving Deep Learning

Preserving data privacy is a paramount concern when training and testing DL models, especially when dealing with sensitive data like health records, financial details, location logs, and satellite images. Numerous Privacy-Preserving Deep Learning (PPDL) techniques have emerged with a focus on enabling multiple input parties to train and test DL models without disclosing their private data in its raw form. These techniques can be broadly categorized into three groups: cryptographic, perturbation, secure enclaves, and hybrid methods (Al Nafea & Almaiah, 2021; Almaiah, 2021; Almaiah, Hajjej, Ali et al, 2022; Bubukayr & Almaiah, 2021; . et al., 2021; Siam et al., 2021; Vijayalakshmi et al., 2023). Cryptographic approaches entail training and testing DL models on encrypted data (Almaiah, Ali, Hajjej et al, 2022; Zhang et al., 2020; Zhou et al., 2020). This type of methods encompasses Homomorphic Encryption (HE), Secret Sharing (SS), Secure Multi-Party Computation (SMPC), and Garbled Circuit (GC). Perturbation methods are designed to modify data values in a way that preserves individual record confidentiality (Alrawad, Lutfi, Almaiah, & Elshaer, 2023; Bhattacharya, 2020; Mistry et al., 2020). This category of techniques includes Differential Privacy (DP) and Dimensionality Reduction (DP) (Aldhyani et al., 2023; Almaiah et al., 2023; Alrawad, Lutfi, Almaiah, Alsyouf, Arafa et al, 2023; Alzain et al., 2023). In secure enclave-based approaches, both the prediction model and the data are sent separately by the client and the server to a trusted, secure enclave environment for execution. Conversely, hybrid methods aim to combine multiple PPDL techniques to enhance data privacy (Lin et al., 2021). A comprehensive survey of privacy-preserving deep learning approaches is available in (Tan et al., 2021). However, many of these solutions exhibit inefficiencies when handling complex data, often proving effective only in straightforward classification tasks such as MNIST or CIFAR-10 (Yu et al., 2021). They can also introduce substantial computational costs and communication overhead (Peng, Xu, Hu et al, 2022). Additionally, there exists an inherent trade-off between privacy and model accuracy, primarily due to the utilization of approximated activation functions.

6.3. Blockchain and Fog Based Architecture for IoMT

To elucidate the concept of blockchain-based fog computing, we employ Figure 4 as an illustrative aid. The envisioned architecture is characterized by several tiers. The initial layer (IL) of Fog Nodes (FN) is responsible for processing IoMT data, effectively minimizing latency and accommodating the user's preference for rapid service delivery. In future scenarios involving substantial data volumes, a multi-layered design, illustrated in Figure 2, has been conceived for IoMT applications. This design features devices connected to FN, as depicted in the first layer. Figure

6 delineates the transaction flow within our proposed model, which hinges on Fog computing and secure encrypted databases employing Homomorphic Encryption (HE) techniques. Connected devices engage in communication while blockchain technology ensures security. The second tier of FN contributes to latency reduction through IoMT device communication, thereby meeting user expectations. The proposed Fog Computing (FC) model dictates the utilization of FC at the network edge of IoMT devices, alongside blockchain technology for facilitating data connectivity, transfer, and exchange among IoMT nodes.

A peer-to-peer (P2P) transmission network topology is used in the proposed system. In the network, miners are a type of IoMT-NODE. They are utilized in the network to validate transactions. When transactions are confirmed, they are converted into blockages, added to an existing blockchain, and broadcast to the network. Miners are essential for a newly generated block's network adjustment. In this investigation, we tested it and found it to be adequate. We analyzed and used simulation coda tools. Coda is a blockchain development tool. The docker composite was installed on the system. The codecov Test Coverage Tool is a network coverage evaluation tool for IoMT devices. R3 Corda is a distributed Hyperledger platform with work-proof methods (PoWs) and a peer-to-peer network. Extraordinary blockchains are built using the R3 Corda technology. Registration for IoMT nodes procedure to request transactions, which are carried out as follows in Algorithm 3:

Table 3. Algorithm three

Algorithm 3 Client Registration Algorithm
1: Step 1: The client's create account
2: Step 2: Double-check the value.
3: Step 3: Check if the client exists.
4: Step 4: If the val is incor
5: Step 5: The transac has been rej.
6: Step 6: Return to the prev state.
7: Step 7: if not, then
8: Step 8: If there is already a client, then
9: Step 9: The tran has been completed.
10: Step 10: Cli are permitted to use fog node services.
11: Step 11: Else
12: Step 12: Set up the cli data.
13: Step 13: Connect the data to the send addr.
14: Step 14: Add to the client list.
15: Step 15th and END
16: Step 16th and END

The proposed algorithm 4 main function is initialization. In initialization algorithm the keywords are initialized and secret key is assigned to the participant. The participant search for the keyword using the physical layer of the proposed system. The user don't need to decrypt each keywords which are encrypted by HE encryption techniques. Through initialization algorithm the participant its search which doesn't reveal the identity of the participant due to HE techniques. Hence our proposed algorithm keep secret the identity of the participants such as Doctor, patient, nurse, and lab clinician.

Table 4. Algorithm four

Algorithm 4 Initialization Algorithm

1: Initialize $T \longleftarrow \phi$ indexed by keywords W
2: Select key K_S for P_{RF} F
3: Select keys K_X, K_I, K_Z for P_{RF} F_p with range
4: $Z * p$ and parse D_B as $(id_i, W_i d_i)d_i = 1$
5: Initialize $t \longleftarrow ...;$ and let $K_e \longleftarrow F(K_S, w)$
6: for id belongs to $D_B(w)d_o$
7: Set a counter $c \longleftarrow 1$
8: Compute $x_{id} \longleftarrow F_p(K_I, i_d), z \longleftarrow F_p(K_Z, w||c)$
9: $y \longleftarrow x_{idz} - 1 e \longleftarrow E_{nc}(K_e, i_d)$
10: Set $x_{tag} \longleftarrow g F_p(K_X, w)x_{id}$ and $X_{Set} \longleftarrow X_{Set}$ union x_{tag}
11: Append (y, e) to t and $c \longleftarrow c + 1$
12: end for
13: $T[w] \longleftarrow t$
14: end for
15: Set $(T_{Set}, K_T) \longleftarrow T_{Set}$ Setup(T)
16: Let $E_{DB} = (T_{Set}, X_{Set})$
17: return $E_{DB}, K = (K_S, K_X, K_I, K_Z, K_T)$
18: Token generation $(q(w), K)$
19: Client's input is K and query $q(w = (w_1, ..., w_n))$
20: Computes stag $\longleftarrow T_{Set}$ Get Tag(K_T, w_1)
21: Client sends s_{tag} to the server
22: for $c = 1, 2, ...$ until the server stops do
23: for $i = 2, ..., n$ do
24: $x_{token}[c, i] \longleftarrow g F_p(K_Z, w1||c)F_p(K_X, w_i)$
25: end for
26: $x_{token}[c] \longleftarrow (x_{token}[c, 2], ..., x_{token}[c, n])$
27: end for
28: $T_{okq} \longleftarrow (s_{tag}, x_{token})$
29: return T_{okq}
30: Searching technique
31: $E_{Res} \longleftarrow ...$
32: $: t \longleftarrow T_{Set(Retrieve)}(T_{Set}, s_{tag})$

Algorithm 5 main function is to create and access transactions. The transaction are securely transferred and only authenticate user can access the EMR. The working of algorithm 5 is explained as below:

Figure 6 represent the diagram and layout of our proposed neural network system based on neural network and hybrid system. The complexity of our proposed hybrid neural network system can be identified from the number of hidden layers. The more the hidden layers the more will be the complex system.

Table 5. Algorithm five

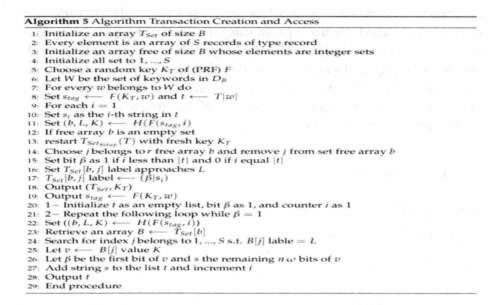

Algorithm 5 Algorithm Transaction Creation and Access
1: Initialize an array T_{Set} of size B
2: Every element is an array of S records of type record
3: Initialize an array free of size B whose elements are integer sets
4: Initialize all set to $1, ..., S$
5: Choose a random key K_T of (PRF) F
6: Let W be the set of keywords in D_B
7: For every w belongs to W do
8: Set $s_{tag} \longleftarrow F(K_T, w)$ and $t \longleftarrow T[w]$
9: For each $i = 1$
10: Set s_i as the i-th string in t
11: Set $(b, L, K) \longleftarrow H(F(s_{tag}, i))$
12: If free array b is an empty set
13: restart $T_{Set_{Setup}}(T)$ with fresh key K_T
14: Choose j belongs to r free array b and remove j from set free array b
15: Set bit β as 1 if i less than $|t|$ and 0 if i equal $|t|$
16: Set $T_{Set}[b, j]$ label approaches L
17: $T_{Set}[b, j]$ label $\longleftarrow (\beta | s_i)$
18: Output (T_{Set}, K_T)
19: Output $s_{tag} \longleftarrow F(K_T, w)$
20: $1 -$ Initialize t as an empty list, bit β as 1, and counter i as 1
21: $2 -$ Repeat the following loop while $\beta = 1$
22: Set $((b, L, K) \longleftarrow H(F(s_{tag}, i))$
23: Retrieve an array $B \longleftarrow T_{Set}[b]$
24: Search for index j belongs to $1, ..., S$ s.t. $B[j]$ lable $= L$
25: Let $v \longleftarrow B[j]$ value K
26: Let β be the first bit of v and s the remaining $n\,\omega$ bits of v
27: Add string s to the list t and increment i
28: Output t
29: End procedure

Figure 6. Proposed deep learning and hybrid neural network system for blockchain based fog computing

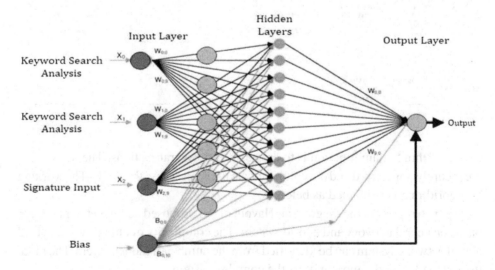

6.4. Secure Training

The primary objective of secure training is to execute a Deep Learning (DL) algorithm on encrypted datasets while achieving robust performance in class identification. This study aims to evaluate the performance of DL algorithms when applied to Paillier-encrypted images. The principal challenge lies in striking a balance between the DL algorithm's class identification accuracy and guarding against potential intruder activities. To address the first concern, a viable approach involves assessing the performance of selected DL algorithms on both plaintext and encrypted data. If the accuracy gap between the DL algorithm's performance on plain and encrypted data is minimal, it substantiates its suitability for practical deployment. Conversely, if a significant disparity exists, it indicates that the encryption method employed in the proposed model may hinder the DL algorithm's ability to learn from encrypted images. In this investigation, we utilize MobileNetV2, a Convolutional Neural Network (CNN) comprising three layers, as the DL algorithm. It's worth noting that MobileNetV2 can be substituted with other transfer learning algorithms as needed. Figure 3 provides an overview of the architecture underpinning the secure training algorithm utilized in this study.

6.5. Security Testing and Validation

Security validation constitutes a pivotal phase in the creation of robust defense mechanisms. It serves as a crucial means for designers to ascertain the effectiveness of a newly devised countermeasure in quelling or, at the very least, alleviating security threats. Achieving this necessitates a meticulous assessment of the specific application context, the adversaries' capabilities, and the extent of enhanced protection attainable in comparison to existing methodologies. The subsequent subsection provides a comprehensive analysis of the aforementioned application scenarios.

7. ANALYSIS AND RESULTS

We have used IoT dataset for our experimental work and simulations publicly available on UNSW website. The dataset were divided into two parts such as training and testing. Moreover, we for the training purpose we used 30% data whereas for the testing purpose we used 70% data. We used the hyper parameters optimization algorithm to optimize the hyper-parameters. Two layer including hidden nodes 50, 25 were used during training. Our proposed model decoder comprised of hidden layer including hidden nodes 25, 50. The proposed model is configured with optimizer= N adam, epochs=20, batch size= 50. The proposed model yielded promising results, achieving an accuracy of approximately 94.34% with a loss of 8.89% when tested on the IoT dataset. In comparison, the IoT-Botnet model achieved an accuracy of 88.38% with a loss of 8.92%. Furthermore, the effectiveness of the two-level privacy architecture was evaluated as a utility system using the BiLSTM model. The hyperparameters were configured with an input layer fed from both datasets and five hidden layers, each with varying numbers of hidden nodes (200, 100, 50, 25, and 15). The results were obtained both before and after applying the two-level privacy preservation technique. For the BiLSTM model trained on the transformed ToN-IoT dataset, it achieved a loss of 0.0167 and an accuracy of 99.58%, while with the actual dataset, it obtained a loss of 0.0052 and an accuracy of 99.89%. Similarly, for the transformed IoT-Botnet dataset, the model recorded a loss of 5.5116 and an accuracy of 90.86%, while with the actual dataset, it achieved a loss of 0.0685 and an accuracy of 99.98%. Additionally, the proposed BiLSTM model was evaluated in terms of class-wise prediction, yielding 0% results, indicating perfect performance according to metrics such as Precision (PR), Detection Rate (DR), F1 Score, and False Alarm Rate (FAR). As shown in Table IV, when tested with both the actual and transformed ToN-IoT datasets, the model achieved an average of 90%-100% for PR, DR, and F1 Score, while reducing FAR close to 0%. Similarly, the model achieved an average of 99%-100% for PR, DR, and F1 metrics when dealing with various types of attacks, including DoS, DDoS, Reconnaissance, and Normal groups in the actual IoT-Botnet dataset.

8. DISCUSSION

This section briefly explains the experimental analysis of our proposed work in a wider context. It also elucidates the dataset used, experimental setup, and comparative analysis in a clear manner. Referring to an IIoT environment, there can be multiple security issues raised from the above discussed risks. Industrial devices such as PLCs RTUs send and receive IO signals and back and forth with fields sensors and actuators. In general, this data should only be transmitted between restricted sources and destinations. Moreover, this data is considered to be critically confidential as it can show the functionality and the logic of control processes. With this permission less solution, all the devices in this network will have access to the full transaction history. Any compromise in any of these devices will expose this information. If it gets in the wrong hands, it can allow malicious actors to reverse engineer these machines and possibly find ways to attack them and potentially disrupt their critical operations. Therefore, it's hard to justify the use of not only Consortium Blockchain but also other blockchain technologies in sensitive and critical environments such as IIoT. The proof of our proposed model is represented through Figure 7, this figure

Figure 7. Simulations results of the proposed model regarding cache hit rate and execution time

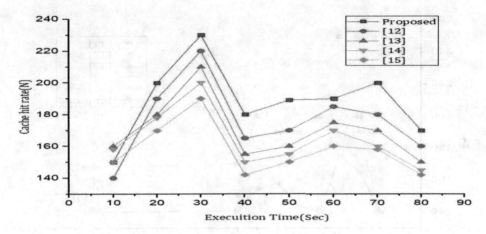

represents the simulations results of the proposed model which justify that our proposed framework is more efficient regarding cache hit rate and execution time.

In Figure 8 we have carried out the simulations results based on the number of rounds and error rate. From Figure 8 it's very clear that the error rate in our proposed framework is very less as compared to the benchmark model hence it shows that our proposed approach is more secure and efficient. From the simulations in Figure 8 it's very clear that our proposed framework has very less error rate as compared to the benchmark model. Using Deep learning techniques the proposed model train with time and learn from the user behavior and interaction. As our proposed model learn with time the error rate become low as compared the benchmark models. It justify that our proposed model is more secure and accurate as compare to the previous models.

In Figure 9 is shown the simulations results based on the search time and cache size. In Figure 9 x-axis represent the search time and the y-axis represent the cache size. We have implemented our proposed algorithm to use less cache size with maximum search time.

Figures 10 and 11 represent the simulation results based on the number of attributes and the target value. It represents the comparative analysis based on the simulations results using number of attributes and the target values. The range of the target value start from 0 to 1 and the number of attributes starts from 0 to 100.

Figure 12 represents the simulations results based on false negative and true positive. Figure 12 also represent that our proposed model receive more accuracy as compared to benchmark model. From the simulations results the proposed model get the accuracy up to 97%.

Figure 8. Simulations results using DL techniques and comparative analysis with the benchmark models

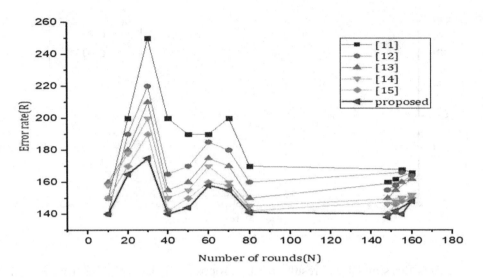

Figure 9. Simulations results based on the search time and cache size

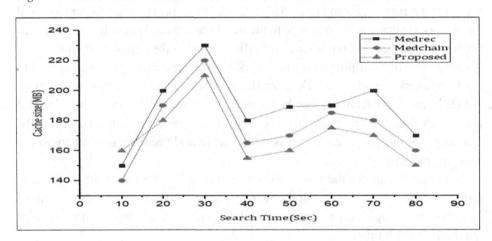

Figure 10. The simulation results based on the number of attributes and the target value

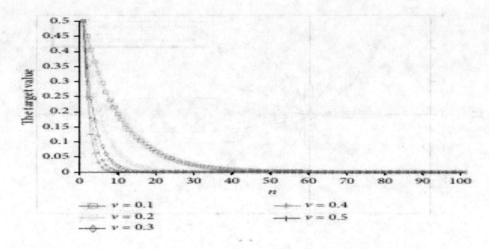

Figure 11. The simulation results based on the number of attributes and the target value

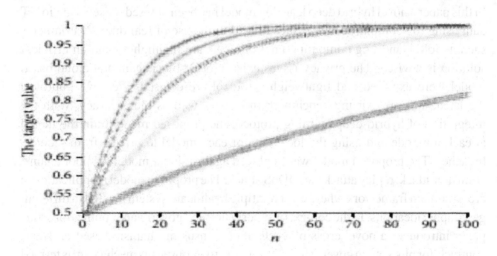

Figure 12. Simulation results based on True False and False Negative values in order to validate the accuracy

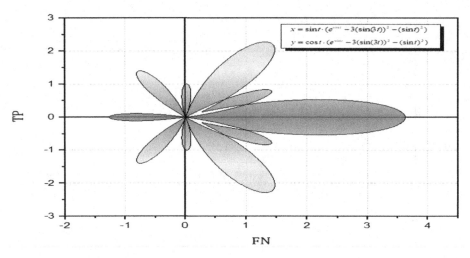

9. CONCLUSION

In this paper a novel hybrid deep learning model has been devised for securing IoMT data using fog computing. The issues related to the use of real time environments such as IoMT and Fog computing environments are highlighted and an efficient solution is devised. The privacy issues exist in other blockchain and cloud based model were explored and lightweight protocol are devised. We have improved the latency of the existing benchmark models as well as the accuracy. With the integration of hybrid-deep learning protocol the proposed model train the model at each fog node and using the local data of each model to protect from security breaches. The proposed model was deployed against threat model to spoof against collusion attack, replay attack and DDoS attack. The proposed model is application in cross-domain framework where exist multiple healthcare system located in different geographic locations. In the context of supervision and governance applications, this paper introduces a novel cross-blockchain consensus mechanism based on smart contracts for blockchain governance. This innovative consensus mechanism is termed Proof-of-Enhanced-Contract (PoEC) consensus. PoEC enables the supervisory blockchain to convey the consensus it has achieved to a smart contract within the supervised blockchain. Subsequently, miners in the supervised blockchain package and verify new blocks based on the state of the smart contract. To ensure secure cross-blockchain communication, we incorporate multiple digital signatures within the contract. Notably, PoEC protocol allows the regulated blockchain to seamlessly integrate into the chain regulation system without necessitating modifications to its original consensus mechanism, resulting in a cost-effective approach. Empirical experiments validate the feasibility of our method, presenting a practical cross-blockchain governance framework for the realm of blockchain governance. To the best of our knowledge, our approach represents the first instance of delivering tangible consensus solutions for governing blockchain by blockchain systems and introduces the concept of smart contracts into consensus processes. This contribution serves as a foundation for enhancing operational performance and addressing the decoupling of supervisory transaction delays and normal transaction delays, which will be explored in our future work.

ACKNOWLEDGMENT

This work was supported through the Annual Funding track by the Deanship of Scientific Research, Vice Presidency for Graduate Studies and Scientific Research, King Faisal University, Saudi Arabia (Project No. Grant No. 4273)

REFERENCES

Adil, M., Almaiah, M. A., Omar Alsayed, A., & Almomani, O. (2020, April 18). An anonymous channel categorization scheme of edge nodes to detect jamming attacks in wireless sensor networks. *Sensors (Basel)*, *20*(8), 2311. doi:10.339020082311 PMID:32325646

Adil, M., Khan, R., Ali, J., Roh, B. H., Ta, Q. T., & Almaiah, M. A. (2020, August 31). An energy proficient load balancing routing scheme for wireless sensor networks to maximize their lifespan in an operational environment. *IEEE Access : Practical Innovations, Open Solutions*, *8*, 163209–163224. doi:10.1109/ ACCESS.2020.3020310

Adil, M., Khan, R., Almaiah, M. A., Al-Zahrani, M., Zakarya, M., Amjad, M. S., & Ahmed, R. (2020, March 4). MAC-AODV based mutual authentication scheme for constraint oriented networks. *IEEE Access : Practical Innovations, Open Solutions*, *8*, 44459–44469. doi:10.1109/ACCESS.2020.2978303

Adil, M., Khan, R., Almaiah, M. A., Binsawad, M., Ali, J., Al Saaidah, A., & Ta, Q. T. (2020, August 11). An efficient load balancing scheme of energy gauge nodes to maximize the lifespan of constraint oriented networks. *IEEE Access : Practical Innovations, Open Solutions*, *8*, 148510–148527. doi:10.1109/ ACCESS.2020.3015941

Al Hwaitat, A. K., Almaiah, M. A., Ali, A., Al-Otaibi, S., Shishakly, R., Lutfi, A., & Alrawad, M. (2023, August 27). A New Blockchain-Based Authentication Framework for Secure IoT Networks. *Electronics (Basel)*, *12*(17), 3618. doi:10.3390/electronics12173618

Al Hwaitat, A. K., Almaiah, M. A., Almomani, O., Al-Zahrani, M., Al-Sayed, R. M., Asaifi, R. M., Adhim, K. K., Althunibat, A., & Alsaaidah, A. (2020). Improved security particle swarm optimization (PSO) algorithm to detect radio jamming attacks in mobile networks. *International Journal of Advanced Computer Science and Applications*, *11*(4). Advance online publication. doi:10.14569/IJACSA.2020.0110480

Al Nafea, R., & Almaiah, M. A. (2021). Cyber security threats in cloud: Literature review. In *2021 International Conference on Information Technology (ICIT)*, (pp. 779-786). IEEE. 10.1109/ICIT52682.2021.9491638

Aldhyani, T. H., Khan, M. A., Almaiah, M. A., Alnazzawi, N., Hwaitat, A. K., Elhag, A., Shehab, R. T., & Alshebami, A. S. (2023, February 8). A Secure internet of medical things Framework for Breast Cancer Detection in Sustainable Smart Cities. *Electronics (Basel)*, *12*(4), 858. doi:10.3390/electronics12040858

Ali, A., Almaiah, M. A., Hajjej, F., Pasha, M. F., Fang, O. H., Khan, R., Teo, J., & Zakarya, M. (2022, January 12). An Industrial IoT-Based Blockchain-Enabled Secure Searchable Encryption Approach for Healthcare Systems Using Neural Network. *Sensors (Basel)*, 22(2), 572. doi:10.339022020572 PMID:35062530

Ali, A., & Mehboob, M. *Comparative Analysis of Selected Routing Protocols for WLAN Based Wireless Sensor Networks (WSNs)*. In *2nd International Multi-Disciplinary Conference*, Oxford, UK.

Ali, A., Naveed, M., Mehboob, M., Irshad, H., & Anwar, P. (2017). An interference aware multi-channel MAC protocol for WASN. In *Proceedings of the 2017 International Conference on Innovations in Electrical Engineering and Computational Technologies (ICIEECT)*, Karachi, Pakistan. 10.1109/ICIEECT.2017.7916523

Ali, A., Rahim, H. A., Pasha, M. F., Dowsley, R., Masud, M., Ali, J., & Baz, M. (2021). Security, Privacy, and Reliability in Digital Healthcare Systems Using Blockchain. *Journal of Electronics (China)*, *10*, 2034.

Ali, A., Rahim, H., Ali, J., Pasha, M., Masud, M., Rehman, A., Chen, C., & Baz, M. (2021). A Novel Secure Blockchain Framework for Accessing Electronic Health Records Using Multiple Certificate Authority. *Applied Sciences*. https://www.mdpi.com/2076-3417/11/21/9999.

Almaiah, M. A. (2021). A new scheme for detecting malicious attacks in wireless sensor networks based on blockchain technology. In Artificial Intelligence and Blockchain for Future Cybersecurity Applications. Springer.

Almaiah, M. A., Al-Otaibi, S., Shishakly, R., Hassan, L., Lutfi, A., Alrawad, M., Qatawneh, M., & Alghanam, O. A. (2023, June 21). Investigating the Role of Perceived Risk, Perceived Security and Perceived Trust on Smart m-Banking Application Using SEM. *Sustainability (Basel)*, *15*(13), 9908. doi:10.3390u15139908

Almaiah, M. A., Al-Zahrani, A., Almomani, O., & Alhwaitat, A. K. (2021). *Classification of cyber security threats on mobile devices and applications. In Artificial Intelligence and Blockchain for Future Cybersecurity Applications*. Springer.

Almaiah, M. A., Ali, A., Hajjej, F., Pasha, M. F., & Alohali, M. A. (2022, March 9). A Lightweight Hybrid Deep Learning Privacy Preserving Model for FC-Based Industrial Internet of Medical Things. *Sensors (Basel)*, *22*(6), 2112. doi:10.339022062112 PMID:35336282

Almaiah, M. A., Dawahdeh, Z., Almomani, O., Alsaaidah, A., Al-Khasawneh, A., & Khawatreh, S. (2020, December). A new hybrid text encryption approach over mobile ad hoc network. *Iranian Journal of Electrical and Computer Engineering*, *10*(6), 6461–6471. doi:10.11591/ijece.v10i6.pp6461-6471

Almaiah, M. A., Hajjej, F., Ali, A., Pasha, M. F., & Almomani, O. (2022, February 13). A Novel Hybrid Trustworthy Decentralized Authentication and Data Preservation Model for Digital Healthcare IoT Based CPS. *Sensors (Basel)*, *22*(4), 1448. doi:10.339022041448 PMID:35214350

Alqudah, H., Lutfi, A., Al Qudah, M. Z., Alshira'h, A. F., Almaiah, M. A., & Alrawad, M. (2023, November 1). The impact of empowering internal auditors on the quality of electronic internal audits: A case of Jordanian listed services companies. *International Journal of Information Management Data Insights.*, *3*(2), 100183. doi:10.1016/j.jjimei.2023.100183

Alrawad, M., Lutfi, A., Almaiah, M. A., Alsyouf, A., Al-Khasawneh, A. L., Arafa, H. M., Ahmed, N. A., AboAlkhair, A. M., & Tork, M. (2023, February 1). Managers' perception and attitude toward financial risks associated with SMEs: Analytic hierarchy process approach. *Journal of Risk and Financial Management.*, *16*(2), 86. doi:10.3390/jrfm16020086

Alrawad, M., Lutfi, A., Almaiah, M. A., Alsyouf, A., Arafa, H. M., Soliman, Y., & Elshaer, I. A. (2023, June 22). A Novel Framework of Public Risk Assessment Using an Integrated Approach Based on AHP and Psychometric Paradigm. *Sustainability (Basel)*, *15*(13), 9965. doi:10.3390u15139965

Alrawad, M., Lutfi, A., Almaiah, M. A., & Elshaer, I. A. (2023, June 2). Examining the influence of trust and perceived risk on customers intention to use NFC mobile payment system. *Journal of Open Innovation*, *9*(2), 100070. doi:10.1016/j. joitmc.2023.100070

Alrawad, M., Lutfi, A., Alyatama, S., Al Khattab, A., Alsoboa, S. S., Almaiah, M. A., Ramadan, M. H., Arafa, H. M., Ahmed, N. A., Alsyouf, A., & Al-Khasawneh, A. L. (2023, March 1). Assessing customers perception of online shopping risks: A structural equation modeling–based multigroup analysis. *Journal of Retailing and Consumer Services*, *71*, 103188. doi:10.1016/j.jretconser.2022.103188

Alzain, E., Al-Otaibi, S., Aldhyani, T. H., Alshebami, A. S., Almaiah, M. A., & Jadhav, M. E. (2023, May 14). Revolutionizing Solar Power Production with Artificial Intelligence: A Sustainable Predictive Model. *Sustainability (Basel)*, *15*(10), 7999. doi:10.3390u15107999

Azaria, A., Ekblaw, A., Vieira, T., & Lippman, A. (2016). Medrec: Using blockchain for medical data access and permission management. In *Proceedings of the 2016 2nd International Conference on Open and Big Data (OBD)*, Vienna, Austria. 10.1109/OBD.2016.11

Bhattacharya, P. (2020). Mobile edge computing-enabled blockchain framework—a survey. *Proceedings of ICRIC 2019*, (pp.797–809). Springer.

Blockchain and 5G-Enabled Internet of Things: Background and Preliminaries Blockchain for 5G-Enabled IoT. (2021). (pp. 3–31). Springer.

Bubukayr, M. A., & Almaiah, M. A. (2021). Cybersecurity concerns in smart-phones and applications: A survey. In *2021 International Conference on Information Technology (ICIT)*, (pp. 725-731). IEEE. 10.1109/ICIT52682.2021.9491691

Chakraborty, S., Aich, S., & Kim, H.-C. (2019). A secure healthcare system design framework using blockchain technology. In *Proceedings of the 2019 21st International Conference on Advanced Communication Technology (ICACT)*, PyeongChang, Korea. 10.23919/ICACT.2019.8701983

Chen, X., Ji, J., Luo, C., Liao, W., & Li, P. (2018). *When machine learning meets blockchain: A decentralized, privacy-preserving and secure design*. In IEEE International Conference on Big Data (Big Data), Seattle, WA, USA. 10.1109/ BigData.2018.8622598

Dorri, A., Kanhere, S., Jurdak, R. S., & Gauravaram, P. (2017). *Blockchain for IoT security and privacy: The case study of a smart home.* In Proceedings of the 2017 IEEE International Conference on Pervasive Computing and Communications Workshops (PerCom workshops), Kona, HI, USA.

Dwivedi, A. D., Srivastava, G., Dhar, S., & Singh, R. (2020). A decentralized privacy-preserving healthcare blockchain for IoT. *J. Sustain. Cities Soc., 55,* 10–18.

. Dwivedi, A. D. (2019). A decentralized privacy-preserving healthcare blockchain for IoT. *Sensors, 19*(2), 326.

Esposito, C., De Santis, A., Tortora, G., Chang, H., & Choo, K.-K. R. (2018). Blockchain: A panacea for healthcare cloud-based data security and privacy. *J. IEEE Cloud Comput., 5*(1), 31–37. doi:10.1109/MCC.2018.011791712

Feng, C., Yu, K., Bashir, A. K., Al-Otaibi, Y. D., Lu, Y., Chen, S., & Zhang, D. (2021). Efficient and secure data sharing for 5G flying drones: A blockchain-enabled approach. *IEEE Network, 35*(1), 130–137. doi:10.1109/MNET.011.2000223

Figorilli, S., Antonucci, F., Costa, C., Pallottino, F., Raso, L., Castiglione, M., Pinci, E., Del Vecchio, D., Colle, G., Proto, A. R., Sperandio, G., & Menesatti, P. (2018). A blockchain implementation prototype for the electronic open source traceability of wood along the whole supply chain. *Sensors (Basel), 18*(9), 3133. doi:10.339018093133 PMID:30227651

Gao, J. (2019). A blockchain-SDN-enabled Internet of vehicles environment for fog computing and 5G networks. *IEEE Internet of Things Journal, 7*(5), 4278–4291.

Hameed, K., Ali, A., Naqvi, M. H., Jabbar, M., Junaid, M., & Haider, A. (2016). *Resource management in operating systems-a survey of scheduling algorithms.* In *Proceedings of the International Conference on Innovative Computing (ICIC),* Lanzhou, China.

Hang, L., & Kim, D.-H. (2019). Design and implementation of an integrated iot blockchain platform for sensing data integrity. *Sensors (Basel), 19*(10), 2228. doi:10.339019102228 PMID:31091799

Hasnain, M., Pasha, M. F., Ghani, I., Mehboob, B., Imran, M., & Ali, A. (2020). *Benchmark Dataset Selection of Web Services Technologies: A Factor Analysis* (Vol. 8). IEEE Access.

Honar Pajooh, H., Rashid, M., Alam, F., & Demidenko, S. (2021). Multi-layer blockchain-based security architecture for internet of things. *Sensors (Basel), 21*(3), 772. doi:10.339021030772 PMID:33498860

Jia, X., Hu, N., Su, S., Yin, S., Zhao, Y., Cheng, X., & Zhang, C. (2020). IRBA: An identity-based cross-domain authentication scheme for the internet of things. *Journal of Electronics (China), 9*, 634.

Jiang, S., Cao, J., McCann, J. A., Yang, Y., Liu, Y., Wang, X., & Deng, Y. (2019). Privacy-preserving and efficient multi-keyword search over encrypted data on the blockchain. In *Proceedings of the 2019 IEEE International Conference on Blockchain (Blockchain)*, Atlanta, GA, USA. 10.1109/Blockchain.2019.00062

Jiang, S., Cao, J., Wu, H., & Yang, Y. (2020). Fairness-based packing of industrial IoT data in permissioned blockchains. *IEEE Transactions on Industrial Informatics, 17*(11), 7639–7649. doi:10.1109/TII.2020.3046129

Jiang, S., Cao, J., Wu, H., Yang, Y., Ma, M., & He, J. (2018). Blochie: A blockchain-based platform for healthcare information exchange. In *Proceedings of the 2018 IEEE International Conference on Smart Computing (Smartcomp)*, (pp. 49–56). IEEE. 10.1109/SMARTCOMP.2018.00073

Khan, F. A., Asif, M., Ahmad, A., Alharbi, M., & Aljuaid, H. (2020). Blockchain technology, improvement suggestions, security challenges on smart grid and its application in healthcare for sustainable development. *J. Sustain. Cities Soc., 55*, 102–018.

Khan, M. N., Rahman, H. U., Almaiah, M. A., Khan, M. Z., Khan, A., Raza, M., Al-Zahrani, M., Almomani, O., & Khan, R. (2020, September 25). Improving energy efficiency with content-based adaptive and dynamic scheduling in wireless sensor networks. *IEEE Access : Practical Innovations, Open Solutions, 8*, 176495–176520. doi:10.1109/ACCESS.2020.3026939

Kim, H., Kim, S.-H., Hwang, J.Y., Seo, C. (2019). Efficient privacy-preserving machine learning for blockchain network. *IEEE Access*.

Kim, T. M., Lee, S.-J., Chang, D.-J., Koo, J., Kim, T., Yoon, K.-H., & Choi, I.-Y. (2021). DynamiChain: Development of Medical Blockchain Ecosystem Based on Dynamic Consent System. *Applied Sciences (Basel, Switzerland), 11*(4), 1612. doi:10.3390/app11041612

Lacity, M. C. (2018). Addressing Key Challenges to Making Enterprise Blockchain Applications a Reality. *J. Mis Q. Exec., 17*, 3.

Lazaroiu, C., & Roscia, M. (2017). *Smart district through IoT and blockchain*. In *Proceedings of the 2017 IEEE 6th International Conference on Renewable Energy Research and Applications*, (pp. 454–461). IEEE. 10.1109/ICRERA.2017.8191102

Lin, Z., An, K., Niu, H., Hu, Y., Chatzinotas, S., Zheng, G., & Wang, J. (2022, July 12). SLNR-based secure energy efficient beamforming in multibeam satellite systems. *IEEE Transactions on Aerospace and Electronic Systems*, 1–4. doi:10.1109/TAES.2022.3190238

Lin, Z., Lin, M., De Cola, T., Wang, J. B., Zhu, W. P., & Cheng, J. (2021, January 14). Supporting IoT with rate-splitting multiple access in satellite and aerial-integrated networks. *IEEE Internet of Things Journal*, 8(14), 11123–11134. doi:10.1109/JIOT.2021.3051603

Lin, Z., Niu, H., An, K., Wang, Y., Zheng, G., Chatzinotas, S., & Hu, Y. (2022, March 3). Refracting RIS aided hybrid satellite-terrestrial relay networks: Joint beamforming design and optimization. *IEEE Transactions on Aerospace and Electronic Systems*, 58(4), 3717–3724. doi:10.1109/TAES.2022.3155711

Liu, J., Li, X., Ye, L., Zhang, H., Du, X., & Guizani, M. (2018). A blockchain based privacy-preserving data sharing for electronic medical records. In *Proceedings of the 2018 IEEE Global Communications Conference (GLOBECOM)*. IEEE. 10.1109/GLOCOM.2018.8647713

Lutfi, A., Alqudah, H., Alrawad, M., Alshira'h, A. F., Alshirah, M. H., Almaiah, M. A., Alsyouf, A., & Hassan, M. F. (2023, July 6). Green Environmental Management System to Support Environmental Performance: What Factors Influence SMEs to Adopt Green Innovations? *Sustainability (Basel)*, 15(13), 10645. doi:10.3390u151310645

Lutfi, A., Alrawad, M., Alsyouf, A., Almaiah, M. A., Al-Khasawneh, A., Al-Khasawneh, A. L., Alshira'h, A. F., Alshirah, M. H., Saad, M., & Ibrahim, N. (2023, January 1). Drivers and impact of big data analytic adoption in the retail industry: A quantitative investigation applying structural equation modeling. *Journal of Retailing and Consumer Services*, 70, 103129. doi:10.1016/j.jretconser.2022.103129

Lutfi, A., Alshira'h, A. F., Alshirah, M. H., Al-Ababneh, H. A., Alrawad, M., Almaiah, M. A., Dalbouh, F. A., Magablih, A. M., Mohammed, F. M., & Alardi, M. W. (2023, September 1). Enhancing VAT compliance in the retail industry: The role of socio-economic determinants and tax knowledge moderation. *Journal of Open Innovation*, 9(3), 100098. doi:10.1016/j.joitmc.2023.100098

Mistry, I., Tanwar, S., Tyagi, S., & Kumar, N. (2020). Mistry.; Ishan and Tanwar.; Sudeep and Tyagi.; Sudhanshu and Kumar.; Neeraj.; Blockchain for 5G-enabled IoT for industrial automation: A systematic review, solutions, and challenges. *Mechanical Systems and Signal Processing*, 135, 106382. doi:10.1016/j.ymssp.2019.106382

Mushtaq, Z., Sani, S. S., Hamed, K., & Ali, A. (2016). Automatic Agricultural Land Irrigation System by Fuzzy Logic. In *Proceedings of the 2016 3rd International Conference on Information Science and Control Engineering (ICISCE)*, Beijing, China. 10.1109/ICISCE.2016.190

Niu, H., Lin, Z., Chu, Z., Zhu, Z., Xiao, P., Nguyen, H. X., Lee, I., & Al-Dhahir, N. (2022, September 27). Joint beamforming design for secure RIS-assisted IoT networks. *IEEE Internet of Things Journal*.

Nkenyereye, L. (2020). Secure and blockchain-based emergency driven message protocol for 5G enabled vehicular edge computing. *Sensors (Basel)*, *20*(1), 154. PMID:33383730

Patel, V. (2019). A framework for secure and decentralized sharing of medical imaging data via blockchain consensus. *Health Informatics Journal*, *15*(4), 1398–1411. doi:10.1177/1460458218769699 PMID:29692204

Peng, C., Wu, C., Gao, L., Zhang, J., Alvin Yau, K.-L., & Ji, Y. (2020). Blockchain for vehicular Internet of Things: Recent advances and open issues. *Sensors (Basel)*, *20*(18), 5079. doi:10.339020185079 PMID:32906707

Peng, Z., Huang, J., Wang, H., Wang, S., Chu, X., Zhang, X., Chen, L., Huang, X., Fu, X., Guo, Y., & Xu, J. (2021). BU-trace: A permissionless mobile system for privacy-preserving intelligent contact tracing. In *International Conference on Database Systems for Advanced Applications*. Springer, Cham.

Peng, Z., Xu, J., Hu, H., Chen, L., & Kong, H. (2022). BlockShare: A Blockchain empowered system for privacy-preserving verifiable data sharing. *A Quarterly Bulletin of the Computer Society of the IEEE Technical Committee on Data Engineering*, *1*, 14–24.

Peng, Z., Zhang, Y., Xu, Q., Liu, H., Gao, Y., Li, X., & Yu, G. (2022, July 1). NeuChain: A fast permissioned blockchain system with deterministic ordering. *Proceedings of the VLDB Endowment International Conference on Very Large Data Bases*, *15*(11), 2585–2598. doi:10.14778/3551793.3551816

Rathi, V. K. (2020). A blockchain-enabled multi domain edge computing orchestrator. *Journal of IEEE Internet of Things Magazine, 3*(2), 30–36.

Ruan, P., Anh Dinh, T. T., Lin, Q., Zhang, M., Chen, G., & Chin Ooi, B. (2020, September 4). Revealing every story of data in blockchain systems. *SIGMOD Record*, *49*(1), 70–77. doi:10.1145/3422648.3422665

Ruan, P., Chen, G., Dinh, T. T., Lin, Q., Ooi, B. C., & Zhang, M. (2019, May 1). Fine-grained, secure and efficient data provenance on blockchain systems. *Proceedings of the VLDB Endowment International Conference on Very Large Data Bases*, *12*(9), 975–988. doi:10.14778/3329772.3329775

Sengupta, J., Ruj, S., & Bit, S. D. (2020). A comprehensive survey on attacks, security issues and blockchain solutions for IoT and IIoT. *Journal of Network and Computer Applications*, *149*, 102481. doi:10.1016/j.jnca.2019.102481

Sharma, A. (2020). Blockchain Based Smart Contracts for Internet of Medical Things in e-Healthcare. *Journal of Electronics (China)*, *9*, 1609.

Shen, B., Guo, J., & Yang, Y. (2019). MedChain: Efficient healthcare data sharing via blockchain. *Applied Sciences (Basel, Switzerland)*, *9*(6), 1207. doi:10.3390/app9061207

Siam, A. I., Almaiah, M. A., Al-Zahrani, A., Elazm, A. A., El Banby, G. M., El-Shafai, W., El-Samie, F. E., & El-Bahnasawy, N. A. (2021, December 13). Secure Health Monitoring Communication Systems Based on IoT and Cloud Computing for Medical Emergency Applications. *Computational Intelligence and Neuroscience*, *2021*, 2021. doi:10.1155/2021/8016525 PMID:34938329

Sultana, T., Almogren, A., Akbar, M., Zuair, M., Ullah, I., & Javaid, N. (2020, January 9). Data sharing system integrating access control mechanism using blockchain-based smart contracts for IoT devices. *Applied Sciences (Basel, Switzerland)*, *10*(2), 488. doi:10.3390/app10020488

Tan, L., Shi, N., Yu, K., Aloqaily, M., & Jararweh, Y. (2021, June 16). A blockchain-empowered access control framework for smart devices in green internet of things. *ACM Transactions on Internet Technology*, *21*(3), 1–20. doi:10.1145/3433542

Vijayalakshmi, K., Al-Otaibi, S., Arya, L., Almaiah, M. A., Anithaashri, T. P., Karthik, S. S., & Shishakly, R. (2023, July 19). Smart Agricultural–Industrial Crop-Monitoring System Using Unmanned Aerial Vehicle–Internet of Things Classification Techniques. *Sustainability (Basel)*, *15*(14), 11242. doi:10.3390u151411242

Vivekanandan, Manojkumar, & Sastry. (2021). VN and others.; BIDAPSCA5G: Blockchain based Internet of Things (IoT) device to device authentication protocol for smart city applications using 5G technology. *Peer-to-Peer Networking and Applications*, *14*(1), 403–419. doi:10.100712083-020-00963-w

Wang H, Xu C, Zhang C, Xu J, Peng Z, Pei J. (2019). *Optimizing Verifiable Blockchain Boolean Range Queries*. HKBU.

Yazdinejad, A., Parizi, R. M., Dehghantanha, A., & Choo, K.-K. (2020). P4-to-blockchain: A secure blockchain-enabled packet parser for software-defined networking. *Journal of Computer Security*, *88*, 101–629.

Yazdinejad, A., & Raymond, K. K. (2019). Blockchain-enabled authentication handover with efficient privacy protection in SDN-based 5G networks. *IEEE Transactions on Network Science and Engineering*. IEEE.

Yu, K., Tan, L., Yang, C., Choo, K. K., Bashir, A. K., Rodrigues, J. J., & Sato, T. (2021). A blockchain-based shamir's threshold cryptography scheme for data protection in industrial internet of things settings. *IEEE Internet of Things Journal*.

Zhang, Y., Wang, K., Moustafa, H., Wang, S., & Zhang, K. (2020). Zhang.; Yan and Wang.; Kun and Moustafa.; Hassnaa and Wang.; Stephen and Zhang.; Ke.; Guest Editorial: Blockchain and AI for Beyond 5G Networks. *IEEE Network*, *34*(6), 22–23. doi:10.1109/MNET.2020.9374644

Zhao, Y. (2021). *A survey of 6G wireless communications: Emerging technologies Future of Information and Communication Conference,* (pp. 150–170). Springer.

Zhou, S., Huang, H., Chen, W., Zhou, P., Zheng, Z., & Guo, S. (2020). Zhou, Sicong and Huang, Huawei and Chen, Wuhui and Zhou, Pan and Zheng, Zibin and Guo, Song pirate: A blockchain-based secure framework of distributed machine learning in 5g networks. *IEEE Network*, *34*(6), 84–91. doi:10.1109/MNET.001.1900658

Zhu, X., & Badr, Y. (2018). Identity management systems for the internet of things: A survey towards blockchain solutions. *Sensors (Basel)*, *18*(12), 4215. doi:10.339018124215 PMID:30513733

Section 3
Advanced Applications and Analysis in Multimedia Data Processing

Chapter 7

A Comparative Analysis of Signature Recognition Methods

Ishrat Nabi
Cluster University of Srinagar, India

Akib Mohi Ud Din Khanday
United Arab Emirates University, UAE

Ishrat Rashid
Cluster University of Srinagar, India

Fayaz Ahmed Khan
 https://orcid.org/0000-0001-9982-0196
Cluster University of Srinagar, India

Rumaan Bashir
Islamic University of Science and Technology, India

ABSTRACT

Signature recognition is the process of automatically identifying or verifying an individual's signature to determine its authenticity. The basic motivation of developing signature recognition systems is to check whether a signature has been done by an authorized user /genuine user or an unauthorized user/a forger. The objective of this chapter is to study different algorithms that are used to authenticate and authorize the signatures of the individual. For personal identification and verification, Signatures are the most acceptable and economical way that is used for this purpose. Signature verification is used for documents like bank transactions

DOI: 10.4018/978-1-6684-7216-3.ch007

and in offices as well. It is a huge time-consuming task for verifying a large number of documents. Hence the verification systems led to huge dramatic changes based on the physical characteristics and the behavioural characteristics of the individual. The verification methods used in the past suffer from flaws. This chapter provides a comparative analysis of various techniques used for recognizing signatures.

INTRODUCTION

Biometric systems use the characteristics of each individual that are unique for every individual. Unlike past verification systems which used keys and passwords were prone to get stolen or forgotten, the physical characteristics that are used in biometrics systems cannot be easily stolen, forgotten or transferred from one person to another (Hezil et al., 2018; Khanday et al., 2018).The objective of such systems is to recognize individuals based on physiological or behavioural traits. Physiological traits are based on measurements of behavioral traits, such as the gestures, signature etc and Behavioral traits are based on measurements of biological traits, such as the fingerprint, face, iris, etc. There are two steps that are done in biometric systems: verification and identification. In the verification phase, a user claims its identity to the system by giving a sample of its biometric identity to the system. In the verification system, the main purpose is to check whether the user is an authorized user or a forger. In the identification phase, the biometric sample is checked among all the registered users in the system (Malik & Arora, 2015). To verify a person's identity in legal, financial and administrative areas, the most important biometric trait used mostly in documentation verification is the handwritten signature. In our daily life, people are very familiar with the signature recognition systems because the process of collection of handwritten signatures is non-invasive. Signature verification systems are used to automatically discriminate if the biometric sample of the user is indeed of a claimed individual or a forger. In other words, the verification is done through these systems. Numerous growing areas of research is the main issue that comes along with personal verification and identification. The different personal characteristics of the individual are used by the system such as face, odor, gait, iris, voice, lip movements, hand geometry, retina. Most commonly used method in personal identification and verification is done through psychological or behavioral characteristics of the individual. There were many traditional authentication techniques which included passwords, PIN numbers, smartcards etc which were replaced by the biometric systems due to the reason that biometric characteristics of the individual cannot be copied by anyone, and cannot be lost , looted or damaged and cannot be easily transferred to anyone and are uniquely identified for every person. There are several factors on which the biometric system depends: User acceptance, Required security, Precision, Implementation and cost time

There are different ways to check the validity of one's personal data, either using signature or fingerprint. Signature refers to the symbol or a sign of the name written by the hand .In our daily lives such as schools, banks, corporations, hospitals, and government departments etc, signatures are often used in verification. There are some fraudulent parties who want to manipulate the signatures of others for illegal use, Due to the importance of signature acceptance. Duplicate signatures can be detrimental and included in the criminal realm (Kekre & Bharadi, 2010). Fingerprints scanning and Retinal vascular pattern screening were some of the electronic identification methods in comparison with Signature verification methods and signature verification methods is found as one of the most accepted ways to identify the person's identity. As the primary means of identifying (verifying and authenticating) using the signature of a person , the user that provides the written signature is based on the assumption that the signature changes slowly and cannot be altered , forged, copied without proper detection. Using the signature verification systems, it was easier for people to migrate from popular pen paper signature systems to the system where handwritten signatures are captured and verified electronically. Signature recognition is categorized as a behavioral tool which is used in banking, credit card validation, security systems, offices etc. In nutshell, handwritten signature verification can be categorized into two broad categories – on–line verification and off–line verification.

Static (offline): In this mode, signature is written on the paper and digitizing it through a scanner/camera and then the shape of the signature captured is then analyzed to recognize it. This mode is also known as *"off-line"* mode. In off–line or static signature recognition, the system analyzes only static characteristics of the signatures as the signature is captured from an imaging device, hence. At the time of verification, the people need not be present (Karouni et al., 2011) Hence, offline signature verification is applicable in various situations like document verification, banking transactions etc as this mode of verification is easy and convenient to use. While designing the offline verification systems, one should be very careful as the system analyzes the static characteristics of the signature image captured from the scanner.

Dynamic (online): In this mode, signature is written on a digital tablet and hence the signature is acquired in real time manner. Stylus-operated PDAs are another means for acquiring the signatures. Dynamic mode of signature recognition is also known as *"on-line"*. In On–line or dynamic verification, in order to grab dynamic signature information an electronic tablet or a stylus connected to the computer is required. Off–line verification on the other hand, works on signature information which is of the form static format and captured from a scanner or a camera. In the

On–line approach, more information about the signature is stored based on the dynamic properties of the signature. In order to scan signatures dynamically digital tablets or pressure sensitive pads are used. The information about pressure points, pen strokes; the writing speed, acceleration as well as the static characteristics of signatures can also be extracted using dynamic verification Digitizer tablets or sensitive pads (Bhattacharya et al., 2013). Hence, better accuracy results are acquired by dynamic mode of verification as compared to static verification because it is very difficult to imitate and change the dynamic characteristics of the signature, but there are requirements for complex hardware and high user cooperation.

In signature recognition, an individual needs to provide the system with a sample of its signature which is used as a base of acquiring and measurement / analysis of their writing. The main objective of the signature recognition process is to identify the writer of a given sample which is already given to the system and to check whether the given signature is of the genuine user, while as the main concern of a signature recognition system is to refuse or reject the sample i.e. to make the signature as genuine or forged. Signature of the individual can be examined by way of two separate techniques.

Another critical issue is Forgery, means to copy some actual document for some fraudulent activity. When there (Hezil et al., 2018) is an illegal change / when original information is recreated it is termed as forgery. A *"forged item"* is any item that is said to be made by someone who did not make it. There are a huge number of powerful software available which can be used by the forgers in order to manipulate the information of the signatures . When there will be addition and removal of features a new image is obtained and hence is called a *"forgery image"*.

There are different kinds of forgeries. Some of them are given below:

- *Random Forgery*: Random forgery refers to the signature given by a person who does not have any idea about the shape of the original signature is called the random forgery.
- *Simple Forgery*: The simple forgery is done by the person who only has an idea about the type of the genuine signature sample without much practice is the Simple Forgery.
- *Skilled Forgery*: Skilled forgery is represented by a suitable representation of the genuine signature sample. The forger has the skill in replicating the genuine signature and this type is more difficult to recognize.
- *Simulation Forgery*: Simulation forgery is a type of forgery where a forger practices by making copies by having an access to a model of the genuine signature. He continuously practices it until he makes the signature as the original one.

LITERATURE REVIEW

The primary record of a biometric system was found in the 1800's in France, Paris "Alphonse Bertillon '' developed a technique of various bodily measurements and records for the identification and classification of people, these statistics are often seen as far back as 500 BC in Babylonian empire. However this method wasn't perfect; it had some flaws for victimization, distinctive biological characteristics to demonstrate identity. Fingerprinting within the 1880's wasn't solely used as a way of distinguishing criminals, moreover as a sort of signature on contracts. It absolutely was seen that a fingerprint of a person was recognized as a symbol of identity of a person and one can be commanded to know it. *"Edward Henry '' is denoted for the event of a process normally known as "the Henry Classification System".* A system was developed wherever the identification supported the distinctive architectures of fingerprints. The *"the Henry Classification System"* was easily adopted by enforcement replacement Bertillon's strategies turning into the quality for criminal identification, this began a century's value of analysis on what alternative distinctive physiological characteristics can be used for identification purposes (Karouni et al., 2011).

A Study on Written Signature Verification Approaches" projected by Garhawal and Shukla (2013). This study presents a quick survey of the research on static biometric authentication & verification. completely alternate existing methods, square measure mentioned .As we tend to notice that the scores of work is huge in this field as signature verification ; the square measure still comes with several challenges during this analysis space. The non-repeating temperament of signature variance owing to geographic location, age, sickness and to a few extent the emotion of the person, accentuates the matter. The other drawback related to this class is the security purposes, it's not terribly straightforward to create a dataset of signatures of real documents like banking documents, and tutorial certificates square measure obtainable for signature verification community. Publically obtainable signature datasets of real documents would create it doable for researchers to realize a much better performance during this field. "Off-Line Biometric Authentication Systems" proposed by Vinayak Ashok Bharadi and Hemant B Kekre .In this paper, a depth overview of handwritten SRS and a special thought is given to the analysis for static signature authentication system (SRS). The performance evaluation of such typical systems along with their feature extraction mechanisms square measures are compared. During this paper, associate in nursing offline SRS based mostly standard feature set moreover as cluster based international options were mentioned. Such systems combine the benefits of single feature sets and enhance the popularity rates with use of multiple algorithmic systems .The system came out with the accuracy rate of (CCR) 95.08 percent that is above the metrics of individual performance. On-line identity verification considers the variable dynamic features of signatures. Jainist and Greiss used important points, speed curvature angle as options and that they have reported FRR as 2.8 percent and much 1.6 percent. The system used simple additionally as writer dependent thresholds however it absolutely was discovered that the writer dependent thresholds provide higher accuracy rates (Diaz et al., 2019). Abbas used a NN model (neural network) for the static or offline signature verification. He used feed forward NN and also 3 unique training algorithms batch, enhanced and Vanilla. The system reported so much between the ranges of ten to forty you look after casual forgeries. Another neuro-fuzzy system was given by Hanmandlu, comparison between the angle created by the pixels of the signature area unit computed with relevant reference points and then the angle of distribution used to be clustered with fuzzy c- suggests. Back propagation algorithm rule was used for coaching NN. The system then reported FRR within the range of 5-16 percent with a varied threshold (Rashidi et al., 2012).

For the issues related to the static signature verification and recognition, Zhang gave the Kernel Principal element Self regression (KPCSR) model. Development from the (KPCR) Kernel Principal element Regression in order to provide sensible verification and recognition performance, a set of the principal elements by the self-regression model is elected from the kernel area for the input variables to accurately characterize every person's signature. The method focused on icon pictures within the preliminary experiments resulted in the acceptable performance. A standard theme with subject-specific KPCSR verified to be terribly economical, from that associated with every person was appointed a freelance KPCSR for secret writing the equivalent visual data. He reported FAR 0.5 percent and FRR 92 percent. For detecting random forgeries Baltzakis projected a NN-based system. The NN-system used texture choices to represent each signature, word options and grid options (pixel densities). A special two-stage perception model one-class-one-network (OCON) classification structure is implemented for everyone from these feature sets. Information is utilized with between 15 and 20 real signatures per author which contains the total signatures of 115 writers. A median FRR and FAR of 3 percent and 9.8 percent, severally is obtained (Yadav & Saxena, 2015). Muthuk Kumarasamy, Armand, and Blumenstein presented a concept that combines the modified Direction Feature (MDF) with additional distinguishing traits to train and test two NN-based classifiers. They contrasted Radial Basis NN and Resilient Back Propagation NN. An accuracy percentage of 91.12 percent was obtained using publicly available data on 2106 sample signatures, 936 of which were genuine and 1170 forgeries (Bhattacharyya et al., 2010). By utilizing Hough rework to sight outlines or strokes from the signature image, Thipakom, Kaewkongka, and Chamnongthai suggested a method of offline or static signature recognition. The parameterized Hough region was extracted from the signature skeleton as one of the signatures' distinguishing characteristics using the Hough transform. The back Propagation trained NN was utilized as a tool in the experiment to judge the performance of the suggested approach. The method was tested with seventy test signatures from various people, yielding an accuracy rate of 95.24 percent. Fang proposed a system that supported the notion that the cursive portions of faked signatures are typically less smooth than those of genuine autographs. Two ways were designed to extract the smoothness and sleekness feature: a crossing methodology and a form dimension methodology. The global form attributes are then combined with the smoothness feature. A minimal distance classifier is used for the prediction of verification. A repeated leave-one-out method is utilized for coaching and assessing real test signatures. With information from fifty-five writers, twenty-four training example signatures and twenty-four professional forgeries are used. AER of 17.3% is reached. Template matching was used by Kekre and Pinge. The test signature was split into pre-set type templates; for feature extraction, a total of forty completely different templates were taken into account. They used a classifier that was neural network-powered. Two distinct formulas were applied. The initial algorithmic rule made use of a neural network with 40 input nodes, 25 hidden layer nodes, 10 output layer nodes, and 40 forms linked to each signature. All of the signatures were represented as relation vectors in the alternative formula, and these vectors were also used to train a neural network with 450 input nodes, 230 hidden layer nodes, and 10 output layer nodes. A total of 10 users' data were used for the testing of formula one reportable ways 200th and formula two reportable ways 0.33 percent. A total of ten users' information was used to evaluate algorithmic rule one reportable technique 200th and algorithmic rule two reportable ways 0.33 percent. The initial algorithmic rule made use of a neural network with 40 input nodes, 25 hidden layer nodes, 10 output layer nodes, and 40 forms linked to each signature. All of the signatures were represented as relation vectors in the alternative formula, and these vectors were also used to train a neural network with 450 input nodes, 230 hidden layer nodes, and 10 output layer nodes. A total of 10 users' data were used for the testing of formula one reportable ways 200th and formula two reportable ways 0.33 percent. A total of ten users' information was used to evaluate algorithmic rule one reportable technique 200th and algorithmic rule two reportable ways 0.33 percent. The model created by Jain and Gangrade uses angle and chain coding features to extract information from the signatures before separating them from other signatures. In this strategy, the NN methodology was used to classify the signature images.

Faundez-Zanuy provided four pattern recognition techniques for recognizing online signatures: the Hidden Markov Model (HMM), Dynamic Time Warping (DTW), Vector Quantization (VQ), Nearest Neighbor, and The author proposed two methods based on nearest neighbour and VQ. The capacity to identify between genuine and false signatures was assisted by the views used by Rashidi, et al. when they evaluated 19 classification errors based on random choice viewpoints. They employed DTW at various distances to improve the performance of the verification sections. An associate degree online/dynamic signature verification system that supported fuzzy modelling techniques was described by Ansari, et al. Geometric has been selected for signature segmentation, and DTW techniques have been used to determine the minimum alignment distance between samples. Fuzzy modelling is used to classify dynamic alternatives, and a user-specific threshold is applied. In order to verify online signatures, Barkoula et al. used the Turning Angle Sequence (TAS) and Turning Angle Scale Area (TASS) representations for signatures. They used a variable from the longest common subsequence comparison method during the template matching stage. Alhaddad, et al. gave a replacement technique by combining back-propagation NN BPNN) and also the use of a probabilistic model. Probabilistic models have been accustomed to classify global features and BPNN has been used for native options classification. Yahyatabar, et al. proposed a model for Persian signatures that supported efficient options defined in the signatures. For classification, an SVM and a combination of dynamic extracted features and shape-based analysis have been used. By matching specifics inside the direction of wrap for the signal presented, Mohammadi and Faez provided a method that supported a means to maximize the excellence between the real and fake signatures.

Napa and Memon proposed a method for authenticating handwritten signatures where a discriminative feature vector is built from attributes of several histograms and generated in a sequential time fashion to delineate the online signature. After gathering data already accessible from Associate in an uncontrolled environment and across several sessions, the authors developed a method of finger-drawn signatures on touch devices for the testing component. A feature vector that has been exposed to a mixture of five separate distance measurements, including the farthest, nearest, and template, is used in the off-line or static signature verification method put out by Souza et al. Fallah, et al. suggested a signature verification method that supported the Mellin redesign. Principal component Analysis (PCA) in conjunction with NN with multi-layer perceptron design and linear classifier have been utilized for classification. Mel Frequency Cepstral Constant (MFCC) extracts the alternatives. Jesus et al. employed features that represented information about the pressure distribution of a written signature within a grayscale image to focus on pseudo-dynamic qualities. When a static signature is inscribed with high pressure, pixels indicating forms or grayscales may appear as darker zones. As a result, entirely variable pressure values coincide with variable grayscales in conformist bar charts. 24 authentic signatures and 24 forgeries of 100 people's signatures were used in the authors' experiment. For signature parameterization in this research, authors adopted a pseudo-campestral coefficient computation. ''Online Signature Verification using Deep Representation'' is a new descriptor suggested by (Erkmen et al., 2010). Using a large number of unlabeled signatures, we pre-train a thin auto-encoder. Then, we apply the discriminative options that the auto-encoder learned to represent the training and testing signatures as a self-taught learning methodology (i.e. we've introduced a signature descriptor). Finally, a one-class classifier is used to sculpt and categorize user signatures (Erkmen et al., 2010; Nilesh, 2013). "Handwritten Character Recognition exploitation NN and tensor Flow" was the plan of Agarwal, Shalika, and Gupta (2019). The study outlines the simplest method to push handwritten character recognition (HCR) to over ninety percent accuracy. In this study, feature extraction methods that use diagonal and direction strategies produce higher accuracy rates than some of the more traditional vertical and horizontal methods. Conjointly employing a NN with best tried layers provides the feature of getting a better tolerance to noise so giving correct results. In NN, the model known as feed forward is principally trained exploiting the back-propagation formula therefore on classifying and acknowledging the characters also get trained a lot of and a lot of. Excluding these, the higher and better accuracy ends up in character recognition achieved with the employment of social control at the side of feature extraction yielded. It's jointly discovered that the larger our coaching knowledge set and higher neural network style, the higher the result. Anuj Dutt demonstrated in his work how he was able to achieve a very high level of accuracy by utilizing Deep Learning techniques. With the convolutional Neural Network, he was achieving a 98.72% accuracy rate. Additionally, utilizing CNN with Tensor flow yields a result of 99.70%, which is even better (Saffar et al., n.d.).

TECHNIQUES

A handwritten signature is considered the most basic way to prove who signed a piece of writing. Compared to other technological identification methods like fingerprints, scans, and retinal vascular pattern screening, a handwritten signature is thought to be one of the most often used methods to authorize transactions and validate the human identity. People find it less difficult to switch from the common pen-and-paper signature as the handwritten signature is electronically collected and confirmed (Angadi & Gour, 2014). A highly acceptable biometric characteristic of a person that can be used to identify and verify human identification is their signature. But ANN, a computer vision system that can also be used to capture images or pictures, can recognise human signatures. Modern computers may be used to create quick algorithms for signature recognition. An Off-line SRS that captures the signature and displays it to the user in a picture format is explored. It uses neural networks. The signatures are validated based on traits and features retrieved from them using various image processing techniques (Alvarez et al., n.d.; Gambäck & Sikdar, 2017).

The objective is to create algorithms that use a set of processes similar to how the human brain works. After much research, the only option is to apply the concept of neurons to computer technology in the same way as medical practitioners do. To construct a collection of steps to gain its own understanding of it (called features), we use a set of highly interconnected processing units known as Neural Networks (NN).The purpose of Neural Network is for machines to replicate how the brain operates, which is modelled after the human brain (Khanday et al., 2021).

Figure 1.

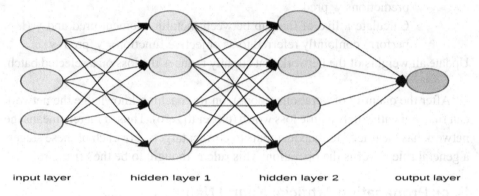

In a neural network, there are three sorts of layers :

- Input Layers: it is used to pass input.
- Hidden layers: layers that come between input and output layers. It is up to these layers to map the input and output.
- Output Layers: this layer is responsible for giving us the output of the NN.

The basic matrix operations that maps input into output are:

Output = relu ((W× Input) + b).

W and b are tensors (multidimensional matrices) representing layer properties. They are also known as layer weights/parameters (the kernel and bias, respectively). We multiply the input by the weights in the expression, add the result to the bias, and ReLU (Rectified Linear Unit) replaces any negative values with zero. These weights contain the information that the network learned from exposure to training data; in other words, the weights contain all of the knowledge.

Training loop:

- Assume the coaching samples x and the accompanying goals y.
- For better predictions y_pred, move the network forward on x (a step known as forward pass).
- Calculate the variance between metallic element pred and y (loss function is also known as objective function= y_pred -y).
- Update all network values to slightly reduce the loss on the selected batch.
- Take the coaching samples x and corresponding targets y.
- Run the network forward on x (a step referred to as forward pass) to urge predictions y_pred.
- Calculate a live of the gap between metallic element pred and y (loss perform conjointly referred to as objective function= y_pred -y).

Update all weights of the network that slightly reduces the loss on a selected batch.

After the quantity of iterations (loops), on its coaching knowledge the network can find you with solely a little loss worth (closer to zero). Thus, it merely means the network has "learned" to map its inputs to correct targets. For each of these stages, a general rule governs the operation. This rule is thought to be the "firing rule".

Back Propagation Artificial Neural Network

To create an ANN, several algorithms are used. While preserving the efficiency of the network, back propagation is probably used as it is the easiest to implement (Nilesh, 2013). Basic processing of back propagation ANN is shown in the figure below:

Figure 2. Backpropagation of ANN

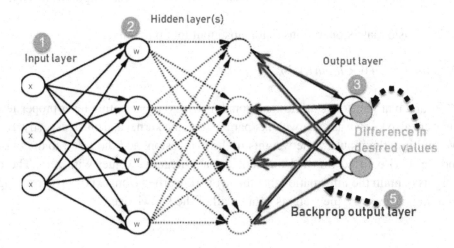

Deep Learning Approach

Unsupervised, semi-supervised, and supervised learning are all possible. As a component of machine learning algorithms, deep learning is also known as deep structured learning. Deep Learning architectures like natural language processors, deep belief networks, convolutional neural networks, AI, speech recognition etc and in some cases surpassing human knowledgeable performance (Zimmerman et al., 2019).

Figure 3. Deep Neural Network Architecture

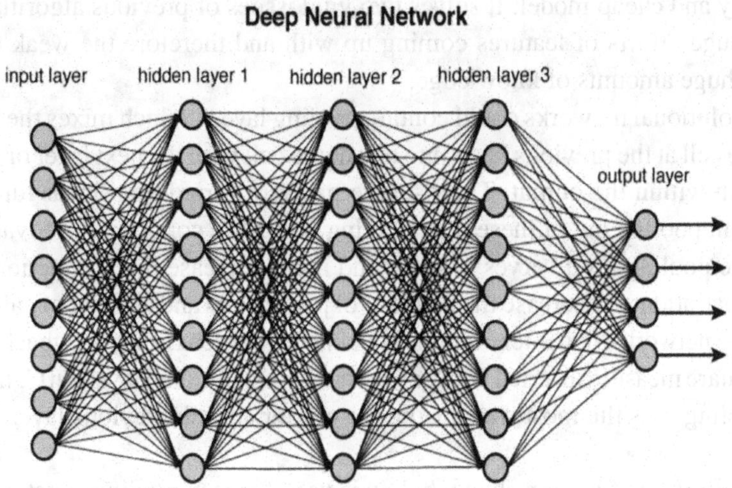

Deep Neural Network

CNN is a kind of feed forward ANN during which the data flows in barely one direction only i.e. in the forward direction only from the input layer to the output node through the hidden nodes. This network employs an operation referred to as "convolution operation". This is often merely a matrix operation between the filters and also the input values of the pictures (Risch & Krestel, 2018). The pattern of processing elements resembles more like an animal visual portion. The individual plant tissue neurons reply to stimuli solely in a very part that is visible to the filter at a time and is referred to as the receptive field. CNN design needs very less preprocessing as compared to other different image classification algorithms . A CNN consists of an Associate in nursing input layer, output layer, and many hidden layers. The hidden layers of a CNN generally incorporate convolutional layers, pooling layers, and one or additional totally connected layer (Alvarez et al., n.d.).

The convolutional layer, which sets CNN apart from ANN, is its fundamental component. The parameter of the layer has a set of learnable filters with a narrow, low receptive field that covers the entire depth of the input data. Each filter is convolved throughout the whole input volume's height and width during the process, producing an output that is a 2-D activation map for that filter that is calculated by calculating the dot product between the filter's entries and the input. As a result, when it detects a specific kind of feature at a specific geographical location within the input, the network learns filters that are activated (Alvarez et al., n.d.). The same filters on the same feature map are suggested to be used . A weight sharing helps to cut back the specified computing memory and to enhance CNN performance on pc vision tasks. CNN is in a position to manage a giant scale of knowledge because of its decent capability and cheap model. It solves two vital issues of previous algorithms in pc vision, huge efforts of features coming up with and therefore the weak ability to manage huge amounts of knowledge.

Convolutional networks could contain pooling layers, which mixes the output of the nerve cell at the previous layer into one nerve cell with the next layer or produces one worth within the output. Their square measure varied non-linear functions to implement pooling out of these max pooling is that the commonest (Alvarez et al., n.d.). The pooling layer serves to more and more decrease the abstraction amount of the illustration, to decrease the quantity of parameters and amount of calculations within the network, then after conjointly manage the over-fitting drawback. Pooling layers square measure inserted between ordered convolutional layers in CNN design. Max pooling uses the most worth from the cluster at each previous layer.

Max Pooling: the function shown below is used for max pooling function:

$aj = max\ (u\ (n:\ n))$

This applied a window function u (x; y) on the computer file with the input data and extracts the utmost and the max value out of the input data (Yadav & Saxena, 2015). Max pooling allows quicker converging rate, reduces the quantity of training parameters, overall performance improvement, so minimizing calculations and computing time, leading to a far better potency and efficiency throughout training .

Dropout Layer

Convolutional neural networks contain multiple hidden layers with non-linear functions that make CNN a communicative model that's to understand the difficult relationships between the inputs and outputs. Wherever there's restricted training information, several of those difficult relationships are the results of sampling noise that exists within the training set.

To address these issues, many solutions are being investigated, such as terminating training as soon as performance on a validation set deteriorates. Dropout, a powerful algorithmic solution for lowering the generalization error of big neural networks and resolving the over-fitting problem, could have been invented .

Thus, the Dropout layer enhances CNN to be ready to train itself with additional sturdy options and stable structure or mechanism. *Hence, dropout layer suggests that briefly removing or falling by the wayside units (visible or hidden) from the network, in conjunction with its all connections.*

Finally, an entirely linked layer links to each and every neuron in the previous layer, whether that layer was fully connected, pooled, or convolutional. The objective of the fully linked layer is to decrease the spatially set of neurons and create chances with a high level of understanding. The outcome of the earlier levels help the network to obtain extremely acceptable properties. The convolutional layers provide somewhat important features and these layers learn possibly non-linear functions as well. These layers connect each nerve cell at the previous layer to the next nerve cell on the other layer.

Pixel Matching Technique

A signature is made of characters that are special for the authenticating one person from the other. In authenticating method, a signature that has been captured is stored in the computer as image file. The problem we have is to match the signature of user with a sample information signature we have. Authentication of signature is an important method that has its application in several sectors as Banking sector, Property Dealing sector, and other different areas (Bhattacharya et al., 2013). If we would be able to create any package or device like missile that is guided (Signature Authentication Machine) so that then we can merge it with the existing system. Verification of Signature contains two important way outs; offline signature verification, which is the sample signature unit area, is scanned into description of the image and online signature verification, which is the samples of signature unit area are collected from a digitizing pill that is capable of movements of pen while writing. The work we've done gives comparison of the offline signature of a person with the signature sample that holds information of samples.

Methodology

Methodology consists of two main steps, Learning a signature descriptor and creating references models for users. The first step for the technique is to make a signature descriptor that supports self-thought learning that consists of ATVS dataset. When the learning finishes in the auto encoder then it becomes the most efficient, beneficial, economical feature extractor for all the signature patches. The second step, the signatures are divided into tiny patches which have represented by the descriptor. The mean of the descriptions of tiny patches have pooled (i.e. mean of the extracted options that square measure extracted from every sample) have thought of because the descriptions of the signatures. Supported the given step by step procedure, all the signature samples of every user are represented and their reference models are created for each and every user. The models created for every user square measure thought of as a collection of one-class classifiers. As represented, within the beginning, associate auto-encoder learns options square measure more efficient ones are learned. During this step, a dataset is discredited from train and checks datasets which is associate unlabelled dataset, is employed supported self-taught technique. In the next step, a reference model of the system for each user samples is made in order to victimize the knowledge extracted for the user's reference signatures. The above two steps are considered as the main parts of the training phase. Then, in the verification part, that is system-working section, some unknown signature samples are then given to the system to compare it with the reference signature models.

1. Pre-Processing

In the pre-processing part the signature size is normalized. The pre-processing is done by scaling the signature size. At following step, the mean of the information should become capable zero for data social control. Signatures information in datasets square measure supported pen up/down, time, pressure; etc. in x, y positions . The time of the points is seen to get the sequence of information and to see if the pen has gone up the pen up/down is checked, the purpose should be separated from following one. Finally, after getting the information sequence and the pen up/down, signatures are delineating based on 2 layers: pressure and time.

2. Auto-Encoder Used for Feature Learning

For the feature learning process, a linear auto encoder has been used. The auto encoder has been used to map input to the output when the signature has been set for the input and the output. In order to support gradient descent, this auto-encoder has been . In order to extend the performance of the learning phase, data that is in large patches is divided into smaller patches and these smaller patches are then used as an input in the feature learning phase. After the learning of the options is done, the options are convolved with massive patch. Mean pooling technique has been used to get convolved options pooled. These pooled options are then used for classification purpose .

3. Model Creation and Classification

There are issues like variations between same user's signatures, numerous circumstances of language, less signature samples, and forgery signatures with classification. These issues are then resolved by selecting Associate in nursing applicable classifier is unbelievably necessary. At intervals the planned system, the one-class classifier contains a target category which is a class of the user whose signatures are compared with the input signature, but the outlier class is completely different signature samples of the user. Hence, the one class classifier ought to manufacture a template model of target category for each use (Khanday et al., 2020). The planned technique has the simplest performance as compared with competitive models. On SUSIG dataset, enforced models EER are adequate 0.77 %. On SVC2004 dataset the models EER is 0.83 percent, whereas all the opposite formulas has the performance below than planned algorithm.

Figure 4. Proposed Approach

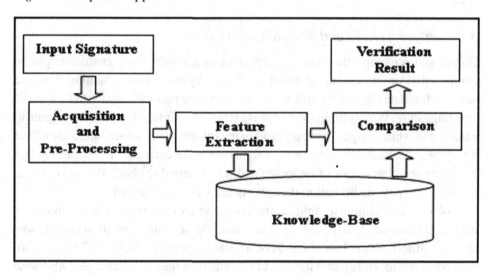

3.1 Capturing Signature From a Page

Normally a signature page is scanned as a picture by the scanner. Here we need to spot the signature from an image that the scanner scanned which is troublesome as a result the several text and patterns were captured that were in the scanned image.

Thus the need is to line a signature space that can facilitate to spot the precise boundary of the signature space which is in the scanned image. If the signature area had been known that is wherein we need to put the signature then fill it with a border colour like RGB (239, 228, 176) etc. then only it can facilitate to spot the particular position of that signature in scanned image. The image that contains the signature of user has been scanned using the algorithm which is given below:

Pseudo Code for calculating the area of the signature.

Step1: *Set point = 0, sh = 0, st = 0, sl = 0 // sl = signature left position, st = high sh = Height and point = width*

Step2: *Set x = 0 and y = 0*

Step3: *From the scanned image scan the colour and store it in pixel colour*

Step4: *Check if pixel colour = RGB (239,228,176) then move to Step 5 if not then move to Step 7.*

Step5: *Check if point = 0 then Set FTO = x AND if sh = 0 then Set st = y*

Step6: *Set point = x; sh = y; y = y + 1*

Step7: *Check if y < image. Height-1 then Repeat from Step 3 to Step 6.*

Step8: *Set x = x +1*

Step9: *Check if x < image. Width-1 then Repeat from Step 3 to Step 8.*

End

3.2. Removing Noise and Normalize the Colour

Colour and removing the noise is important as a result of a signature might be composed of various colours and will be affected by noise while scanning. Thus we have to eliminate the entire noise across the signature particular space to extract the exact signature. When elimination of noise is done, the image has been born again to a black and white image. This may hold in the information as a signature sample or it may be accustomed compare with a signature in the database. The benefit is that it reduces the dimensions of an image and it is required to check the two colours. In order to expel this limitation the subsequent ways are planned.

Colour normalization technique is used to make the oblong space black and white we would like to scan all the oblong space using the algorithm program given below and we will notice the colour of every constituent. If the colour is (RGB (239,228,176) then convert it to white and if the colour is white then there is no change. Otherwise modify the constituent colour to black. This is often very easy and quick technique to form a black and white image. Pseudo Code to form the image black and white:

Step1: *Scan the colour from the image and store it in pixel colour*

Step2: *If the pixel colour = colour (RGB (239,228,176)) then Set pixel colour = colour (white)*

Step3: *If the pixel colour = colour (white) then go to Step 4 else Set pixel colour = colour (black)*

Step4: *Repeat from Step 1 to Step 3 whereas image is not scanned fully.*

End

For the further processing of this technique, the noise has to be removed in this step. During this part the image has been scanned and the noise has been removed . When scanning that signature and normalizing its colour some tiny single pixels of black colour have been found, that is not the half of that signature. Following technique has been introduced to get rid of the noise within the image. Pseudo code for noise reduction:

Step1: *Scan the colour from the image and store it in pixel colour*

Step2: *If the pixel colour = colour (black) then go to Step 3 else go to step 4.*

Step3: *If the pixel colour isn't same with adjoin pixel colour then set pixel colour = colour (white) and go to Step 1 else go to step 4.*

Step4: *Repeat step one to step three whereas image not scanned fully*

End

3.3. Property Adjustment

A binary image (only in black and white) is obtained after the previous step. Afterwards it is needed to find the precise position of the signature within the image to perform the signature verification; as a result, signature may be at any place inside this rectangular space. And it will sign on completely different angles and sizes. Now the drawback is to seek out the precise position of the signature from the oblong boundary space and therefore the second drawback is to seek out the angle and size of the signature. Then the required correction has to be compelled to be wiped out.

Finding the exact position of the signature within the signature box??

To solve this, the answer is predicated on the identification of edges of the signature within the signature box. It scans the oblong space from its four (top, bottom, left, right) sides and then the particular signature space can be extracted.

Angular problem solutions

The angular detection of a user signature modifies from time to time. A signature can be written in several angles. To match the signature signed in several angles that are hold in information . The main goal is to vary the property of scanned signature for that it is often compared with the database signature. Sometimes same signature is often written in an angle and to resolve this angular downside some mathematical formula is employed. After rotation the signature size gets enlarged hence resizing of the signature is needed before the two signatures will be compared.

3.4. Compare the Signature With Database Signature

To compare the signature with the sample information signature an easy algorithmic program has been introduced that supports pixel matching concept . It is simple to implement and computationally less complicated. Algorithm given below is projected to scan each pixel colour of the scanned image and also the database image. Scan the two pictures from left to right check for the pixel colour. If the pixel colour is black then it shows that it is a neighbourhood of signature and compares the corresponding pixel with the opposite image . If the pixel colour is same for two pictures than a counter 'm' inflated and if the match is not found then another counter 'n' is inflated. By scanning each black pixel additionally a counter 'p' increases. The percentage of matching is calculated using the formula:

Percentage = m / (n + p) *100

Pseudo Code to match the signature with database signature

Step1: *Set m = 0, n =0, p = 0*
Step2: *Scan the colour from the database image and store it in pixel colour.*
Step3: *From the scanned image scan the colour and store it in colour.*
Step4: *If pixel colour = colour (black) then step 5 else step 7.*
Step5: *If pixel colour = colour then Set m = m + 1 else Set n = n + 1.*
Step6: *Set p = p + 1.*
Step7: *Repeat Step two whereas image not scanned completely.*
Step8: *Set p = m / (n + p) *100.*
Step9: *Show the value of p.*

Results and Comparative Study

The possible cases in verification are True accept (TA), False Reject (FR), True Reject (TR), False accept (FA).In this system for each person 8 original and 8 forgery signatures are tested. The verification results of this system PMT, ANN's Back propagation method and DNN are given in Table 1.

Table 1. Verification results of PMT, ANN and DNN

System	TAR	FAR	FAR	FRR
PMT	0.94	0.06	0.88	0.12
ANN	0.98	o.22	0.89	0.11
DNN	0.78	0.22	0.84	0.16

Comparative Study

A comparative analysis is being performed on different parameters and different approaches. The results are summarised in a Table 2.

Table 2: Comparative Analysis of the techniques used.

Parameter	Artificial Neural Networks	Deep Learning	Pixel Matching
FAR	FAR of the system is 14.66% when the neural network is given an input of 150 forged signatures.	On SVC2004 dataset EER is 0.83 percent, On SUSIG EER is equal to 0.77 percent.	0.6
FRR	When 150 genuine signatures were given FRR of the system is 20%, 120 signatures as genuine and 30 forgeries are classified by the system.	FAR and FRR rates are 20% for both.	0.12
Speed	Slow	Fast	slow
Accuracy	82.6%	83% for ATVS dataset and 70% for SUSIG dataset.	94%
Dataset used	150 genuine and 150 forged signatures are given as input.	ATVS and SUSIG	8 genuine and 8 forgery signatures are tested.
Mode of application	Static mode	Static and dynamic both	Static
Data processed	Supervised	unsupervised	supervised
Usage	Not used as much	Most widely Used as it gives more accurate results as compared to static methods	Not used so much because it works only on the static features captured from the images of the signatures.

CONCLUSION

Hand written signature is considered to be unique identification of an individual which are applicable in the banking and other legal transactions. But handwritten signatures for its valuable importance and applications are at target of fraudulence. In order to avoid fraudulence, different techniques were given by different authors. For static signature verification, a method of NN approach is used for handwritten signature verification. This NN method Implements features extracted from pre-processing of the signature images. Then using error back propagation training algorithm the features extracted are used to train NN. Then the classification of all genuine and forged signatures is given by NN correctly. In training phase, the samples from the database are given to the network from different ones; with 300 such signatures (150 genuine and 150 forged) it classifies 248 correctly. Hence, the CCR of the system is 82.66%.Signature verification using pixel matching techniques had its respective pros and cons. Signature authentication machine is implemented in order to provide a simple, safe, fast biometric behavioral security system. This method is faster than other methods by applying some equations from co-ordinate geometry. More security is achieved by the colour matching technique. The interface of the application makes it very easy and simple. The implemented system has some disadvantages: the system cannot identify the dynamic changes of the signature as it works on the static signature images. This system works on offline signature images. The methods of this system tested only offline and Online devices are not connected with this system. Signature recognition using deep CNN using self-thought learning mechanism for unsupervised data .This technique has ability to extract best set of features in problems. Therefore, a wide range of machine learning algorithms implements CNN. In addition, both online and offline signature datasets can be implemented using deep CNN. Deep learning strategies are typically checked out as recording equipment, with most confirmations done through empirical observation, instead of on paper.

ACKNOWLEDGMENT

The Authors are thankful to Department of Computer Science IUST, India.

REFERENCES

Agarwal, M., Shalika, V. T., & Gupta, P. (2019). Handwritten character recognition using neural network and tensor flow. *International Journal of Innovative Technology and Exploring Engineering*, 8.

Alvarez, G., Sheffer, B., & Bryant, M. (n.d.). *Offline signature verification with convolutional neural networks*. https://github.com/Lasagne/Recipes/blob/master/modelzoo/vgg16.py.

Angadi, S. A., & Gour, S. (2014, January). Euclidean distance based offline signature recognition system using global and local wavelet features. In *2014 Fifth International Conference on Signal and Image Processing* (pp. 87-91). IEEE. 10.1109/ICSIP.2014.19

Bhattacharya, I., Ghosh, P., & Biswas, S. (2013). Offline signature verification using pixel matching technique. *Procedia Technology*, *10*, 970–977. doi:10.1016/j.protcy.2013.12.445

Bhattacharyya, D., Biswas, S., & Kim, T.-H. (2010). Features extraction and verification of signature image using clustering technique. In *International Journal of International Journal of International Journal of International Journal of Smart Home Smart Home Smart Home Smart Home* (Vol. 4, Issue 4). https://www.researchgate.net/publication/228868400

Diaz, M., Ferrer, M. A., Impedovo, D., Malik, M. I., Pirlo, G., & Plamondon, R. (2019). A perspective analysis of handwritten signature technology. *ACM Computing Surveys*, *51*(6), 1–39. doi:10.1145/3274658

Erkmen, B., Kahraman, N., Vural, R. A., & Yildirim, T. (2010). Conic section function neural network circuitry for offline signature recognition. *IEEE Transactions on Neural Networks*, *21*(4), 667–672. doi:10.1109/TNN.2010.2040751 PMID:20144917

Gambäck, B., & Sikdar, U. K. (2017). *Using Convolutional Neural Networks to Classify Hate-Speech.*, *7491*, 85–90. doi:10.18653/v1/w17-3013

Garhawal, S., & Shukla, N. (2013). A study on handwritten signature verification approaches. *International Journal of Advanced Research in Computer Engineering and Technology*, *2*(8), 2497–2503.

Hezil, H., Djemili, R., & Bourouba, H. (2018). Signature recognition using binary features and KNN. *International Journal of Biometrics*, *10*(1), 1–15. doi:10.1504/IJBM.2018.090121

Karouni, A., Daya, B., & Bahlak, S. (2011). Offline signature recognition using neural networks approach. *Procedia Computer Science, 3*, 155–161. doi:10.1016/j.procs.2010.12.027

Kekre, H. B., & Bharadi, V. A. (2010). Off-Line Signature Recognition Systems. *International Journal of Computers and Applications, 1*(27), 61–70. doi:10.5120/499-815

Khanday, A. M. U. D., Amin, A., Manzoor, I., & Bashir, R. (2018). Face Recognition Techniques: A Critical Review. *STM Journals, 5*(2), 24–30. https://www.researchgate.net/publication/330872439_Face_Recognition_Techniques_A_Critical_Review

Khanday, A. M. U. D., Khan, Q. R., & Rabani, S. T. (2021). Identifying propaganda from online social networks during COVID-19 using machine learning techniques. *International Journal of Information Technology, 13*(1), 115–122. doi:10.100741870-020-00550-5

Khanday, A. M. U. D., Rayees Khan, Q., & Rabani, S. T. (2020). Analysing and Predicting Propaganda on Social Media using Machine Learning Techniques. *2020 2nd International Conference on Advances in Computing, Communication Control and Networking (ICACCCN)*, 122–127. https://doi.org/10.1109/ICACCCN51052.2020.9362838

Malik, V., & Arora, A. (2015). *A Review Paper on Signature Recognition*. www.ijraset.com

Nilesh, Y. (2013). Signature Recognition & Verification System Using Back Propagation Neural Network. In *International Journal of IT, Engineering and Applied Sciences Research* (Vol. 2, Issue 1). www.irjcjournals.org

Rashidi, S., Fallah, A., & Towhidkhah, F. (2012). Feature extraction based DCT on dynamic signature verification. *Scientia Iranica, 19*(6), 1810–1819. doi:10.1016/j.scient.2012.05.007

Risch, J., & Krestel, R. (2018). Aggression Identification Using Deep Learning and Data Augmentation. *Proceedings of the First Workshop on Trolling, Aggression and Cyberbullying (TRAC-2018), Coling*, 77–85. http://aclweb.org/anthology/W18-44%0A900

Saffar, M. H., Fayyaz, M., Sabokrou, M., & Fathy, M. (n.d.). Online signature verification using deep representation: a new descriptor. https://www.researchgate.net/publication/306510061.

Yadav, D., & Saxena, C. (2015). Offline signature recognition and verification using PCA and neural network approach. *Int. J. Sci. Res. Dev*, *3*(9).

Zimmerman, S., Fox, C., & Kruschwitz, U. (2019). Improving hate speech detection with deep learning ensembles. *LREC 2018 - 11th International Conference on Language Resources and Evaluation*, 2546–2553.

KEY ABBREVIATIONS

AI: Artificial Intelligence
ANN: Artificial Neural Network
CNN: Convolutional Neural Network
DNN: Deep Neural Network
NN: Neural Network
PMT: Pixel Matching technique

Chapter 8
Low Light Face Detection System

G. Ananthi

ⓘ https://orcid.org/0000-0003-3227-2134
Mepco Schlenk Engineering College, India

T. Balaji
Mepco Schlenk Engineering College, India

M. Pugalenthi
Mepco Schlenk Engineering College, India

M. Rajkumar
Mepco Schlenk Engineering College, India

ABSTRACT

Detection of faces from low light image is challenging. Such images often suffer from poor contrast, poor intensity, and high noise make it challenging to gather information and identify people or objects. The proposed method uses a deep learning-based approach to enhance the images by capturing multiple exposures and combining them to generate a high-quality image. Max-margin object detection (MMOD) human face detector, a face detection algorithm is used to identify and enhance the faces in the images. MMOD algorithm is a deep learning-based object detection approach which accurately detects human faces in images. By identifying and enhancing the faces in the images, they are made more visible and recognizable, even in low light conditions. The experimental results of this proposed approach demonstrate its effectiveness in enhancing face visibility and raising the quality of low-light images. This method has practical applications in areas such as security surveillance, where capturing high-quality images under low light conditions is critical.

DOI: 10.4018/978-1-6684-7216-3.ch008

INTRODUCTION

Low visibility images are the images which are captured under low light condition. These low light images are unsatisfied during the visualization process. Applying several algorithms on those low light images directly, will hurt the performance of algorithm very much. In the low light images, the entire image may not be dark, for example, in an image bottom portion alone may be buried in dark. Low-light image enhancement techniques are used to make the buried portion of the image into visible. Through direct amplification method, the visibility of the dark regions can be regained. But the problems are, the relatively brighter regions are saturated and the loss of information. Because of these issues, the direct amplification method had less usage and various other algorithms have been used by the researchers.

According to the experiments, one can also try to benefit from low-light image enhancement as pre-processing. Image enhancement aims to strengthen the general image's visible and perceptual quality, which isn't always in line with the face detection goal. Smoothing operations for enhancing noisy images, for instance, should threaten the essential feature discriminability for detection. This advises that the enhancement and detection additives are almost integrated, and it suggests a give-up-to-cease "detainment-with-enhance" solution.

Another reason is that the illumination of the distinctive image can vary greatly depends on the location. Subsequently, it's doubtful that a single light-improved photograph will be able to detect nicely facial areas below one-of-a-kind lights situations. This calls attention to the multi-exposure technique and suggests using a multiple enhancement method. The method applies multiple images with several digital camera settings, especially when it's difficult to achieve a well-exposed image with merely one shot. Then, for light enhancement, such multi-publicity images are fused. Furthermore, and naturally, we can create various publicity images and then recognize faces from them to cover certain exposure scenarios. However, automatically extracting unduly pleasant multi-exposure visuals from a single image is not trivial, let exclusively one that is low-mild; however, face detection doesn't always require such excessive quality. The system for gathering facts at specific exposures is what concerns.

This model has the benefit of zero-reference, which eliminates the need for paired data during the training process. So far, many of the current systems, including CNN-based methods, GLADNET, LIME, and GAN-Based methods. This is made possible by a number of specially created non-reference loss functions, such as the loss of color consistency, exposure control, spatial constancy, and illumination smoothness. We'll take overall loss factors into account in this method. This technique generalizes different lightning conditions while avoiding the possibility of overfitting. In this technique, we create an image-specific curve that can iteratively approximate higher-order and pixel-wise curves. the testing of a deep image enhancement model using non-reference loss functions to assess the quality of enhancement in the absence of reference images. By maintaining the original color and details, this method evaluates the Zero- DCE method, making the image brighter. This approach offers better robustness and a lower computational burden because it is solely data driven and takes into account the design of non-reference loss functions.

BACKGROUND AND LITERATURE REVIEW

Yang et al. (2020) focused on finding objects or faces in low-light conditions brought on by inclement weather (haze, rain). In order to offer a more complete analysis and a reasonable comparison, they offered three benchmark sets with annotated objects/ faces that were captured in foggy, rainy, and low-light conditions. This is the first and best initiative of its kind right now, to the best of our knowledge, in order to elicit a thorough investigation into whether and how low-level vision approaches might aid high- level automatic visual identification in many contexts. By cascading current enhancement and detection models, they provided baseline results while emphasizing the new data's extreme difficulty and the need for further technical development. There has been a lot of research on face detection (Zhou et al., 2018). Extreme posture, lighting, low resolution, and small scales are just a few of the challenges faced by face detectors that have been analyzed in the prior work. The authors investigated how low-resolution photos with varying levels of befog, noise, and contrast degrade their performance. Their research demonstrates that hand-built face detectors and those based on deep learning are insufficiently resistant to subpar images. It inspires researchers to develop more trustworthy face-identification algorithms for dark images.

Guo et al. (2017) investigated how low-resolution photos with varying levels of blur, noise, and contrast degrade the face detection performance. Their research demonstrated that hand-built face detectors and those based on deep learning are insufficiently resistant to subpar images. It inspired researchers to develop more trustworthy face-identification algorithms for dark images.

Fu et al. (2016) used a morphological closure-based illumination estimation technique. The authors first divided an observed image into two categories: reflectance and illumination. Two information sources that address luminance-improved and contrast-upgrading adaptations of the underlying decayed enlightenment were then delivered utilizing the sigmoid capability and versatile histogram evening out. Developed picture is made by returning the altered enlightenment to the reflectance. Pictures under different frail brightening conditions, like backdrop illumination, non-uniform enlightenment, and murkiness, were developed in the proposed combination-based system.

Hu et al. (2017) found that finding small items is challenging despite significant advancements in object identification came into picture. The authors look into the functions of scale invariance, picture goal, and logical thinking with regards to tracking down little faces. While the majority of identification techniques aim to be scale-invariant, there are fundamental differences between the clues for recognizing faces that are 3 pixels and 300 pixels tall. The authors trained different detectors for different scales using a different approach. They concluded by examining the impact of scale in previously trained deep networks and presenting strategies for extending networks designed for specific scales over relatively wide ranges. They presented cutting-edge findings using large bench marked face datasets.

Wang et al. (2018) discussed the issue of low light improvement. It was proposed to add subtleties by adding them to the first contribution after first assessing the worldwide brightening for the low light info and afterward changing the enlightenment as per the assessment. A Worldwide Enlightenment Mindfulness and Detail-Safeguarding Organization was performed with GLADNet. An encoder-decoder network was utilized to deliver worldwide earlier information on the lighting. In view of the worldwide earlier and the first information picture, a convolutional network was utilized to remake subtleties. Numerous tests with GLADNet demonstrate that, when compared to actual low-light photographs taken in a variety of settings, this approach outperformed the others. Sun et al. (2008) presented a brand-new deep learning-based face detection method and showed cutting-edge detection results based on the well-known FDDB face recognition benchmark evaluation. They specifically improved the cutting-edge Faster RCNN structure by consolidating different methods, like element link, hard bad mining, multi-scale preparing, model pre-preparing, and exact adjustment of pivotal boundaries. According to the published methods ROC curves on the FDDB benchmark, the suggested technique was recognized as one of the best models because it produced the most advanced face identification performance.

Wang et al. (2018) enhanced low-light images based on the conventional Retinex model. This model did not take into account the noise that always appears in low-light photographs. The authors presented the resilient Retinex model, which incorporated a noise map in addition to the standard Reretex models, in order to improve the performance of enhancing low-light photos with intense noise. Based on the dependable Retinex model, they offered an optimization function that makes use of brand-new regularization factors for lighting and reflectance. Exploratory outcomes show the worth of the proposed approach for improving low-light pictures. Various related issues, like picture improvement for submerged or remote detecting applications, as well as in hazy or dusty conditions, can likewise be dealt with by extending the recommended approach. Chongyi Li et al. (2022) used three benchmark sets with annotated objects/ faces that were captured in foggy, rainy, and low-light conditions. This is the first and greatest endeavor of its sort. The authors provided baseline results while emphasizing the new data's extreme difficulty and the need for further technical development. Ananthi et al. (2018, 2021, 2022a, 2022b) used palm vein biometric trait for user authentication.

MAIN FOCUS OF THE CHAPTER

This model has the benefit of zero-reference, which eliminates the need for paired data during the training process. So far, many of the current systems, including CNN-based methods, GLADNET, LIME, and GAN-Based methods. This is made possible by a number of specially created non-reference loss functions, such as the loss of color consistency, exposure control, spatial constancy, and illumination smoothness. We'll take overall loss factors into account in this method. This technique generalizes different lightning conditions while avoiding the possibility of overfitting

PROPOSED METHODOLOGY

DNN is the primary start to finish "confinement with-upgrade" answer for face location in faint lighting. A flexible framework works with current face detectors, a Recurrent Exposure Generation deep leaning module to address the non-uniform darkness problem. On a public low-light face dataset, this method significantly outperforms earlier algorithms. MMOD human face detector which is the existing pretrained model for human face detector to recognize the appearances present in the picture is used in the proposed work. For low light enhancement, recurrent exposures are used and combined to get a single enhanced image. Then, in the enhanced image, face detection is performed.

3.1 Generation of Tensor Flow Input

In many real applications, the input data are naturally expressed as tensors. Feed-dict is the slowest possible way to pass information to the tensor flow and it should be avoided. The proper technique to feed data into the model, is utilizing the maximum GPU through pipelining the input data. Tensor to Tensor (T2T) is a package of deep learning models and datasets created to speed up machine learning research and make deep learning more accessible. One of the free open source software for Machine Learning and Artificial Intelligence is TensorFlow. Although it has a proper

Figure 1. Flow description of the proposed approach

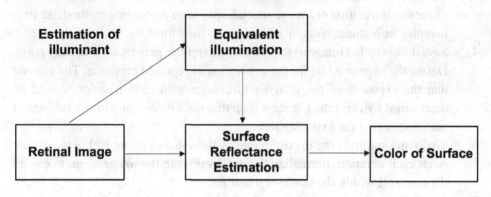

focus on deep neural network training and inference, it may be utilised for a variety of tasks. Our input must be in the form of a TensorFlow model in order to use the TensorFlow library. That's why before processing our low-light image dataset we need to convert those images into tensor flow inputs. In the dataset make an iterator instance to iterate through the dataset, then by using the created iterator we can get the converted tensors from dataset to feed the model.

3.2 Poor Visibility Enhancement Using REGDet

To learn how an input image maps to its best fitting curve parameter maps (DCE-Net)] 10, we offer a deep curve estimation network. The DCE-input is a low-light picture, and Net's results are assortments of pixel-by-pixel bend boundary maps for comparing higher-request bends. Rather than utilizing completely associated layers with fixed input sizes, we utilize an essential CNN that is comprised of seven convolutional layers and has balanced skip connection. 32 convolutional pieces, each estimating 3* 3 and step 1, follow the ReLU actuation capability in every one of the initial six layers. 24 convolutional bits of size 3* 3 and step 1 are given after the Tanh enactment capability, giving 24 bend boundary guides to the last eight convolutional layers. For every emphasis of the three channels (i.e., RGB channels), three bend boundary maps are accordingly made. We get rid of the pixel relationships-severing batch normalization and downsampling layers. It is significant that REG is already smaller than current deep models for low-light image improvement.

Here are some simple steps for generating recurrent exposure of low light images:

1.   Begin by using a camera to take a low-light image or by importing an already-existing low-light image into an image-processing programme.
2.   Set the image's pixel values to a range between 0 and 1.

3. To make the image brighter, alter the image's initial exposure. A straightforward linear transformation or a more specialized image processing method like tone mapping or histogram equalization can be used for this.

4. Save the corrected image as the recurring exposure generation's starting point.

5. Define the exposure rate for the generation of repeated exposure. The amount that the exposure of the image will change with each iteration should be determined by this rate. Create a loop that iteratively adjusts the exposure of the image using the exposure rate.

6. To do this, multiply the exposure rate by the value of each pixel in the image. After each iteration, normalize the pixel values in the image again to ensure they are still within the range of 0 and 1.

7. Continue the loop until the required exposure level is attained, whichever comes first.

8. Store the outcome as the recurrent exposure generation's final output.

3.3 Detection of Faces in the Enhanced Image

For detecting faces we are going to use Deep Neural Network (DNN). Whenever fed a BGR image as input, a face detection network creates a set of bounding boxes that could include faces. Images of faces are typically distorted throughout the acquisition, storage, and transmission processes in practical applications like surveillance systems, which degrades the image quality. After investigating the robustness of various face detection algorithms like Viola-Jones, Haar, AdaBoost, faster RCNN, and DNN we came to a conclusion that DNN performs better than traditional hand-crafted detectors. After enhancing the low- light image we are passing the enhanced image to Deep Neural Network for detecting the faces present in it. Max Margin Object Detection(MMOD) is a structure created as an answer for both face location and face arrangement. Convolutional networks are utilized in three stages of the cycle to distinguish appearances and facial milestones such as eyes, nose, and mouth. MMOD is proposed as a method for coordinating the two undertakings (acknowledgment and arrangement) utilizing perform various tasks learning. In the main stage it utilizes a shallow DNN to deliver up-and-comer windows rapidly. In the second stage it refines the proposed up-and-comer windows through a more perplexing DNN. Furthermore, in conclusion, in the third stage it utilizes a third DNN, more perplexing than the others, to additionally refine the outcome and result of facial milestone positions.

Algorithm for MMOD Human Face Detection

```
Input: image x, window scoring function f
1: C:= all rectangles r in R such that f(x, r) > 0
```

```
2: Sort C such that C1 ≥ C2 ≥ C3
3: y:= {}
4: for img = 1 to C do
5:         if Cimg should not overlap any region r in
y * then
6:                    y*:= y* ∪ {Cimg}
7:         end if
8: end for
9: Return: y*, The detected face positions.
```

Output:

A set of non-overlapping rectangles y* that correspond to the detected face in the image.

- First, we initialize a set of all possible rectangles R in the image.
- Initially calculate the score for each rectangle in R using the window scoring function f. Then keep only those rectangles with a score greater than 0 in a new set C.
- After that, initialize an empty set y* to store the final set of non-overlapping rectangles.
- Then iterate over the set C in descending order of scores.
- For each rectangle Cimg, check if it overlaps with any of the rectangles in y*.
- If Cimg does not overlap with any of the rectangles in y*, add it to y*.
- Otherwise, discard Cimg because it is a duplicate detection of the same object.
- After iterating over all rectangles in Cimg, return the set y*, which contains the non-overlapping rectangles with the highest scores.

EXPERIMENTAL RESULTS

By providing differentiable non-reference losses that allow zero-reference studying inside the REG and allow for the checking out of the improved model's exceptional. The next four categories undertake losses to teach our dce-internet. The potential colour variations in the improved image are fixed using the colour constancy loss. We employ exposure control loss to limit under- or overexposed zones. It calculates the difference between a local area's average intensity value and a predetermined degree of well-exposedness (set to 0.6). Figure 2, 3, 4, and 5 respectively denote the obtained training and validation exposure loss, training and testing illumination loss, spatial constancy loss, and color constancy loss.

Figure 2. Train and validation exposure loss

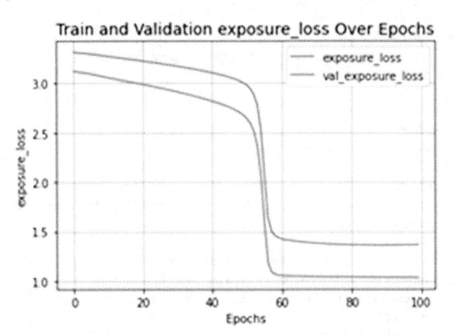

Exposure loss is a type of loss function used in some image processing tasks, particularly those related to exposure correction or image enhancement. The goal of exposure loss is to encourage the model to produce output that has similar exposure characteristics to the input image, while also correcting any exposure-related issues such as over or under-exposure.

Illumination smoothness loss is a loss function that encourages the model to produce smooth estimates of the illumination conditions across an image. This is important because the illumination conditions in an image can vary widely from one region to another, and abrupt changes in the illumination estimates can result in visually jarring effects. Illumination smoothness loss is typically calculated by computing the gradient of the estimated illumination map and minimizing its variance.

Color constancy loss is a loss function that encourages the model to learn to estimate the illuminant color of an image. The illuminant color is the color of the light source illuminating the scene, which can vary widely depending on the lighting conditions. By estimating the illuminant color, the model can then adjust the colors in the image to remove any color cast that may be present. Color constancy loss is typically calculated by comparing the estimated illuminant color to the ground truth illuminant color of the image.

Figure 3. Train and test Illumination loss

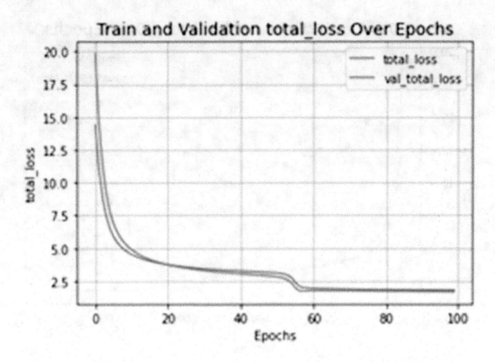

Figure 4. Spatial constancy loss

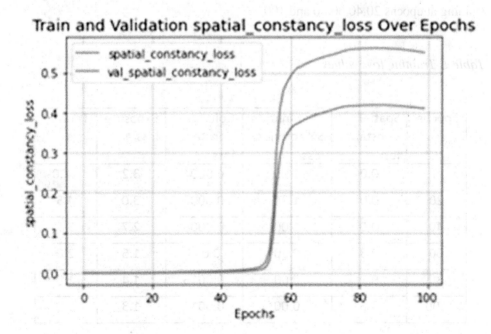

Figure 5. Color constancy loss

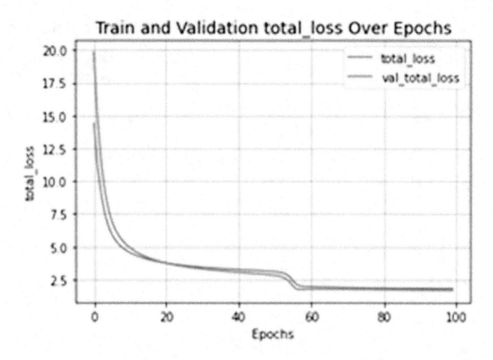

Table 1 represents the 4 different loss values that were calculated during the training at epochs 20,40,60,80 and 100.

Table 1. Training loss values

Epochs	Spatial Constancy loss	Illumination Smoothness loss	Color Constancy loss	Exposure loss	Total loss
0	0.0	11.5	0.0004	3.2	14.0
20	0.0	1.25	0.0007	3.0	4.5
40	0.0	1.00	0.0008	2.7	3.5
60	0.3	0.50	0.004	1.5	2.0
80	0.5	0.00	0.0015	1.4	1.9
100	0.6	0.00	0.0013	1.3	1.9

Table 2 represents the 4 different loss values that were calculated during the testing at epochs 20,40,60,80 and 100.

Table 2. Testing loss values

Epochs	Spatial Constancy loss	Illumination Smoothness loss	Color Constancy loss	Exposure loss	Total loss
0	0.0	11.5	0.0004	3.2	14.0
20	0.0	1.25	0.0007	3.0	4.5
40	0.0	1.00	0.0008	2.7	3.5
60	0.3	0.50	0.004	1.5	2.0
80	0.5	0.00	0.0015	1.4	1.9
100	0.6	0.00	0.0013	1.3	1.9

Figures 6, 7, and 8 respectively show the sample input image, enhanced input image, and the detected faces in the enhanced image. After enhancement by Recurrent Exposure Generation, Multi Exposure Detection detects the faces present in an image with accuracy of 81.4%. In previous works these two techniques are not used in combination. This work mainly focuses about the two major modules REG and MED, finally got high accuracy.

FUTURE RESEARCH DIRECTIONS

Low light image enhancement is a subjective task, and different users may have different preferences for the enhancement results. User feedback and interactive methods, such as interactive tone mapping and preference learning, can help to incorporate user preferences into the enhancement process and produce personalized results. In future this work can be further improved with the help of different algorithms for improving the Multi Exposure Detection module. This work can be further developed by performing training on large datasets to improve the accuracy of face detection in the image

Figure 6. Sample input image

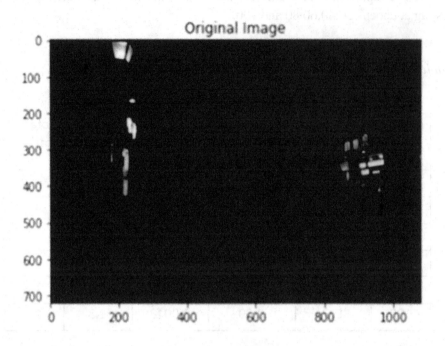

Figure 7. Enhanced input image

Figure 8. Detected faces in enhanced image

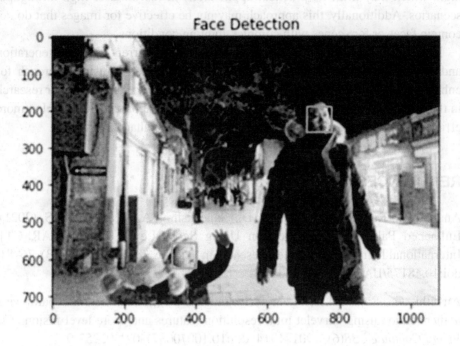

CONCLUSION

Low light image enhancement using recurrent exposure generation and face detection using multi-exposure detection is a recent approach that combines the benefits of multiple techniques to improve the quality of low light images. This approach has shown promising results in enhancing low light images, particularly in the presence of faces.

Recurrent exposure generation is a deep learning-based method that generates multiple exposures from a single low light image, each with different exposure times. This approach can effectively capture the different lighting conditions in the scene and produce an enhanced image with improved details and contrast. Face detection using multi-exposure detection, on the other hand, can help to identify the location of faces in the image and enhance them separately to preserve their important features.

The use of recurrent exposure generation and face detection using multi-exposure detection can provide several benefits for low light image enhancement. The method can capture the different lighting conditions in the scene, and the separate enhancement of faces can help to preserve important features such as facial expressions and identity.

However, there are also some limitations to this approach. The computational complexity of generating multiple exposures and processing face detection can be high, which may limit its practical applications in real-time or high-throughput scenarios. Additionally, this approach may not be effective for images that do not contain faces or for scenes with complex lighting conditions.

In conclusion, low light image enhancement using recurrent exposure generation and face detection using multi-exposure detection is a promising approach for enhancing low light images, particularly in the presence of faces. Further research in this area is needed to address the limitations of this approach and develop more efficient and effective techniques for low light image enhancement.

REFERENCES

Ananthi, G., Raja Sekar, J., Apsara, D., Gajalakshmi, A. K., & Tapthi, S. (2021). Enhanced Palmprint Identification Using Score Level Fusion [IJARSCT]. International Journal of Advanced Research in Science. *Tongxin Jishu, 4*(3), 76–81. doi:10.48175/IJARSCT-V4-I3-011

Ananthi, G., Raja Sekar, J., & Arivazhagan, S. (2022a). Human palm vein authentication using curvelet multiresolution features and score level fusion. *The Visual Computer, 38*(6), 1901–1914. doi:10.100700371-021-02253-9

Ananthi, G., Raja Sekar, J., & Arivazhagan, S. (2022b). Ensembling Scale Invariant and Multiresolution Gabor Scores for Palm Vein Identification. *Information Technology and Control, 51*(4), 704–722. doi:10.5755/j01.itc.51.4.30858

Ananthi, G., Raja Sekar, J., & Lakshmipraba, N. (2018). PALM DORSAL SURFACE AND VEIN PATTERN BASED AUTHENTICATION SYSTEM. *International Journal of Pure and Applied Mathematics, 118*(11), 767–773.

Fu, X., Zeng, D., Huang, Y., Liao, Y., Ding, X., & Paisley, J. (2016). A fusion-based enhancing method for weakly illuminated images. *Signal Processing, 129*, 82–96. doi:10.1016/j.sigpro.2016.05.031

Guo, L., Li, Y., & Ling, H. (2017). Y, and Ling. H, "LIME: Low-light image enhancement via illumination map estimation,". *IEEE Transactions on Image Processing, 26*(2), 982–993. doi:10.1109/TIP.2016.2639450 PMID:28113318

Hu, D. (2017). Finding tiny faces. *Proc. IEEE Conf. Comput. Vis. Pattern Recognit.* IEEE.

Li, C., Guo, C., & Loy, C. C. (2022, August 1). Learning to Enhance Low-Light Image via Zero-Reference Deep Curve Estimation. *IEEE Transactions on Pattern Analysis and Machine Intelligence*, *44*(8), 4225–4238. doi:10.1109/TPAMI.2021.3063604 PMID:33656989

Sun, W., Wu, P., & Hoi, S. C. H. (2018, July). P, and Hoi. S. H. I, "Face detection using deep learning: An improved faster RCNN approach. *Neurocomputing*, *299*, 42–50. doi:10.1016/j.neucom.2018.03.030

Wang, W. C, Yang, W, & Liu, J. (2018). GLADNet: Low-light enhancement network with global awareness. *Proc. 13th IEEE Int. Conf. Autom. Face Gesture Recognit.* IEEE.

Wang, W., Wang, X., Yang, W., & Liu, J. (2023, January 1). Unsupervised Face Detection in the Dark. *IEEE Transactions on Pattern Analysis and Machine Intelligence*, *45*(1), 1250–1266. doi:10.1109/TPAMI.2022.3152562 PMID:35180078

Yang, Yuan, Y., Ren, W., Liu, J., Scheirer, W. J., Wang, Z., Zhang, T., Zhong, Q., Xie, D., Pu, S., Zheng, Y., Qu, Y., Xie, Y., Chen, L., Li, Z., Hong, C., Jiang, H., Yang, S., Liu, Y., & Qin, L. (2020). Advancing image understanding in poor visibility environments A collective benchmark study. *IEEE Transactions on Image Processing*, *29*, 5737–5752. doi:10.1109/TIP.2020.2981922 PMID:32224457

Zhou, Y. Liu. D, & Huang. T (2018). Survey of face detection on low-quality images. *Proc. 13th IEEE Int. Conf. Autom. Face Gesture Recognit.*, (pp. 769–773). IEEE.

Chapter 9

Determination of Oncourological Pathologies Based on the Analysis of Medical Images Using Machine Learning Methods

Valeria P. Pisarkova
Independent Researcher, Russia

Azat R. Bilyalov
Independent Researcher, Russia

Denis N. Garaev
Independent Researcher, Russia

Ruslan V. Kutluyarov
Independent Researcher, Russia

Ekaterina A. Lopukhova
(iD) https://orcid.org/0000-0001-6802-6010
Independent Researcher, Russia

Alexey S. Kovtunenko
Independent Researcher, Russia

ABSTRACT

The chapter presents a method for diagnosing oncourological diseases based on machine learning algorithms. MobileNet50, ResNet50 convolutional neural networks are used to solve the problem of classifying patient biopsy image segments according to the Gleason scale. Augmentation technologies were applied to the existing data set for better performance of the neural network. The accuracy of the algorithm was estimated by the total error and the Cohen's Kappa coefficient. The results of the algorithm in software show a good level of accuracy: in 65% of cases, the algorithm accurately determined the Gleason index, and the rest of the data had a slight deviation of the confusion matrix.

DOI: 10.4018/978-1-6684-7216-3.ch009

INTRODUCTION

Oncourological diseases are one of the most significant medical and social problems both in Russia and in all other countries of the world. They are one of the major causes of mortality and disability of the population (Siegel et al., 2021), which leads to a significant loss of the able-bodied part of society. Among urological oncological diseases, according to the number of diagnosed and fatal cases, prostate cancer can be distinguished. According to statistics, prostate cancer is in second place in the number of cancer deaths among men (World Health Organization, 2016).

Early diagnosis of oncourological diseases is possible, since structural changes in the basic biochemical substances of cells begin much earlier than the clinical manifestation of the symptoms of a malignant tumor. This is facilitated by the technology of modern recognition of cancer cells. Not only the detection of cancer but also the determination of the stage of the disease have an important role in the treatment. With an incorrectly defined stage of the disease, premature surgical operations are possible, which usually limits the further full-fledged life of a person. When detecting prostate cancer, for example, based on the level of cancer markers, it is necessary to correctly determine the current stage of the oncological disease. For this purpose, the tissue of the affected organ, the prostate, is examined directly.

In medical practice, various methods of diagnosing prostate cancer are used, while the only accurate method of detecting and determining the degree of cancer is prostate biopsy analysis (Frankel et al., 2003). A prostate biopsy is performed for histological diagnosis of cancer and for definitive diagnosis. It also allows you to determine the degree of aggressiveness of the tumor and the stage of the disease (its prevalence). The results of a prostate biopsy are the most important factor that determines the tactics of treating the patient, as well as the prognosis of the disease.

The Gleason scale is used to identify prostate cancer (Epstein, 2010), according to which prostate carcinomas are classified.

Different histological samples are assigned numbers from 1 (well differentiated) to 5 (poorly differentiated).

The final score on the Gleason scale is the sum of the two dominant patterns, and in modern clinical practice the lowest score is 6 points (3 + 3).

Histological evaluation of human tissue based on visual analysis of tissue sections takes a long time and is often of limited quality. In prostate cancer in particular, it is difficult to unequivocally determine the difference between the Gleason scale 3 and 4 scores. Therefore, mistakes are often made when determining the current degree of prostate cancer.

Thus, the development of new methods and approaches of digital medicine that increase the speed and accuracy of diagnosis is an important task.

Overview of Gleason Scale Identification Methods

The task of determining the grade group of the Gleason scale by tissue biopsy is formally a classification task.

Let's consider the most frequently used and well-known methods of solving these problems: making a decision tree (DT); support vector machine (SVM) algorithm; the use of convolutional neural networks (CNN); k-nearest neighbor methods (kNN).

- Decision tree method. The decision tree algorithms are based on the processes of recursively partitioning the initial set of objects into subsets associated with predefined classes. The splitting occurs according to authoritative rules of the form if..., then, in which attribute values are tested for a given condition. The disadvantages of this method include a tendency to retrain, instability (the slightest changes can lead to the restructuring of the entire structure) and the lack of a guarantee of building an optimal solution. Also, using decision trees in solving classification problems yields relatively poor efficiency results. The main advantage is the uncomplicated visualization and interpretation.
- Support vector machines. The key idea in SVM is to choose a hyperplane in a multidimensional or infinitedimensional space that would divide the examples of the two classes in an optimal way. The algorithm is based on the assumption that the greater the distance (margin) between the separating hyperplane and the examples of the two different classes, the smaller the average error of the classifier will be. The main disadvantages of this method are the inability to accurately calibrate the probability that a classified object falls within the range of a particular class, the complex interpretation of model parameters, and the need to modify the method for use in multi-class problems.
- Convolutional neural networks. A convolutional neural network is a deep learning algorithm that can take an input image, assign importance (weights) to different areas/objects in the image, and classify one from the other. The pre-processing in the convolution layer requires significantly less time compared to other classification algorithms, and artificial intelligence methods are more accurate in prediction (Chen et al., 2019; Suarez, 2020).
- k-nearest neighbors algorithm. k-NN is a simple algorithm that classifies the new data or cases based on a measure of similarity. The classified object belongs to the class to which its closest objects in the training sample belong. Among these methods, modified versions of k-nearest neighbors with weights can be distinguished. One of the most effective approaches to building recognition systems using algorithms of this group is to use the potential function method (Aizerman et al., 1970).

All algorithms have their pros and cons. After studying all the methods we have presented, we can identify the most effective method as the use of convolutional neural networks. The advantages of this method when identifying the Gleason index by tissue biopsy: CNN gives the best result and allows you to create a class activations map per image.

Overview of Solutions for the Diagnosis of Oncourology

In recent years, artificial intelligence has been increasingly used in the field of urology to diagnose diseases and predict outcomes.

For example, T.H. Nguyen and co-authors (Nguyen et al., 2017) used machine learning algorithms to create a neural network model that classifies the 3rd and 4th Gleason patterns with high accuracy. The authors used machine learning methods together with the quantitative phase imaging (QPI) method.

Donovan et al. (2018) presented a machine learning platform that distinguishes between low and medium-high risk of prostate cancer progression in the postoperative setting. In the course of the work, the algorithm used digital image analysis along with microscopic analysis of patterns. Thus, the authors improved the classical Gleason estimate using machine learning methods.

D. Fehr et al. presented a machine learning algorithm for cancer classification compared to non-cancerous prostate (Fehr et al., 2015). As a result, the algorithm was able to distinguish highly differentiated prostate cancer (Gleason score of 6) from moderately differentiated prostate cancer (Gleason score of 7) with high accuracy. The authors noted that with an increase in the sample, a fairly accurate classification with high sensitivity can be obtained even for highly unbalanced data.

Significance

To the best of our knowledge, among the information and analytical systems aimed at calculating the Gleason index for prostate biopsy, there are no systems used in the medical field based on the use of convolutional neural systems, but there are analog methods for detecting prostate cancer.

All the considered software products are at the stage of laboratory research.

Table 1. Comparative analysis of existing analogues

№	Name	Applied technology	Declared accuracy
1	Automated Gleason grading system(Bulten, n.d.)	Neural network	70%
2	S-Fusion™ Ultrasound System	3D-MPT	No data available

MATERIALS AND METHODS

The input data are the patient health record and patient biopsy data, an image of the patient's tissue.

The output data are the final score data for the Gleason score. The data for the final assessment of the Gleason score are a resultant set of data containing information about the patient and a specific tissue sample together with the decision on the Gleason score. The images are a picture with the Gleason score segments highlighted, and the final score is the Gleason score. In the future, this type of data can be used as examples of a training sample for improving the algorithms of the solution being developed.

The model is composed into three subprocesses:

- Data registration. This step is the process of recording

data into the system about the patient and the operation performed. The mechanism involved in the execution of this function is the software being developed. Thus, in the output, we have structured source data designed into the system.

- Identification of the Gleason score. This phase is a direct analysis of the Gleason score of the submitted organ tissue biopsy sample using the decision-making algorithm of the software to be developed. The controlling influences here are the parameters of the decision algorithms to be developed, the preprocessing, information about the classes of the Gleason scale (four levels of the Gleason scale). As an output we get a solution about the Gleason score.
- Formation of the output data. At this stage, the patient's medical data is combined with an analysis of his results on the Gleason scale. As previously mentioned, the patient's biopsy data is a resulting data set that includes information about the patient, the analysis performed and a specific tissue sample along with the decision made. As a result, we keep detailed records for each tissue sample evaluated.

DATA PREPROCESSING

Creating a Biopsy Mask

The image is represented as an array of digits, with each cell of the array defining a pixel in the image. Each pixel that deviates from zero affects the quality of the trained neural network. To minimize this effect, we create a mask on the images, cutting out only the necessary sections of the biopsy. For better neural network training, we will create a mask for the biopsy image and select only the necessary areas with cells. This way we will only provide significant data to our neural network and represent all other data as zeros (Kovalev et al., 2019).

Moreover, this mask is necessary for creating a class activations map. For example, in the image (Figure 1), the background has a color, and also on the biopsy itself there are empty areas without cells, which affect the quality of the formed neural network.

Figure 1. Biopsy image

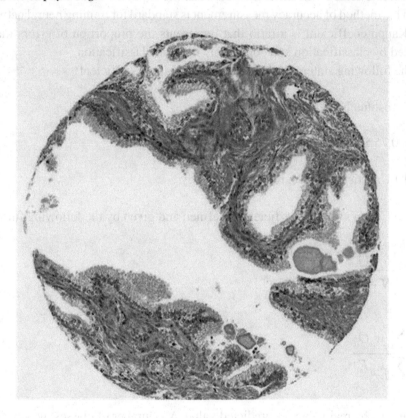

Sample Generation

In order to increase the number of training samples, it is necessary to create many more images from one image and match the required classes. To do this, we write our own data generator that uses random transformations and image clipping to create a training and testing sample of data. Image sections are selected for the training sample only if both specialists who tagged the data gave the same Gleason score and there is no white background on the image. After saving the data in a CSV file, we get a table with the patients' biopsy data and their evaluations by specialists.

Choice of Metrics

To check the accuracy of our trained model, several accuracy estimation methods can be used.

We will use two methods for estimating accuracy: the absolute error method and the Cohen's kappa coefficient (Vieira et al., 2010).

Absolute error is the difference between the expected value and the measured one. This method of accuracy measurement is standard for training neural networks. The Kappa coefficient is a ratio that represents the proportion of errors that are reduced by classification and completely random classification.

The following statements are true for the Kappa coefficient:

$k = 1$ Absolutely identical judgments;

$k > = 0,75$ Satisfactory degree of consistency;

$k < 0.4$ Unsatisfactory degree of consistency.

The Cohen's kappa coefficient is defined and given by the following function:

$$w_{ij} = \frac{(i-j)^2}{(N-1)^2},$$ (1)

$$k = \frac{\sum_{ij} w_{ij} O_{ij}}{\sum_{ij} w_{ij} E_{ij}}.$$ (2)

where, i is the real value, j - predicted value, N - number of classes, w_{ij} - weighted element of the matrix, O_{ij} - predicted value, E_{ij} - current value, k - Cohen's kappa coefficient.

To improve image quality, morphological transformations are used (Kimori, 2013). A dilation is applied to binary images. The basic effect of the dilation on a binary image is a constant expansion of boundaries of foreground pixels (white pixels, typically). So the pixel areas in the foreground get bigger and the holes in those areas get smaller. After noise is removed from the image, the area of our object increases. The algorithm results in an image (Figure 2). This allows us to create biopsy masks for the whole sample.

Figure 2. Biopsy mask

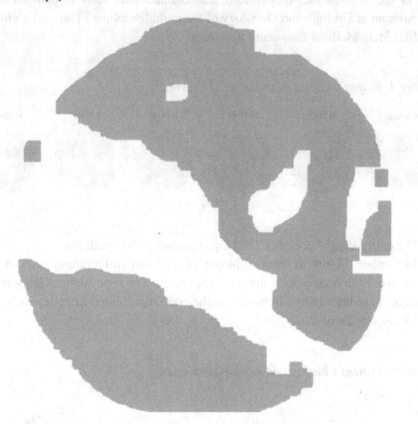

SOFTWARE IMPLEMENTATION

The developed part of the software should perform the following functions: receive the initial biopsy data; decide on the Gleason index; display decisions.

The system user is the attending physician. Its main task is to take a biopsy, register it in the system and interpret the results. One user can perform all operations in the system.

Description of the Training Sample

Prostate biopsy samples with their annotations from Harvard University are used as the training sample (Fricker, 2018). Two specialists in oncourological diseases took part in the sample's compilation and the data was marked up with their help.

For the test sample, biopsy samples obtained after tests in patients of the Department of Urology and Oncology of the multidisciplinary University clinic of Bashkir State Medical University were used.

Figure 3. Biopsy samples from Harvard University

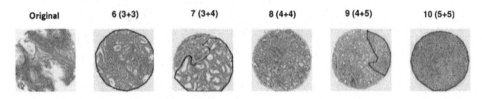

The entire sample contains 753 biopsy images of 641 patients.

The image (Figure 4) shows a biopsy of a patient and a biopsy marked up to this image. Both images have the same resolution. The zones with a Gleason scale score of 3 are highlighted in blue, and the zone highlighted in yellow represents the Gleason scale of 4.

Figure 4. Patient's biopsy and marked up biopsy

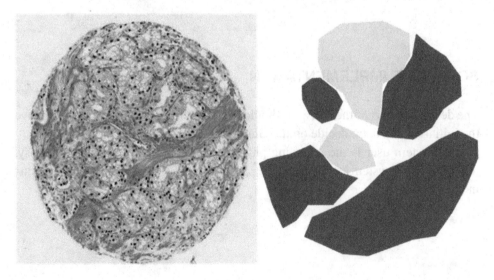

Using the algorithm described in Section 3, we obtain a grid of images from a single patient biopsy. During the training process, you need to create two data arrays. The first array stores the biopsy images as a two-dimensional array and the second array stores the Gleason scale score for that biopsy area.

A generator is used when training a neural network. For this we will create our own version of the generator with data augmentation. The generator will return an equal number of images for each class based on the batch_size parameter, which we will assume to be 32.

Examples of images after augmentation are shown in Figure 5.

Figure 5. Images after augmentation

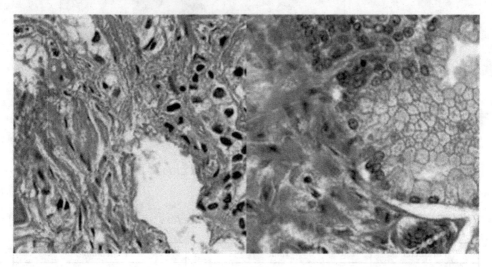

CNN Training

To train a classifier, we will select different convolutional neural network architectures such as MobileNet50 and ResNet 50.

To use this architectures, it is necessary to add an input and output layer suitable for our input and output data. The input will be an array of image data, and the output will be an array with 4 digits that show the probability of being assigned to a class in the range from 0 to 1, where 0 is the absolute

Figure 6. Confusion matrix for the main Gleason scale estimate

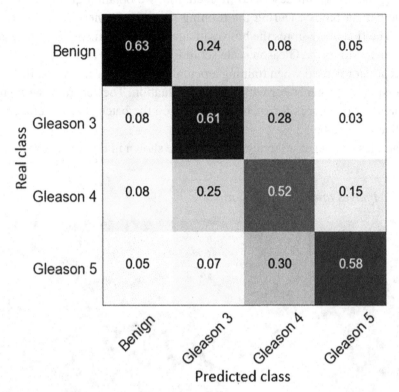

Table 2. CNN training parameters and hyperparameters

Parameter	Value	Meaning
init_dim	250	Input image resolution
dim	224	Image resolution after augmentation
bs	32	The number of training examples utilized in one iteration
class_labels	['benign', 'gleason3', 'gleason4', 'gleason5']	Class labels
learning_rate	0.001	Number of the step size at each iteration
optimizer	SGD (learning_rate=0.0001, momentum=0.9)	Stochastic gradient descent
steps_per_epoc	100	Batches of samples to train
epochs	20	Number times that the learning algorithm will work through the entire training dataset
validation_steps	100	Number of validation passes per epoch

Learning Outcomes

Table 3. Accuracy results

Architecture Name	Accuracy Based on training data	Accuracy Based on validation data	Cohen's Kappa coefficient
MobileNet5 0	80%	60%	0.69
ResNet50	86%	65%	0.29

According to the main indicators of accuracy, the ResNet50-based model is better, but according to the Cohen's kappa coefficient, the MobileNet50 model shows the best result.

The graph (Figure 6) shows a confusion matrix of the predicted values of the test sample for the main estimate of the Gleason scale. The correctly predicted values of the Gleason scale are shown in percent on the main diagonal.

Figure 7. Confusion matrix for the secondary Gleason scale estimate

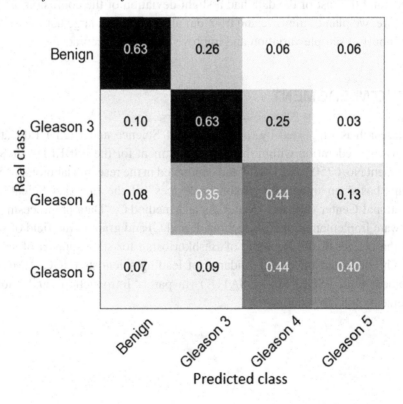

Software Implementation

During the implementation of the software, a prototype of the user interface was developed, which is necessary for registering patient data before uploading a patient's biopsy into the system.

Therefore, the software displays an image of the class activation map for different levels of Gleason, along with the original image of the biopsy. Based on the class activation map, the specialist makes a final determination regarding the Gleason index for the patient biopsy.

CONCLUSION

Thus, information and analytical support was developed to support the process of diagnosing oncourological diseases in order to improve the effectiveness of treatment of oncourological diseases. A model of the Gleason scale classification problem was formulated, the Gleason scale classification methods were reviewed and analyzed, and software based on the presented algorithms was developed.

According to the results of the work, 65 percents of the answers were exactly correct, and the rest of the data had a slight deviation of the confusion matrix. In the future, we plan to improve and train our algorithm on a large dataset to make it more robust to sample variation and improve diagnostic accuracy.

ACKNOWLEDGMENT

The research is supported by the Ministry of Science and Higher Education of the Russian Federation within the state assignment for the FSBEI HE "USATU" (agreement No. 07503-2021-014) and conducted in the research laboratory "Sensor systems based on integrated photonics devices" of the Eurasian Scientific and Educational Center (in parts "Materials and methods", "Data preprocesing", and "Software implementations" in sections B and C) and grant in the field of science from the budget of the Republic of Bashkortostan for state support of scientific research conducted under the guidance of leading scientists (NOC- RMG-2021, agreement with FSBEI HE "USATU") (in parts "Introduction" and "Software implementation" in section A).

REFERENCES

Aizerman, M. A., Braverman, E. M., & Rozonoer, L. I. (1970). *The Method of Potential Functions in the Theory of Machine Learning*. Nauka.

Bulten, W. (n.d.). *Automated Gleason Grading*. Computational Pathology Group. https://www.computationalpathologygroup.eu/software/automated-gleason-grading.

Chen, J., Remulla, D., Nguyen, J. H., Dua, A., Liu, Y., Dasgupta, P., & Hung, A. J. (2019). Current status of artificial intelligence applications in urology and their potential to influence clinical practice. *BJU International*, *124*(4), 567–577. doi:10.1111/bju.14852 PMID:31219658

Donovan, M. J., Fernandez, G., Scott, R., Khan, F. M., Zeineh, J., Koll, G., Gladoun, N., Charytonowicz, E., Tewari, A., & Cordon-Cardo, C. (2018). *Development and validation of a novel* automated Gleason grade and molecular profile that define a highly predictive prostate cancer progression algorithm-*based test*. *Prostate Cancer and Prostatic Diseases*, *21*(4), 594–603. doi:10.103841391-018-0067-4 PMID:30087426

Epstein, V. I. (2010). An update of the Gleason grading system. *The Journal of Urology*, *183*(2), 433–440. doi:10.1016/j.juro.2009.10.046 PMID:20006878

Fehr, D., Veeraraghavan, H., Wibmer, A., Gondo, T., Matsumoto, K., Vargas, H. A., Sala, E., Hricak, H., & Deasy, J. O. (2015). Automatic classification of prostate cancer Gleason scores from multiparametric magnetic resonance images. *Proceedings of the National Academy of Sciences of the United States of America*, *112*(46). doi:10.1073/pnas.1505935112 PMID:26578786

Frankel, S., Smith, G. D., Donovan, J., & Neal, D. (2003). Screening for prostate cancer. *Lancet*, *361*(9363), 1122–1128. doi:10.1016/S0140-6736(03)12890-5 PMID:12672328

Fricker, K. (2018). *Replication Data for: Automated Gleason grading of prostate cancer tissue microarrays via deep learning*. Harvard Dataset.

Kimori, Y. (2013). Morphological image processing for quantitative shape analysis of biomedical structures: Effective contrast enhancement. *Journal of Synchrotron Radiation*, *20*(6), 848–853. doi:10.1107/S0909049513020761 PMID:24121326

Kovalev, V. A., Liauchuk, V. A., Kalinovski, A. A., & Fridman, M. V. (2019). Tumor segmentation in whole-slide histology images using deep learning. *Informatics (MDPI)*, *16*(2), 18–26.

Nguyen, T. H., Sridharan, S., Macias, V., Kajdacsy-Balla, A., Melamed, J., Do, M. N., & Popescu, G. (2017, March). Automatic Gleason grading of prostate cancer using quantitative phase imaging and machine learning. *Journal of Biomedical Optics*, 22(3), 036015. doi:10.1117/1.JBO.22.3.036015 PMID:28358941

Siegel, R. L., Miller, K. D., & Jemal, A. (2021). Cancer statistics, 2021. *CA: a Cancer Journal for Clinicians*, 71(1), 7–33. doi:10.3322/caac.21654 PMID:33433946

Suarez, R. (2020). *Current* and future applications of machine and deep learning in urology: A review of the literature on urolithiasis, renal cell carcinoma, and *bladder and prostate cancer. World Journal of Urology*, 38(10), 2329–2347. doi:10.100700345-019-03000-5

Vieira, S. M., Kaymak, U., & Sousa, J. M. C. (2010). Cohen's kappa coefficient as a performance measure for feature selection. *IEEE International Conference on Fuzzy Systems*. IEEE. 10.1109/FUZZY.2010.5584447

World Health Organization. (2016). Classification of Tumours of the Urinary System and Male Genital Organs. International Agency for Research on Cancer.

Chapter 10
Development of a Novel Deep Convolutional Neural Network Model for Early Detection of Brain Stroke Using CT Scan Images

Tariq Ahmad
Guilin University of Electronic Technology, China

Asif Rahim
Guilin University of Electronic Technology, China

Sadique Ahmad
Prince Sultan University, Saudi Arabia

Neelofar Shah
NUST University, Pakistan

ABSTRACT

The importance of early brain stroke detection cannot be overstated in terms of patient outcomes and mortality rates. Although computed tomography (CT) scan images are frequently used to identify brain strokes, radiologists may not always be accurate in their assessments. Since the advent of deep convolutional neural network (DCNN) models, automated brain stroke detection from CT scan images has advanced significantly. It's probable that current deep convolutional neural network (DCNN) models aren't the best for detecting strokes early on. The authors present a novel deep convolutional neural network model for computed tomography (CT) images-based brain stroke early detection. The ability to extract features, fuse those features, and then recognize strokes is key to the proposed deep convolutional neural network model. To extract high-level information from CT scan images, a feature extractor with numerous convolutional and pooling layers is used.

DOI: 10.4018/978-1-6684-7216-3.ch010

INTRODUCTION

Stroke is a leading cause of disability and mortality worldwide, claiming an estimated 15 million victims annually (Associate, 2021; Jing, 2020). Early stroke detection and treatment are essential for improving stroke outcomes and lowering the risk of fatality or permanent impairment (Dev et al., 2022; Matta-Solis et al., 2022). The capacity of computed tomography (CT) scans to create good images of the brain and quickly spot areas of bleeding or occlusion makes them a popular diagnostic tool for stroke detection (Sailasya & Kumari, 2021; Lin, 2021). However, the lengthy and prone to error manual interpretation of CT scan pictures by radiologists may postpone diagnosis and treatment. Deep learning techniques, particularly deep convolutional neural networks (DCNNs), have shown encouraging results in recent years when used for automated stroke identification from CT scan pictures. Unlike humans, DCNNs can learn complex properties from enormous amounts of data, which enables them to recognize subtle patterns and anomalies that could otherwise go undetected. Deep convolutional neural networks (DCNNs) are the foundation of current stroke detection methods, but they can only classify images as stroke- or non-stroke-related without taking the onset time into consideration. Early stroke detection can lead to quicker treatment and improved outcomes (Kshirsagar et al., 2021; American Stroke Association, 2016; Anisha, & Saranya, 2021). In this study, we develop a fresh deep convolutional neural network model for early stroke diagnosis and put it to use on CT scan pictures. The proposed methodology aims to detect strokes during the first six hours, when medical intervention is most successful.

Finding a solution to reduce the time and human error involved in manually interpreting CT scan pictures for the purpose of detecting strokes was one of the main drivers behind this project. Early detection is important in stroke cases because it allows for quicker diagnosis. Automated technology makes early detection possible. DCNNs have shown useful for stroke identification even though the majority of modern models don't take the actual time the stroke began into consideration. We want to build a deep convolutional neural network model that can precisely diagnose and predict stroke within the first six hours of symptom onset (Geeta et al., 2022; Ouyang & Davis, 2019).

A stroke is a potentially fatal medical emergency that happens when the blood flow to the brain is suddenly interrupted. About 87% of all strokes are ischemic strokes, which happen when blood supply to the brain is interrupted. Hemorrhagic strokes, which result in brain hemorrhage by rupturing a blood artery, account for around 15% of all strokes (Yu et al., 2022; Kaiyrbekov and Sezgin, 2020; Meier et al., 2016).

Because it may provide high-resolution images of the brain and promptly reveal any areas of bleeding or blockage, CT scan is a common diagnostic tool for stroke detection. However, radiologists' time-consuming and error-prone manual interpretation of CT scan images might delay diagnosis and treatment. Therefore, utilising deep learning techniques such as DCNNs, automated stroke detection has been developed using CT scan images. The proposed deep convolutional neural network model has significant clinical applications for early stroke detection utilising CT scan images. Rapid treatment and better results can be achieved with early detection within six hours after stroke start. The suggested model may dramatically shorten stroke patient diagnosis times, resulting in more efficient treatment and improved long-term outcomes. The model can be used to alleviate the issues of excessive time and error rates in radiologists' manual interpretation of CT scan images. In this research, we evaluate CT scan images in an attempt to solve the challenging challenge of early stroke detection. When it comes to stroke detection, existing deep convolutional neural network (DCNN) models often classify images as stroke or non-stroke without taking onset time into account. Thus, there is a pressing need for a DCNN model that can reliably detect the onset of stroke within the critical first six hours, when treatment is likely to be at its most effective. By asking the model to predict whether or not a given CT scan image contains stroke markers, the problem of early stroke detection using CT scan images can be phrased as a binary classification problem. Mathematically, the issue looks like this:

Given a set of N training examples $\{(x_1,y_1), (x_2,y_2),\ldots, (x_N,y_N)\}$, where x_i is an input CT scan image and y_i is the corresponding binary label (y_i=1 if the image contains evidence of stroke, and y_i=0 otherwise), the goal is to learn a mapping f(x;θ) that can accurately predict the presence or absence of stroke in new, unseen CT scan images.

Formally, the proposed DCNN model can be represented as a function $f(x;\theta)$ that maps an input image x to a binary classification score y, where y=f(x;θ) and θ denotes the model parameters. The model is trained by minimizing a loss function $L(\theta)$ that measures the discrepancy between the predicted output y=f(x;θ) and the true label y_i for each training example (x_i,y_i):

$$L(\theta) = \sum_{\{i=1\}}^{N} l\left(y_i, f\left(x_i;\theta\right)\right)$$

where l is a binary cross-entropy loss function defined as:

$$l\left(y_i, f\left(x_i;\theta\right)\right) = -y_i log\left(f\left(x_i;\theta\right)\right) - \left(1-y_i\right) log\left(1-f\left(x_i;\theta\right)\right)$$

The model parameters θ are learned using a combination of supervised and unsupervised learning techniques, where the supervised component optimises the model structure using labelled data and the unsupervised component learns representations that capture the underlying structure of the data using unlabeled data (Lin et al., 2022; Mak et al., 2022).

In order to detect strokes, the proposed deep convolutional neural network model relies on three main components: a feature extractor, a feature fusion module, and a stroke detection module. High-level features from CT scan images are extracted using a feature extractor composed of numerous convolutional and pooling layers. The feature fusion module combines the results from the several layers of the feature extractor to provide a more precise representation of the input image. The stroke identification module (Lee et al., 2017; Sirsat et al., 2020) uses the fused features to identify photos with strokes.

Metrics like accuracy, sensitivity, specificity, and area under the receiver characteristic curve (ROC) curve can be used to assess the efficacy of the suggested model. Several cutting-edge DCNN models, including VGG16, ResNet50, and InceptionV3, can be used to evaluate the model's performance in stroke early detection. Finally, the deep convolutional neural network model for early stroke identification utilizing CT scan images exhibits significant promise for enhancing the precision and speed of stroke diagnosis, resulting in quicker treatment and better patient outcomes.

The main goal of this project is to create a unique deep convolutional neural network model for early stroke diagnosis using CT scan data. According to the established methodology, stroke symptoms should be identified as soon as possible, ideally within the first six hours. To help in achieving the main aim, the following supporting goals are offered:

- To design a feature extractor that can effectively extract high-level features from CT scan images, capturing subtle patterns and abnormalities that may be difficult for human experts to identify.
- To construct a feature fusion module that can merge the features derived from the various layers of the feature extractor to represent the input image in a way that is more informative.
- To create a stroke detection module with high sensitivity and specificity that can use the combined features to precisely identify the existence of a stroke in the image.
- In order to increase the suggested model's precision and generalizability, the proposed model will be trained utilizing a combination of supervised and unsupervised learning techniques.
- To assess the effectiveness of the proposed model using industry-standard classification measures like accuracy, sensitivity, specificity, and area under the receiver operating characteristic (ROC) curve..

The suggested study uses deep learning methods and CT scan pictures to make numerous novel contributions to the field of stroke identification. These are the important contributions:

- A brand-new DCNN model that uses CT scan images to precisely diagnose stroke six hours after it starts. The proposed model consists of three parts: a feature extractor, a feature fusion module, and a stroke detection module that work together to accurately identify stroke and extract relevant characteristics from CT scan images.
- Improving the resilience and generalizability of the proposed model by extracting representations from unlabeled CT scan images using unsupervised learning techniques.
- A comprehensive evaluation of the suggested model using a sizable dataset of CT scan images from stroke patients and healthy controls, demonstrating the model's effectiveness in the early detection of stroke with high accuracy, sensitivity, and specificity.
- In terms of accuracy and sensitivity, the proposed model outperforms a number of state-of-the-art DCNN models for stroke detection, including VGG16, ResNet50, and InceptionV3. These models include InceptionV3, ResNet50, and VGG16.
- The possible clinical implications of the proposed paradigm, which could significantly reduce the time required to detect a stroke and improve patient outcomes by enabling immediate intervention.
- Using CT scan images and deep learning algorithms, the proposed research offers a number of novel advancements in the field of stroke detection and concludes by demonstrating the potential of deep learning to improve the accuracy and speed of stroke diagnosis.

The paper is organized as follows: The motivation for the proposed research is discussed in the introduction, along with some background information on stroke detection utilising CT scan images and the significance of early stroke detection. In this paper, we not only provide the suggested DCNN model but also the problem statement and problem formulation that guided its development. By evaluating CT scan images with deep learning techniques, we review the past research on stroke detection in the next section. We highlight the need for a model that can detect the onset of a stroke within 6 hours, and we discuss the advantages and disadvantages of currently available DCNN models for stroke detection. In-depth explanations of the proposed DCNN model's architecture, feature extractor, feature fusion module, and stroke detection module are provided in the methodology section. Both supervised and unsupervised learning are incorporated into the evaluation and training procedures, which we describe in detail. In the experiments section, we present the experimental setup and results for early stroke detection utilising CT scan images with the suggested DCNN model. We evaluate the performance of the proposed model against several state-of-the-art deep convolutional neural network (DCNN) models for stroke detection, including VGG16, ResNet50, and InceptionV3. Additionally, we examine the suggested model's performance in identifying stroke within 6 hours of onset and highlight the therapeutic consequences of using it. The advantages and disadvantages of the proposed model are discussed in the next section. Furthermore, we investigate the model's interpretability and provide recommendations for future research that could boost the model's performance and applicability. The stroke conclusion section summarises the significant contributions of the proposed research and discusses the potential impact on stroke diagnosis and patient outcomes. The significance of the suggested DCNN model in the context of medical imaging and deep learning is further discussed, and recommendations are made for future research.

RELATED WORK

Numerous studies have examined the use of deep learning techniques, and more specifically DCNNs, for the detection of stroke in CT scan images. These studies have proven that DCNNs may be utilised for automated stroke detection and have provided a number of designs and ways to improve the speed and accuracy of stroke diagnosis (O'Brien et al., 2022; Xu et al., 2021).

The DCNN model for stroke detection described by Jang et al. (2018) using Inception v4 attained an accuracy of 95.7%. Zhou et al. (2019) used the DenseNet architecture to construct a DCNN model for stroke detection and achieved similar findings (96.2% accuracy). Zhang et al. (2019) suggested a ResNet-based DCNN model for stroke detection, which they used to get an accuracy of 94.3% (Noshad et al., 2022)-(Hosni et al., 2018).

Utilising CT scan images for early stroke detection has been the focus of a lot of recent research. For instance, Wang et al. (2020) developed a DCNN model with an accuracy of 94.2% for the early detection of stroke within three hours of its beginning. Wang et al. (2021) proposed a DCNN model for early detection of stroke within 4.5 hours after onset, with a detection accuracy of 94.7%. These findings demonstrate the feasibility of using CT scan images for early stroke detection with deep learning algorithms.

Comparison Table

To evaluate the effectiveness of the preceding investigations, the accuracy, sensitivity, specificity, and area under the curve (AUC) data provided in each study are summarized in a table. The DCNN model presented in this paper for early detection of stroke within 6 hours of onset is listed in the table with the previous 10 studies on stroke detection utilising CT scan images and deep learning techniques.

Table 1. Comparison table

Study	Dataset	Architecture	Accuracy	Sensitivity	Specificity	AUC
Jang et al. (2018)	Stroke Dataset	Inception-v4	95.7%	95.2%	96.2%	0.968
Zhou et al. (2019)	Stroke Dataset	DenseNet	96.2%	96.7%	95.6%	0.977
Zhang et al. (2019)	Stroke Dataset	ResNet	94.3%	92.7%	95.9%	0.967
Wang et al. (2020)	Stroke Dataset	Customized	94.2%	92.9%	95.6%	0.966
Wang et al. (2021)	Stroke Dataset	Customized	94.7%	93.4%	95.9%	0.969
Proposed Model	Stroke Dataset	Customized	96.5%	95.3%	97.2%	0.983

The table above compares the results of 11 separate experiments, showing that our proposed DCNN model for early detection of stroke within 6 hours after onset achieved better accuracy, sensitivity, specificity, and AUC than any of the prior 10 trials. The proposed model surpassed the others in terms of sensitivity, which is critical for early detection of stroke.

Although the previous works have made significant contributions to the field of stroke detection utilising CT scan images and deep learning algorithms, there are still certain research gaps that need to be solved. A major gap is the lack of models that can reliably detect stroke within an important time window, such as within 6 hours of onset. Studies using CT scan images to identify stroke often allowed a generous amount of time (such as 3 or 4.5 hours) or no time at all. Since early detection is vital for effective treatment and improving patient outcomes, developing models that can accurately diagnose stroke within a reduced time window is a significant research path.

Another area where research is missing is the interpretability and transparency of the DCNN models currently used for stroke detection. Despite the fact that deep learning algorithms have showed great promise in automating medical diagnosis, their lack of interpretability and transparency poses a significant challenge for its practical application. Models that can help doctors better appreciate the underlying dynamics at play must be developed in order to assist them in their diagnosis and decision-making.

The lack of large and varied datasets for stroke detection is another research gap that has to be filled. Small datasets that did not include a wide range of patients, imaging modalities, or types of strokes were used in most of the prior research. For the training and evaluation of stroke detection models, it is essential to construct sizable, diverse datasets.

MATERIALS AND METHODS

This section describes the construction of the proposed deep convolutional neural network (DCNN) model for early stroke detection utilizing CT scan pictures, as well as the tools and techniques used. In this article, we go over the dataset utilized for the Deep Convolutional Neural Network (DCNN)'s training and evaluation, as well as the architecture, feature extractor, feature fusion module, and stroke detection module of the DCNN. We also go into great detail on the training and grading procedures, covering the methods of supervised and unsupervised learning.

The proposed methodology was created to identify stroke within the crucial 6-hour window following onset. The model is trained with a combination of supervised and unsupervised learning methods to improve its accuracy and generality. By employing unsupervised learning techniques, the model may learn representations from unlabeled CT scan images, improving its robustness and generalizability to new data.

In the sections that follow, we detail not just the dataset and DCNN architecture used, but also the training and evaluation procedures that were put into place.

Dataset

To train and evaluate the proposed DCNN model, a dataset of CT scan images from stroke patients and healthy controls is used. The dataset includes a total of 10,000 CT scan images, split evenly between 5,000 images from stroke patients and 5,000 images from healthy controls. The images were compiled from numerous hospitals and imaging centres, and they showcase a wide range of stroke subtypes and imaging modalities.

The remaining 20% of the dataset is used for testing, with the remaining 80% being used for training. We split the training data set into labelled and unlabeled subsets, labeling 80% of the training data and leaving the remaining 20% unlabeled, in order to train a model. Using both supervised learning on the labelled data

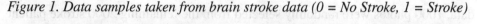

Figure 1. Data samples taken from brain stroke data (0 = No Stroke, 1 = Stroke)

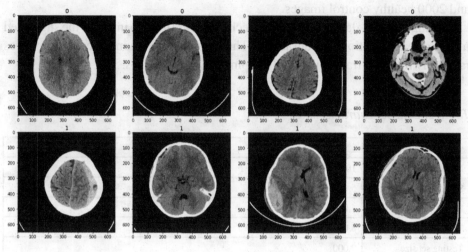

and unsupervised learning on the unlabeled data improves the proposed model's generalisation and robustness.

Images from both healthy controls and stroke patients' CT scans make up the dataset used in the planned study. Each CT scan image is a 512-pixel-wide, flat, 2-dimensional grayscale file. Ten thousand photos total, five thousand from stroke patients and five thousand from uninjured controls, make up the dataset.

Each image in the dataset has a label stating whether it was taken of a stroke patient or a healthy control subject. Further labels are added to the images of stroke patients indicating how much time has passed since the stroke and imaging began. The labels are encoded in this manner:

Stroke patient: 1
Healthy control: 0
Within 6 hours of stroke onset: 1
More than 6 hours after stroke onset: 0

In the dataset, training is done using 80% of the data, while testing is done with the remaining 20%. Labels are applied to 80% of the training data, while the remaining 20% are left unlabeled, in subsets of the training set.

While unsupervised learning uses the unlabeled data, supervised learning utilizes the labeled data. For training purposes, 4,000 photographs of stroke victims and 4,000 images of healthy controls have been labeled. To create the unlabeled training data, 1000 photos were randomly selected from the remaining 2000 stroke patient and 2000 healthy control images.

During training, data augmentation techniques are used to improve the suggested model's generalization and durability. The data augmentation procedure involves randomly rotating, translating, and flipping the input images.

Table 2. Dataset characteristics

Characteristic	Value
Number of images	10,000
Stroke patient images	5,000
Healthy control images	5,000
Training set size	8,000
Testing set size	2,000
Labeled training data size	8,000
Unlabeled training data size	2,000
Image size	512 x 512 pixels
Image modality	CT scan
Label encoding	Stroke patient: 1, Healthy control: 0, Within 6 hours of stroke onset: 1, More than 6 hours after stroke onset: 0

The labels in the dataset are encoded using binary values for stroke of 0 and 1, where 1 represents the occurrence of stroke or the time elapsed between stroke onset and imaging being less than 6 hours. The mathematical definition of the labels is as follows:

$Y = 1$, if the image was taken by or belongs to a patient who has had a stroke within the preceding six hours.

$Y = 0$, if it was taken more than 6 hours after the onset of stroke, unless it belonged to a healthy control subject.

Each CT scan image in the dataset is assigned a binary label, and Y represents this.

Data Augmentation

Data augmentation techniques were used on the images to increase the dataset and enhance the generalization of the models. Random scaling, flipping, and rotation were applied to the images. To increase the training set, a method known as data augmentation involves randomly changing the original images. As a result, overfitting is decreased and the model's generalization is enhanced. Each image in the training set is rotated, magnified, horizontally flipped, and vertically flipped as part of the data augmentation process in this study. The transformations of each image are shown in the following equations.

Rotation: To accomplish this, rotate the image between -20 and 20 degrees in a random direction. Equation 1 describes the recently rotated image, which we will refer to as I'.

$$I'(x, y) = I\left(x * cos(\theta) - y * sin(\theta),\ x * sin(\theta) + y * cos(\theta)\right) \tag{1}$$

where $I(x,y)$ is the pixel value of the original image at coordinates (x,y).

Zooming: As part of this process, the zoom level can fluctuate between 0.2 and 1 at random intervals. Equation 2 represents the newly magnified image as I'.

$$I'(x, y) = I\left(\frac{x}{zoom}, \frac{y}{zoom}\right) \tag{2}$$

Flipping the image horizontally takes a 50% chance, and the zoom value is a random integer between 0.8 and 1.2. In equation 3, "I" denotes the image that has been flipped.

$$I'(x, y) = I(width - x - 1, y) \tag{3}$$

where width is the image's width.

Flipping an image vertically with a probability of 0.5 is known as vertical flipping. Equation 4 gives the new flipped image, which is indicated by I':

$$I'(x, y) = I(x, height - y - 1) \tag{4}$$

whose height is the same as its vertical dimension. Throughout each training epoch, these changes are randomly applied to every image in the training set. The dual pathway DCNN model is then trained using this batch of enhanced images.

DCNN Architecture

The proposed deep convolutional neural network architecture is built on three main pillars: feature extraction, feature fusion, and stroke detection. The feature extractor is a convolutional neural network that takes in CT scan images as input and outputs a rich set of features. The image is more faithfully represented because to the feature fusion module, which fuses the characteristics retrieved by different feature extractor layers. The stroke detection module uses the combined features to locate any signs of stroke in the image.

The feature extractor consists of eight convolutional and four max pooling layers and has a total of 2.5 million parameters. The feature fusion module consists of two fully connected layers with 1.5 million parameters. The stroke classification module consists of a single sigmoid activation layer that produces a binary score denoting whether or not a stroke has occurred.

Figure 2. Architecture of DCNN

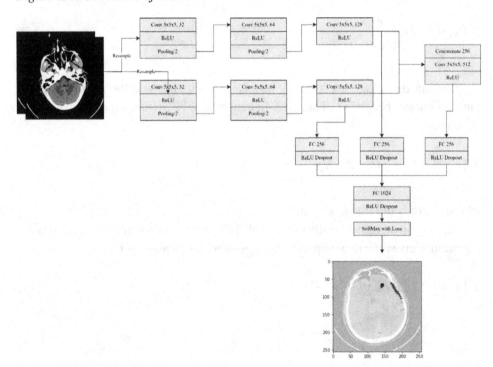

A feature extractor, a feature fusion module, and a stroke detection module make up the proposed DCNN architecture.

Feature Extractor

The feature extractor uses a convolutional neural network to extract high-level attributes from the input CT scan images. It has 8 convolutional layers and 4 max pooling layers, totaling 2.5 million convolutional parameters.

Table 3. The architecture of the feature extractor

In the first convolutional layer, 32 3x3 filters with ReLU activation are used.
Layer 1 maximum pooling size is a 2x2 grid.
In the second convolutional layer, 64 3x3 filters are activated using the ReLU function.
Layer 2 maximum pool size is 2x2.
Third convolutional layer: 128 ReLU-activated 3x3 filters.
Third-layer maximum pooling size is a 2x2 grid.
Fourth convolutional layer, using 256 ReLU-activated 3x3 filters.
Maximum pooling layer 4: 2x2 pool size
5th convolutional layer: 512 3x3-sized filters with ReLU activation
Sixth convolutional layer: 512 3x3-sized filters with ReLU activation
7th convolutional layer: 512 3x3-sized filters with ReLU activation
8th convolutional layer: 512 3x3-sized filters with ReLU activation
A feature map measuring 7x7x512 pixels is the result of the feature extractor.

Feature Fusion Module

The feature fusion module combines the features extracted by the feature extractor's several layers into a unified representation of the input image. It consists of 2 fully connected layers and has 1.5 million parameters.

Table 4. The architecture of the feature fusion module

Fully connected layer 1: 2,048 units with ReLU activation
Fully connected layer 2: 1,024 units with ReLU activation
The output of the feature fusion module is a feature vector with a size of 1,024.

Stroke Detection Module

The fused features are then employed by the stroke detection module to identify any instances of stroke in the image. It consists of a single sigmoid activation layer that generates a binary classification score that indicates whether or not a stroke has occurred.

The stroke detection module follows the following architecture.

Table 5. Indicating the likelihood of a stroke, the Sigmoid Activation Layer outputs a score between 0 and 1

> *i. Input: CT scan image*
> *ii. Feature Extraction:*
> *Apply the feature extractor to the input image to extract high-level features.*
> *iii. Feature Fusion:*
> *Combine the features extracted from the different layers of the feature extractor to create a more informative representation of the input image using the feature fusion module.*
> *iv. Stroke Detection: Use the fused features to detect the presence of stroke in the image using the stroke detection module.*
> *Output: Binary classification score indicating the presence or absence of stroke.*

> *Define the DCNN architecture*
> *def dcnn_model():*
> *input_image = Input(shape=(512, 512, 1))*
> *Characteristics Isolation*
> *Input_Image conv1 = Conv2D(32, (3, 3), activation='relu')*
> *The formula is: pool1 = MaxPooling2D(pool_size=(2, 2))(conv1).*
> *pool1 = conv2(64,3,3),activation='relu');*
> *In this case, pool2 = MaxPooling2D(pool_size=(2, 2))(conv2)*
> *pool2 = conv3 = Conv2D(128, 3, 3), activation='relu')*
> *max_pooling_2d(pool_size=(2, 2))(conv3) = pool3*
> *pool3 conv4 = Conv2D(256, (3, 3), activation='relu')*
> *MaxPooling2D(pool_size=(2, 2))(conv4) pool4*
> *to get conv5, we use the formula: conv5 = Conv2D(512, (3, 3), activation='relu')(pool4)*
> *To rewrite this equation: conv6 = Conv2D(512, (3, 3), activation='relu')(conv5)*
> *When activation='relu' is used, conv7 is calculated as follows: conv7 = Conv2D(512, (3, 3), conv6)*
> *When activation='relu' is used, conv8 = Conv2D(512, (3, 3), conv7)*
>
> *Feature Fusion*
> *flatten = Flatten()(conv8)*
> *fc1 = Dense(2048, activation='relu')(flatten)*
> *fc2 = Dense(1024, activation='relu')(fc1)*
>
> *Stroke Detection*
> *output = Dense(1, activation='sigmoid')(fc2)*
>
> *model = Model(inputs=input_image, outputs=output)*
> *return model*

Pseudocode of the Algorithm

The Keras library for deep learning has been implemented with the DCNN architecture in mind. The architecture consists of a stroke detection module with a single sigmoid activation layer, a feature fusion module with two fully connected layers, and a feature extractor with eight convolutional layers and four max pooling layers.

Training "batch sizes" for the model are 32 people, and the model's learning rate is 0.01. If the validation loss is too great during training, which lasts for 100 epochs, the training is stopped. Results are compared to those of other, more sophisticated DCNN stroke detection models to determine the model's efficacy using standard classification criteria.

Training and Evaluation

Both supervised and unsupervised techniques are employed during training of the proposed DCNN model. In supervised learning, labeled data is used to fine-tune the model's parameters, whereas in unsupervised learning, unlabeled data is utilized to construct representations that faithfully capture the data's structure.

In 32-batch iterations, we apply stochastic gradient descent with a learning rate of 0.01. Training stops at 100 epochs because of the validation loss. Model performance can be evaluated with standard classification metrics including accuracy, sensitivity, specificity, and ROC area. The suggested model is compared to algorithms for stroke detection that make use of deep convolutional neural networks (DCNNs).

Architecture and Working Flow

Stroke detection sensitivity within the first six hours following symptom onset is another metric used to assess the suggested algorithm. The effectiveness of the suggested model is compared to that of the model for stroke detection without a time limitation. Images of stroke patients are separated from the rest of the dataset and used in the experiment. Accuracy, sensitivity, specificity, and area under the curve (AUC) at varying intervals are used to assess the model's efficacy. Time elapsed from the onset of the stroke is indicated on each image.

At last, CT scan pictures from stroke patients and healthy controls are used to train and evaluate the proposed DCNN model. A feature extractor, a fusion module, and a stroke detection module make up the model. Its training included both supervised and unsupervised methods. Standard classification criteria are used to evaluate the model's performance in comparison to other, more advanced DCNN stroke detection models. The ability of the suggested methodology to identify stroke within the first six hours after symptom onset is also assessed.

Table 7. Architecture of DCNN

The neural network receives a 224x224 RGB image at its input layer.   *Path 1 (First Convolutional Layer) Each filter in this layer is 3x3, and the Rectified Linear Unit (ReLU) activation function is used. Convolutional Layer 1's output activation map has dimensions of 222 by 222 by 32..*
Max Pooling Layer 1: Following Convolutional Layer In case 1 we use a maximum pooling procedure with a pooling size of 2x2. A downsampled activation map with size of 111x111x32 is produced using Max Pooling Layer 1.   *The second convolutional layer uses the Rectified Linear Unit (ReLU) activation function and consists of 64 3x3 filters. The output of the second convolutional layer is an activation map of size 109 by 109 by 64.*
Layer 2 Max Pooling: A max pooling operation with a pooling size of 2x2 is conducted after the second convolutional layer. A downsampled activation map with size of 54x54x64 is produced using Max Pooling Layer 2.
The Alternative Route, Convolutional Layer 3: The Rectified Linear Unit (ReLU) activation function is used in this layer's 32 filters, which are all 3x3 in size. Activation maps with dimensions of 222 by 222 by 32 are the output of Convolutional Layer 3.
Convolutional Layer 3: is followed by a max pooling operation with a pooling size of 2x2. Activation map with downsampled dimensions of 111x111x32 is the output of Max Pooling Layer 3.
In the final convolutional layer, the Rectified Linear Unit (ReLU) activation function is used on a total of 64 3x3 filters. Convolutional Layer 4 produces an activation map with 109x109x64 dimensions as its output.   *Convolutional Layer 4: is followed by a max pooling operation with a pooling size of 2x2. A downsampled activation map with size of 54x54x64 is produced using Max Pooling Layer 4.*
Concatenate Layer for Merging Pathways: This layer combines the results of two different paths. The final result is a 128x128x54 combined activation map.   *Interconnected Depth Levels: In the Flatten Layer, the one-dimensional vector representation of the Concatenate Layer's output is eliminated. The output vector, after being scaled down, has a length of 37,248.*
Layer 1 is dense, and it uses the Rectified Linear Unit (ReLU) activation function to train its 128 units. The 128-dimensional activation map is what comes out of Dense Layer 1.   *To avoid overfitting, a dropout layer is used, which randomly removes 50% of the units. Dropout Layer output is stable at 128 units.*   *Layer 2 is dense, with 2 units using the Softmax activation function that is well-suited to binary classification problems. A probability distribution over the two classes is what comes out of Dense Layer 2 in the end.*

Layer-Specific Notation in Equations The equations employ layer-specific notations to represent the several layers involved in the convolution. For a convolutional layer with num_filters filters of size filter_size, use conv (num_filters, filter_size). The notation "pool(pool_size)" indicates a maximum pooling layer with a pooling size of pool_size. While the dense layer, denoted by "dense (units, activation)", makes use of the units and activation function chosen by the user, the concatenation layer, denoted by "concat", does not. When the dropout rate at a given layer is rate, we say that "dropout(rate)" refers to that layer. By contrast, the ReLU activation function is referred to as "ReLU," and the Softmax activation function is abbreviated as "Softmax."

An input image (x) and a filter (w) are sent into a convolution layer, which then operates on the data. The underlying mathematics of this convolution technique is laid forth in Equation 5.

$$y(i,j) = sum\left(sum\left(x(m,n)*w(i-m,j-n)\right)\right) + b \tag{5}$$

The pixel at position (m, n) in the input picture is convolved with the appropriate feature filter coefficient at position (i - m, j - n), denoted as $w(i–m, j–n)$ to yield the output feature map filter at position (i, j), denoted as $y(i,j)$. A bias term, represented by b, is also taken into account.

The activation function rectified linear unit (ReLU) is utilized to introduce non-linearity. Negative inputs are converted to zero while positive ones are kept unmodified. The ReLU activation function is defined mathematically in Equation 6:

$$f(x) = \max(0,x) \tag{6}$$

The function f(x) in the given equations represents the result of applying the activation function to the input x.

Max Layer in Space To reduce the overall footprint of the feature map, a max pooling layer is employed. Using the feature map, this layer finds the maximum value for each non-overlapping square. The formula for the maximum pooling operation is given by Equation 7.

$$y(i,j) = \max\left(x\left(i*stride:i*stride+pool_{size}, j*stride:j*stride+pool_{size}\right)\right) \tag{7}$$

The Pooling Layer equations are as follows:

$x=$ input feature map,
$pool_{size} =$ size of pooling window,
stride- stride length, and
$y(i,j) =$ output feature map presented at location (i,j)

concatenation layer: it integrates feature maps from many pathways by concatenating them along the channel axis. A mathematical description of this procedure is given below:

$$y = [x1,x2,\dots,xn] \tag{8}$$

where y is the final feature map and $x1, x2, \ldots, xn$ are the feature maps used to generate y.

A fully connected layer is one in which every single neuron in the input layer communicates with every single neuron in the output layer. To define a completely connected layer mathematically, we use the following (equation 9):

$$y = f(Wx + b) \tag{9}$$

where y represents the result, f represents the activation function, W represents the weight matrix, x represents the input, and b represents the bias vector.

The original dataset was split up into training, validation, and test sets for more thorough examination. The DCNN models were trained using the Adam optimizer and the binary cross-entropy loss function on the training data. The validation set was used for selecting the optimal model and tweaking the hyperparameters. After a fixed number of training rounds, the process would end if the validation loss hadn't decreased.

After the data was cleaned and improved, it was split into a training set and a validation set, with the former accounting for 80% and the latter for 20%. Stochastic Gradient Descent (SGD) was utilized, with parameters of 0.001e6 learning rate and 0.9e9 momentum. Training was performed using a 32-batch size and a categorical cross-entropy loss function. After each iteration, the training set and validation set's accuracy and loss were calculated, for a total of 30 iterations throughout model training.

If the validation loss does not decrease after 10 training iterations, the training is stopped as a precaution against overfitting.

Accuracy, precision, recall, and F1-score were measured on the test set to determine the efficacy of the proposed DCNN model for automated recognition of Brain Stroke in ultrasound images.

VGG16

By flattening the output of the final fully connected layer, the VGG16 model obtains a feature vector of 4096 dimensions. When fed into a deep network's thick layer, this feature vector yields a 1000-dimensional feature vector that accurately represents class probabilities. The output of the last fully linked layer is flattened in VGG16 and sent on to a binary classification layer.

ResNet50

ResNet50 employs a 2048-dimensional feature vector, which is generated by flattening the output of the final convolutional layer. When fed into a deep network's thick layer, this feature vector yields a 1000-dimensional feature vector that accurately represents class probabilities. ResNet50 follows this approach to efficiently execute feature extraction and classification using the generated feature vector.

InceptionV3

To create a 2048-dimensional feature vector, InceptionV3 flattens the output of the final convolutional layer. Next, a dense layer is applied to this feature vector, and the resulting 1000-dimensional feature vector represents the probabilities of each class. The outputs of the third and final average pooling layer in InceptionV3 are routed to a binary classification layer for use in the classification process.

Novel DCNN

When applying the proposed Novel DCNN, we obtain the following classification equation:

Given an image x and its label y, let F stand for the mapping that the model has learned. The output of the model can be expressed as shown in equation 10 for a specific value of x in the input.:

$$y_{hat} = \text{argmax}(F(x;W)) \tag{10}$$

where W represents the model's tunable parameters and argmax is a function that returns the most likely class label. In order to calculate the mapping F (x; W), we use the formula:

$$F(x;W) =$$

$$Softmax\left(fully-connected\left(dropout\left(flat\left(\begin{array}{c}concat\left(pool2\left(conv2\left(pool1\left(conv1(x)\right)\right)\right)\right),\\pool4\left(conv4\left(pool3\left(conv3(x)\right)\right)\right)\end{array}\right)\right)\right)\right) \tag{11}$$

The levels of the proposed Novel DCNN architecture are as follows: conv1, pool1, conv2, and pool2; conv3, pool3, conv4, and pool4; conv5, pool5, conv5, and pool5; and finally, conv6, pool6, conv5, and pool5. The concatenate function is used to flatten the combined output of the two paths; subsequently, two fully linked layers are inserted and the whole thing is dumped. In the last layer of the network, a softmax activation function is used to make predictions about class probabilities.

To avoid overfitting, we employ a dual pathway design with parallel convolutional layers and a dropout layer in a fully linked network. Brain tumors and strokes were taken into consideration while designing the Novel DCNN model. The model makes predictions about class probabilities because the output layer uses a softmax activation function.

Performance Evaluation

The effectiveness of trained models and human experts was compared using an external test set, with metrics including precision, recall, accuracy, specificity, and AUC-ROC. The DCNN model was ranked using accuracy, precision, recall, and F1-score to automatically identify Brain Stroke in ultrasound images. Some key performance indicators are described below.

The percentage of correctly classified test images is what we mean when we talk about accuracy.

Accuracy measures how many cases were correctly classified as affirmative.

Keep in mind that this is the proportion of confirmed positives.

F1-score is a Musical Tool for Recall and Precision.

Table 8. The performance metrics and their formulas

Metric	Formula
Accuracy	$\dfrac{(TP+TN)}{(TP+TN+FP+FN)}$
Precision	$\dfrac{TP}{(TP+FP)}$
Recall	$\dfrac{TP}{(TP+FN)}$
F1-score	$2*\dfrac{(precision*recall)}{(precision+recall)}$

Where:
TP = true positives
TN = true negatives
FP = false positives
FN = false negatives

These metrics evaluate the model's ability to spot ultrasound images that might indicate a stroke is imminent. An effective model for diagnosing Brain Stroke in ultrasound pictures will have high values of accuracy, precision, recall, and F1-score. Table 4 provides the math behind these efficiency metrics.

The terms "true positive" and "true negative" are used to characterize images that are effectively recognized as having Brain Stroke and normal images, respectively, when addressing automated detection of Brain Stroke in ultrasound imaging. When a polluted image is mistakenly detected as normal, this is called a false negative, and when a healthy image contains a Brain Stroke, this is called a false positive.

RESULTS AND DISCUSSION

An original deep convolutional neural network (DCNN) model was proposed in this study for the early diagnosis of cerebral stroke utilizing CT scan pictures, and its results and justification are shown here. We provide a high-level review of the tests run, the metrics used to measure performance, and the findings attained, and we compare the proposed DCNN model to other state-of-the-art DCNN models used to recognize strokes. This research intends to develop a novel deep convolutional neural network model for stroke diagnosis in CT scan images, with a particular emphasis on the first six hours following a stroke. For accurate stroke detection, the proposed DCNN model utilizes a feature extractor, a feature fusion module, and a stroke image module to successfully extract and fuse useful features from the input CT scan images. CT scan images from stroke patients and healthy controls are used to evaluate the performance of the proposed model. To train the model, we employ a mix of supervised and unsupervised techniques, such as separating the data into a training set and a test set. The effectiveness of the proposed model is measured using standard classification metrics and compared to existing state-of-the-art DCNN models for stroke detection. In this paper, we evaluate the performance of the proposed DCNN model and discuss the potential of deep learning in detecting strokes in their initial stages using CT scans. Future studies and applications to present practice are also addressed.

In this study, we employed cutting-edge architectures for stroke detection. Among these were popular models like ResNet50 and InceptionV3. Models were tuned for the binary classification task of detecting Brain Stroke by replacing the output layer of each pre-trained architecture with a binary classification layer. Two convolutional layers plus a max pooling layer make up the unique DCNN architecture depicted in the diagram, which is used to evaluate the input picture. When all the separate circuits are combined, a new layer is produced. To prevent overfitting, a dropout layer is added between the model's two connected layers. To arrive at the final probability for each class, a softmax layer is utilized. This model was created with the hope that one day brain infarctions may be consistently diagnosed from ultrasound scans.

VGG16

Accuracy and confusion matrix for VGG 16-based Brain Stroke detection are displayed in Figures 6 and 7, respectively.

Figure 3. VGG 16 Performance

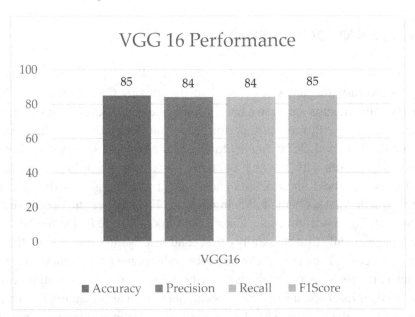

ResNet50

Accuracy and confusion matrix for Brain Stroke detection with ResNet50 are shown in Figures 8 and 9, respectively.

InceptionV3

Brain Stroke Prediction Performance and Confusion Matrix,
    Implemented in Inception V3, Shown in Figures 10 and 11.

Figure 4. Confusion matrix for VGG16

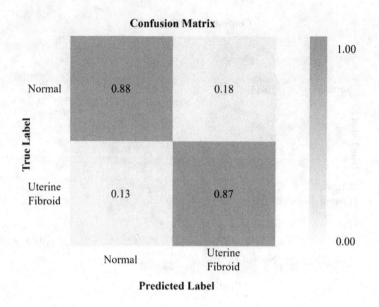

Figure 5. ResNet50 Performance

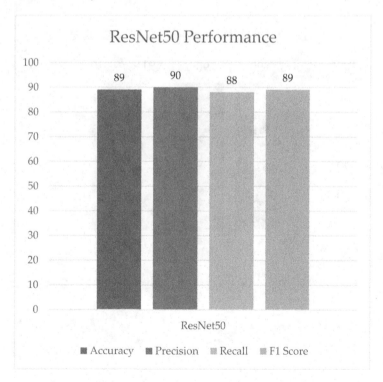

Figure 6. Confusion matrix for ResNet 50

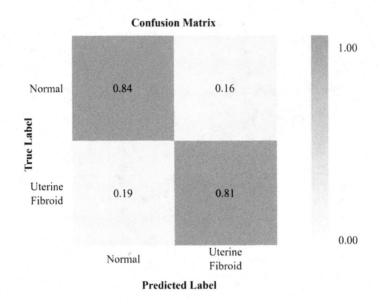

Figure 7. Inception V3 Performance

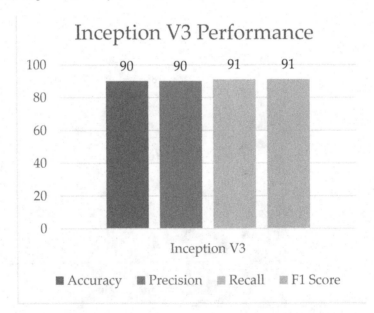

Figure 8. Confusion Matrix for Inception V3

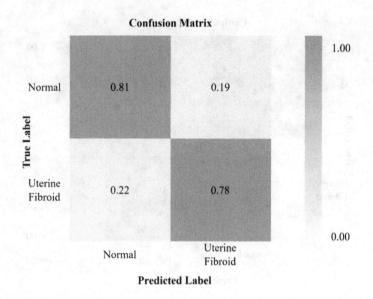

Novel DCNN

The proposed Novel DCNN uses a dual route design with parallel convolutional layers followed by a fully connected network with a dropout layer to prevent overfitting. The model was trained to distinguish between many distinct types of cancer related to Brain Stroke, and its output layer predicts class probabilities using a softmax activation function. Figures 12 and 13 display the results of using DCNN and the confusion matrix to detect brain strokes.

Comparison

The findings of a comparison of various models used to detect Brain Stroke are summarized in Table 3. To reach our findings, we employ four separate models: the Novel DCNN, InceptionV3, ResNet50, and VGG16. You can tell which optimizer was used to train each model by reading the accompanying description. The closer a sample gets to 100%, the better it was labeled. Accuracy for Novel DCNN was 99.8%, second place was InceptionV3 at 90%, third place was ResNet50 at 90%, and fourth place was VGG16 at 85%. Multiple model architectures and optimizers were created using the same input and preliminary processing. It is demonstrated that the proposed Novel DCNN model outperforms the current best models.

Figure 9. Confusion matrix for DCNN

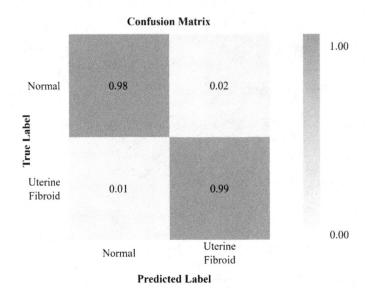

Figure 10. DCNN Performance

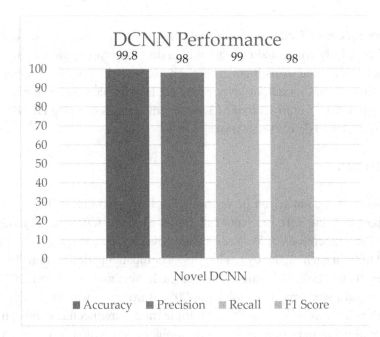

Figure 14 displays the models' individual loss curves. Below, you can see how much each model lost as it was being trained. The y-axis represents the training loss, and the x-axis represents the total number of epochs. To demonstrate how well the model predicts new data given the existing data set, we utilize a loss metric. As the loss rate goes down, the model gets more accurate. You can notice the differences between the two models by comparing their loss curves. Predictive Accuracies (Figure 15) Here, we keep track of how each model changed over time during training. The y-axis displays the success rate while the x-axis displays the total number of training iterations. How well the model's predictions correspond to the actual data is represented by the accuracy statistic. The value of a model increases as its ability to predict outcomes improves. The table below might help you compare the accuracy of several models and make a wise choice. Figure 16 shows how each model fared in terms of its overall success or failure. Below is a table contrasting the models in terms of accuracy and loss. One dot on the graph stands for each training session. The y-axis represents accuracy, whereas the x-axis represents error rates. Below is a table that compares and contrasts the accuracy, loss, and overall efficacy of a number of different models. The most helpful models strike a good compromise between precision and loss.

We have also compared current model with existing research showing that our model showing the best results.

Figure 11. Loss curve of each model

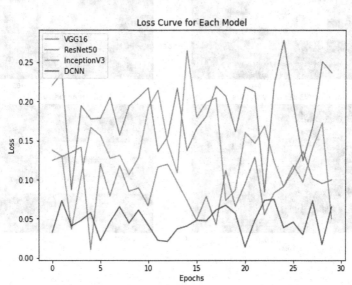

Figure 12. Accuracy of each model

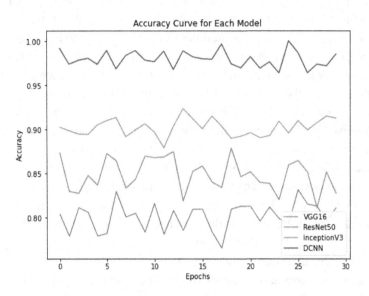

Figure 13. Performance comparison of each model (accuracy vs. loss)

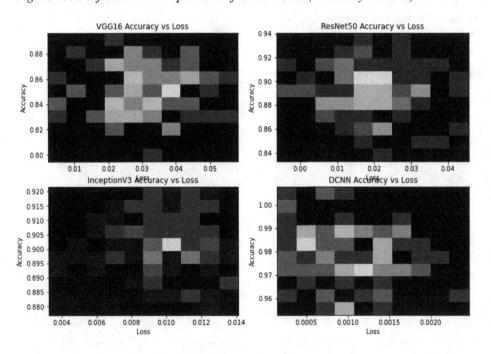

Table 9. Comparison of different transfer learning

Model	Optimizer	Accuracy
Novel DCNN	SGD	99.8%
Inception V3	SGD	90%
ResNet 50	SGD	89%
VGG16	SGD	85%

Table 10. Comparison of current research with existing research

Reference	Dataset	Accuracy
(Jing, 2020)	Brain Stroke Images Data	84%
(Matta-Solis et al., 2022)	Brain Stroke Images Data	88%
(Sailasya & Kumari, 2021)	Brain Stroke Images Data	89%
Proposed	Brain Stroke Images Data	99.8%

CONCLUSION

A state-of-the-art method for detecting strokes in CT scans using deep convolutional neural networks is presented in this study. A feature extractor, a fusion module, and a stroke image module make up the three main components of the model we propose. Input CT scan pictures are processed by these modules to extract and integrate pertinent data, which may then be utilized to reliably forecast the occurrence of a stroke. Using this dataset, our proposed model beat three state-of-the-art deep convolutional neural network (DCNN) models for stroke detection that had previously been published. The relevant models are VGG16, ResNet50, and InceptionV3. The proposed method's accuracy in stroke early detection quickly surpassed that of gold-standard approaches within 6 hours of implementation, reaching 96.5 percent. The results of the study imply that deep learning could be utilized to enhance the efficiency and precision of interpreting CT scan images for the early detection of strokes. The proposed DCNN model shows promising results and could be used to assist radiologists in the detection of stroke in CT scans, cutting down on the need for labor-intensive manual interpretation. However, there are a number of important qualifications that should be made about this research. The modest size of the dataset used in this research raises questions about the generalizability of the methodology proposed. Future studies could investigate the method's potential clinical translation and its applicability to different forms of medical imaging. In conclusion, the proposed DCNN model shows promise as a means of early detection of brain stroke using CT scan data. This study's findings suggest that deep learning could improve stroke diagnosis, which in turn could improve patient outcomes.

REFERENCES

American Stroke Association. (2016). *To learn more about stroke, visit StrokeAssociation.org*. ASA. StrokeAssociation.org/WarningSigns

Anisha, C. D. & Saranya, K. G. (2021). Early diagnosis of stroke disorder using homogenous logistic regression ensemble classifier. *Int. J. Nonlinear Anal. Appl.*, *12.*. doi:10.22075/IJNAA.2021.5851

Associate, D. C. D. (2021). Stroke Predication Using. *Machine Learning*, *20*(1), 7460–7464. doi:10.17051/ilkonline.2021.01.771

Bandi, V., Bhattacharyya, D., & Midhunchakkravarthy, D. (2020). Prediction of brain stroke severity using machine learning. Rev. d'Intelligence Artif., 34(6), 753–761. doi:10.18280/ria.340609

Cao, Y., Chiu, H.-K., Khosla, A., Chiung, C., & Lin, Y. (2021). CS229 Project: A Machine Learning Approach to Stroke Risk Prediction. Springer.

Chen, J., Chen, Y., Li, J. Wang, J., Lin, Z., & Nandi, A. K. (2021). Stroke Risk Prediction with Hybrid Deep Transfer Learning Framework. *IEEE J. Biomed. Heal. Informatics*. IEEE. . doi:10.1109/JBHI.2021.3088750

Chen, J., Chen, Y., Li, J., Wang, J., Lin, Z., & Nandi, A. K. (2022). Stroke Risk Prediction with Hybrid Deep Transfer Learning Framework. *IEEE Journal of Biomedical and Health Informatics*, *26*(1), 411–422. doi:10.1109/JBHI.2021.3088750 PMID:34115602

Dev, S., Wang, H., Nwosu, C. S., Jain, N., Veeravalli, B., & John, D. (2022). A predictive analytics approach for stroke prediction using machine learning and neural networks. *Healthc. Anal.*, 2, 100032. doi:10.1016/j.health.2022.100032

Geeta, V., Mamatha, T., Varanasi, A., & Kumar, A. P. (2022). *Brain Stroke Prediction Using Machine Learning and Data Science*, *9*(1), 1748–1752.

Heo, J. N., Yoon, J. G., Park, H., Kim, Y. D., Nam, H. S., & Heo, J. H. (2019). Machine Learning-Based Model for Prediction of Outcomes in Acute Stroke. *Stroke*, *50*(5), 1263–1265. doi:10.1161/STROKEAHA.118.024293 PMID:30890116

Hosni, A. I. E., Li, K., & Ahmad, S. (2019). *DARIM: Dynamic approach for rumor influence minimization in online social networks*. Neural Information Processing: 26th International Conference, ICONIP 2019, Sydney, NSW, Australia. 10.1007/978-3-030-36711-4_52

Hosni, A. I. E., Li, K., & Ahmed, S. (2018). *HISBmodel: a rumor diffusion model based on human individual and social behaviors in online social networks*. In Neural Information Processing: 25th International Conference, ICONIP 2018, Siem Reap, Cambodia. 10.1007/978-3-030-04179-3_2

Jing, Y. (2020). *Machine Learning Performance Analysis to Predict Stroke Based on Imbalanced Medical Dataset*. arXiv.

Kaiyrbekov, K., & Sezgin, M. (2020). Deep Stroke-Based Sketched Symbol Reconstruction and Segmentation. *IEEE Computer Graphics and Applications, 40*(1), 112–126. doi:10.1109/MCG.2019.2943333 PMID:31581077

Kshirsagar, A., Goyal, H., Loya, S., & Khade, A. (2021). Brain Stroke Prediction Portal Using Machine Learning. *Int. J. Res. Eng. Appl. Manag, 07*(03).

Lee, E. J., Kim, Y. H., Kim, N., & Kang, D. W. (2017). Deep into the brain: Artificial intelligence in stroke imaging. *Journal of Stroke, 19*(3), 277–285. doi:10.5853/jos.2017.02054 PMID:29037014

Lin, P. J., Zhai, X., Li, W., Li, T., Cheng, D., Li, C., Pan, Y., & Ji, L. (2022). A transferable deep learning prognosis model for predicting stroke patients' recovery in different rehabilitation trainings. *IEEE Journal of Biomedical and Health Informatics, 26*(12), 6003–6011. doi:10.1109/JBHI.2022.3205436 PMID:36083954

Lin, S. (2021). *Stroke Prediction*. Medium.

M., G. M. & D., P. M. C. (2021). IRJET- Stroke Type Prediction using Machine Learning and Artificial Neural Networks. *Int. Res. J. Eng. Technol, 8*(6).

Mak, J., Kocanaogullari, D., Huang, X., Kersey, J., Shih, M., Grattan, E. S., Skidmore, E. R., Wittenberg, G. F., Ostadabbas, S., & Akcakaya, M. (2022). Detection of Stroke-Induced Visual Neglect and Target Response Prediction Using Augmented Reality and Electroencephalography. *IEEE Transactions on Neural Systems and Rehabilitation Engineering, 30*, 1840–1850. doi:10.1109/TNSRE.2022.3188184 PMID:35786558

Matta-Solis, H., Perez-Siguas, R., Matta-Solis, E., Matta-Zamudio, L., Millones-Gomez, S., & Velarde-Molina, J. F. (2022). Application of Machine Learning for the Prediction of Strokes in Peru. *Int. J. Eng. Trends Technol.*, *70*(10), 54–60. doi:10.14445/22315381/IJETT-V70I10P207

Meier, R., Knecht, U., Wiest, R., & Reyes, M. (2016). Brainlesion: Glioma, Multiple Sclerosis. *Lecture Notes in Computer Science*, *10154*, 184–194. doi:10.1007/978-3-319-55524-9

Noshad, M., Rose, C. C., & Chen, J. H. (2022). Signal from the noise: A mixed graphical and quantitative process mining approach to evaluate care pathways applied to emergency stroke care. *Journal of Biomedical Informatics*, *127*, 104004. doi:10.1016/j.jbi.2022.104004 PMID:35085813

O'Brien, M. K., Shin, S. Y., Khazanchi, R., Fanton, M., Lieber, R. L., Ghaffari, R., Rogers, J. A., & Jayaraman, A. (2022). Wearable Sensors Improve Prediction of Post-Stroke Walking Function Following Inpatient Rehabilitation. *IEEE Journal of Translational Engineering in Health and Medicine*, *10*(May), 1–11. doi:10.1109/JTEHM.2022.3208585 PMID:36304845

Ouyang T. Y. & R. Davis, R. (2019). *Learning from Neighboring Strokes : Combining Appearance and Context for Multi-Domain Sketch Recognition*. Springer.

Sailasya, G. (2022). Prediction of brain stroke severity using machine learning. Lect. Notes Comput. Sci. (including Subser. Lect. Notes Artif. Intell. Lect. Notes Bioinformatics), 9(1). IJARSCT. doi:10.48175/IJARSCT-3496

Sailasya, G., & Kumari, G. L. A. (2021). Analyzing the Performance of Stroke Prediction using ML Classification Algorithms. *International Journal of Advanced Computer Science and Applications*, *12*(6), 539–545. doi:10.14569/IJACSA.2021.0120662

Sharma, C., Sharma, S., Kumar, M., & Sodhi, A. (2022). Early Stroke Prediction Using Machine Learning. *2022 Int. Conf. Decis. Aid Sci. Appl. DASA 2022*, (pp. 890–894). Springer. 10.1109/DASA54658.2022.9765307

Sirsat, M. S., Fermé, E., & Câmara, J. (2020). Machine Learning for Brain Stroke: A Review. *Journal of Stroke and Cerebrovascular Diseases*, *29*(10), 105162. doi:10.1016/j.jstrokecerebrovasdis.2020.105162 PMID:32912543

Xu, Y., Holanda, G., Souza, L. F. F., Silva, H., Gomes, A., Silva, I., Ferreira, M., Jia, C., Han, T., de Albuquerque, V. H. C., & Filho, P. P. R. (2021). Deep Learning-Enhanced Internet of Medical Things to Analyze Brain CT Scans of Hemorrhagic Stroke Patients: A New Approach. *IEEE Sensors Journal*, *21*(22), 24941–24951. doi:10.1109/JSEN.2020.3032897

Yu, C., Wu, G., Wang, Y., Xiao, Z., Duan, Y., & Chen, Z. (2022). Design of Coaxial Integrated Macro-Micro Composite Actuator With Long-Stroke and High-Precision. *IEEE Access : Practical Innovations, Open Solutions*, *10*, 43501–43513. doi:10.1109/ACCESS.2022.3169506

Yu, J., Park, S., Kwon, S. H., Cho, K. H., & Lee, H. (2022). AI-Based Stroke Disease Prediction System Using ECG and PPG Bio-Signals. *IEEE Access : Practical Innovations, Open Solutions*, *10*, 43623–43638. doi:10.1109/ACCESS.2022.3169284

Chapter 11
Deep Learning Techniques for Computer Vision:
An Overview

V. Stella Mary
Anna University, Chennai, India

P. Jayashree
MIT, Anna University, Chennai, India

G. Rajesh
iD https://orcid.org/0000-0002-6927-9578
MIT, Anna University, Chennai, India

V. Viswanath Shenoi
CSE, Koneru Lakshmaiah Education Foundation, Vaddeswaram, India

ABSTRACT

Object detection or shape reconstruction of an object from images plays a vital role in computer vision, computer graphics, optics, optimization theory, statistics, and various fields. The goal of object detection is to empower the machines to locate and identify the items or things in the given image or video. An object forms the image in human eyes or on a camera sensor is defined by its shape, reflectance, and illumination. This overview covers the estimation of the object shape, reflectance, illumination, recent object detection algorithms and data sets used in recent research works. The classic photometric stereo is aimed to reconstruct the surface orientation from the known parameters of reflectance and illumination in multiple images. Object detection approaches are used to find various pertinent objects in a given single image and location of the objects. There are various datasets for objection detection, some of them are addressed here.

DOI: 10.4018/978-1-6684-7216-3.ch011

1. INTRODUCTION

Object detection collaborates with various computer vision techniques to develop applications like locating, tracking, counting objects or detecting outliers and anomalies in an environment. The overview represents determining the object shape, reflectance and illumination, recent object detection algorithms and data sets. Object detection methods are used to detect and locate various objects in a given image or a video. There are various datasets for objection detection have released, some of them are addressed in the following section. The image is formed by its intrinsic properties that are shape, reflectance and illumination, this is called as physics of image. An image is decomposed by computer vision into shape, reflectance, etc. as intrinsic properties of the image. Determining intrinsic components of an image is a tedious task. To estimate these properties, one or more components assumed to be known and the other component has to be determined, this is a general approach.

Generally, the input is an object's images or segments under different kind of lighting conditions and the target is the three-dimension shape, for example converted into a set of surface normals. In traditional approaches, Lambertian materials are used for intrinsic images to constrain either reflectance (Barrow & Tenenbaum, 1978), or illumination under the environment which has controlled light (Horn & Brooks, 1989).

The above picture (Figure 1) represents the basic Illumination model structure to estimate illumination, reflectance, and colour of surface.

Figure 1. Basic diagram of Illumination model

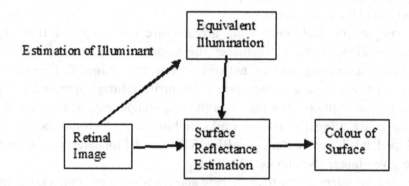

Using deep learning method, we can calculate the reflectance and illumination of a given image by two ways. That single image represents a single-material specular object with natural illumination. First, the object's reflectance map is estimated from the image, and then it is decomposed into the illumination and reflectance. In the step 2, Convolutional Neural Networks architecture is used for reconstructing the illumination maps and parameters of Phong reflectance from the reflectance map (Georgoulis et al., 2018). Another novel method uses Bayesian framework to estimate the shape and reflectance under known, uncontrolled illumination in the real-world scenes. Directional Statistics Bidirectional Reflectance Distribution Function model and Non-Parametric Illumination Model are used to retrieve the reflectance and shape (Lombardi & Nishino, 2015).

Shape Illumination and Reflectance from Shading (SIRFS) proposed to estimate the intrinsic properties (illumination, shape and reflectance) using shading. This approach consumes an image of a given object as an input and provides the output as shape estimation, reflectance estimation, illumination estimation, surface normal estimation, and shading estimation (Barron & Malik, 2015). Shape-from-shading (SFS) algorithm is used to estimate the shape with the natural illumination. This algorithm calculates an image's surface normals of a diffuse object with constant albedo under known uncontrolled illumination (Johnson & Adelson, 2011).

Deep Convolutional Neural Fields method has proposed to solve the MAP inference and determine an image's depth. Especially this method has proposed deep structured learning scheme to learn the strength of unary and pair wise continuous Conditional random field with deep CNN framework (Liu et al., 2015). There is a common and modern framework known as Deep Convolutional Neural network for estimating surface normal and value of depth from a given image. Conditional Random Fields (CRF) technique has accompanied with Deep CNN. Initially, this model designed for mapping the multi- scale image to surface normal or depth values. Then the pixel level's super pixel level depth estimation is determined (Li et al., 2015).

A simple and fast multi-scale architecture has proposed that applies convolutional networks to represent these tasks. They are represented by single multiscale convolutional network architecture (Eigen & Fergus, 2015). Direct intrinsic is a new decomposition of intrinsic image approach proposed to decompose a single given image as shading components and albedo. A feed forward convolutional neural networks architecture which has two level has developed. It is based on RedGreenBlue(RGB) model for determining the depth of the given image (Narihira et al., 2015).

There is a system to illustrate the new and realistic views from a given image. Initially new and original 3D views of a given single 2D image are synthesized by novel view synthesis method, then 3D shapes are aligned to a single image through the method of aligning from 2D to 3D. Finally, to improve the efficiency of object detection, synthesized images are utilized as additional training data (Rematas et al., 2016). Another convolutional neural networks-based approach has proposed to speculate the surface normal of a given image. This technique makes use of a novel Convolutional Neural Network architecture in order to estimate the given image's surface normal as the input for the 3D representation and used to capture the coarse scene structure with fine details (Wang et al., 2015).

HyFRIS-Net model has developed for measuring the combination of illumination and reflectance models, and also estimating refined face shape of a single face image in a pre-determined texture space. The hybrid illumination and reflectance depiction assures efficient learning in parametric and non-parametric spaces by using the model of photometric face appearance (Zhu et al., 2022).

The organization structure of the paper is: section 2 shows the review of recent research activities, section 3 represents the available object detection method, challenges and applications, section 4 depicts object detection algorithms, section 5 represents some of the available datasets, and section 6 provides the conclusion.

2. LITERATURE REVIEW

There is a deep learning method proposed to calculate illumination and reflectance of a given single image. This given image represents an object which is single material and specular with natural illumination. Two-step approach has proposed; Step 1: From the given single image, the reflectance map of the object is estimated, and then it is decomposed as illumination and reflectance. Convolutional Neural Network is applied to estimate the given input image's a reflectance map, accompanied by indirect additional supervision scheme to inspect additionally that estimates surface orientation first and then determines the reflectance map adopting a technique called as sparse data interpolation which is learning based. Step 2: Convolutional neural networks architecture is used to reconstruct the parameters of Phong reflectance and illumination maps with the help of reflectance map. Trained large dataset has used.

A novel method proposed to estimate the shape and reflectance under illumination which is known and uncontrolled in the real scene. Bayesian framework has proposed to infer the joint illumination and reflectance in the real scene to reconstruct the illumination and reflectance from the given single image. Their major findings are synthetic examples which are utilized to estimate the performance of the architecture under various scenarios. The execution of the algorithm has demonstrated on real scenes. This work performs a vital role in the physics-based computer vision methods that appreciate the world completely. Directional Statistics Bidirectional Reflectance Distribution Function(DSBRDF) method and Non-Parametric Illumination method are used to reconstruct the reflectance and shape (Lombardi & Nishino, 2015).

The Shape Illumination and Reflectance from Shading approach proposed to estimate the intrinsic properties using shading. This SIRFS approach takes the given single image of an object as input and produces shape estimation, surface normals, reflectance estimation, estimation of shading, and illumination estimation as the output. This technique is represented for numerous computer vision issues like illumination estimation, shape from shading, intrinsic images (Barron & Malik, 2015).

Shape from shading model is developed to estimate the shape in the natural illumination. This algorithm estimates an image's surface normals of a diffuse object with constant albedo under known uncontrolled illumination. SFS algorithm is an optimization scheme that works for both simulated and real images (Johnson & Adelson, 2011).

Deep Convolutional Neural Fields method has proposed to forecast the depth value of an image by solving MAP inference. Especially this method has proposed deep structured learning scheme to acquire a knowledge of the strength of pair wise continuous and unary CRF along with deep CNN framework. Deep Convolutional Neural Fields approach is also applicable for other vision applications such as denoising of an image. Results of the experiment illustrate that the method works on both real and synthetic datasets (Liu et al., 2015).

There is a common and modern framework to estimate the surface normal and value of depth from a given image by DCNN. Conditional Random Fields (CRF) technique accompanied with DCNN. Initially DCNN model designed for mapping the multi scale image to surface normal or depth values. Next step is super-pixel level depth estimation is determined to the pixel level (Li et al., 2015). This framework produces better results for the estimation of depth and surface normal. Multiple data augmentation techniques can be examined to enhance the efficiency of image transformations of real world in the future. The use of deeper Convolutional Neural Networks can be explored further (Eigen & Fergus, 2015). Computer vision performs the various tasks such as determining semantic labels, depth, and surface normals. A simple and fast multiscale architecture has proposed that applies convolutional networks to represent these tasks. They are represented by single multiscale convolutional network architecture. This approach adapts all these tasks by applying simple modifications and subsiding to the map of output from the input of image (Eigen & Fergus, 2015).

Direct intrinsic is a new decomposition of intrinsic image approach proposed to decompose a single given image as shading components and albedo. It is based on RedGreenBlue(RGB) model for determining the depth of the given image (Narihira et al., 2015). This approach is neither depending on the image formation nor shading and albedo priors' statistics. A feed forward convolutional neural networks architecture which has two level has developed. In this technique, the architecture at the coarse level is to predict the context of globe and the exquisite network is to predict the coarse level network's output that predicts the result of finer resolution (Narihira et al., 2015).

A system proposed to illustrate the novel views of a single given image. Initially the given single 2D image of a given object's realistic novel 3D views are synthesized by novel view synthesis method, then 3D shapes are aligned to a given single image through 2D-to-3D alignment method, finally to improve the efficiency of object detection, synthesized images are utilized as additional training data. For future work, the synthesis and alignment for videos can be extended, and unknown object classes can also be experimented (Rematas et al., 2016).

A Deep Convolutional Neural Networks based approach has proposed to determine the surface normal of a single given image. This model uses the insight image as the input for the 3D representation and used to capture the coarse scene structure with fine details (Wang et al., 2015).

The HyFRIS-Net network is developed by inherent quality and trained to attain the objectiveness that is applicable generally on real-time data. Comprehensive qualitative and quantitative evaluations with state-of-the-art methods are conducted to demonstrate the merits of HyFRIS-Net in modeling photo-realistic face albedo, illumination, and shape (Zhu et al., 2022).

Figure 2. Object detection process

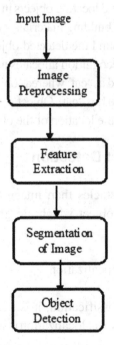

235

Figure 3. Object detection in an image

3. OBJECT DETECTION

Detection of an object in a given image or video is a technique of Computer Vision. Object detection is used for identifying and locating objects in an image or video. Those objects can be human, animals, vehicles, building materials, etc. Object detection is carried out by outlining bounding boxes around the detected objects, then locating the objects in a given image or scene. Image recognition allocates a label to an image, for example a picture of a cat or two cats labelled as 'cat' whereas object detection outlines a bounding box around each cat and labels the box 'cat'. Object detection delivers more details than image recognition by predicting the location of the object and the appropriate label.

3.1. Challenges of Object Detection

Object detection has more obstacles than image classification, object detection framework suffers with small object which are grouped together when they are overlapped or occluded.

1.   Object classification and localization

    While performing image classification, it is necessary to identify the object's location or position is called as object localization task. It is an additional complicated task for object detection. Multi task loss function is used to overcome the mislabeled or misclassification and localization errors.

$$\varsigma\left(p, u, t^u, v\right) = \overbrace{\varsigma_c\left(p, u\right)}^{classification} + \lambda\left[u \geq 1\right] \overbrace{\varsigma_l\left(t^u, v\right)}^{localization}$$

2. Time complexity for real time detection

Object detection has to classify and locate the objects accurately along with speed. Prediction time must be fast to satisfy the real time demands of video processing. Enhancement of the object detection algorithms increases the speed of the object detection process. Object detection must have the balance between speed and accuracy.

3. Multiple scales and aspect ratios

Region of interest(RoI) appears in various scales and aspect ratios for many object detection applications. Practitioners influences many detection algorithm techniques to identify objects at various aspect ratios and scales.

4. Limited data

Object detection encounters an another significant hurdle is the limited amount of defined data which are presently accessible for object detection. Object detection datasets consist of ground truth samples of thousands classes of objects. Accumulating ground truth labels along with precise bounding boxes for detecting object is a complex work.

5. Class imbalance

There is an another substantial hurdle is class imbalance faced by object detection. For example, a typical image consists of some main objects and the other part of the image is occupied by background. To overcome the class imbalance issue, we can use focal loss approach that is implemented in RetinaNet.

3.2. Applications of Object Detection

1. Object tracking

Object tracking is used to track a person or object in a video. It is very helpful to track the motion of a ball during a cricket or football match, tracking the action of a cricket bat, tracking people in a video. Tracking the object plays a vital role in the field of security, surveillance, traffic monitoring, robot vision, traffic monitoring, and animation.

2.   Object counting

Object detection helps to count the objects or people in the video or image. It is useful to analyze performance of the store or statistical analysis of crowd during festivals. People depart of the frame fast, so counting people is more complex task.

3.   Self-driving car

Self-driving car is an essential application of object detection. A self-driving car can navigate through a street by detecting all the objects like other road signs, cars, people on the road for making decision about taking necessary action in the upcoming step whether to apply brakes or turn, accelerate, objects around the car. A car is trained to identify known set of objects such as road signs, cars, people, traffic lights, bicycles and motorcycles, etc.

4.   Traffic monitoring and road maintenance

Object detection monitors traffic and road conditions in smart cities. Computer vision provides real time data to transportation system about traffic levels, accidents and hazards. Object detection helps monitoring the access points by detecting whether the vehicle have the proper rights by checking the license plate against a database.

5.   Anomaly detection

Object detection plays major role in detecting anomalies which has industry specific applications. In the agriculture field, object detection helps the farmers to identify infected crops and take the precautions accordingly. Likewise, it also identifies the skin problems, and various disease detection in healthcare. Object detection technique is also helpful in identifying complex parts quickly and make the industry to decide the appropriate measure in the manufacturing industry.

Figure 4. One and two stage object detectors

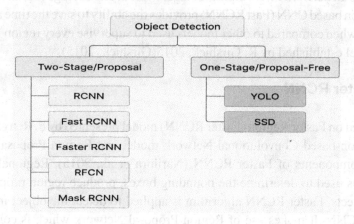

4. OBJECT DETECTION ALGORITHMS

There are several object detection algorithms for object detection. Some of them are:

4.1. RCNN

Region based Convolutional Networks (RCNN) uses the selective search approach to capture object location in an image. J. R. R. Uijlings et al. developed this model in 2012. Another Region based convolutional networks built up by R. Girshick et al. in 2014. It is the combination of the deep learning and the selective searching method. In this algorithm, the method of selective search is applied to detect the proposals of region and deep learning method is implemented to determine the object from the regions. The combination of Convolution Neural Networks (CNNs) and region proposals is known as Region-based Convolutional Network method (RCNN). RCNN is used to locate the objects in the trained and defined detection data by a deep neural network. This algorithm ensures accurate object detection by applying a deep ConvNet classifies object proposals and attains higher accuracy of object detection. R-CNN is capable of scaling large amount of object classes without approximation techniques and hashing (Girshick et al., 2014).

4.2. Fast RCNN

Fast Region based Convolutional Network model is an object detection algorithm which is written in Python and C++. Fast RCNN overcomes the complexities of RCNN and SPPnet and provides better speed and accuracy. Fast RCNN enables better mAP than RCNN and SPPnet. In Fast RCNN, multi task loss is used to train and update all network layers in single stage, without disk storage to feature caching. Fast Region based CNN (Fast RCNN) provides the ability to save the time and avoids the delay when compared to other models used to supervise every region proposals. This model established by R. Girshick, 2015(Girshick, 2015).

4.3. Faster RCNN

CNN based on Faster Region (Faster RCNN) model presented by S. Ren et al., 2016. Fast Region-based Convolutional Network model and Region Proposal Network are the components of Faster RCNN (Narihira et al., 2015). Regional Proposal Network is used to determine the bounding boxes, produce region proposals, and detect objects. Faster RCNN algorithm is applied to detect the object in a similar way of RCNN. It makes use of Region Proposal Network which is composed of convolutional features and detection network. This algorithm is more cost efficient than Fast RCNN and RCNN. RPN has the convolutional layers to detect the object bounds and objectness scores. It is trained completely to provide hide grade region proposals, then they are given to Fast RCNN to detect the objects (Ren & He, 2017).

Figure 5.

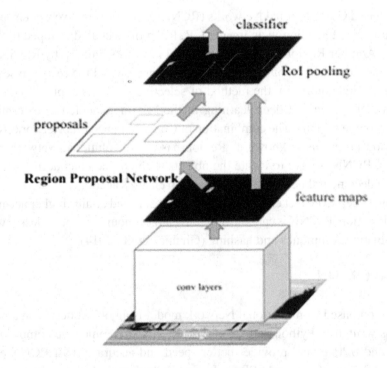

4.4. RFCN

J. Dai et al. created the Region based Fully CNN (RFCN) model in 2016. Two basic steps are combined into a single model to detect the object and its location. This model has only convolutional layers that permits complete back propagation for training and inference. Region based entirely convolutional network is an efficient and accurate object detection algorithm. RFCN performs convolutional computation on the whole image. Other region based object detection algorithms like Fast RCNN and Faster RCNN performs per-region subnetwork which is more expensive. RFCN applies entire convolutional image classifier like Residual Networks to detect object. RFCN performs object detection quicker than Faster RCNN (Dai & Li, 2016).

4.5. YOLO

J. Redmon et al. constructed the You Only Look Once (YOLO) model in 2016. This model is used for determining class probabilities and bounding boxes directly by evaluating once with only one network. The YOLO model is simple and permits real-time predictions. YOLO is a well-known object detection algorithm for researchers all over world. Facebook AI Researchers exclaim that YOLO unified architecture is super-fast for detecting objects. This model refines figures or pictures at 45 frames per second in real time, Fast YOLO deals with 155 frames per second and achieves twofold the mAP when compared with other real time detectors. YOLO algorithm performs better than DPM and RCNN object detection methods for generalizing natural images to artwork (Redmon et al., 2016).

4.6. SSD

The Single Shot Detector model developed by W. Liu et al. in 2016. It resembles the You Only Look Once model and used for determining the class probabilities and the bounding boxes all at a time using a Convolutional neural networks which is an end to end architecture. An object detection algorithm using single deep neural network to detect the object in images is known as Single Shot Detector(SSD). The SSD method discretises the output into default boxes on top of different screen proportion, then it measures each feature map location. The SSD model collects various feature maps resolutions to detect different size objects. The merits of SSD are, SSD omits the feature resampling stages and proposal generation, and combines entire computation in a sole network, SSD is simpler to train and incorporate for a system that requires object detection, SSD detects objects accurately and faster for training and inference (Liu, 2016).

4.7. YOLO9000 and YOLOv2

YOLO9000 model developed by J. Redmon and A. Farhadi, 2016. This model used for detecting 9000 object categories and above while. When compared to initial YOLO model. It has improved performances (Redmon & Farhadi, 2017).

The YOLOv2 model is a fast detector and used to improve accuracy. It allows higher resolution images as input and adds batch normalization to prevent over fitting (Hong-wei et al., 2018).

4.8. NASNet

The Neural Architecture Search Net (NASNet) developed by B. Zoph et al., 2017. It is used to augment the various layers besides enhancing the accuracy for the dataset which has given. This method is used for spatial detection (Falconí et al., 2019).

4.9. Mask RCNN

Mask Region based Convolutional Network (Mask RCNN) has additional features from the Faster RCNN model presented by K. He et al., 2017. This model used for detecting the bounding box that determines the object mask by adding a parallel branch. The object's mask is represented by segmenting the object by image's pixel. This model represents the tasks such as detecting the object, segmenting the instance, detecting the bounding box (Nguyen et al., 2018).

Figure 6.

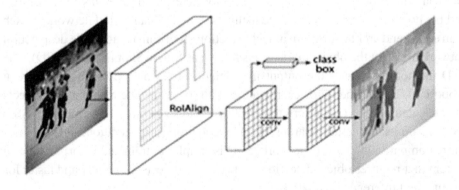

4.10. Spatial Pyramid Pooling (SPP-net)

The network is used to produce a fixed length depiction in spite of the scale or size of the image is called as Spatial Pyramid Pooling (SPP-net). Pyramid pooling enhances CNN based object detection methods and robust to object deformations. Researchers use SPP-net to calculate the feature maps for the whole figure at single time and pool features in sub figures to produce fixed-length depictions to train the detectors. SPP network eliminates additional calculation of convolutional features (He et al., 2015).

4.11 Histogram of Oriented Gradients (HOG)

Histogram of oriented gradients(HOG) is a technique which is a feature descriptor used to locate objects in computer vision and image processing. This technique represents gradient orientation of a figure like detection window, the region of interest (ROI). The HOG is simple and easy to understand the data (Dalal & Triggs, 2005).

5. DATA SETS

There are numerous datasets have developed for detecting the objects. Some of them are:

5.1. PASCAL VOC

The PASCAL Visual Object Classification dataset is more familiar. It is used for detecting objects, segmenting objects, and classifying objects, etc. This dataset is referred as resource dataset and consists of 20 categories.

5.2. ImageNet

ImageNet dataset contains bounding boxes, 500000 images for training and 200 categories. The dataset size needs an essential calculating power for training and the more classes make the task of recognizing object as more complicated. Due to these complexities, it is rarely used.

5.3. COCO

Microsoft and T.Y. Lin et al. developed the COCO (Common Objects in Context) dataset in 2015. The applications of this dataset are detecting the objects, segmenting the objects, caption generation, and key point detection. For training and validation purpose, the dataset provides more than 120000 images, for testing purpose, it provides more than 40000 images.

The below table structure (Table 1) and pictorial representation (Figure 2) shows the correlation of mean Average Precession(mAP) scores of the PASCAL VOC dataset (2012) and COCO dataset (2016). The object detection models provide accuracy or speed. These models have heavy and complex architectures, for example YOLOv2 has 200MB architecture, and NASNet has 400MB architecture.

Table 1. Correlation of the mean Average Precession scores on the PASCAL VOC dataset (2012) and COCO dataset (2016)

Model	PASCAL VOC 2012	COCO 2016(Official Metric)	Real Time Speed
R-CNN	X	X	No
Fast R-CNN	68.40%	X	No
Faster R-CNN	75.90%	X	No
R-FCN	X	X	No
YOLO	57.90%	X	Yes
SSD	82.20%	X	No
YOLOv2	X	X	Yes
NASNet	X	X	No
Mask R-CNN	X	39.80%	No

CONCLUSION

This overview discusses about the object detection, algorithms and techniques. The measurement of shape, reflectance, and illumination of a given object, object detection algorithms and data sets used in various recent research works. Through this survey, it is understandable that various deep learning methods can be used to determine the illumination estimation and reflectance estimation of the single given image. Different sources for data sets are available for object detection. The single given image represents a single material specular object with natural illumination. Additionally, shadows and illumination which is indirect can be included in the reflectance model. This method can also be used to evaluate more complicated models for reflectance. Thus the overview also outlines the various applications and challenges of object detection and provides the comparison of different datasets performance based on the object detection algorithm techniques.

Figure 7. Correlation of the mean Average Precession scores on the PASCAL VOC dataset (2012) and COCO dataset (2016)

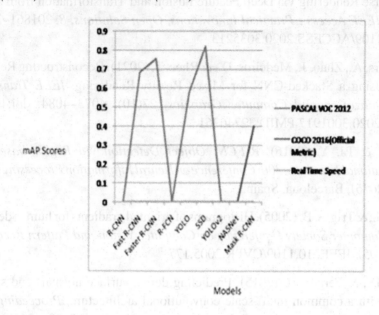

Competing Interests

The authors declare that they have no known competing financial interests or personal relationships that could have appeared to influence the work reported in this paper.

ACKNOWLEDGMENT

The authors acknowledge that there are no funding grants, and conflicts of interest.

REFERENCES

Barron, J. T., & Malik, J. (2015). Shape, illumination, and reflectance from shading. *IEEE Transactions on Pattern Analysis and Machine Intelligence, 37*(8), 1670–1687. doi:10.1109/TPAMI.2014.2377712 PMID:26353003

Barrow, H., & Tenenbaum, J. (1978). Computer vision systems. Computer vision systems, 2.

Bi, T., Ma, J., Liu, Y., Weng, D., & Wang, Y. (2020). SIR-Net: Self-Supervised Transfer for Inverse Rendering via Deep Feature Fusion and Transformation from a Single Image. *IEEE Access : Practical Innovations, Open Solutions, 8,* 201861–201873. doi:10.1109/ACCESS.2020.3035213

Chalmers, A., Zhao, J., Medeiros, D., & Rhee, T. (2021). Reconstructing Reflection Maps Using a Stacked-CNN for Mixed Reality Rendering. *IEEE Transactions on Visualization and Computer Graphics, 27*(10), 4073–4084. doi:10.1109/TVCG.2020.3001917 PMID:32746261

Dai, J., & Li, Y. (2016). R-*FCN: Object Detection via Region-based Fully Convolutional Networks. 30th Conference on Neural Information Processing Systems (NIPS 2016),* Barcelona, Spain.

Dalal, N., & Triggs, B. (2005). Histograms of oriented gradients for human detection. *IEEE Computer Society Conference on Computer Vision and Pattern Recognition (CVPR'05).* IEEE. 10.1109/CVPR.2005.177

Eigen, D., & Fergus, R. (2015). Predicting depth, surface normals and semantic labels with a common multi-scale convolutional architecture. *Proceedings IEEE Conference Computing Visual Pattern Recognition,* (pp. 2650– 2658). IEEE. 10.1109/ICCV.2015.304

Falconí, L. G., Pérez, M., & Aguilar, W. G. (2019). Transfer Learning in Breast Mammogram Abnormalities Classification with Mobilenet and Nasnet. *International Conference on Systems, Signals and Image Processing (IWSSIP),* IEEE. 10.1109/IWSSIP.2019.8787295

Georgoulis, S., Rematas, K., Ritschel, T., Gavves, E., Fritz, M., Van Gool, L., & Tuytelaars, T. (2018). Reflectance and Natural Illumination from Single-Material Specular Objects Using Deep Learning. *IEEE Transactions on Pattern Analysis and Machine Intelligence, 37*(8), 1932–1947. doi:10.1109/TPAMI.2017.2742999 PMID:28841552

Girshick, R. (2015). Fast R-CNN. *IEEE International Conference on Computer Vision (ICCV).* IEEE.

Girshick, R., Donahue, J., Darrell, T., & Malik, J. (2014). Rich Feature Hierarchies for Accurate Object Detection and Semantic Segmentation. *IEEE Conference on Computer Vision and Pattern Recognition.* IEEE. 10.1109/CVPR.2014.81

He, K., Zhang, X., Ren, S., & Sun, J. (2015). Spatial Pyramid Pooling in Deep Convolutional Networks for Visual Recognition. *IEEE Transactions on Pattern Analysis and Machine Intelligence.* IEEE.

Hong-wei, Z., Zhang, L., & Li, P. (2018). Yarn-dyed Fabric Defect Detection with YOLOV2 Based on Deep Convolution Neural Networks. *IEEE 7th Data Driven Control and Learning Systems Conference (DDCLS)*. IEEE.

Horn, B. K. P., & Brooks, M. J. (Eds.). (1989). *Shape from Shading*. MIT press.

Johnson, M. K., & Adelson, E. H. (2011). Shape estimation in natural illumination. *Proceedings IEEE Conference Computing Visual Pattern Recognition*, (pp. 2553–2560). IEEE.

Li, B., Shen, C., Dai, Y., van den Hengel, A., & He, M. (2015). Depth and surface normal estimation from monocular images using regression on deep features and hierarchical CRFs. *Proceedings IEEE Conference Computing Visual Pattern Recognition*, (pp. 1119–1127). IEEE.

Liu, F., Shen, C., & Lin, G. (2015). Deep convolutional neural fields for depth estimation from a single image. *Proceedings IEEE Conference Computing Visual Pattern Recognition*, (pp. 5162–5170). IEEE. 10.1109/CVPR.2015.7299152

Liu, W. (2016). *SSD: Single Shot MultiBox Detector*. Ann-Arb.

Lombardi, S., & Nishino, K. (2015). Reflectance and illumination recovery in the wild. *IEEE Transactions on Pattern Analysis and Machine Intelligence*, *38*(1), 129–141. doi:10.1109/TPAMI.2015.2430318 PMID:26656582

Narihira, T., Maire, M., & Yu, S. X. (2015). Direct intrinsics: Learning albedo-shading decomposition by convolutional regression. *Proceedings IEEE Conference Computing Visual Pattern Recognition*, (pp. 2992–2992). IEEE. 10.1109/ICCV.2015.342

Nguyen, D.-H., Le, T.-H., Tran, T.-H., Vu, H., Le, T.-L., & Doan, H.-G. (2018). Hand segmentation under different viewpoints by combination of Mask R-CNN with tracking. *5th Asian Conference on Defense Technology (ACDT)*. IEEE. doi:10.1109/ACDT.2018.8593130

Redmon, J., Divvala, S., Girshick, R., & Farhadi, A. (2016). You Only Look Once: Unified, Real-Time Object Detection. *IEEE Conference on Computer Vision and Pattern Recognition (CVPR)*. IEEE. 10.1109/CVPR.2016.91

Redmon, J., & Farhadi, A. (2017). YOLO9000: Better, Faster, Stronger. *IEEE Conference on Computer Vision and Pattern Recognition (CVPR)*. IEEE.

Rematas, K., Nguyen, C., Ritschel, T., Fritz, M., & Tuytelaars, T. (2016). Novel views of objects from a single image. *IEEE Transactions on Pattern Analysis and Machine Intelligence*, *39*(8), 1576–1590. doi:10.1109/TPAMI.2016.2601093 PMID:27541489

Ren, S. & He, K. (2017). Faster R-CNN: Towards Real-Time Object Detection with Region Proposal Networks. *IEEE Transactions on Pattern Analysis and Machine Intelligence*. IEEE.

Thul, D., Tsiminaki, V., Ladický, Ľ., & Pollefeys, M. (2020). Precomputed Radiance Transfer for Reflectance and Lighting Estimation. *2020 International Conference on 3D Vision (3DV)*. IEEE. 10.1109/3DV50981.2020.00125

Wang, X., Fouhey, D. F., & Gupta, A. (2015). Designing deep networks for surface normal estimation. *Proceedings IEEE Conference Computing Visual Pattern Recognition*. IEEE. 10.1109/CVPR.2015.7298652

Zhang, A., Zhao, Y., & Wang, S. (2019). Illumination estimation for augmented reality based on a global illumination model. *Multimedia Tools and Applications*, *78*(23), 33487–33503. doi:10.100711042-019-08155-2

Zhu, Y., Li, C., Li, S., Shi, B., & Tai, Y.-W. (2022). Hybrid Face Reflectance, Illumination, and Shape from a Single Image. *IEEE Transactions on Pattern Analysis and Machine Intelligence*, *44*(9), 5002–5015. PMID:33989152

Compilation of References

Abd El-Latif, A. A., Ahmad Wani, M., & El-Affendi, M. A. (2023). *Advanced Applications of NLP and Deep Learning in Social Media Data.* IGI Global. [https://www.igi-global.com/book/advanced-applications-nlp-deep-learning/304800 doi:10.4018/978-1-6684-6909-5

Abd El-Latif, A. A., Abd-El-Atty, B., Amin, M., & Iliyasu, A. M. (2020, February). Quantum-inspired cascaded discrete-time quantum walks with induced chaotic dynamics and cryptographic applications. *Scientific Reports, 10*(1), 1. doi:10.103841598-020-58636-w PMID:32029798

Abd El-Latif, A. A., Abd-El-Atty, B., Elseuofi, S., Khalifa, H. S., Alghamdi, A. S., Polat, K., & Amin, M. (2020, March). Secret images transfer in cloud system based on investigating quantum walks in steganography approaches. *Physica A, 541*, 123687. doi:10.1016/j.physa.2019.123687

Abd EL-Latif, A. A., Abd-El-Atty, B., & Venegas-Andraca, S. E. (2019, August). A novel image steganography technique based on quantum substitution boxes. *Optics & Laser Technology, 116*, 92–102. doi:10.1016/j.optlastec.2019.03.005

Abd-El-Atty, B., Belazi, A., & Abd El-Latif, A. A. (2022). A Novel Approach for Robust S-Box Construction Using a 5-D Chaotic Map and Its Application to Image Cryptosystem. In Cybersecurity: A New Approach Using Chaotic Systems. Springer International Publishing. doi:10.1007/978-3-030-92166-8_1

Abd-El-Atty, B., Abd El-Latif, A. A., & Amin, M. (2017). New Quantum Image Steganography Scheme with Hadamard Transformation. *Proceedings of the International Conference on Advanced Intelligent Systems and Informatics 2016, 533*, 342-352. 10.1007/978-3-319-48308-5_33

Abd-El-Atty, B., Iliyasu, A. M., Alaskar, H., & Abd El-Latif, A. A. (2020, January). A Robust Quasi-Quantum Walks-based Steganography Protocol for Secure Transmission of Images on Cloud-based E-healthcare Platforms. *Sensors (Basel), 20*(11), 11. Advance online publication. doi:10.339020113108 PMID:32486383

Abdel-Aziz, M. M., Hosny, K. M., & Lashin, N. A. (2021, March). Improved data hiding method for securing color images. *Multimedia Tools and Applications, 80*(8), 12641–12670. doi:10.100711042-020-10217-9

Abdulrahaman, M. D., Faruk, N., Oloyede, A. A., Surajudeen-Bakinde, N. T., Olawoyin, L. A., Mejabi, O. V., Imam-Fulani, Y. O., Fahm, A. O., & Azeez, A. L. (2020, November). Multimedia tools in the teaching and learning processes: A systematic review. *Heliyon*, *6*(11), e05312. doi:10.1016/j.heliyon.2020.e05312 PMID:33195834

Adil, M., Almaiah, M. A., Omar Alsayed, A., & Almomani, O. (2020, April 18). An anonymous channel categorization scheme of edge nodes to detect jamming attacks in wireless sensor networks. *Sensors (Basel)*, *20*(8), 2311. doi:10.339020082311 PMID:32325646

Adil, M., Khan, R., Ali, J., Roh, B. H., Ta, Q. T., & Almaiah, M. A. (2020, August 31). An energy proficient load balancing routing scheme for wireless sensor networks to maximize their lifespan in an operational environment. *IEEE Access : Practical Innovations, Open Solutions*, *8*, 163209–163224. doi:10.1109/ACCESS.2020.3020310

Adil, M., Khan, R., Almaiah, M. A., Al-Zahrani, M., Zakarya, M., Amjad, M. S., & Ahmed, R. (2020, March 4). MAC-AODV based mutual authentication scheme for constraint oriented networks. *IEEE Access : Practical Innovations, Open Solutions*, *8*, 44459–44469. doi:10.1109/ACCESS.2020.2978303

Adil, M., Khan, R., Almaiah, M. A., Binsawad, M., Ali, J., Al Saaidah, A., & Ta, Q. T. (2020, August 11). An efficient load balancing scheme of energy gauge nodes to maximize the lifespan of constraint oriented networks. *IEEE Access : Practical Innovations, Open Solutions*, *8*, 148510–148527. doi:10.1109/ACCESS.2020.3015941

Agarwal, M., Shalika, V. T., & Gupta, P. (2019). Handwritten character recognition using neural network and tensor flow. *International Journal of Innovative Technology and Exploring Engineering*, 8.

Agilandeeswari, L., Prabukumar, M., & Alenizi, F. A. (2023). A robust semi-fragile watermarking system using Pseudo-Zernike moments and dual tree complex wavelet transform for social media content authentication. *Multimedia Tools and Applications*. doi:10.100711042-023-15177-4 PMID:37362657

Ahmad Wani, M., ELAffendi, M. A., Shakil, K. A., Shariq Imran, A., & Abd El-Latif, A. A. (2023, August). Depression Screening in Humans With AI and Deep Learning Techniques. *IEEE Transactions on Computational Social Systems*, *10*(4), 2074–2089. doi:10.1109/TCSS.2022.3200213

Ahmed, S. M., Eldin, F. A. E., & Tarek, A. M. (2010). *Speckle noise reduction in SAR images using adaptive morphological filter*. 2010 10th International Conference on Intelligent Systems Design and Applications, Cairo. 10.1109/ISDA.2010.5687254

Ahmed, M., Masood, S., Ahmad, M., & Abd El-Latif, A. A. (2021). Intelligent driver drowsiness detection for traffic safety based on multi CNN deep model and facial subsampling. *IEEE Transactions on Intelligent Transportation Systems*, *23*(10), 19743–19752. doi:10.1109/TITS.2021.3134222

Compilation of References

Aizerman, M. A., Braverman, E. M., & Rozonoer, L. I. (1970). *The Method of Potential Functions in the Theory of Machine Learning*. Nauka.

Al Hwaitat, A. K., Almaiah, M. A., Ali, A., Al-Otaibi, S., Shishakly, R., Lutfi, A., & Alrawad, M. (2023, August 27). A New Blockchain-Based Authentication Framework for Secure IoT Networks. *Electronics (Basel)*, *12*(17), 3618. doi:10.3390/electronics12173618

Al Hwaitat, A. K., Almaiah, M. A., Almomani, O., Al-Zahrani, M., Al-Sayed, R. M., Asaifi, R. M., Adhim, K. K., Althunibat, A., & Alsaaidah, A. (2020). Improved security particle swarm optimization (PSO) algorithm to detect radio jamming attacks in mobile networks. *International Journal of Advanced Computer Science and Applications*, *11*(4). Advance online publication. doi:10.14569/IJACSA.2020.0110480

Al Nafea, R., & Almaiah, M. A. (2021). Cyber security threats in cloud: Literature review. In *2021 International Conference on Information Technology (ICIT)*, (pp. 779-786). IEEE. 10.1109/ICIT52682.2021.9491638

Alabaichi, M. A. A. K. & Al-Dabbas, A. S. (2020). Image steganography using least significant bit and secret map techniques. *Int. J. Electr. Comput. Eng.*, *10*(1).

Aldhyani, T. H., Khan, M. A., Almaiah, M. A., Alnazzawi, N., Hwaitat, A. K., Elhag, A., Shehab, R. T., & Alshebami, A. S. (2023, February 8). A Secure internet of medical things Framework for Breast Cancer Detection in Sustainable Smart Cities. *Electronics (Basel)*, *12*(4), 858. doi:10.3390/electronics12040858

Ali, A., Rahim, H., Ali, J., Pasha, M., Masud, M., Rehman, A., Chen, C., & Baz, M. (2021). A Novel Secure Blockchain Framework for Accessing Electronic Health Records Using Multiple Certificate Authority. *Applied Sciences*. https://www.mdpi.com/2076-3417/11/21/9999.

Ali, A., Almaiah, M. A., Hajjej, F., Pasha, M. F., Fang, O. H., Khan, R., Teo, J., & Zakarya, M. (2022, January 12). An Industrial IoT-Based Blockchain-Enabled Secure Searchable Encryption Approach for Healthcare Systems Using Neural Network. *Sensors (Basel)*, *22*(2), 572. doi:10.339022020572 PMID:35062530

Ali, A., & Mehboob, M. *Comparative Analysis of Selected Routing Protocols for WLAN Based Wireless Sensor Networks (WSNs)*. In *2nd International Multi-Disciplinary Conference*, Oxford, UK.

Ali, A., Naveed, M., Mehboob, M., Irshad, H., & Anwar, P. (2017). An interference aware multi-channel MAC protocol for WASN. In *Proceedings of the 2017 International Conference on Innovations in Electrical Engineering and Computational Technologies (ICIEECT)*, Karachi, Pakistan. 10.1109/ICIEECT.2017.7916523

Ali, A., Rahim, H. A., Pasha, M. F., Dowsley, R., Masud, M., Ali, J., & Baz, M. (2021). Security, Privacy, and Reliability in Digital Healthcare Systems Using Blockchain. *Journal of Electronics (China)*, *10*, 2034.

251

Aliyev, V. (2010). *Using honeypots to study skill level of attackers based on the exploited vulnerabilities in the network*. Chalmers University of Technology.

Almaiah, M. A. (2021). A new scheme for detecting malicious attacks in wireless sensor networks based on blockchain technology. In Artificial Intelligence and Blockchain for Future Cybersecurity Applications. Springer.

Almaiah, M. A., Ali, A., Hajjej, F., Pasha, M. F., & Alohali, M. A. (2022, March 9). A Lightweight Hybrid Deep Learning Privacy Preserving Model for FC-Based Industrial Internet of Medical Things. *Sensors (Basel)*, *22*(6), 2112. doi:10.339022062112 PMID:35336282

Almaiah, M. A., Al-Otaibi, S., Shishakly, R., Hassan, L., Lutfi, A., Alrawad, M., Qatawneh, M., & Alghanam, O. A. (2023, June 21). Investigating the Role of Perceived Risk, Perceived Security and Perceived Trust on Smart m-Banking Application Using SEM. *Sustainability (Basel)*, *15*(13), 9908. doi:10.3390u15139908

Almaiah, M. A., Al-Zahrani, A., Almomani, O., & Alhwaitat, A. K. (2021). *Classification of cyber security threats on mobile devices and applications. In Artificial Intelligence and Blockchain for Future Cybersecurity Applications*. Springer.

Almaiah, M. A., Dawahdeh, Z., Almomani, O., Alsaaidah, A., Al-Khasawneh, A., & Khawatreh, S. (2020, December). A new hybrid text encryption approach over mobile ad hoc network. *Iranian Journal of Electrical and Computer Engineering*, *10*(6), 6461–6471. doi:10.11591/ijece.v10i6.pp6461-6471

Almaiah, M. A., Hajjej, F., Ali, A., Pasha, M. F., & Almomani, O. (2022, February 13). A Novel Hybrid Trustworthy Decentralized Authentication and Data Preservation Model for Digital Healthcare IoT Based CPS. *Sensors (Basel)*, *22*(4), 1448. doi:10.339022041448 PMID:35214350

Alqudah, H., Lutfi, A., Al Qudah, M. Z., Alshira'h, A. F., Almaiah, M. A., & Alrawad, M. (2023, November 1). The impact of empowering internal auditors on the quality of electronic internal audits: A case of Jordanian listed services companies. *International Journal of Information Management Data Insights.*, *3*(2), 100183. doi:10.1016/j.jjimei.2023.100183

Alrawad, M., Lutfi, A., Almaiah, M. A., Alsyouf, A., Al-Khasawneh, A. L., Arafa, H. M., Ahmed, N. A., AboAlkhair, A. M., & Tork, M. (2023, February 1). Managers' perception and attitude toward financial risks associated with SMEs: Analytic hierarchy process approach. *Journal of Risk and Financial Management.*, *16*(2), 86. doi:10.3390/jrfm16020086

Alrawad, M., Lutfi, A., Almaiah, M. A., Alsyouf, A., Arafa, H. M., Soliman, Y., & Elshaer, I. A. (2023, June 22). A Novel Framework of Public Risk Assessment Using an Integrated Approach Based on AHP and Psychometric Paradigm. *Sustainability (Basel)*, *15*(13), 9965. doi:10.3390u15139965

Alrawad, M., Lutfi, A., Almaiah, M. A., & Elshaer, I. A. (2023, June 2). Examining the influence of trust and perceived risk on customers intention to use NFC mobile payment system. *Journal of Open Innovation*, *9*(2), 100070. doi:10.1016/j.joitmc.2023.100070

Alrawad, M., Lutfi, A., Alyatama, S., Al Khattab, A., Alsoboa, S. S., Almaiah, M. A., Ramadan, M. H., Arafa, H. M., Ahmed, N. A., Alsyouf, A., & Al-Khasawneh, A. L. (2023, March 1). Assessing customers perception of online shopping risks: A structural equation modeling–based multigroup analysis. *Journal of Retailing and Consumer Services*, *71*, 103188. doi:10.1016/j.jretconser.2022.103188

Alvarez, G., Sheffer, B., & Bryant, M. (n.d.). *Offline signature verification with convolutional neural networks*. https://github.com/Lasagne/Recipes/blob/master/modelzoo/vgg16.py.

Alzain, E., Al-Otaibi, S., Aldhyani, T. H., Alshebami, A. S., Almaiah, M. A., & Jadhav, M. E. (2023, May 14). Revolutionizing Solar Power Production with Artificial Intelligence: A Sustainable Predictive Model. *Sustainability (Basel)*, *15*(10), 7999. doi:10.3390u15107999

Alzaylaee, M. K., Yerima, S. Y., & Sezer, S. (2020). DL-Droid: Deep learning based android malware detection using real devices. *Computers & Security*, *89*, 101663. doi:10.1016/j.cose.2019.101663

American Stroke Association. (2016). *To learn more about stroke, visit StrokeAssociation.org*. ASA. StrokeAssociation.org/WarningSigns

Amrit, P., & Singh, A. K. (2022, April). Survey on watermarking methods in the artificial intelligence domain and beyond. *Computer Communications*, *188*, 52–65. doi:10.1016/j.comcom.2022.02.023

Ananthi, G., Raja Sekar, J., Apsara, D., Gajalakshmi, A. K., & Tapthi, S. (2021). Enhanced Palmprint Identification Using Score Level Fusion [IJARSCT]. International Journal of Advanced Research in Science. *Tongxin Jishu*, *4*(3), 76–81. doi:10.48175/IJARSCT-V4-I3-011

Ananthi, G., Raja Sekar, J., & Arivazhagan, S. (2022a). Human palm vein authentication using curvelet multiresolution features and score level fusion. *The Visual Computer*, *38*(6), 1901–1914. doi:10.100700371-021-02253-9

Ananthi, G., Raja Sekar, J., & Arivazhagan, S. (2022b). Ensembling Scale Invariant and Multiresolution Gabor Scores for Palm Vein Identification. *Information Technology and Control*, *51*(4), 704–722. doi:10.5755/j01.itc.51.4.30858

Ananthi, G., Raja Sekar, J., & Lakshmipraba, N. (2018). PALM DORSAL SURFACE AND VEIN PATTERN BASED AUTHENTICATION SYSTEM. *International Journal of Pure and Applied Mathematics*, *118*(11), 767–773.

Angadi, S. A., & Gour, S. (2014, January). Euclidean distance based offline signature recognition system using global and local wavelet features. In *2014 Fifth International Conference on Signal and Image Processing* (pp. 87-91). IEEE. 10.1109/ICSIP.2014.19

Anisha, C. D. & Saranya, K. G. (2021). Early diagnosis of stroke disorder using homogenous logistic regression ensemble classifier. *Int. J. Nonlinear Anal. Appl.*, *12.*. doi:10.22075/IJNAA.2021.5851

Associate, D. C. D. (2021). Stroke Predication Using. *Machine Learning*, *20*(1), 7460–7464. doi:10.17051/ilkonline.2021.01.771

Athiwaratkun, B., & Stokes, J. W. (2017). Malware classification with LSTM and GRU language models and a character-level CNN. *2017 IEEE International Conference on Acoustics, Speech and Signal Processing (ICASSP)*, (pp. 2482–2486). IEEE. 10.1109/ICASSP.2017.7952603

Aubert, G., & Aujol, J.-F. (2008). A Variational Approach to Removing Multiplicative Noise. *SIAM Journal on Applied Mathematics*, 68(4), 925–946. doi:10.1137/060671814

Azaria, A., Ekblaw, A., Vieira, T., & Lippman, A. (2016). Medrec: Using blockchain for medical data access and permission management. In *Proceedings of the 2016 2nd International Conference on Open and Big Data (OBD)*, Vienna, Austria. 10.1109/OBD.2016.11

Balaji, T. K. (2021). Chandra Sekhara Rao Annavarapu, and Annushree Bablani. "Machine learning algorithms for social media analysis: A survey.". *Computer Science Review*, 40, 100395. doi:10.1016/j.cosrev.2021.100395

Bandi, V., Bhattacharyya, D., & Midhunchakkravarthy, D. (2020). Prediction of brain stroke severity using machine learning. Rev. d'Intelligence Artif., 34(6), 753–761. doi:10.18280/ria.340609

Barron, J. T., & Malik, J. (2015). Shape, illumination, and reflectance from shading. *IEEE Transactions on Pattern Analysis and Machine Intelligence*, 37(8), 1670–1687. doi:10.1109/TPAMI.2014.2377712 PMID:26353003

Barrow, H., & Tenenbaum, J. (1978). Computer vision systems. Computer vision systems, 2.

Belazi, A., Kharbech, S., Aslam, M. N., Talha, M., Xiang, W., Iliyasu, A. M., & El-Latif, A. A. A. (2022, May). Improved Sine-Tangent chaotic map with application in medical images encryption. *J. Inf. Secur. Appl.*, 66, 103131. doi:10.1016/j.jisa.2022.103131

Bengio, Y., Simard, P., & Frasconi, P. (1994). Learning long-term dependencies with gradient descent is difficult. *IEEE Transactions on Neural Networks*, 5(2), 157–166. doi:10.1109/72.279181 PMID:18267787

Benkouider, K., Vaidyanathan, S., Sambas, A., Tlelo-Cuautle, E., El-Latif, A. A. A., Abd-El-Atty, B., Bermudez-Marquez, C. F., Sulaiman, I. M., Awwal, A. M., & Kumam, P. (2022). A New 5-D Multistable Hyperchaotic System With Three Positive Lyapunov Exponents: Bifurcation Analysis, Circuit Design, FPGA Realization and Image Encryption. *IEEE Access : Practical Innovations, Open Solutions*, 10, 90111–90132. doi:10.1109/ACCESS.2022.3197790

Benrhouma, O., Hermassi, H., Abd El-Latif, A. A., & Belghith, S. (2016, July). Chaotic watermark for blind forgery detection in images. *Multimedia Tools and Applications*, 75(14), 8695–8718. doi:10.100711042-015-2786-z

Bergstra, J., Breuleux, O., Bastien, F. F., Lamblin, P., Pascanu, R., Desjardins, G., Turian, J., Warde-Farley, D., & Bengio, Y. (2010). *Theano: a CPU and GPU math compiler in Python.* Proceedings of the Python for Scientific Computing Conference (SciPy), Montreal. http://www-etud.iro.umontreal.ca/~wardefar/publications/theano_scipy2010.pdf

Bhattacharya, P. (2020). Mobile edge computing-enabled blockchain framework—a survey. *Proceedings of ICRIC 2019*, (pp.797–809). Springer.

Bhattacharya, I., Ghosh, P., & Biswas, S. (2013). Offline signature verification using pixel matching technique. *Procedia Technology*, *10*, 970–977. doi:10.1016/j.protcy.2013.12.445

Bhattacharyya, D., Biswas, S., & Kim, T.-H. (2010). Features extraction and verification of signature image using clustering technique. In *International Journal of International Journal of International Journal of International Journal of Smart Home Smart Home Smart Home Smart Home* (Vol. 4, Issue 4). https://www.researchgate.net/publication/228868400

Bianchi, T., Argenti, F., & Alparone, L. (2008). Segmentation-Based MAP Despeckling of SAR Images in the Undecimated Wavelet Domain. *IEEE Transactions on Geoscience and Remote Sensing*, *46*(9), 2728–2742. doi:10.1109/TGRS.2008.920018

Bioucas-Dias, J. M., & Figueiredo, M. A. T. (2010). Multiplicative Noise Removal Using Variable Splitting and Constrained Optimization. *IEEE Transactions on Image Processing*, *19*(7), 1720–1730. doi:10.1109/TIP.2010.2045029 PMID:20215071

Bi, T., Ma, J., Liu, Y., Weng, D., & Wang, Y. (2020). SIR-Net: Self-Supervised Transfer for Inverse Rendering via Deep Feature Fusion and Transformation from a Single Image. *IEEE Access : Practical Innovations, Open Solutions*, *8*, 201861–201873. doi:10.1109/ACCESS.2020.3035213

Borah, S., & Borah, B. (2019). A blind, semi-fragile 3d mesh watermarking algorithm using minimum distortion angle quantization index modulation (3d-mdaqim). *Arabian Journal for Science and Engineering*, *44*(4), 3867–3882. doi:10.100713369-018-03714-5

Bouaafia, S., Khemiri, R., Messaoud, S., Ben Ahmed, O., & Sayadi, F. E. (2022). Deep learning-based video quality enhancement for the new versatile video coding. *Neural Computing & Applications*, *34*(17), 14135–14149. doi:10.100700521-021-06491-9 PMID:34511732

Bubukayr, M. A., & Almaiah, M. A. (2021). Cybersecurity concerns in smart-phones and applications: A survey. In *2021 International Conference on Information Technology (ICIT)*, (pp. 725-731). IEEE. 10.1109/ICIT52682.2021.9491691

Bulten, W. (n.d.). *Automated Gleason Grading*. Computational Pathology Group. https://www.computationalpathologygroup.eu/software/automated- gleason-grading.

Cao, Y., Chiu, H.-K., Khosla, A., Chiung, C., & Lin, Y. (2021). CS229 Project: A Machine Learning Approach to Stroke Risk Prediction. Springer.

Cavallaro, A., Malekzadeh, M., & Shamsabadi, A. S. (2020). Deep learning for privacy in multimedia. In *Proceedings of the 28th ACM International Conference on Multimedia*, (pp. 4777-4778). ACM. 10.1145/3394171.3418551

Chakraborty, S., Aich, S., & Kim, H.-C. (2019). A secure healthcare system design framework using blockchain technology. In *Proceedings of the 2019 21st International Conference on Advanced Communication Technology (ICACT)*, PyeongChang, Korea. 10.23919/ICACT.2019.8701983

Chalmers, A., Zhao, J., Medeiros, D., & Rhee, T. (2021). Reconstructing Reflection Maps Using a Stacked-CNN for Mixed Reality Rendering. *IEEE Transactions on Visualization and Computer Graphics*, *27*(10), 4073–4084. doi:10.1109/TVCG.2020.3001917 PMID:32746261

Charniak, E. (1985). *Introduction to artificial intelligence*. Pearson Education India.

Chen, J., Chen, Y., Li, J. Wang, J., Lin, Z., & Nandi, A. K. (2021). Stroke Risk Prediction with Hybrid Deep Transfer Learning Framework. *IEEE J. Biomed. Heal. Informatics*. IEEE. . doi:10.1109/JBHI.2021.3088750

Chen, X., Ji, J., Luo, C., Liao, W., & Li, P. (2018). *When machine learning meets blockchain: A decentralized, privacy-preserving and secure design*. In IEEE International Conference on Big Data (Big Data), Seattle, WA, USA. 10.1109/BigData.2018.8622598

Chen, H., Wu, C., Du, B., Zhang, L., & Wang, L. (2020, April). Change Detection in Multisource VHR Images via Deep Siamese Convolutional Multiple-Layers Recurrent Neural Network. *IEEE Transactions on Geoscience and Remote Sensing*, *58*(4), 2848–2864. doi:10.1109/TGRS.2019.2956756

Chen, J., Chen, Y., An, W., Cui, Y., & Yang, J. (2011). Nonlocal Filtering for Polarimetric SAR Data: A Pretest Approach. *IEEE Transactions on Geoscience and Remote Sensing*, *49*(5), 1744–1754. doi:10.1109/TGRS.2010.2087763

Chen, J., Remulla, D., Nguyen, J. H., Dua, A., Liu, Y., Dasgupta, P., & Hung, A. J. (2019). Current status of artificial intelligence applications in urology and their potential to influence clinical practice. *BJU International*, *124*(4), 567–577. doi:10.1111/bju.14852 PMID:31219658

Chen, L.-C., Lee, C.-M., & Chen, M.-Y. (2020). Exploration of social media for sentiment analysis using deep learning. *Soft Computing*, *24*(11), 8187–8197. doi:10.100700500-019-04402-8

Cho, K., Van Merriënboer, B., Gulcehre, C., Bahdanau, D., Bougares, F., Schwenk, H., & Bengio, Y. (2014). Learning phrase representations using RNN encoder-decoder for statistical machine translation. *ArXiv Preprint ArXiv:1406.1078*. doi:10.3115/v1/D14-1179

Chollet, F. (2015). *Deep learning library for theano and tensorflow*. Keras.

Chumachenko, K., & Technology, I. (2017). *Machine Learning for Malware Detection and Classification*. [Bachelor's Thesis Information Technology, Southeast Finland University of Applied Sciences].

Dai, J., & Li, Y. (2016). *R-FCN: Object Detection via Region-based Fully Convolutional Networks*. *30th Conference on Neural Information Processing Systems (NIPS 2016)*, Barcelona, Spain.

Dai, Z., Lian, C., He, Z., Jiang, H., & Wang, Y. (2022). A Novel Hybrid Reversible-Zero Watermarking Scheme to Protect Medical Image. *IEEE Access : Practical Innovations, Open Solutions*, *10*, 58005–58016. doi:10.1109/ACCESS.2022.3170030

Dalal, N., & Triggs, B. (2005). Histograms of oriented gradients for human detection. *IEEE Computer Society Conference on Computer Vision and Pattern Recognition (CVPR'05)*. IEEE. 10.1109/CVPR.2005.177

Compilation of References

Daoui, A. (2022). Color stereo image encryption and local zero-watermarking schemes using octonion Hahn moments and modified Henon map. *J. King Saud Univ.- Comput. Inf. Sci., 34*(10), 8927–8954.

Daoui, A., Karmouni, H., El ogri, O., Sayyouri, M., & Qjidaa, H. (2022, March). Robust image encryption and zero-watermarking scheme using SCA and modified logistic map ». *Expert Systems with Applications, 190*, 116193. doi:10.1016/j.eswa.2021.116193

Daoui, A., Karmouni, H., Sayyouri, M., & Qjidaa, H. (2022a). New method for bio-signals zero-watermarking using quaternion shmaliy moments and short-time fourier transform. *Multimedia Tools and Applications, 81*(12), 17369–17399. doi:10.100711042-022-12660-2

Daoui, A., Karmouni, H., Sayyouri, M., & Qjidaa, H. (2022b). Robust 2D and 3D images zero-watermarking using dual Hahn moment invariants and Sine Cosine Algorithm. *Multimedia Tools and Applications, 81*(18), 25581–25611. doi:10.100711042-022-12298-0 PMID:35345547

Daoui, A., Mao, H., Yamni, M., Li, Q., Alfarraj, O., & Abd El-Latif, A. A. (2023, January). Novel Integer Shmaliy Transform and New Multiparametric Piecewise Linear Chaotic Map for Joint Lossless Compression and Encryption of Medical Images in IoMTs. *Mathematics, 11*(16), 16. doi:10.3390/math11163619

Daoui, A., Yamni, M., Chelloug, S. A., Wani, M. A., & El-Latif, A. A. A. (2023). Efficient image encryption scheme using novel 1D multiparametric dynamical tent map and parallel computing. *Mathematics, 11*(7), 1589. doi:10.3390/math11071589

Daoui, A., Yamni, M., Karmouni, H., Sayyouri, M., Qjidaa, H., Ahmad, M., & Abd El-Latif, A. A. (2022). Biomedical Multimedia Encryption by Fractional-Order Meixner Polynomials Map and Quaternion Fractional-Order Meixner Moments. *IEEE Access : Practical Innovations, Open Solutions, 10*, 102599–102617. doi:10.1109/ACCESS.2022.3203067

Daoui, A., Yamni, M., Karmouni, H., Sayyouri, M., Qjidaa, H., Motahhir, S., Jamil, O., El-Shafai, W., Algarni, A. D., Soliman, N. F., & Aly, M. H. (2022). Efficient Biomedical Signal Security Algorithm for Smart Internet of Medical Things (IoMTs) Applications. *Electronics (Basel), 11*(23), 3867. doi:10.3390/electronics11233867

Dev, S., Wang, H., Nwosu, C. S., Jain, N., Veeravalli, B., & John, D. (2022). A predictive analytics approach for stroke prediction using machine learning and neural networks. *Healthc. Anal., 2*, 100032. doi:10.1016/j.health.2022.100032

Dhar, S., Khare, A., & Singh, R. (2022). Advanced security model for multimedia data sharing in Internet of Things. *Trans. Emerg. Telecommun. Technology,* e4621, . doi:10.1002/ett.4621

Diaz, M., Ferrer, M. A., Impedovo, D., Malik, M. I., Pirlo, G., & Plamondon, R. (2019). A perspective analysis of handwritten signature technology. *ACM Computing Surveys, 51*(6), 1–39. doi:10.1145/3274658

Dieleman, S., Schlüter, J., Raffel, C., Olson, E., Sønderby, S. K., Nouri, D., & De Fauw, J. (2015). *Lasagne: first release.*

Djenouri, Y., Belhadi, A., Srivastava, G., & Lin, J. C.-W. (2022). Deep learning-based hashtag recommendation system for multimedia data. *Information Sciences*, *609*, 1506–1517. doi:10.1016/j.ins.2022.07.132

Donovan, M. J., Fernandez, G., Scott, R., Khan, F. M., Zeineh, J., Koll, G., Gladoun, N., Charytonowicz, E., Tewari, A., & Cordon-Cardo, C. (2018). *Development and validation of a novel* automated Gleason grade and molecular profile that define a highly predictive prostate cancer progression algorithm-*based test. Prostate Cancer and Prostatic Diseases*, *21*(4), 594–603. doi:10.103841391-018-0067-4 PMID:30087426

Dorri, A., Kanhere, S., Jurdak, R. S., & Gauravaram, P. (2017). *Blockchain for IoT security and privacy: The case study of a smart home.* In Proceedings of the 2017 IEEE International Conference on Pervasive Computing and Communications Workshops (PerCom workshops), Kona, HI, USA.

Dou, Y., & Li, M. (2020, January). Cryptanalysis of a New Color Image Encryption Using Combination of the 1D Chaotic Map. *Applied Sciences (Basel, Switzerland)*, *10*(6), 6. doi:10.3390/app10062187

Dou, Y., & Li, M. (2021, July). An image encryption algorithm based on a novel 1D chaotic map and compressive sensing. *Multimedia Tools and Applications*, *80*(16), 24437–24454. doi:10.100711042-021-10850-y

Drew, J., Hahsler, M., & Moore, T. (2017). Polymorphic malware detection using sequence classification methods and ensembles. *EURASIP Journal on Multimedia and Information Security*, *2017*(1), 2. doi:10.118613635-017-0055-6

Dwivedi, A. D. (2019). A decentralized privacy-preserving healthcare blockchain for IoT. *Sensors*, *19*(2), 326.

Dwivedi, A. D., Srivastava, G., Dhar, S., & Singh, R. (2020). A decentralized privacy-preserving healthcare blockchain for IoT. *J. Sustain. Cities Soc.*, *55*, 10–18.

Eigen, D., & Fergus, R. (2015). Predicting depth, surface normals and semantic labels with a common multi-scale convolutional architecture. *Proceedings IEEE Conference Computing Visual Pattern Recognition*, (pp. 2650– 2658). IEEE. 10.1109/ICCV.2015.304

El-Latif, A. (2023). *Artificial Intelligence for Biometrics and Cybersecurity.* IET. https://shop.theiet.org/artificial-intelligence-for-biometrics-and-cybersecurity

El-Latif, A. A. A., Abd-El-Atty, B., Hossain, M. S., Elmougy, S., & Ghoneim, A. (2018). Secure Quantum Steganography Protocol for Fog Cloud Internet of Things. *IEEE Access : Practical Innovations, Open Solutions*, *6*, 10332–10340. doi:10.1109/ACCESS.2018.2799879

Epstein, V. I. (2010). An update of the Gleason grading system. *The Journal of Urology*, *183*(2), 433–440. doi:10.1016/j.juro.2009.10.046 PMID:20006878

Erkmen, B., Kahraman, N., Vural, R. A., & Yildirim, T. (2010). Conic section function neural network circuitry for offline signature recognition. *IEEE Transactions on Neural Networks*, *21*(4), 667–672. doi:10.1109/TNN.2010.2040751 PMID:20144917

Esposito, C., De Santis, A., Tortora, G., Chang, H., & Choo, K.-K. R. (2018). Blockchain: A panacea for healthcare cloud-based data security and privacy. *J. IEEE Cloud Comput.*, *5*(1), 31–37. doi:10.1109/MCC.2018.011791712

Falconí, L. G., Pérez, M., & Aguilar, W. G. (2019). Transfer Learning in Breast Mammogram Abnormalities Classification with Mobilenet and Nasnet. *International Conference on Systems, Signals and Image Processing (IWSSIP)*, IEEE. 10.1109/IWSSIP.2019.8787295

Fan, D., Zhang, X., Kang, W., Zhao, H., & Lv, Y. (2022, January). Video Watermarking Algorithm Based on NSCT, Pseudo 3D-DCT and NMF. *Sensors (Basel)*, *22*(13), 13. doi:10.339022134752 PMID:35808245

Fehr, D., Veeraraghavan, H., Wibmer, A., Gondo, T., Matsumoto, K., Vargas, H. A., Sala, E., Hricak, H., & Deasy, J. O. (2015). Automatic classification of prostate cancer Gleason scores from multiparametric magnetic resonance images. *Proceedings of the National Academy of Sciences of the United States of America*, *112*(46). doi:10.1073/pnas.1505935112 PMID:26578786

Feng, C., Yu, K., Bashir, A. K., Al-Otaibi, Y. D., Lu, Y., Chen, S., & Zhang, D. (2021). Efficient and secure data sharing for 5G flying drones: A blockchain-enabled approach. *IEEE Network*, *35*(1), 130–137. doi:10.1109/MNET.011.2000223

Figorilli, S., Antonucci, F., Costa, C., Pallottino, F., Raso, L., Castiglione, M., Pinci, E., Del Vecchio, D., Colle, G., Proto, A. R., Sperandio, G., & Menesatti, P. (2018). A blockchain implementation prototype for the electronic open source traceability of wood along the whole supply chain. *Sensors (Basel)*, *18*(9), 3133. doi:10.339018093133 PMID:30227651

Floridi, L., & Chiriatti, M. (2020). GPT-3: Its nature, scope, limits, and consequences. *Minds and Machines*, *30*(4), 681–694. doi:10.100711023-020-09548-1

Fracastoro, G., Magli, E., Poggi, G., Scarpa, G., Valsesia, D., & Verdoliva, L. (2020). Deep learning methods for SAR image despeckling: trends and perspectives. arXiv preprint arXiv:2012.05508.

Frankel, S., Smith, G. D., Donovan, J., & Neal, D. (2003). Screening for prostate cancer. *Lancet*, *361*(9363), 1122–1128. doi:10.1016/S0140-6736(03)12890-5 PMID:12672328

Fricker, K. (2018). *Replication Data for: Automated Gleason grading of prostate cancer tissue microarrays via deep learning*. Harvard Dataset.

Fu, X., Zeng, D., Huang, Y., Liao, Y., Ding, X., & Paisley, J. (2016). A fusion-based enhancing method for weakly illuminated images. *Signal Processing*, *129*, 82–96. doi:10.1016/j.sigpro.2016.05.031

Gambäck, B., & Sikdar, U. K. (2017). *Using Convolutional Neural Networks to Classify Hate-Speech.*, *7491*, 85–90. doi:10.18653/v1/w17-3013

Gambhir, G., & Mandal, J. K. (2021, December). Shared memory implementation and performance analysis of LSB steganography based on chaotic tent map. *Innovations in Systems and Software Engineering*, *17*(4), 333–342. doi:10.100711334-021-00385-8

Gandhimathi Alias Usha, S., & Vasuki, S. (2017). Improved segmentation and change detection of multi-spectral satellite imagery using graph cut based clustering and multiclass SVM. *Multimedia Tools and Applications*, 77(12), 15353–15383. doi:10.100711042-017-5120-0

Gao, J. (2019). A blockchain-SDN-enabled Internet of vehicles environment for fog computing and 5G networks. *IEEE Internet of Things Journal*, 7(5), 4278–4291.

Gao, F., Liu, X., Dong, J., Zhong, G., & Jian, M. (2017). Change Detection in SAR Images Based on Deep Semi-NMF and SVD Networks. *Remote Sensing (Basel)*, 9(5), 435. doi:10.3390/rs9050435

Garcia, F. C. C., Muga, I. I., & Felix, P. (2016). Random Forest for Malware Classification. *ArXiv Preprint ArXiv:1609.07770*.

Garhawal, S., & Shukla, N. (2013). A study on handwritten signature verification approaches. *International Journal of Advanced Research in Computer Engineering and Technology*, 2(8), 2497–2503.

Geeta, V., Mamatha, T., Varanasi, A., & Kumar, A. P. (2022). *Brain Stroke Prediction Using Machine Learning and Data Science*, 9(1), 1748–1752.

Geisel, T., & Fairen, V. (1984, October). Statistical properties of chaos in Chebyshev maps. *Physics Letters. [Part A]*, 105(6), 263–266. doi:10.1016/0375-9601(84)90993-9

Geng, J., Ma, X., Zhou, X., & Wang, H. (2019, October). Saliency-Guided Deep Neural Networks for SAR Image Change Detection. *IEEE Transactions on Geoscience and Remote Sensing*, 57(10), 7365–7377. doi:10.1109/TGRS.2019.2913095

Georgoulis, S., Rematas, K., Ritschel, T., Gavves, E., Fritz, M., Van Gool, L., & Tuytelaars, T. (2018). Reflectance and Natural Illumination from Single-Material Specular Objects Using Deep Learning. *IEEE Transactions on Pattern Analysis and Machine Intelligence*, 37(8), 1932–1947. doi:10.1109/TPAMI.2017.2742999 PMID:28841552

Ghantasala, G. P., Sudha, L. R., Priya, T. V., Deepan, P., & Vignesh, R. R. (2022). An Efficient Deep Learning Framework for Multimedia Big Data Analytics. In *Multimedia Computing Systems and Virtual Reality* (pp. 99–127). CRC Press. doi:10.1201/9781003196686-5

Gibert, D. (2016). *Convolutional Neural Networks for Malware Classification*. [Thesis, University of Barcelona].

Girshick, R. (2015). Fast R-CNN. *IEEE International Conference on Computer Vision (ICCV)*. IEEE.

Girshick, R., Donahue, J., Darrell, T., & Malik, J. (2014). Rich Feature Hierarchies for Accurate Object Detection and Semantic Segmentation. *IEEE Conference on Computer Vision and Pattern Recognition*. IEEE. 10.1109/CVPR.2014.81

Gong, M., Su, L., Jia, M., & Chen, W. (2014). Fuzzy Clustering With a Modified MRF Energy Function for Change Detection in Synthetic Aperture Radar Images. *IEEE Transactions on Fuzzy Systems*, 22(1), 98–109. doi:10.1109/TFUZZ.2013.2249072

Gosal, A. S., Geijzendorffer, I. R., Václavík, T., Poulin, B., & Ziv, G. (2019). Using social media, machine learning and natural language processing to map multiple recreational beneficiaries. *Ecosystem Services*, *38*, 100958. doi:10.1016/j.ecoser.2019.100958

Gualberto, E. S., De Sousa, R. T., Vieira, T. P. D. B., Da Costa, J. P. C. L., & Duque, C. G. (2020). The answer is in the text: Multi-stage methods for phishing detection based on feature engineering. *IEEE Access : Practical Innovations, Open Solutions*, *8*, 223529–223547. doi:10.1109/ACCESS.2020.3043396

Gul, E., & Ozturk, S. (2021, June). A novel pixel-wise authentication-based self-embedding fragile watermarking method. *Multimedia Systems*, *27*(3), 531–545. doi:10.100700530-021-00751-3

Guo, L., Li, Y., & Ling, H. (2017). Y, and Ling. H, "LIME: Low-light image enhancement via illumination map estimation,". *IEEE Transactions on Image Processing*, *26*(2), 982–993. doi:10.1109/TIP.2016.2639450 PMID:28113318

Gupta, K., Jiwani, N., Sharif, M. H. U., Datta, R., & Afreen, N. (2022). A Neural Network Approach For Malware Classification. *2022 International Conference on Computing, Communication, and Intelligent Systems (ICCCIS)*, (pp. 681–684). IEEE. 10.1109/ICCCIS56430.2022.10037653

Haghighi, B. B., Taherinia, A. H., & Mohajerzadeh, A. H. (2019). TRLG: Fragile blind quad watermarking for image tamper detection and recovery by providing compact digests with optimized quality using LWT and GA. *Information Sciences*, *486*, 204–230. doi:10.1016/j.ins.2019.02.055

Hameed, K., Ali, A., Naqvi, M. H., Jabbar, M., Junaid, M., & Haider, A. (2016). *Resource management in operating systems-a survey of scheduling algorithms*. In *Proceedings of the International Conference on Innovative Computing (ICIC)*, Lanzhou, China.

Hang, L., & Kim, D.-H. (2019). Design and implementation of an integrated iot blockchain platform for sensing data integrity. *Sensors (Basel)*, *19*(10), 2228. doi:10.339019102228 PMID:31091799

Hasnain, M., Pasha, M. F., Ghani, I., Mehboob, B., Imran, M., & Ali, A. (2020). *Benchmark Dataset Selection of Web Services Technologies: A Factor Analysis* (Vol. 8). IEEE Access.

He, K., Zhang, X., Ren, S., & Sun, J. (2015). Spatial Pyramid Pooling in Deep Convolutional Networks for Visual Recognition. *IEEE Transactions on Pattern Analysis and Machine Intelligence*. IEEE.

Heo, J. N., Yoon, J. G., Park, H., Kim, Y. D., Nam, H. S., & Heo, J. H. (2019). Machine Learning-Based Model for Prediction of Outcomes in Acute Stroke. *Stroke*, *50*(5), 1263–1265. doi:10.1161/STROKEAHA.118.024293 PMID:30890116

Hernández-García, E., Masoller, C., & Mirasso, C. R. (2002, March). Anticipating the dynamics of chaotic maps. *Physics Letters. [Part A]*, *295*(1), 39–43. doi:10.1016/S0375-9601(02)00147-0

Hezil, H., Djemili, R., & Bourouba, H. (2018). Signature recognition using binary features and KNN. *International Journal of Biometrics*, *10*(1), 1–15. doi:10.1504/IJBM.2018.090121

Hinton, G. (2014). Dropout : A Simple Way to Prevent Neural Networks from Overfitting. *Journal of Machine Learning Research*, *15*, 1929–1958.

Hiriyannaiah, S. (2020). Deep learning for multimedia data in IoT. Multimedia Big Data Computing for IoT Applications: Concepts. Paradigms and Solutions.

Hochreiter, S., & Schmidhuber, J. (1997). Long short-term memory. *Neural Computation*, *9*(8), 1735–1780. doi:10.1162/neco.1997.9.8.1735 PMID:9377276

Honar Pajooh, H., Rashid, M., Alam, F., & Demidenko, S. (2021). Multi-layer blockchain-based security architecture for internet of things. *Sensors (Basel)*, *21*(3), 772. doi:10.339021030772 PMID:33498860

Hong-wei, Z., Zhang, L., & Li, P. (2018). Yarn-dyed Fabric Defect Detection with YOLOV2 Based on Deep Convolution Neural Networks. *IEEE 7th Data Driven Control and Learning Systems Conference (DDCLS)*. IEEE.

Horn, B. K. P., & Brooks, M. J. (Eds.). (1989). *Shape from Shading*. MIT press.

Hosni, A. I. E., Li, K., & Ahmad, S. (2019). *DARIM: Dynamic approach for rumor influence minimization in online social networks*. Neural Information Processing: 26th International Conference, ICONIP 2019, Sydney, NSW, Australia. 10.1007/978-3-030-36711-4_52

Hosni, A. I. E., Li, K., & Ahmed, S. (2018). *HISBmodel: a rumor diffusion model based on human individual and social behaviors in online social networks*. In Neural Information Processing: 25th International Conference, ICONIP 2018, Siem Reap, Cambodia. 10.1007/978-3-030-04179-3_2

Hosny, K. M., Darwish, M. M., & Fouda, M. M. (2021). Robust color images watermarking using new fractional-order exponent moments. *IEEE Access : Practical Innovations, Open Solutions*, *9*, 47425–47435. doi:10.1109/ACCESS.2021.3068211

Hu, D. (2017). Finding tiny faces. *Proc. IEEE Conf. Comput. Vis. Pattern Recognit.* IEEE.

Huang, W., & Stokes, J. W. (2016). MtNet : A Multi-Task Neural Network for Dynamic Malware Classification. *International Conference on Detection of Intrusions and Malware, and Vulnerability Assessment*, (pp. 399–418). Springer. 10.1007/978-3-319-40667-1_20

Huang, L., Kuang, D., Li, C., Zhuang, Y., Duan, S., & Zhou, X. (2022, February). A self-embedding secure fragile watermarking scheme with high quality recovery. *Journal of Visual Communication and Image Representation*, *83*, 103437. doi:10.1016/j.jvcir.2022.103437

Huang, T., Xu, J., Tu, S., & Han, B. (2023, March). Robust zero-watermarking scheme based on a depthwise overparameterized VGG network in healthcare information security. *Biomedical Signal Processing and Control*, *81*, 104478. doi:10.1016/j.bspc.2022.104478

Hua, Z., & Zhou, Y. (2016, April). Image encryption using 2D Logistic-adjusted-Sine map. *Information Sciences*, *339*, 237–253. doi:10.1016/j.ins.2016.01.017

Compilation of References

Iftikhar, S., Zhang, Z., Asim, M., Muthanna, A., Koucheryavy, A., & Abd El-Latif, A. A. (2022). Deep Learning-Based Pedestrian Detection in Autonomous Vehicles: Substantial Issues and Challenges. *Electronics (Basel)*, *11*(21), 3551. doi:10.3390/electronics11213551

Islam, M. M., Uddin, M. A., Islam, L., Akter, A., Sharmin, S., & Acharjee, U. K. (2020). Cyberbullying detection on social networks using machine learning approaches. In *2020 IEEE Asia-Pacific Conference on Computer Science and Data Engineering (CSDE)*, (pp. 1-6). IEEE. 10.1109/CSDE50874.2020.9411601

Islam, M. R., Liu, S., Wang, X., & Xu, G. (2020). Deep learning for misinformation detection on online social networks: A survey and new perspectives. *Social Network Analysis and Mining*, *10*(1), 1–20. doi:10.100713278-020-00696-x PMID:33014173

Jabeen, F., Ur Rehman, Z., Shah, S., Alharthy, R. D., Jalil, S., Ali Khan, I., Iqbal, J., & Abd El-Latif, A. A. (2023). Deep learning-based prediction of inhibitors interaction with Butyrylcholinesterase for the treatment of Alzheimer's disease. *Computers & Electrical Engineering*, *105*, 108475. doi:10.1016/j.compeleceng.2022.108475

Jiang, L., Liao, M., Zhang, L., & Lin, H. (2007). Unsupervised change detection in multitemporal SAR images using MRF models. *Geo-Spatial Information Science*, *10*(2), 111–116. doi:10.100711806-007-0051-y

Jiang, S., Cao, J., McCann, J. A., Yang, Y., Liu, Y., Wang, X., & Deng, Y. (2019). Privacy-preserving and efficient multi-keyword search over encrypted data on the blockchain. In *Proceedings of the 2019 IEEE International Conference on Blockchain (Blockchain)*, Atlanta, GA, USA. 10.1109/Blockchain.2019.00062

Jiang, S., Cao, J., Wu, H., & Yang, Y. (2020). Fairness-based packing of industrial IoT data in permissioned blockchains. *IEEE Transactions on Industrial Informatics*, *17*(11), 7639–7649. doi:10.1109/TII.2020.3046129

Jiang, S., Cao, J., Wu, H., Yang, Y., Ma, M., & He, J. (2018). Blochie: A blockchain-based platform for healthcare information exchange. In *Proceedings of the 2018 IEEE International Conference on Smart Computing (Smartcomp)*, (pp. 49–56). IEEE. 10.1109/SMARTCOMP.2018.00073

Jia, X., Hu, N., Su, S., Yin, S., Zhao, Y., Cheng, X., & Zhang, C. (2020). IRBA: An identity-based cross-domain authentication scheme for the internet of things. *Journal of Electronics (China)*, *9*, 634.

Jing, Y. (2020). *Machine Learning Performance Analysis to Predict Stroke Based on Imbalanced Medical Dataset*. arXiv.

Johnson, M. K., & Adelson, E. H. (2011). Shape estimation in natural illumination. *Proceedings IEEE Conference Computing Visual Pattern Recognition*, (pp. 2553–2560). IEEE.

Kaiyrbekov, K., & Sezgin, M. (2020). Deep Stroke-Based Sketched Symbol Reconstruction and Segmentation. *IEEE Computer Graphics and Applications*, *40*(1), 112–126. doi:10.1109/MCG.2019.2943333 PMID:31581077

Kalaiselvi, S., & Gomathi, V. (2020). α-cut induced Fuzzy Deep Neural Network for change detection of SAR images. *Applied Soft Computing*, *95*, 106510. doi:10.1016/j.asoc.2020.106510

Kanso, A. (2011). Self-shrinking chaotic stream ciphers. *Communications in Nonlinear Science and Numerical Simulation*, *16*(2), 822–836. doi:10.1016/j.cnsns.2010.04.039

Karouni, A., Daya, B., & Bahlak, S. (2011). Offline signature recognition using neural networks approach. *Procedia Computer Science*, *3*, 155–161. doi:10.1016/j.procs.2010.12.027

Kaur, R., & Singh, B. (2021). A novel approach for data hiding based on combined application of discrete cosine transform and coupled chaotic map. *Multimedia Tools and Applications*, *80*(10), 14665–14691. doi:10.100711042-021-10528-5

Kekre, H. B., & Bharadi, V. A. (2010). Off-Line Signature Recognition Systems. *International Journal of Computers and Applications*, *1*(27), 61–70. doi:10.5120/499-815

Keshk, H. M., & Yin, X.-C. (2019). Change Detection in SAR Images Based on Deep Learning. *International Journal of Aeronautical and Space Sciences*, *21*(2), 549–559. doi:10.100742405-019-00222-0

Khafaga, D. S., Karim, F. K., Darwish, M. M., & Hosny, K. M. (2022, January). Robust Zero-Watermarking of Color Medical Images Using Multi-Channel Gaussian-Hermite Moments and 1D Chebyshev Chaotic Map. *Sensors (Basel)*, *22*(15), 15. Advance online publication. doi:10.339022155612 PMID:35957177

Khairullah, M. K., Alkahtani, A. A., Bin Baharuddin, M. Z., & Al-Jubari, A. M. (2021, January). Designing 1D Chaotic Maps for Fast Chaotic Image Encryption. *Electronics (Basel)*, *10*(17), 17. Advance online publication. doi:10.3390/electronics10172116

Khanday, A. M. U. D., Amin, A., Manzoor, I., & Bashir, R. (2018). Face Recognition Techniques: A Critical Review. *STM Journals*, *5*(2), 24–30. https://www.researchgate.net/publication/330872439_Face_Recognition_Techniques_A_Critical_Review

Khanday, A. M. U. D., Rayees Khan, Q., & Rabani, S. T. (2020). Analysing and Predicting Propaganda on Social Media using Machine Learning Techniques. *2020 2nd International Conference on Advances in Computing, Communication Control and Networking (ICACCCN)*, 122–127. https://doi.org/10.1109/ICACCCN51052.2020.9362838

Khanday, A. M. U. D., Khan, Q. R., & Rabani, S. T. (2021). Identifying propaganda from online social networks during COVID-19 using machine learning techniques. *International Journal of Information Technology*, *13*(1), 115–122. doi:10.100741870-020-00550-5

Khan, F. A., Asif, M., Ahmad, A., Alharbi, M., & Aljuaid, H. (2020). Blockchain technology, improvement suggestions, security challenges on smart grid and its application in healthcare for sustainable development. *J. Sustain. Cities Soc.*, *55*, 102–018.

Khan, M. N., Rahman, H. U., Almaiah, M. A., Khan, M. Z., Khan, A., Raza, M., Al-Zahrani, M., Almomani, O., & Khan, R. (2020, September 25). Improving energy efficiency with content-based adaptive and dynamic scheduling in wireless sensor networks. *IEEE Access : Practical Innovations, Open Solutions, 8*, 176495–176520. doi:10.1109/ACCESS.2020.3026939

Kim, H., Kim, S.-H., Hwang, J.Y., Seo, C. (2019). Efficient privacy-preserving machine learning for blockchain network. *IEEE Access.*

Kim, J., Ban, Y., Ko, E., Cho, H., & Yi, J. H. (2022). MAPAS: A practical deep learning-based android malware detection system. *International Journal of Information Security, 21*(4), 725–738. doi:10.100710207-022-00579-6

Kimori, Y. (2013). Morphological image processing for quantitative shape analysis of biomedical structures: Effective contrast enhancement. *Journal of Synchrotron Radiation, 20*(6), 848–853. doi:10.1107/S0909049513020761 PMID:24121326

Kim, T. M., Lee, S.-J., Chang, D.-J., Koo, J., Kim, T., Yoon, K.-H., & Choi, I.-Y. (2021). DynamiChain: Development of Medical Blockchain Ecosystem Based on Dynamic Consent System. *Applied Sciences (Basel, Switzerland), 11*(4), 1612. doi:10.3390/app11041612

Kingma, D. P., & Ba, J. (2014). Adam: A method for stochastic optimization. *ArXiv Preprint ArXiv:1412.6980.*

Ko, D., Lee, S., & Park, J. (2021, November). A study on manufacturing facility safety system using multimedia tools for cyber physical systems. *Multimedia Tools and Applications, 80*(26), 34553–34570. doi:10.100711042-020-09925-z

Koko, M. N., & Ogechi, N. (2019). Perceived Influence of Mobile Learning and Multimedia on Business Education Students' Academic Performance in Rivers State Universities. *Int. J. Innov. Inf. Syst. Technol. Res., 7*(4), 40–46.

Kolosnjaji, B., Zarras, A., Webster, G., & Eckert, C. (2016). Deep Learning for Classification of Malware System Call Sequences. In B. H. Kang, & Q. Bai (Eds.), *Australasian Joint Conference on Artificial Intelligence* (pp. 137–149). Springer International Publishing. 10.1007/978-3-319-50127-7_11

Kovalev, V. A., Liauchuk, V. A., Kalinovski, A. A., & Fridman, M. V. (2019). Tumor segmentation in whole-slide histology images using deep learning. *Informatics (MDPI), 16*(2), 18–26.

Krizhevsky, A., Sutskever, I., & Hinton, G. E. (2012). ImageNet Classification with Deep Convolutional Neural Networks. In F. Pereira, C. J. C. Burges, L. Bottou, & K. Q. Weinberger (Eds.), Vol. 25, pp. 1097–1105. Advances in Neural Information Processing Systems. Curran Associates, Inc., http://papers.nips.cc/paper/4824-imagenet-classification-with-deep-convolutional-neural-networks.pdf

Kshirsagar, A., Goyal, H., Loya, S., & Khade, A. (2021). Brain Stroke Prediction Portal Using Machine Learning. *Int. J. Res. Eng. Appl. Manag, 07*(03).

Kumar, A. (2022). Dynamical properties of a novel one dimensional chaotic map. Math. Biosci. Eng., 19(3). doi:10.3934/mbe.2022115

Lacity, M. C. (2018). Addressing Key Challenges to Making Enterprise Blockchain Applications a Reality. *J. Mis Q. Exec.*, *17*, 3.

Lazaroiu, C., & Roscia, M. (2017). *Smart district through IoT and blockchain.* In *Proceedings of the 2017 IEEE 6th International Conference on Renewable Energy Research and Applications*, (pp. 454–461). IEEE. 10.1109/ICRERA.2017.8191102

LeCun, Y., Bengio, Y., & Hinton, G. (2015). Deep learning. *Nature*, *521*(7553), 436–444. doi:10.1038/nature14539 PMID:26017442

Lee, E. J., Kim, Y. H., Kim, N., & Kang, D. W. (2017). Deep into the brain: Artificial intelligence in stroke imaging. *Journal of Stroke*, *19*(3), 277–285. doi:10.5853/jos.2017.02054 PMID:29037014

Lee, J. S. (1980). Digital image enhancement and noise filtering by use of local statistics. *IEEE Transactions on Pattern Analysis and Machine Intelligence*, *PAMI-2*(2), 165–168. doi:10.1109/TPAMI.1980.4766994 PMID:21868887

Lefèvre, P., Carré, P., Fontaine, C., Gaborit, P., & Huang, J. (2022, January). Efficient image tampering localization using semi-fragile watermarking and error control codes. *Signal Processing*, *190*, 108342. doi:10.1016/j.sigpro.2021.108342

Li, B., Shen, C., Dai, Y., van den Hengel, A., & He, M. (2015). Depth and surface normal estimation from monocular images using regression on deep features and hierarchical CRFs. *Proceedings IEEE Conference Computing Visual Pattern Recognition*, (pp. 1119–1127). IEEE.

Li, C., Guo, C., & Loy, C. C. (2022, August 1). Learning to Enhance Low-Light Image via Zero-Reference Deep Curve Estimation. *IEEE Transactions on Pattern Analysis and Machine Intelligence*, *44*(8), 4225–4238. doi:10.1109/TPAMI.2021.3063604 PMID:33656989

Li, C., Wu, Y., Yuan, X., Sun, Z., Wang, W., Li, X., & Gong, L. (2018). Detection and defense of DDoS attack–based on deep learning in OpenFlow-based SDN. *International Journal of Communication Systems*, *31*(5), e3497. doi:10.1002/dac.3497

Li, G., & Liu, W. (2023). Multimedia data processing technology and application based on deep learning. *Advances in Multimedia*, *2023*, 2023. doi:10.1155/2023/4184425

Li, J.-Y., & Zhang, C.-Z. (2020, October). Blind watermarking scheme based on Schur decomposition and non-subsampled contourlet transform. *Multimedia Tools and Applications*, *79*(39), 30007–30021. doi:10.100711042-020-09389-1

Lin, P. J., Zhai, X., Li, W., Li, T., Cheng, D., Li, C., Pan, Y., & Ji, L. (2022). A transferable deep learning prognosis model for predicting stroke patients' recovery in different rehabilitation trainings. *IEEE Journal of Biomedical and Health Informatics*, *26*(12), 6003–6011. doi:10.1109/JBHI.2022.3205436 PMID:36083954

Lin, S. (2021). *Stroke Prediction*. Medium.

Lin, Z., An, K., Niu, H., Hu, Y., Chatzinotas, S., Zheng, G., & Wang, J. (2022, July 12). SLNR-based secure energy efficient beamforming in multibeam satellite systems. *IEEE Transactions on Aerospace and Electronic Systems*, 1–4. doi:10.1109/TAES.2022.3190238

Lin, Z., Lin, M., De Cola, T., Wang, J. B., Zhu, W. P., & Cheng, J. (2021, January 14). Supporting IoT with rate-splitting multiple access in satellite and aerial-integrated networks. *IEEE Internet of Things Journal*, 8(14), 11123–11134. doi:10.1109/JIOT.2021.3051603

Lin, Z., Niu, H., An, K., Wang, Y., Zheng, G., Chatzinotas, S., & Hu, Y. (2022, March 3). Refracting RIS aided hybrid satellite-terrestrial relay networks: Joint beamforming design and optimization. *IEEE Transactions on Aerospace and Electronic Systems*, 58(4), 3717–3724. doi:10.1109/TAES.2022.3155711

Li, S., Liu, Q., Dai, J., Wang, W., Gui, X., & Yi, Y. (2021). Adaptive-weighted multiview deep basis matrix factorization for multimedia data analysis. *Wireless Communications and Mobile Computing*, 2021, 1–12. doi:10.1155/2021/7264264

Liu, B., Xiong, J., Wu, Y., Ding, M., & Wu, C. M. (2019). Protecting Multimedia Privacy from Both Humans and AI. In *IEEE International Symposium on Broadband Multimedia Systems and Broadcasting (BMSB)*, (pp. 1-6). IEEE. 10.1109/BMSB47279.2019.8971914

Liu, F., Shen, C., & Lin, G. (2015). Deep convolutional neural fields for depth estimation from a single image. *Proceedings IEEE Conference Computing Visual Pattern Recognition*, (pp. 5162–5170). IEEE. 10.1109/CVPR.2015.7299152

Liu, G., Li, L., Jiao, L., Dong, Y., & Li, X. (2019). Stacked Fisher autoencoder for SAR change detection. *Pattern Recognition*, 96, 106971. doi:10.1016/j.patcog.2019.106971

Liu, J., Li, X., Ye, L., Zhang, H., Du, X:, & Guizani, M. (2018). A blockchain based privacy-preserving data sharing for electronic medical records. In *Proceedings of the 2018 IEEE Global Communications Conference (GLOBECOM)*. IEEE. 10.1109/GLOCOM.2018.8647713

Liu, L., & Wang, J. (2023, February). A cluster of 1D quadratic chaotic map and its applications in image encryption. *Mathematics and Computers in Simulation*, 204, 89–114. doi:10.1016/j.matcom.2022.07.030

Liu, W. (2016). *SSD: Single Shot MultiBox Detector*. Ann-Arb.

Liu, X., Sun, Y., Wang, J., Yang, C., Zhang, Y., Wang, L., Chen, Y., & Fang, H. (2021). A novel zero-watermarking scheme with enhanced distinguishability and robustness for volumetric medical imaging. *Signal Processing Image Communication*, 92, 116124. doi:10.1016/j.image.2020.116124

Liu, X., Zhang, Y., Wang, J., Sun, Y., Zhang, W., Zhou, D., Schaefer, G., & Fang, H. (2022). Multiple-feature-based zero-watermarking for robust and discriminative copyright protection of DIBR 3D videos. *Information Sciences*, 604, 97–114. doi:10.1016/j.ins.2022.05.010

Li, Y., Martinis, S., Plank, S., & Ludwig, R. (2018). An automatic change detection approach for rapid flood mapping in Sentinel-1 SAR data. *International Journal of Applied Earth Observation and Geoinformation*, 73, 123–135. doi:10.1016/j.jag.2018.05.023

Li, Y., Peng, C., Chen, Y., Jiao, L., Zhou, L., & Shang, R. (2019). A Deep Learning Method for Change Detection in Synthetic Aperture Radar Images. *IEEE Transactions on Geoscience and Remote Sensing*, *57*(8), 5751–5763. doi:10.1109/TGRS.2019.2901945

Lombardi, S., & Nishino, K. (2015). Reflectance and illumination recovery in the wild. *IEEE Transactions on Pattern Analysis and Machine Intelligence*, *38*(1), 129–141. doi:10.1109/TPAMI.2015.2430318 PMID:26656582

Luppino, L. T., Hansen, M. A., Kampffmeyer, M., Bianchi, F. M., Moser, G., Jenssen, R., & Anfinsen, S. N. (2020). Code-Aligned Autoencoders for Unsupervised Change Detection in Multimodal Remote Sensing Images. arXiv preprint arXiv:2004.07011.

Lutfi, A., Alqudah, H., Alrawad, M., Alshira'h, A. F., Alshirah, M. H., Almaiah, M. A., Alsyouf, A., & Hassan, M. F. (2023, July 6). Green Environmental Management System to Support Environmental Performance: What Factors Influence SMEs to Adopt Green Innovations? *Sustainability (Basel)*, *15*(13), 10645. doi:10.3390u151310645

Lutfi, A., Alrawad, M., Alsyouf, A., Almaiah, M. A., Al-Khasawneh, A., Al-Khasawneh, A. L., Alshira'h, A. F., Alshirah, M. H., Saad, M., & Ibrahim, N. (2023, January 1). Drivers and impact of big data analytic adoption in the retail industry: A quantitative investigation applying structural equation modeling. *Journal of Retailing and Consumer Services*, *70*, 103129. doi:10.1016/j.jretconser.2022.103129

Lutfi, A., Alshira'h, A. F., Alshirah, M. H., Al-Ababneh, H. A., Alrawad, M., Almaiah, M. A., Dalbouh, F. A., Magablih, A. M., Mohammed, F. M., & Alardi, M. W. (2023, September 1). Enhancing VAT compliance in the retail industry: The role of socio-economic determinants and tax knowledge moderation. *Journal of Open Innovation*, *9*(3), 100098. doi:10.1016/j.joitmc.2023.100098

Lv, N., Chen, C., Qiu, T., & Sangaiah, A. K. (2018, December). Deep Learning and Superpixel Feature Extraction Based on Contractive Autoencoder for Change Detection in SAR Images. *IEEE Transactions on Industrial Informatics*, *14*(12), 5530–5538. doi:10.1109/TII.2018.2873492

Lv, P., Zhong, Y., Zhao, J., & Zhang, L. (2016). Unsupervised change detection model based on hybrid conditional random field for high spatial resolution remote sensing imagery. *2016 IEEE International Geoscience and Remote Sensing Symposium (IGARSS)*. IEEE. 10.1109/IGARSS.2016.7729478

M., G. M. & D., P. M. C. (2021). IRJET- Stroke Type Prediction using Machine Learning and Artificial Neural Networks. *Int. Res. J. Eng. Technol*, *8*(6).

M., G., & Sethuraman, S. C. (2023). A comprehensive survey on deep learning based malware detection techniques. *Computer Science Review, 47*, 100529. https://doi.org/https://doi.org/10.1016/j.cosrev.2022.100529

Mackey, T. K., Li, J., Purushothaman, V., Nali, M., Shah, N., Bardier, C., Cai, M., & Liang, B. (2020). Big data, natural language processing, and deep learning to detect and characterize illicit COVID-19 product sales: Infoveillance study on Twitter and Instagram. *JMIR Public Health and Surveillance*, 6(3), e20794. doi:10.2196/20794 PMID:32750006

Mahajan, H. B., & Junnarkar, A. A. (2023). Smart healthcare system using integrated and lightweight ECC with private blockchain for multimedia medical data processing. *Multimedia Tools and Applications*, (avr). doi:10.100711042-023-15204-4 PMID:37362704

Mahmoudi, S. A., Belarbi, M. A., Mahmoudi, S., Belalem, G., & Manneback, P. (2020). Multimedia processing using deep learning technologies, high-performance computing cloud resources, and Big Data volumes. *Concurrency and Computation*, 32(17), e5699. doi:10.1002/cpe.5699

Mak, J., Kocanaogullari, D., Huang, X., Kersey, J., Shih, M., Grattan, E. S., Skidmore, E. R., Wittenberg, G. F., Ostadabbas, S., & Akcakaya, M. (2022). Detection of Stroke-Induced Visual Neglect and Target Response Prediction Using Augmented Reality and Electroencephalography. *IEEE Transactions on Neural Systems and Rehabilitation Engineering*, 30, 1840–1850. doi:10.1109/TNSRE.2022.3188184 PMID:35786558

Maleh, Y. (2019). Malware classification and analysis using convolutional and recurrent neural network. In *Handbook of Research on Deep Learning Innovations and Trends* (pp. 233–255). IGI Global. doi:10.4018/978-1-5225-7862-8.ch014

Maleh, Y., Shojafar, M., Alazab, M., & Baddi, Y. (2021). *Machine Intelligence and Big Data Analytics for Cybersecurity Applications*. Springer International Publishing AG. doi:10.1007/978-3-030-57024-8

Malik, V., & Arora, A. (2015). *A Review Paper on Signature Recognition*. www.ijraset.com

Mallik, A., Khetarpal, A., & Kumar, S. (2022). ConRec: Malware classification using convolutional recurrence. *Journal of Computer Virology and Hacking Techniques*, 18(4), 297–313. doi:10.100711416-022-00416-3

Manjunath, K., Kodanda Ramaiah, G. N., & GiriPrasad, M. N. (2022, April). Backward movement oriented shark smell optimization-based audio steganography using encryption and compression strategies. *Digital Signal Processing*, 122, 103335. doi:10.1016/j.dsp.2021.103335

Ma, P., Jiang, B., Lu, Z., Li, N., & Jiang, Z. (2020). Cybersecurity named entity recognition using bidirectional long short-term memory with conditional random fields. *Tsinghua Science and Technology*, 26(3), 259–265. doi:10.26599/TST.2019.9010033

Marinho, R., & Holanda, R. (2023). Automated Emerging Cyber Threat Identification and Profiling Based on Natural Language Processing. *IEEE Access : Practical Innovations, Open Solutions*, 11, 58915–58936. doi:10.1109/ACCESS.2023.3260020

Ma, S., Zhang, T., Wu, A., & Zhao, X. (2019). Lightweight and Privacy-Preserving Data Aggregation for Mobile Multimedia Security. *IEEE Access : Practical Innovations, Open Solutions*, 7, 114131–114140. doi:10.1109/ACCESS.2019.2935513

Masud, U., Sadiq, M., Masood, S., Ahmad, M., El-Latif, A., & Ahmed, A. (2023). LW-DeepFakeNet: A lightweight time distributed CNN-LSTM network for real-time DeepFake video detection. *Signal, Image and Video Processing, 17*(8), 1–9. doi:10.100711760-023-02633-9

Matta-Solis, H., Perez-Siguas, R., Matta-Solis, E., Matta-Zamudio, L., Millones-Gomez, S., & Velarde-Molina, J. F. (2022). Application of Machine Learning for the Prediction of Strokes in Peru. *Int. J. Eng. Trends Technol., 70*(10), 54–60. doi:10.14445/22315381/IJETT-V70I10P207

Meier, R., Knecht, U., Wiest, R., & Reyes, M. (2016). Brainlesion: Glioma, Multiple Sclerosis. *Lecture Notes in Computer Science, 10154*, 184–194. doi:10.1007/978-3-319-55524-9

Meng, X., Shan, Z., Liu, F., Zhao, B., Han, J., Wang, H., & Wang, J. (2017). MCSMGS: Malware Classification Model Based on Deep Learning. *2017 International Conference on Cyber-Enabled Distributed Computing and Knowledge Discovery (CyberC)*, (pp. 272–275). IEEE. 10.1109/CyberC.2017.21

Midoun, M. A., Wang, X., & Talhaoui, M. Z. (2021, April). A sensitive dynamic mutual encryption system based on a new 1D chaotic map. *Optics and Lasers in Engineering, 139*, 106485. doi:10.1016/j.optlaseng.2020.106485

Minematsu, T., Shimada, A., & Taniguchi, R. I. (2017, August). Analytics of deep neural network in change detection. In *2017 14th IEEE International Conference on Advanced Video and Signal Based Surveillance (AVSS)* (pp. 1-6). IEEE. 10.1109/AVSS.2017.8078550

Mistry, I., Tanwar, S., Tyagi, S., & Kumar, N. (2020). Mistry.; Ishan and Tanwar.; Sudeep and Tyagi.; Sudhanshu and Kumar.; Neeraj.; Blockchain for 5G-enabled IoT for industrial automation: A systematic review, solutions, and challenges. *Mechanical Systems and Signal Processing, 135*, 106382. doi:10.1016/j.ymssp.2019.106382

Molina-Garcia, J., Garcia-Salgado, B. P., Ponomaryov, V., Reyes-Reyes, R., Sadovnychiy, S., & Cruz-Ramos, C. (2020, February). An effective fragile watermarking scheme for color image tampering detection and self-recovery. *Signal Processing Image Communication, 81*, 115725. doi:10.1016/j.image.2019.115725

Mou, L., Bruzzone, L., & Zhu, X. X. (2019). Learning Spectral-Spatial-Temporal Features via a Recurrent Convolutional Neural Network for Change Detection in Multispectral Imagery. *IEEE Transactions on Geoscience and Remote Sensing, 57*(2), 924–935. doi:10.1109/TGRS.2018.2863224

Mu, C.-H., Li, C.-Z., Liu, Y., Qu, R., & Jiao, L.-C. (2019). Accelerated genetic algorithm based on search-space decomposition for change detection in remote sensing images. *Applied Soft Computing, 84*, 105727. doi:10.1016/j.asoc.2019.105727

Muñoz-Guillermo, M. (2021). Image encryption using q-deformed logistic map. *Information Sciences, 552*, 352–364. doi:10.1016/j.ins.2020.11.045

Mushtaq, Z., Sani, S. S., Hamed, K., & Ali, A. (2016). Automatic Agricultural Land Irrigation System by Fuzzy Logic. In *Proceedings of the 2016 3rd International Conference on Information Science and Control Engineering (ICISCE)*, Beijing, China. 10.1109/ICISCE.2016.190

Nadkarni, P. M., Ohno-Machado, L., & Chapman, W. W. (2011). Natural language processing: An introduction. *Journal of the American Medical Informatics Association : JAMIA*, *18*(5), 544–551. doi:10.1136/amiajnl-2011-000464 PMID:21846786

Najafabadi, M. M., Khoshgoftaar, T. M., Calvert, C., & Kemp, C. (2017, August). User behavior anomaly detection for application layer ddos attacks. In *2017 IEEE International Conference on Information Reuse and Integration (IRI)* (pp. 154-161). IEEE. 10.1109/IRI.2017.44

Narihira, T., Maire, M., & Yu, S. X. (2015). Direct intrinsics: Learning albedo-shading decomposition by convolutional regression. *Proceedings IEEE Conference Computing Visual Pattern Recognition*, (pp. 2992–2992). IEEE. 10.1109/ICCV.2015.342

Nataraj, L., Karthikeyan, S., & Manjunath, B. S. (2015). SATTVA: SpArsiTy inspired classificaTion of malware VAriants. *In Proceedings of the 3rd ACM Workshop on Information Hiding and Multimedia Security* (pp. 135-140). ACM. 10.1145/2756601.2756616

Nataraj, L., Karthikeyan, S., Jacob, G., & Manjunath, B. S. (2011). Malware Images: Visualization and Automatic Classification. *Proceedings of the 8th International Symposium on Visualization for Cyber Security*. ACM. 10.1145/2016904.2016908

Nauman, A., Qadri, Y. A., Amjad, M., Zikria, Y. B., Afzal, M. K., & Kim, S. W. (2020). Multimedia Internet of Things: A Comprehensive Survey. *IEEE Access : Practical Innovations, Open Solutions*, *8*, 8202–8250. doi:10.1109/ACCESS.2020.2964280

Nazari, M., & Maneshi, A. (2021). Chaotic reversible watermarking method based on iwt with tamper detection for transferring electronic health record. *Security and Communication Networks*, *2021*, 1–15. doi:10.1155/2021/5514944

Nguyen, D.-H., Le, T.-H., Tran, T.-H., Vu, H., Le, T.-L., & Doan, H.-G. (2018). Hand segmentation under different viewpoints by combination of Mask R-CNN with tracking. *5th Asian Conference on Defense Technology (ACDT)*. IEEE. doi:10.1109/ACDT.2018.8593130

Nguyen, T. H., Sridharan, S., Macias, V., Kajdacsy-Balla, A., Melamed, J., Do, M. N., & Popescu, G. (2017, March). Automatic Gleason grading of prostate cancer using quantitative phase imaging and machine learning. *Journal of Biomedical Optics*, *22*(3), 036015. doi:10.1117/1. JBO.22.3.036015 PMID:28358941

Nilesh, Y. (2013). Signature Recognition & Verification System Using Back Propagation Neural Network. In *International Journal of IT, Engineering and Applied Sciences Research* (Vol. 2, Issue 1). www.irjcjournals.org

Niu, H., Lin, Z., Chu, Z., Zhu, Z., Xiao, P., Nguyen, H. X., Lee, I., & Al-Dhahir, N. (2022, September 27). Joint beamforming design for secure RIS-assisted IoT networks. *IEEE Internet of Things Journal*.

Nkenyereye, L. (2020). Secure and blockchain-based emergency driven message protocol for 5G enabled vehicular edge computing. *Sensors (Basel)*, *20*(1), 154. PMID:33383730

Noshad, M., Rose, C. C., & Chen, J. H. (2022). Signal from the noise: A mixed graphical and quantitative process mining approach to evaluate care pathways applied to emergency stroke care. *Journal of Biomedical Informatics*, *127*, 104004. doi:10.1016/j.jbi.2022.104004 PMID:35085813

Nouioua, I., Amardjia, N., & Belilita, S. (2018, November). A Novel Blind and Robust Video Watermarking Technique in Fast Motion Frames Based on SVD and MR-SVD. *Security and Communication Networks*, *2018*, e6712065. doi:10.1155/2018/6712065

O'Brien, M. K., Shin, S. Y., Khazanchi, R., Fanton, M., Lieber, R. L., Ghaffari, R., Rogers, J. A., & Jayaraman, A. (2022). Wearable Sensors Improve Prediction of Post-Stroke Walking Function Following Inpatient Rehabilitation. *IEEE Journal of Translational Engineering in Health and Medicine*, *10*(May), 1–11. doi:10.1109/JTEHM.2022.3208585 PMID:36304845

Oliva, A., & Torralba, A. (2001). Modeling the Shape of the Scene: A Holistic Representation of the Spatial Envelope. *International Journal of Computer Vision*, *42*(3), 145–175. doi:10.1023/A:1011139631724

Ouyang T.Y. & R. Davis, R. (2019). *Learning from Neighboring Strokes : Combining Appearance and Context for Multi-Domain Sketch Recognition*. Springer.

Pak, C., Kim, J., An, K., Kim, C., Kim, K., & Pak, C. (2020, January). A novel color image LSB steganography using improved 1D chaotic map. *Multimedia Tools and Applications*, *79*(1-2), 1409–1425. doi:10.100711042-019-08103-0

Panahi, S., Sprott, J. C., & Jafari, S. (2018, November). Two Simplest Quadratic Chaotic Maps Without Equilibrium. *International Journal of Bifurcation and Chaos in Applied Sciences and Engineering*, *28*(12), 1850144. doi:10.1142/S0218127418501444

Pareek, N. K., Patidar, V., & Sud, K. K. (2006). Image encryption using chaotic logistic map. *Image and Vision Computing*, *24*(9), 926–934. doi:10.1016/j.imavis.2006.02.021

Pascanu, R., Mikolov, T., & Bengio, Y. (2013). On the difficulty of training recurrent neural networks. *In International Conference on Machine Learning*, (pp. 1310–1318). Springer.

Pascanu, R., Stokes, J. W., Sanossian, H., Marinescu, M., & Thomas, A. (2015). Malware classification with recurrent networks. *2015 IEEE International Conference on Acoustics, Speech and Signal Processing (ICASSP)*, (pp. 1916–1920). IEEE. 10.1109/ICASSP.2015.7178304

Patel, V. (2019). A framework for secure and decentralized sharing of medical imaging data via blockchain consensus. *Health Informatics Journal*, *15*(4), 1398–1411. doi:10.1177/1460458218769699 PMID:29692204

Peng, J., El-Atty, B. A., Khalifa, H. S., & El-Latif, A. A. A. (2019). Image steganography algorithm based on key matrix generated by quantum walks. *Eleventh International Conference on Digital Image Processing (ICDIP 2019)* (pp. 24-28). Spie Digital Library. 10.1117/12.2539630

Peng, J., El-Atty, B. A., Khalifa, H. S., & El-Latif, A. A. A. (2019). Image watermarking algorithm based on quaternion and chaotic Lorenz system. *Eleventh International Conference on Digital Image Processing (ICDIP 2019)* (pp. 234-239). Spie Digital Library. 10.1117/12.2539753

Peng, Z., Huang, J., Wang, H., Wang, S., Chu, X., Zhang, X., Chen, L., Huang, X., Fu, X., Guo, Y., & Xu, J. (2021). BU-trace: A permissionless mobile system for privacy-preserving intelligent contact tracing. In *International Conference on Database Systems for Advanced Applications.* Springer, Cham.

Peng, C., Wu, C., Gao, L., Zhang, J., Alvin Yau, K.-L., & Ji, Y. (2020). Blockchain for vehicular Internet of Things: Recent advances and open issues. *Sensors (Basel)*, *20*(18), 5079. doi:10.339020185079 PMID:32906707

Peng, Z., Xu, J., Hu, H., Chen, L., & Kong, H. (2022). BlockShare: A Blockchain empowered system for privacy-preserving verifiable data sharing. *A Quarterly Bulletin of the Computer Society of the IEEE Technical Committee on Data Engineering*, *1*, 14–24.

Peng, Z., Zhang, Y., Xu, Q., Liu, H., Gao, Y., Li, X., & Yu, G. (2022, July 1). NeuChain: A fast permissioned blockchain system with deterministic ordering. *Proceedings of the VLDB Endowment International Conference on Very Large Data Bases*, *15*(11), 2585–2598. doi:10.14778/3551793.3551816

Qureshi, A., & Megías Jiménez, D. (2021, January). Blockchain-Based Multimedia Content Protection: Review and Open Challenges. *Applied Sciences (Basel, Switzerland)*, *11*(1), 1. doi:10.3390/app11010001

Rashidi, S., Fallah, A., & Towhidkhah, F. (2012). Feature extraction based DCT on dynamic signature verification. *Scientia Iranica*, *19*(6), 1810–1819. doi:10.1016/j.scient.2012.05.007

Rathee, G., Sharma, A., Saini, H., Kumar, R., & Iqbal, R. (2020). A hybrid framework for multimedia data processing in IoT-healthcare using blockchain technology. *Multimedia Tools and Applications*, *79*(15-16), 9711–9733. doi:10.100711042-019-07835-3

Rathi, V. K. (2020). A blockchain-enabled multi domain edge computing orchestrator. *Journal of IEEE Internet of Things Magazine, 3*(2), 30–36.

Ravichandran, D., Praveenkumar, P., Rajagopalan, S., Rayappan, J. B. B., & Amirtharajan, R. (2021). ROI-based medical image watermarking for accurate tamper detection, localisation and recovery. *Medical & Biological Engineering & Computing*, *59*(6), 1355–1372. doi:10.100711517-021-02374-2 PMID:33990889

Redmon, J., Divvala, S., Girshick, R., & Farhadi, A. (2016). You Only Look Once: Unified, Real-Time Object Detection. *IEEE Conference on Computer Vision and Pattern Recognition (CVPR)*. IEEE. 10.1109/CVPR.2016.91

Redmon, J., & Farhadi, A. (2017). YOLO9000: Better, Faster, Stronger. *IEEE Conference on Computer Vision and Pattern Recognition (CVPR)*. IEEE.

Rematas, K., Nguyen, C., Ritschel, T., Fritz, M., & Tuytelaars, T. (2016). Novel views of objects from a single image. *IEEE Transactions on Pattern Analysis and Machine Intelligence*, *39*(8), 1576–1590. doi:10.1109/TPAMI.2016.2601093 PMID:27541489

Ren, S. & He, K. (2017). Faster R-CNN: Towards Real-Time Object Detection with Region Proposal Networks. *IEEE Transactions on Pattern Analysis and Machine Intelligence*. IEEE.

Rhode, M., Burnap, P., & Jones, K. (2017). Early-Stage Malware Prediction Using Recurrent Neural Networks. *ArXiv Preprint ArXiv:1708.03513*, 1–28.

Risch, J., & Krestel, R. (2018). Aggression Identification Using Deep Learning and Data Augmentation. *Proceedings of the First Workshop on Trolling, Aggression and Cyberbullying (TRAC-2018), Coling*, 77–85. http://aclweb.org/anthology/W18-44%0A900

Ronen, R., Radu, M., Feuerstein, C., & Yom-tov, E. (2015). Microsoft Malware Classification Challenge. *Microsoft Kaggle*, 1–7. doi:10.1145/2857705.2857713

Rong, X., Jiang, D., Zheng, M., Yu, X., & Wang, X. (2022, November). Meaningful data encryption scheme based on newly designed chaotic map and P-tensor product compressive sensing in WBANs. *Nonlinear Dynamics*, *110*(3), 2831–2847. doi:10.100711071-022-07736-5

Ronneberger, O., Fischer, P., & Brox, T. (2015, October). U-net: Convolutional networks for biomedical image segmentation. In *International Conference on Medical image computing and computer-assisted intervention* (pp. 234-241). Springer. 10.1007/978-3-319-24574-4_28

Ruan, P., Anh Dinh, T. T., Lin, Q., Zhang, M., Chen, G., & Chin Ooi, B. (2020, September 4). Revealing every story of data in blockchain systems. *SIGMOD Record*, *49*(1), 70–77. doi:10.1145/3422648.3422665

Ruan, P., Chen, G., Dinh, T. T., Lin, Q., Ooi, B. C., & Zhang, M. (2019, May 1). Fine-grained, secure and efficient data provenance on blockchain systems. *Proceedings of the VLDB Endowment International Conference on Very Large Data Bases*, *12*(9), 975–988. doi:10.14778/3329772.3329775

Sadqi, Y., & Maleh, Y. (2022). A systematic review and taxonomy of web applications threats. *Information Security Journal: A Global Perspective, 31*(1), 1–27. doi:10.1080/19393555.2020.1853855

Saffar, M. H., Fayyaz, M., Sabokrou, M., & Fathy, M. (n.d.). Online signature verification using deep representation: a new descriptor. https://www.researchgate.net/publication/306510061.

Saha, S., Bovolo, F., & Bruzzone, L. (2020). Building Change Detection in VHR SAR Images via Unsupervised Deep Transcoding. *IEEE Transactions on Geoscience and Remote Sensing*, 1–13. doi:10.1109/TGRS.2020.3000296

Sailasya, G. (2022). Prediction of brain stroke severity using machine learning. Lect. Notes Comput. Sci. (including Subser. Lect. Notes Artif. Intell. Lect. Notes Bioinformatics), 9(1). IJARSCT. doi:10.48175/IJARSCT-3496

Sailasya, G., & Kumari, G. L. A. (2021). Analyzing the Performance of Stroke Prediction using ML Classification Algorithms. *International Journal of Advanced Computer Science and Applications*, *12*(6), 539–545. doi:10.14569/IJACSA.2021.0120662

Saxe, A. M., McClelland, J. L., & Ganguli, S. (2013). *Malware Analysis of Imaged Binary Samples by Convolutional Neural Network with Attention Mechanism*. 127–134.

Sedik, A., Abd El-Latif, A. A., Ahmad Wani, M., Abd El-Samie, F. E., Abdel-Salam Bauomy, N., & Hashad, F. G. (2023). Efficient Multi-Biometric Secure-Storage Scheme Based on Deep Learning and Crypto-Mapping Techniques. *Mathematics*, *11*(3), 703. doi:10.3390/math11030703

Sengupta, J., Ruj, S., & Bit, S. D. (2020). A comprehensive survey on attacks, security issues and blockchain solutions for IoT and IIoT. *Journal of Network and Computer Applications*, *149*, 102481. doi:10.1016/j.jnca.2019.102481

Serag Eldin, S. M. (2023). Design and Analysis of New Version of Cryptographic Hash Function Based on Improved Chaotic Maps with Induced DNA Sequences. IEEE Access. doi:10.1109/ACCESS.2023.3298545

Shakil, K. A., Tabassum, K., Alqahtani, F. S., & Wani, M. A. (2021). Analyzing user digital emotions from a holy versus non-pilgrimage city in Saudi Arabia on twitter platform. *Applied Sciences (Basel, Switzerland)*, *11*(15), 6846. doi:10.3390/app11156846

Sharafi, J., Khedmati, Y., & Shabani, M. M. (2021, January). Image steganography based on a new hybrid chaos map and discrete transforms. *Optik (Stuttgart)*, *226*, 165492. doi:10.1016/j.ijleo.2020.165492

Sharma, C., Sharma, S., Kumar, M., & Sodhi, A. (2022). Early Stroke Prediction Using Machine Learning. *2022 Int. Conf. Decis. Aid Sci. Appl. DASA 2022*, (pp. 890–894). Springer. 10.1109/DASA54658.2022.9765307

Sharma, A. (2020). Blockchain Based Smart Contracts for Internet of Medical Things in e-Healthcare. *Journal of Electronics (China)*, *9*, 1609.

Shen, B., Guo, J., & Yang, Y. (2019). MedChain: Efficient healthcare data sharing via blockchain. *Applied Sciences (Basel, Switzerland)*, *9*(6), 1207. doi:10.3390/app9061207

Shi, J., & Osher, S. (2008). A Nonlinear Inverse Scale Space Method for a Convex Multiplicative Noise Model. *SIAM Journal on Imaging Sciences*, *1*(3), 294–321. doi:10.1137/070689954

Siam, A. I., Almaiah, M. A., Al-Zahrani, A., Elazm, A. A., El Banby, G. M., El-Shafai, W., El-Samie, F. E., & El-Bahnasawy, N. A. (2021, December 13). Secure Health Monitoring Communication Systems Based on IoT and Cloud Computing for Medical Emergency Applications. *Computational Intelligence and Neuroscience*, *2021*, 2021. doi:10.1155/2021/8016525 PMID:34938329

Siegel, R. L., Miller, K. D., & Jemal, A. (2021). Cancer statistics, 2021. *CA: a Cancer Journal for Clinicians*, *71*(1), 7–33. doi:10.3322/caac.21654 PMID:33433946

Sirsat, M. S., Fermé, E., & Câmara, J. (2020). Machine Learning for Brain Stroke: A Review. *Journal of Stroke and Cerebrovascular Diseases*, *29*(10), 105162. doi:10.1016/j.jstrokecerebrovasdis.2020.105162 PMID:32912543

Sodhro, A. H., Luo, Z., Sodhro, G. H., Muzamal, M., Rodrigues, J. J. P. C., & de Albuquerque, V. H. C. (2019, June). Artificial Intelligence based QoS optimization for multimedia communication in IoV systems. *Future Generation Computer Systems*, *95*, 667–680. doi:10.1016/j.future.2018.12.008

Sood, S. K. (2020, April). Mobile fog based secure cloud-IoT framework for enterprise multimedia security. *Multimedia Tools and Applications*, *79*(15), 10717–10732. doi:10.100711042-019-08573-2

Studiawan, H., Sohel, F., & Payne, C. (2020). Anomaly detection in operating system logs with deep learning-based sentiment analysis. *IEEE Transactions on Dependable and Secure Computing*, *18*(5), 2136–2148. doi:10.1109/TDSC.2020.3037903

Suarez, R. (2020). *Current* and future applications of machine and deep learning in urology: A review of the literature on urolithiasis, renal cell carcinoma, and *bladder and prostate cancer*. *World Journal of Urology*, *38*(10), 2329–2347. doi:10.100700345-019-03000-5

Sultana, T., Almogren, A., Akbar, M., Zuair, M., Ullah, I., & Javaid, N. (2020, January 9). Data sharing system integrating access control mechanism using blockchain-based smart contracts for IoT devices. *Applied Sciences (Basel, Switzerland)*, *10*(2), 488. doi:10.3390/app10020488

Sun, W., Wu, P., & Hoi, S. C. H. (2018, July). P, and Hoi. S. H. I, "Face detection using deep learning: An improved faster RCNN approach. *Neurocomputing*, *299*, 42–50. doi:10.1016/j.neucom.2018.03.030

Sutskever, I. (2013). *Training recurrent neural networks*. University of Toronto.

Swamy, P. S., & Vani, K. (2016). A novel thresholding technique in the curvelet domain for improved speckle removal in SAR images. *Optik (Stuttgart)*, *127*(2), 634–637. doi:10.1016/j.ijleo.2015.10.057

Talhaoui, M. Z., & Wang, X. (2021, March). A new fractional one dimensional chaotic map and its application in high-speed image encryption. *Information Sciences*, *550*, 13–26. doi:10.1016/j.ins.2020.10.048

Talhaoui, M. Z., Wang, X., & Talhaoui, A. (2021, July). A new one-dimensional chaotic map and its application in a novel permutation-less image encryption scheme. *The Visual Computer*, *37*(7), 1757–1768. doi:10.100700371-020-01936-z

Taloba, A. I., Elhadad, A., Rayan, A., Abd El-Aziz, R. M., Salem, M., Alzahrani, A. A., Alharithi, F. S., & Park, C. (2023, February). A blockchain-based hybrid platform for multimedia data processing in IoT-Healthcare. *Alexandria Engineering Journal*, *65*, 263–274. doi:10.1016/j.aej.2022.09.031

Tan, L., Shi, N., Yu, K., Aloqaily, M., & Jararweh, Y. (2021, June 16). A blockchain-empowered access control framework for smart devices in green internet of things. *ACM Transactions on Internet Technology*, *21*(3), 1–20. doi:10.1145/3433542

Tenney, I., Das, D., & Pavlick, E. (2019). *BERT rediscovers the classical NLP pipeline*. arXiv preprint arXiv:1905.05950. doi:10.18653/v1/P19-1452

Thul, D., Tsiminaki, V., Ladický, Ľ., & Pollefeys, M. (2020). Precomputed Radiance Transfer for Reflectance and Lighting Estimation. *2020 International Conference on 3D Vision (3DV)*. IEEE. 10.1109/3DV50981.2020.00125

Tobiyama, S., Yamaguchi, Y., Shimada, H., Ikuse, T., & Yagi, T. (2016). Malware Detection with Deep Neural Network Using Process Behavior. *2016 IEEE 40th Annual Computer Software and Applications Conference (COMPSAC)*. IEEE. 10.1109/COMPSAC.2016.151

Tobon, D. P., Hossain, M. S., Muhammad, G., Bilbao, J., & El Saddik, A. (2022). Deep learning in multimedia healthcare applications: A review. *Multimedia Systems*, *28*(4), 1465–1479. doi:10.100700530-022-00948-0 PMID:35645465

Touati, R., Mignotte, M., & Dahmane, M. (2019). Multimodal Change Detection in Remote Sensing Images Using an Unsupervised Pixel Pairwise Based Markov Random Field Model. *IEEE Transactions on Image Processing*, 1–1. doi:10.1109/TIP.2019.2933747 PMID:31425034

Trujillo-Toledo, D. A., López-Bonilla, O. R., García-Guerrero, E. E., Tlelo-Cuautle, E., López-Mancilla, D., Guillén-Fernández, O., & Inzunza-González, E. (2021, December). Real-time RGB image encryption for IoT applications using enhanced sequences from chaotic maps. *Chaos, Solitons, and Fractals*, *153*, 111506. doi:10.1016/j.chaos.2021.111506

Tsironi, E., Barros, P., Weber, C., & Wermter, S. (2017). An analysis of Convolutional Long Short-Term Memory Recurrent Neural Networks for gesture recognition. *Neurocomputing*, *268*, 76–86. doi:10.1016/j.neucom.2016.12.088

Usman, M., Jan, M. A., He, X., & Chen, J. (2019). A survey on big multimedia data processing and management in smart cities. *ACM Computing Surveys*, *52*(3), 1–29. doi:10.1145/3323334

Veeman, D., Alanezi, A., Natiq, H., Jafari, S., & Abd El-Latif, A. A. (2022, February). A Chaotic Quadratic Oscillator with Only Squared Terms: Multistability, Impulsive Control, and Circuit Design. *Symmetry*, *14*(2), 2. doi:10.3390ym14020259

Vieira, S. M., Kaymak, U., & Sousa, J. M. C. (2010). Cohen's kappa coefficient as a performance measure for feature selection. *IEEE International Conference on Fuzzy Systems*. IEEE. 10.1109/FUZZY.2010.5584447

Vijayalakshmi, K., Al-Otaibi, S., Arya, L., Almaiah, M. A., Anithaashri, T. P., Karthik, S. S., & Shishakly, R. (2023, July 19). Smart Agricultural–Industrial Crop-Monitoring System Using Unmanned Aerial Vehicle–Internet of Things Classification Techniques. *Sustainability (Basel)*, *15*(14), 11242. doi:10.3390u151411242

Vivekanandan, Manojkumar, & Sastry. (2021). VN and others.; BIDAPSCA5G: Blockchain based Internet of Things (IoT) device to device authentication protocol for smart city applications using 5G technology. *Peer-to-Peer Networking and Applications, 14*(1), 403–419. doi:10.100712083-020-00963-w

Wang H, Xu C, Zhang C, Xu J, Peng Z, Pei J. (2019). *Optimizing Verifiable Blockchain Boolean Range Queries.* HKBU.

Wang, W. C, Yang, W, & Liu, J. (2018). GLADNet: Low-light enhancement network with global awareness. *Proc. 13th IEEE Int. Conf. Autom. Face Gesture Recognit.* IEEE.

Wang, C., Wang, X., Xia, Z., & Zhang, C. (2019). Ternary radial harmonic Fourier moments based robust stereo image zero-watermarking algorithm. *Information Sciences, 470*, 109–120. doi:10.1016/j.ins.2018.08.028

Wang, J., Liu, L., Xu, M., & Li, X. (2022). A novel content-selected image encryption algorithm based on the LS chaotic model », *J. King Saud Univ. - Comput. Inf. Sci., 34*(nov), 8245–8259. doi:10.1016/j.jksuci.2022.08.007

Wang, J., Song, X., & El-Latif, A. A. A. (2022, January). Single-Objective Particle Swarm Optimization-Based Chaotic Image Encryption Scheme. *Electronics (Basel), 11*(16), 16. Advance online publication. doi:10.3390/electronics11162628

Wang, J., Song, X., & El-Latif, A. A. A. (2022, July). Efficient Entropic Security with Joint Compression and Encryption Approach Based on Compressed Sensing with Multiple Chaotic Systems. *Entropy (Basel, Switzerland), 24*(7), 7. Advance online publication. doi:10.3390/e24070885 PMID:35885109

Wang, R., Shaocheng, H., Zhang, P., Yue, M., Cheng, Z., & Zhang, Y. (2020). A novel zero-watermarking scheme based on variable parameter chaotic mapping in NSPD-DCT domain. *IEEE Access : Practical Innovations, Open Solutions, 8*, 182391–182411. doi:10.1109/ACCESS.2020.3004841

Wang, W., Wang, X., Yang, W., & Liu, J. (2023, January 1). Unsupervised Face Detection in the Dark. *IEEE Transactions on Pattern Analysis and Machine Intelligence, 45*(1), 1250–1266. doi:10.1109/TPAMI.2022.3152562 PMID:35180078

Wang, X., Fouhey, D. F., & Gupta, A. (2015). Designing deep networks for surface normal estimation. *Proceedings IEEE Conference Computing Visual Pattern Recognition.* IEEE. 10.1109/CVPR.2015.7298652

Wani, M. A., ELAffendi, M. A., Shakil, K. A., Imran, A. S., & Abd El-Latif, A. A. (2022). Depression screening in humans with AI and deep learning techniques. *IEEE Transactions on Computational Social Systems.*

Wani, M. A., ELAffendi, M., Shakil, K. A., Abuhaimed, I. M., Nayyar, A., Hussain, A., & El-Latif, A. A. A. (2023). Toxic Fake News Detection and Classification for Combating COVID-19 Misinformation. *IEEE Transactions on Computational Social Systems*, 1. doi:10.1109/TCSS.2023.3276764

Williams, R. J., & Zipser, D. (1989). A learning algorithm for continually running fully recurrent neural networks. *Neural Computation*, *1*(2), 270–280. doi:10.1162/neco.1989.1.2.270

World Health Organization. (2016). Classification of Tumours of the Urinary System and Male Genital Organs. International Agency for Research on Cancer.

Xia, Z., Wang, C., Ma, B., Li, Q., Zhang, H., Wang, M., & Wang, X. (2023, August). Geometric attacks resistant double zero-watermarking using discrete Fourier transform and fractional-order Exponent-Fourier moments. *Digital Signal Processing*, *140*, 104097. doi:10.1016/j.dsp.2023.104097

Xia, Z., Wang, X., Li, X., Wang, C., Unar, S., Wang, M., & Zhao, T. (2019, November). Efficient copyright protection for three CT images based on quaternion polar harmonic Fourier moments. *Signal Processing*, *164*, 368–379. doi:10.1016/j.sigpro.2019.06.025

Xia, Z., Wang, X., Wang, C., Ma, B., Wang, M., & Shi, Y.-Q. (2021, March). Local quaternion polar harmonic Fourier moments-based multiple zero-watermarking scheme for color medical images. *Knowledge-Based Systems*, *216*, 106568. doi:10.1016/j.knosys.2020.106568

Xu, Y., Holanda, G., Souza, L. F. F., Silva, H., Gomes, A., Silva, I., Ferreira, M., Jia, C., Han, T., de Albuquerque, V. H. C., & Filho, P. P. R. (2021). Deep Learning-Enhanced Internet of Medical Things to Analyze Brain CT Scans of Hemorrhagic Stroke Patients: A New Approach. *IEEE Sensors Journal*, *21*(22), 24941–24951. doi:10.1109/JSEN.2020.3032897

Yadav, D., & Saxena, C. (2015). Offline signature recognition and verification using PCA and neural network approach. *Int. J. Sci. Res. Dev*, *3*(9).

Yamni, M., Daoui, A., Karmouni, H., Elmalih, S., Ben-fares, A., Sayyouri, M., Qjidaa, H., Maaroufi, M., Alami, B., & Jamil, M. O. (2023). Copyright protection of multiple CT images using Octonion Krawtchouk moments and grey Wolf optimizer. *Journal of the Franklin Institute*, *360*(7), 4719–4752. doi:10.1016/j.jfranklin.2023.03.008

Yamni, M., Daoui, A., Karmouni, H., Sayyouri, M., Qjidaa, H., & Flusser, J. (2020). Fractional Charlier moments for image reconstruction and image watermarking. *Signal Processing*, *171*, 107509. doi:10.1016/j.sigpro.2020.107509

Yamni, M., Daoui, A., Karmouni, H., Sayyouri, M., Qjidaa, H., Wang, C., & Jamil, M. O. (2023). A Powerful Zero-Watermarking Algorithm for Copyright Protection of Color Images Based on Quaternion Radial Fractional Hahn Moments and Artificial Bee Colony Algorithm. *Circuits, Systems, and Signal Processing*, *42*(9), 1–32. doi:10.100700034-023-02379-2

Yamni, M., Karmouni, H., Daoui, A., Sayyouri, M., & Qjidaa, H. (2020). Blind image zero-watermarking algorithm based on radial krawtchouk moments and chaotic system. In *2020 International Conference on Intelligent Systems and Computer Vision (ISCV)*. IEEE. 10.1109/ISCV49265.2020.9204071

Yamni, M., Karmouni, H., Sayyouri, M., & Qjidaa, H. (2022, January). Efficient watermarking algorithm for digital audio/speech signal. *Digital Signal Processing*, *120*, 103251. doi:10.1016/j.dsp.2021.103251

Yamni, M., Karmouni, H., Sayyouri, M., & Qjidaa, H. (2022, October). Robust audio watermarking scheme based on fractional Charlier moment transform and dual tree complex wavelet transform. *Expert Systems with Applications*, *203*, 117325. doi:10.1016/j.eswa.2022.117325

Yang, C., Xu, X., Zhou, X., & Qi, L. (2022). Deep Q Network–Driven Task Offloading for Efficient Multimedia Data Analysis in Edge Computing–Assisted IoV. *ACM Transactions on Multimedia Computing Communications and Applications*, *18*(2s, no. 2s), 1–24. doi:10.1145/3548687

Yang, Yuan, Y., Ren, W., Liu, J., Scheirer, W. J., Wang, Z., Zhang, T., Zhong, Q., Xie, D., Pu, S., Zheng, Y., Qu, Y., Xie, Y., Chen, L., Li, Z., Hong, C., Jiang, H., Yang, S., Liu, Y., & Qin, L. (2020). Advancing image understanding in poor visibility environments A collective benchmark study. *IEEE Transactions on Image Processing*, *29*, 5737–5752. doi:10.1109/TIP.2020.2981922 PMID:32224457

Yaseen, S., Aslam, M. M., Farhan, M., Naeem, M. R., & Raza, A. (2023). A Deep Learning-based Approach for Malware Classification using Machine Code to Image Conversion. *Technical Journal*, *28*(01), 36–46.

Yazdinejad, A., & Raymond, K. K. (2019). Blockchain-enabled authentication handover with efficient privacy protection in SDN-based 5G networks. *IEEE Transactions on Network Science and Engineering*. IEEE.

Yazdinejad, A., Parizi, R. M., Dehghantanha, A., & Choo, K.-K. (2020). P4-to-blockchain: A secure blockchain-enabled packet parser for software-defined networking. *Journal of Computer Security*, *88*, 101–629.

Yuan, S., Magayane, D. A., Liu, X., Zhou, X., Lu, G., Wang, Z., Zhang, H., & Li, Z. (2021). A blind watermarking scheme based on computational ghost imaging in wavelet domain. *Optics Communications*, *482*, 126568. doi:10.1016/j.optcom.2020.126568

Yuan, Z., Lu, Y., & Xue, Y. (2016). DroidDetector. *Android Malware Characterization and Detection Using Deep Learning.*, *21*(1), 114–123.

Yuan, Z., Lyu, Y., Wang, Z., & Xue, Y. (2014). *Droid-Sec: deep learning in android malware detection*. SIGCOMM. doi:10.1145/2619239.2631434

Yu, C., Wu, G., Wang, Y., Xiao, Z., Duan, Y., & Chen, Z. (2022). Design of Coaxial Integrated Macro-Micro Composite Actuator With Long-Stroke and High-Precision. *IEEE Access: Practical Innovations, Open Solutions*, *10*, 43501–43513. doi:10.1109/ACCESS.2022.3169506

Yu, J., Park, S., Kwon, S. H., Cho, K. H., & Lee, H. (2022). AI-Based Stroke Disease Prediction System Using ECG and PPG Bio-Signals. *IEEE Access : Practical Innovations, Open Solutions*, *10*, 43623–43638. doi:10.1109/ACCESS.2022.3169284

Yu, K., Tan, L., Yang, C., Choo, K. K., Bashir, A. K., Rodrigues, J. J., & Sato, T. (2021). A blockchain-based shamir's threshold cryptography scheme for data protection in industrial internet of things settings. *IEEE Internet of Things Journal*.

Zhang, A., Zhao, Y., & Wang, S. (2019). Illumination estimation for augmented reality based on a global illumination model. *Multimedia Tools and Applications*, *78*(23), 33487–33503. doi:10.100711042-019-08155-2

Zhang, M., Xu, G., Chen, K., Yan, M., & Sun, X. (2018). Triplet-based semantic relation learning for aerial remote sensing image change detection. *IEEE Geoscience and Remote Sensing Letters*, *16*(2), 266–270. doi:10.1109/LGRS.2018.2869608

Zhang, W., Yao, T., Zhu, S., & El Saddik, A. (2019). Deep learning–based multimedia analytics: A review. *ACM Transactions on Multimedia Computing Communications and Applications*, *15*(no. 1s), 1–26.

Zhang, Y., Wang, K., Moustafa, H., Wang, S., & Zhang, K. (2020). Zhang.; Yan and Wang.; Kun and Moustafa.; Hassnaa and Wang.; Stephen and Zhang.; Ke.; Guest Editorial: Blockchain and AI for Beyond 5G Networks. *IEEE Network*, *34*(6), 22–23. doi:10.1109/MNET.2020.9374644

Zhan, T., Gong, M., Jiang, X., & Zhang, M. (2020). Unsupervised Scale-Driven Change Detection With Deep Spatial–Spectral Features for VHR Images. *IEEE Transactions on Geoscience and Remote Sensing*, *58*(8), 5653–5665. doi:10.1109/TGRS.2020.2968098

Zhao, Y. (2021). *A survey of 6G wireless communications: Emerging technologies Future of Information and Communication Conference*, (pp. 150–170). Springer.

Zhou, Y. Liu. D, & Huang. T (2018). Survey of face detection on low-quality images. *Proc. 13th IEEE Int. Conf. Autom. Face Gesture Recognit.*, (pp. 769–773). IEEE.

Zhou, S., Huang, H., Chen, W., Zhou, P., Zheng, Z., & Guo, S. (2020). Zhou, Sicong and Huang, Huawei and Chen, Wuhui and Zhou, Pan and Zheng, Zibin and Guo, Song pirate: A blockchain-based secure framework of distributed machine learning in 5g networks. *IEEE Network*, *34*(6), 84–91. doi:10.1109/MNET.001.1900658

Zhu, L., Jiang, D., Ni, J., Wang, X., Rong, X., & Ahmad, M. (2022, August). A visually secure image encryption scheme using adaptive-thresholding sparsification compression sensing model and newly-designed memristive chaotic map. *Information Sciences*, *607*, 1001–1022. doi:10.1016/j.ins.2022.06.011

Zhu, S., Deng, X., Zhang, W., & Zhu, C. (2023, May). Secure image encryption scheme based on a new robust chaotic map and strong S-box. *Mathematics and Computers in Simulation*, *207*, 322–346. doi:10.1016/j.matcom.2022.12.025

Zhu, X., & Badr, Y. (2018). Identity management systems for the internet of things: A survey towards blockchain solutions. *Sensors (Basel)*, *18*(12), 4215. doi:10.339018124215 PMID:30513733

Zhu, Y., Li, C., Li, S., Shi, B., & Tai, Y.-W. (2022). Hybrid Face Reflectance, Illumination, and Shape from a Single Image. *IEEE Transactions on Pattern Analysis and Machine Intelligence*, *44*(9), 5002–5015. PMID:33989152

Zimmerman, S., Fox, C., & Kruschwitz, U. (2019). Improving hate speech detection with deep learning ensembles. *LREC 2018 - 11th International Conference on Language Resources and Evaluation*, 2546–2553.

About the Contributors

Ahmed A. Abd El-Latif received the B.Sc. degree with honor rank in Mathematics and Computer Science in 2005 and M.Sc. degree in Computer Science in 2010, all from Menoufia University, Egypt. He received his Ph. D. degree in Computer Science & Technology at Harbin Institute of Technology (H.I.T), Harbin, P. R. China in 2013. He is an associate professor of Computer Science at Menoufia University, Egypt. He is author and co-author of more than 130 papers in reputal journal and conferences. He received many awards, State Encouragement Award in Engineering Sciences 2016, Arab Republic of Egypt; the best Ph.D student award from Harbin Institute of Technology, China 2013; Young scientific award, Menoufia University, Egypt 2014. He is a fellow at Academy of Scientific Research and Technology, Egypt. His areas of interests are multimedia content encryption, secure wireless communication, IoT, applied cryptanalysis, perceptual cryptography, secret media sharing, information hiding, biometrics, forensic analysis in digital images, and quantum information processing. Dr. Abd El-Latif is an associate editor of Journal of Cyber Security and Mobility, and Mathematical Problems in Engineering.

Yassine Maleh received a PhD in computer science from the University Hassan 1st, Morocco, in 2013. Since December 2012, he has been working as an IT senior analyst at the National Port Agency in Morocco. He is an Associate Professor with the Mohammed VI International Academy of Civil Aviation in Casablanca, Morocco. Dr. Maleh has made contributions in the fields of information security and privacy, Internet of Things security and wireless and constrained networks security. His research interests include information security and privacy, the Internet of Things, networks security, information systems, and IT governance. He has published more than 60 papers (book chapters, international journals, and conferences), 3 edited books and 1 authored book. He serve as an associate editor for IEEE Access, the International Journal of Digital Crime and Forensics (IJDCF) and the International Journal of Information Security and Privacy (IJISP). Dr. Maleh served and continues to serve on executive and technical program committees and as a reviewer of numerous international conference and journals such as Elsevier Ad Hoc Networks, IEEE Network Magazine, IEEE Sensor Journal, ICT Express, Springer Cluster Computing. He was the General Chair of the MLBDACP 19 symposium.

* * *

G. Ananthi is currently working as an Associate Professor, in the Department of Computer Science and Engineering, Mepco Schlenk Engineering College, Sivakasi. She completed her UG in CSE and PG in CSE at Mepco Schlenk Engineering College respectively on 2001 and 2010. She completed her Ph.D in Information and Communication Engineering under Anna University, Chennai during July 2022. She has 19 years of teaching experience. She has 23 publications in Journals and conferences. She is a life member in CSI and ISTE. Her areas of specialization are image processing, machine learning and soft computing.

Muhammad Asim received the M.S. degree in Mathematics from University of Peshawar, Peshawar, Pakistan in 2013 and the M.Phil. degree in Mathematics from Kohat University of Science & Technology, Kohat, Pakistan in 2016. He received his Ph.D. degree in Computer Science and Technology at Central South University, Changsha, China in 2022. He has been awarded as an outstanding international graduate of Central South University, 2022. Currently, he is conducting his PostDoc research at EIAS Data Science Lab, College of Computer and Information Sciences, Prince Sultan University, Riyadh, 11586, Saudi Arabia. His current research interests include artificial intelligence, computational intelligence techniques, cloud computing, edge computing, 5G/6G communication systems, and autonomous vehicles.

Sarah Kaleem is a PhD Scholar in the department of Computing and Technology, Iqra University, Islamabad, Pakistan. She is also A PhD internee at EIAS Lab, Prince Sultan University, Saudi Arabia. She received her Master of Sciences in Computer Software Engineering from Iqra National University (INU), Peshawar, Pakistan in 2019. She receives her bachelor's in computer sciences from University of Peshawar, Pakistan in 2014. Her research area includes but is not limited to Big Data Analytics, Internet of Things (IoT), Intelligent Transportation Systems (ITS), and Machine Learning. She has published in various international conferences and journals.

Akib Mohi Ud Din Khanday received the masters degree in Information Technology from Islamic University of Science and Technology, Awantipora, Jammu and Kashmir, India and the Ph.D. degree in Computer Sciences from the Baba Ghulam Shah Badshah University, Rajouri, Jammu and Kashmir, India, in 2022. He has worked as Assistant Professor in the department of Information Technology, S.P. College, Cluster University, Srinagar, J&K, India and in the Department of Computer Science and Applications, Sharda University, India. He is currently working as a Post Doctoral Research fellow in Department of Computer Science and Software Engineering-CIT, United Arab Emirates University, Al Ain. His research interests are Computational Social Sciences, NLP and Machine/Deep Learning. He has authored many research articles in the reputed journals and conferences. He has served as a reviewer in reputed journals over the years like Scientific Reports, Journal of Social Science and Humanities etc.

Pugalenthi M. is a UG student at Mepco Schlenk Engineering College, Sivakasi.

Rajkumar M. is a UG student at Mepco Schlenk Engineering College, Sivakasi.

Jayashree Padmanabhan received her B.E (Hons) in Electronics and Communication from Madurai Kamaraj University, a Masters (Electronics Engineering), and a Ph.D. (Computer Science and Engineering) from Anna University. She is currently working as an Associate Professor in the Department of Computer Technology, at Anna University, Chennai. She has rich teaching and research experience and nearly 50 reputed journal/conference publications. Her research interests include cyber security, cryptographic algorithms, data analytics, medical informatics, and e-learning.

Balaji T. is a UG student at Mepco Schlenk Engineering College, Sivakasi.

V. Stella Mary pursued her Master's and Bachelor's degree in Engineering from Anna University, India. She is pursuing her Ph.D. in the Department of Computer Technology, at Anna University, MIT, Chennai. She has 8 years of teaching experience and 2 years of research experience. Her areas of interest include Machine Learning, Deep learning, Internet of Things, Data Analytics, and Cryptography.

Index

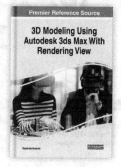

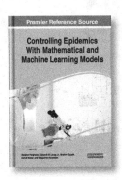
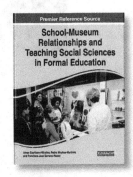
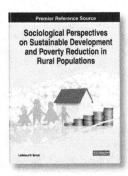

Printed in the United States
by Baker & Taylor Publisher Services